THiS BOOK bELoNGs To

have yourself a

# homemade
# Christmas

Scrumptious recipes, handmade crafts &
heartfelt gifts to make your spirits bright

Oxmoor
House.

have yourself a homemade Christmas

©2012 by Gooseberry Patch
2500 Farmers Dr., #110, Columbus, Ohio 43235
1-800-854-6673, **gooseberrypatch.com**

©2012 by Time Home Entertainment Inc.
135 West 50th Street, New York, NY 10020

ISBN-13: 978-0-8487-3695-8
ISBN-10: 0-8487-3695-8
Library of Congress Control Number: 2012945151
Printed in the United States of America
First Printing 2012

**Oxmoor House**
Editorial Director: Leah McLaughlin
Creative Director: Felicity Keane
Brand Manager: Vanessa Tiongson
Senior Editor: Rebecca Brennan
Managing Editor: Rebecca Benton

**Gooseberry Patch Have Yourself a Homemade Christmas**
Editor: Susan Ray
Project Editor: Emily Chappell
Assistant Designer: Allison Sperando Potter
Director, Test Kitchen: Elizabeth Tyler Austin
Assistant Directors, Test Kitchen: Julie Christopher, Julie Gunter
Recipe Developers and Testers: Wendy Ball, R.D.;
    Victoria E. Cox; Stefanie Maloney; Callie Nash;
    Leah Van Deren
Recipe Editor: Alyson Haynes
Food Stylists: Margaret Monroe Dickey,
    Catherine Crowell Steele
Photography Director: Jim Bathie
Senior Photo Stylist: Kay E. Clarke
Photo Stylist: Katherine Eckert Coyne
Assistant Photo Stylist: Mary Louise Menendez
Production Manager: Theresa Beste-Farley

**Contributors**
Proofreader: Rhonda Lee Lother
Interns: Mackenzie Cogle, Susan Kemp, Emily Robinson

**Time Home Entertainment Inc.**
Publisher: Jim Childs
VP, Strategy & Business Development: Steven Sandonato
Executive Director, Marketing Services: Carol Pittard
Executive Director, Retail & Special Sales: Tom Mifsud
Director, Bookazine Development & Marketing: Laura Adam
Executive Publishing Director: Joy Butts
Finance Director: Glenn Buonocore
Associate General Counsel: Helen Wan

To order additional publications, call 1-800-765-6400 or
    1-800-491-0551.

For more books to enrich your life, visit **oxmoorhouse.com**

To search, savor, and share thousands of recipes, visit
    **myrecipes.com**

Front Cover (left to right): 9-Minute Microwave Peanut
    Brittle (page 154), Ham with Cumberland Sauce (page 258),
    Tree Stocking and Bird Stocking (page 28)
Back Cover (left to right): Cozy Mug Wraps (page 73),
    Vintage Angels Wreath (page 14), Carrot Cake Jam (page 138)

# Our Story

Back in 1984, we were next-door neighbors raising our families in the little town of Delaware, Ohio. Two moms with small children, we were looking for a way to do what we loved and stay home with the kids too. We had always shared a love of home cooking and making memories with family & friends and so, after many a conversation over the backyard fence, **Gooseberry Patch** was born.

We put together our first catalog at our kitchen tables, enlisting the help of our loved ones wherever we could. From that very first mailing, we found an immediate connection with many of our customers and it wasn't long before we began receiving letters, photos and recipes from these new friends. In 1992, we put together our very first cookbook, compiled from hundreds of these recipes and the rest, as they say, is history.

Hard to believe it's been over 25 years since those kitchen-table days! From that original little Gooseberry Patch family, we've grown to include an amazing group of creative folks who love cooking, decorating and creating as much as we do. Today, we're best known for our homestyle, family-friendly cookbooks, now recognized as national bestsellers.

One thing's for sure, we couldn't have done it without our friends all across the country. Each year, we're honored to turn thousands of your recipes into our collectible cookbooks. Our hope is that each book captures the stories and heart of all of you who have shared with us. Whether you've been with us since the beginning or are just discovering us, welcome to the **Gooseberry Patch** family!

## We couldn't make our best-selling cookbooks without YOU!

Each of our books is filled with recipes from cooks just like you, gathered from kitchens all across the country.

Share your tried & true recipes with us on our website and you could be selected for an upcoming cookbook. If your recipe is included, you'll receive a FREE copy of the cookbook when it's published!

## www.gooseberrypatch.com

## We'd love to add YOU to our Circle of Friends!

Get free recipes, crafts, giveaways and so much more when you join our email club...join us online at all the spots below for even more goodies!

Whimsical snowmen always make us smile! This year, celebrate all the fun of the freezing season with a few of the frosty-looking fellows. You'll also find tinsel trees, magical snowflake ornaments and Advent Calendars. The Dapper Doorman greets visitors and assures them they'll find a wonderland of wintry decorations indoors.

Dapper Doorman instructions are on page 324.

Dapper Doorman

9

## Door Basket

Place florist's foam in a hanging basket and arrange greenery and pinecones in the foam. (If using fresh greenery, line the basket with a plastic bag and moisten the foam before placing it in the basket.)

To add the bow and bells, wrap florist's wire around a multi-loop bow and each bell; then, insert the wires in the foam.

Door Basket

Sleigh Bell Strap

## Sleigh Bell Strap

- 4" dia. brass ring
- silver spray paint
- 5"x32" piece of red vinyl
- fabric glue
- 16" length of 3"w apple green ribbon
- four 2½" silver jingle bells
- 45 assorted size silver jingle bells
- 30-gauge silver wire
- artificial greenery
- 1½ yards 1½"w red dotted reversible ribbon

**1.** Working in a well-ventilated area, spray the brass ring silver.
**2.** Enlarge pattern (page 381) to 158%. Use the pattern and cut the strap from the vinyl. Cut the ribbon slits on the front side only of the strap.
**3.** Thread the green ribbon through the slits; glue on the wrong side. Sew the large jingle bells to the ribbon. Thread the strap through the silver ring, match the scalloped edges and glue the vinyl together.
**4.** Thread assorted silver jingle bells onto lengths of wire, wrapping the wire after each bell and allowing a bit of space before adding the next one. Wire the greenery pieces and the bell wires to the ring top. Make a multi-loop bow and attach to the ring top with a ribbon length.

## Lamp Post Banner

- 17½"x45" piece of primed canvas
- transfer paper
- apple green, green, brown, dark brown, red and ivory acrylic paints and paint brushes
- satin interior/exterior varnish
- six 25mm red jingle bells

**1.** Fold the canvas side and bottom edges 1" to the wrong side; machine stitch. For the casing, fold the top edge 3" to the wrong side and machine stitch close to the raw edge.
**2.** Enlarge the pattern (page 381) to 455%. Use transfer paper to transfer the design to both sides of the hemmed canvas. Paint the design on both sides. Apply several coats of varnish to the banner.
**3.** Sew the jingle bells along the banner bottom edge.

Lamp Post Banner

## Cheery Winter Welcome

- roll of copper wire mesh (found in the craft store sculpting department)
- wire cutters
- off-white latex enamel indoor/outdoor paint
- large disposable roasting pan
- disposable foam brush
- garden gloves
- pliers
- medium-gauge wire
- acrylic paints
- paintbrushes
- assorted greenery and ornaments

1. Enlarge the pattern on page 382 as desired. (We enlarged ours to 316% to make a 15"-long finished stocking.) Use the pattern and cut 2 stocking pieces from wire mesh.
2. Pour the enamel paint (to a depth of 1½") in the roasting pan. Dip one mesh stocking. After a few seconds, pick the stocking up from the top, allowing the paint to run down the stocking. Repeat with the second stocking. Hang the stockings to dry. To fill in any holes in the mesh, dip the foam brush into the paint and lightly brush over each stocking; allow to dry.
3. Stack the stockings. Wearing gloves, carefully crimp and bend the side and bottom edges to the back to join the stockings. Squeeze the "seams" flat with the pliers.
4. Open the top to allow for the greenery; turn the top edges to the inside and squeeze flat with the pliers. Add a wire hanger to the back of the stocking.
5. Paint stripes on the front of the stocking. Insert the greenery and ornaments into the top of the stocking.

**Cheery Winter Welcome**

Felted Ball Wreath

## Felted Ball Wreath

- plastic basin
- liquid dishwashing detergent (without scents or dyes)
- shades of green, red, ivory, blue and rust wool roving
- foam balls (we used 13 each of 1½", 2" and 2½" dia. balls)
- rubber gloves (optional)
- embroidery floss
- large-eye needle
- 12" dia. wire wreath form (ours has 4 wire rings)
- hot glue gun
- 1½ yards of 1½"w grosgrain ribbon
- plastic ring or aluminum can pull tab

**1.** Follow Felted Wool Balls (page 320) to cover foam balls with roving.

(continued on page 325)

Wouldn't it be merry to have a wreath on every door in your home? If you don't have time to make all four of these Whimsical Wreaths, most are so simple that you can surely create one for your front door! With just a little more time, you could make two of the same kind and give the second one as a gift!

## Whimsical Wreaths
### Vintage Angels
Dress up a plain 12" greenery wreath by wiring vintage ceramic angel bells along the bottom. Complete the wreath with layered circles (punched from cardstock and favorite holiday cards), vintage ornaments and a twill tape bow.

### Monogrammed Apple
Thread apples (fresh or artificial) on a sturdy 12" wire ring (cut open with wire cutters). Cover a wooden or chipboard letter with scrapbook paper and lightly sand the edges. Glue a craft stick to the letter back and insert into the bottom apple. Glue a small wood block behind the letter to keep it from tilting. Hang the wreath from a pretty ribbon.

### Felt Poinsettia
Begin by wiring pinecones to a 16" wire wreath form (we used an artificial pinecone garland). Enlarge the poinsettia pattern (page 376) to 200% and use it to cut 21 petals from assorted red felted wool and wool felt; cut 9 leaves from green wool felt. For each poinsettia, sew 7 petals together at the center; sew a button to the center. Hot glue the poinsettias and leaves to the pinecone wreath.

### Burlap Holly
Enlarge the holly leaf pattern (page 379) to 215% and 275%. Use the smaller pattern to cut 14 fabric leaves; use the larger pattern to cut 23 burlap leaves. Drybrush (page 318) the burlap leaf edges with green acrylic paint. Layer the fabric leaves on some of the burlap leaves. Work embroidery floss Running Stitches (page 319) through the leaf centers. Sew buttons to felt rounds. Glue the leaves, felt-backed buttons and letter squares to a burlap-wrapped 14" foam wreath. Add a wide twill tape bow to the wreath top.

## Vintage Angels

## Monogrammed Apple

## Felt Poinsettia

## Burlap Holly

"Bell Jar" Ornament

## "Bell Jar" Ornaments

• 5-oz. 2-piece plastic wine glasses
• craft knife or awl
• ornament cap and loop (removed from a purchased ornament)
• ribbon
• super-jumbo bottle cap (available at scrapbook stores) or jar lid
• mementos and other items to encase in ornament
• craft glue
• mica flakes

1. Use the craft knife or awl to make a small hole in the stem of the wine glass piece (discard the base piece). Attach the ornament cap to the glass by inserting the wire loop through the hole. Knot a ribbon length through the wire loop.

2. Place the mementos on the bottle cap or jar lid, gluing as necessary. We enclosed a mini bottle-brush tree and added a little "JOY" banner created with cork stickers and embroidery floss; marked the date with alphabet and number stamps, surrounding them with printed paper tinsel, mini ornaments, and colorful postage stamps; combined red and green postage stamps, a mini clothespin, and a seasonal label for a festive look; and arranged a sentiment rubber stamp with a beribboned key.

3. Glue the wine glass to the bottle cap or jar lid. Run a thin bead of glue around the wine glass rim and sprinkle mica flakes into the wet glue.

Family & friends will be amazed to see all the festive little things on display in the "Bell Jar" Ornaments.

Cardinal Ornament
Bell Mini-Banner Ornament

## Cardinal Ornament

- lightweight aluminum flashing
- utility scissors
- gloves to protect hands when working with flashing
- scrap block of wood
- hammer and small nail
- red spray paint
- black and brown acrylic paints and paintbrushes
- 2½" flat clothespin
- E-6000® adhesive

**1.** Enlarge the patterns (page 390) to 200%. Draw around the patterns on the flashing. Wearing gloves, cut out the pieces with the utility scissors.
**2.** On the wrong side of the paper patterns, draw over the wing, tail and eye with a pencil. Place the patterns, right side up, on the flashing wing, body and tail pieces and draw over the detail lines, transferring them to the flashing. Place the flashing pieces on the wood block; use the hammer and nail to punch the eye and the wing and tail detail lines.
**3.** Working in a well-ventilated area, spray the front and back of each flashing piece red. Paint the face black. Paint the clothespin brown.
**4.** Glue the wing and tail pieces to the body. Glue the clothespin to the cardinal back.

## Bell Mini-Banner Ornament

Instructions are on page 325.

17

Framed in small painted hoops, the 12 Days Ornaments feature easy embroidery and fabric appliqués for extra color.

**12 Days Ornaments**

## 12 Days Ornaments
- paper-backed fusible web
- fabric scraps for appliqués (we used 6 different fabrics)
- tissue paper
- water-soluble fabric marker
- twelve 6" squares of white duck cloth or heavyweight cotton
- embroidery floss
- teal acrylic paint
- paintbrush
- twelve 3" dia. wood embroidery hoops
- sandpaper
- 8" length of 1/8"w silk ribbon

*Read Embroidery Stitches on pages 318-319 before beginning. Use 2 strands of floss.*

**1.** Fuse web to the back of each fabric scrap.
**2.** Follow the Water-Soluble Fabric Marker Method (page 318) and transfer the patterns on page 384 onto duck cloth squares. Using the photos and patterns, cut fabric scrap appliqués. Fuse the appliqués in place.
**3.** Embroider the designs using Stem Stitch, French Knot and Lazy Daisy stitches.
**4.** Paint the hoops teal; then, sand for an aged appearance. Insert the stitched pieces in the hoops; trim excess fabric. Sew a silk ribbon bow to the 5 Golden Rings design.

## Frosted Jars and Tree Centerpiece

- square and round jars
- self-adhesive shelf liner
- assorted size circle stickers
- paper towels
- frosted glass spray
- foam brush
- decoupage glue
- glitter
- yarn
- rickrack
- fresh greenery
- tea lights
- acrylic paint
- paintbrush
- terra cotta flower pots
- sandpaper
- fresh spruce seedlings from the nursery
- heavy-gauge wire and wire cutters

*Don't leave burning candles unattended.*

**1.** Size the patterns on page 389 to fit your jars (see Sizing Patterns on page 318). For each square jar, use the pattern to cut 4 trees from shelf liner. Adhere one tree to each side of the jar. Place circle stickers on the round jars.

**2.** Place paper towels in the jars to protect the insides. Spray the jars with frosted glass spray in a well-ventilated area. When dry, remove the patterns, stickers and towels.

**3.** Brush decoupage glue over the unfrosted areas and sprinkle with glitter.

**4.** Wind small balls of yarn and glue the loose yarn ends to the balls. Tie rickrack or yarn balls and greenery to the jars. Add tea lights.

**5.** For the seedling trees, thin acrylic paint with water; brush over the pots. When dry, lightly sand the pots and transplant the seedlings. Make yarn balls and thread them onto wire. Wrap each tree with a yarn ball garland. We added plain glass jars in various sizes and shapes and used a trio of candlesticks and pillar candles to complete the arrangement.

Frosted Jars and Tree Centerpiece

19

Snowman Trio

If you could capture a bit of winter to keep indoors, it would surely look like this! The little Snowman Trio is pleased to be a part of your holidays. And the Tinsel Wreath is aged with an easy technique before vintage ornaments are added.

## Tinsel Wreath

- fine-gauge wire
- wire cutters
- 12" dia. white foam wreath
- silver tinsel garland
- T-pins or greening pins
- Design Master® Glossy
  Wood Tone Spray
- 2¼"w wire-edged ribbon
- vintage ornaments

This wreath glows with a cheery holiday welcome. Tie a wire hanger around the wreath. Wrap the wreath with garland, pinning as you go. In a well-ventilated area, lightly spray the wreath with wood tone spray to give the tinsel an aged appearance. Pin a bow at the bottom of the wreath and add ornament clusters.

## Snowman Trio
Instructions begin on page 324.

Tinsel Wreath

## Jar Mini-scapes

Any glass container can easily become a miniature Christmas vignette, so why not invite the older kids to assemble Jar Mini-scapes?

### Jar Mini-scapes

Capture a moment in time with these miniature vignettes.

Glue an old-time snowman ornament to the lid of a refrigerator jar. Dot the inside of the jar with craft glue and sprinkle with glitter for a snowy effect. Sprinkle mica flakes at the base of the snowman and glue the lid to the jar. Glue printed paper tinsel around the jar.

A sweet little reindeer is glued in a jar with a dusting of mica-flake snow at his feet. Tie a rickrack length around the jar and add a seasonal message cut from printed paper tinsel.

Nestle a bottle-brush tree in a tin gelatin mold and decorate with assorted buttons, printed paper garland and red Running Stitched (page 319) rickrack. Top off the tree with a vintage brooch.

Next, glue the mold into the lid of a large jar. Scatter mica flakes and buttons in the lid. Adhere dimensional snowflake stickers to the inside of the jar. Place the jar over the tree and tighten the lid.

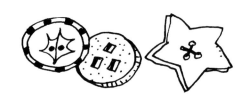

No snow outside? Let it snow inside! A purchased snowflake garland adds the beauty of the season to wrapped packages. Make a curtain of "falling" snow with Window Dressing Garlands. They're simple to create by cutting snowflakes from felt and adding buttons and pom-poms.

**Window Dressing Garlands**
Bring a bit of snowflake magic indoors with this frosty window or mirror dressing.

Enlarge the patterns (page 387) to 200%. Use the enlarged patterns and cut snowflakes from felt. Sew vintage buttons to the snowflake centers. Thread the snowflakes, more vintage buttons and pom-poms onto 30-lb. test weight fishing line lengths, knotting the line above and below each element.

Window Dressing Garlands

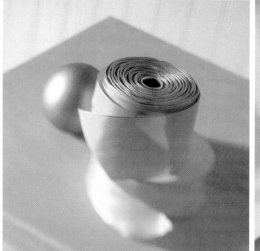

## Fabric Christmas Cookie Ornaments

*Bits of rickrack, seed beads and tiny buttons combine with simple embroidery stitches to make these cookies extra-sweet.*

- tracing paper
- washable marking pen
- cotton muslin fabric
- scraps of thin cotton batting
- embroidery floss in desired colors
- assorted buttons, ⅛" for gingerbread man, others as desired
- red baby rickrack for gingerbread figures
- 6 mm seed beads in assorted colors
- invisible nylon thread
- 7" of ⅜" w ribbon for each hanging loop
- scraps of felted wool, in assorted colors
- scraps of ultra-hold double-sided fusible web
- pinking shears

(continued on page 325)

Fabric Christmas Cookie Ornaments
Vintage Popcorn String

Scraps of muslin turn into dozens of sweet Fabric Christmas Cookie Ornaments using simple patterns and clever embellishments. Fold brown paper, and with a snip of your scissors, you've created a magical Gingerbread House Garland! Add touches of paint and bits of tissue to complete each little house.

Gingerbread House Garland

## Vintage Popcorn String

This vintage look is easy to do and even more fun to do together! String some popcorn and cranberries on dental floss to make a sturdy string garland that will give your tree that welcoming look. The cranberries will dry to become a beautiful dark red. Keep the garland in your freezer to last year after year.

## Gingerbread House Garland

- tracing paper
- one roll of brown kraft paper
- scissors
- scraps of light yellow tissue paper
- crafts glue
- white fabric paint in a tube

**1.** Trace pattern (page 380) onto tracing paper and cut out, being sure that folds on the pattern are marked.

**2.** Cut the brown kraft paper into 3½" x 18" lengths, cutting as many lengths as needed for the tree.

**3.** Fold the paper accordion-style. Lay the pattern on the folded paper with the folds at the side. Cut out the pattern cutting through all of the thicknesses of the paper. Open up the garland.

(continued on page 326)

Fruit-Inspired Luminarias

Create Felted Holly Trims using green felted fabric and red homespun yarn. Light the way with Fruit-Inspired Luminarias…painted fruit jars with votive candles inside.

## Fruit-Inspired Luminarias

- clear, smooth canning jars
- tracing paper
- pencil
- scissors
- tape
- glass paint in desired colors
- paintbrush
- crackle medium, topcoat and dark crackle enhancer, such as Modern Masters
- ribbon

**1.** Trace the desired full-size patterns (page 378). For each jar, cut out the shape and tape it in the desired position on the inside of the jar. Use the pattern to paint the fruit shape on the jar, blending white with the color to make a highlighted top. Let the paint dry.

**2.** Apply the base coat of the crackle mixture to the painted fruit shape as directed by the manufacturer. Follow each of the crackling technique steps as directed, ending with the enhancer to make the appearance of crackling stand out. Let dry. Tie a ribbon bow around jar.

## Felted Holly Trims

- tracing paper
- two 9" x 10" pieces of green wool felt for each ornament
- matching sewing threads
- polyester fiberfill
- contrasting green embroidery floss
- red homespun yarn
- green perle cotton thread

**1.** Enlarge and trace pattern (page 379) onto tracing paper. Cut out. Place felt pieces together and cut out 2 leaf shapes from the pattern.

**2.** With right sides together stitch around outside edges using ¼" seam allowance, leaving an opening for turning. Clip curves and points. Turn right side out, pushing out points of leaves.

**3.** Stuff leaves with a small amount of polyester fiberfill. Sew opening closed with hand stitches. Mark vein lines on leaves with marking pencil. Using 2 strands of embroidery floss, stitch Stem Stitches (page 319).

**4.** Coil short lengths (6"-8") of yarn on top of leaves in center to make berries. Handstitch in place by couching over yarn, using matching thread. Sew a length of perle cotton through leaves and knot at ends to make a hanging loop.

Felted Holly Trims

Santa will be thrilled to see all these felt stockings waiting to be filled. Wool roving makes Santa's beard fluffy.

## Stockings
### Santa
- two 14"x23" pieces of aqua felt
- dressmaker's tracing paper
- red, ivory, peach, pink and black wool roving
- needle felting tool and mat
- ¾" dia. shank button for nose
- fabric glue
- 16"x8" piece of chenille fabric
- 16" length of ball fringe

**1.** Enlarge the pattern (page 379) to 206%. Using the enlarged pattern, cut 2 aqua felt stocking pieces. Using dressmaker's tracing paper, transfer the design to 1 piece. For the hanger, cut a 1"x5" felt piece.

**2.** Follow Needle Felting (page 320) to fill in Santa. For the moustache, needle felt a roving piece above the mouth, leaving the ends loose. Sew Santa's button nose in place. Add ivory roving "snow" to the stocking.

**3.** Leaving the top open, glue the stocking pieces together along the edges. Fold under ¼" along both long edges and 1 short end of the chenille piece. Overlap the short ends and glue, forming a ring. Use Running Stitches (page 319) to gather the chenille piece to about 3½" high. Glue the fringe to the chenille piece bottom edge. Glue the chenille piece top edge to the stocking top, gluing the hanger in the upper right corner.

### Tree
Instructions are on page 326.

Stockings

### Bird
- two 14"x23" pieces of red felt
- fabric scraps
- paper-backed fusible web
- embroidery floss
- buttons
- clear nylon thread

**1.** Enlarge the Bird patterns (page 378) to 200%. Enlarge the Poinsettias Stocking pattern (page 390, ignoring the poinsettia design) to 206%. Using the enlarged stocking pattern, cut 2 red felt stocking pieces. For the hanger, cut a 1"x5" felt piece.

**2.** Fuse web to the back of each fabric scrap. Using the enlarged Bird patterns, cut body, wing, 5 small leaf and 5 large leaf appliqués. Fuse the appliqués to 1 stocking piece. Use floss to work a Running Stitch (page 319) vine, a French Knot eye and to sew on the buttons.

**3.** Leaving the top open, use nylon thread to sew the stocking pieces together along the edges, catching the hanger in the upper right corner.

## Poinsettias

- two 14"x23" pieces of blue felt
- tissue paper
- tan crewel wool
- ivory and tan textured yarns
- fabric glue

*Read Embroidery Stitches on pages 318-319 before beginning.*

**1.** Enlarge the pattern (page 390) to 206%. Using the enlarged pattern, cut 2 blue felt stocking pieces. For the hanger, cut a 1"x5" felt piece.

**2.** Transfer (page 318) the design to 1 felt stocking. Embroider the design using the crewel wool for the Chain Stitches, Straight Stitches and small French Knots. Work additional larger French Knot flower centers with the ivory textured yarn.

**3.** Using crewel wool, work Couching Stitches and French Knots to attach lengths of ivory and tan yarn to the cuff and toe. Leaving the top open, glue the stocking pieces together along the edges, gluing the hanger in the upper right corner.

29

**Counting the Days Calendar**

Advent Calendars bring out the kid in everyone. That's because we all remember the excitement of counting the days 'til Christmas! With these ideas, you can track the days with colorful tags, bags of candy and other treats or a variety of clever magnets with fun messages hidden underneath.

### Advent Calendars
#### A Jolly Christmas Countdown

A simple enamel-ware tray is transformed into a countdown to Christmas with fun magnets. Make magnets from cardstock, tags, covered buttons, dominos, dice, vintage tags and wrappings, rub-on numbers, rubber stamps, playing cards, small numeral stencils and all kinds of scrapbooking supplies. Place a small printed reward, such as "Bake cookies with Mom," under each magnet.

### Counting the Days Calendar
### Matchbox Garland
### Mini Gift Sacks
Instructions begin on page 326.

**Matchbox Garland**

Mini Gift Sacks

A Jolly Christmas Countdown

It is LATER

DEC. 23rd

than you think.

Papier-Mâché Ornament

Glittered Snowflake Ornament

## Papier-Mâché Ornament

- hot glue gun
- 5/8" and 1/4" dia. wooden beads
- 2 1/2" dia. onion-shaped papier-mâché ornament
- ball-head straight pin
- spray primer
- red spray paint
- white acrylic paint
- paintbrush
- 1/8" dia. self-adhesive rhinestones
- small foam brush
- decoupage glue
- mica flakes
- paper plate
- tinsel chenille stem

Hot glue the large bead to the top of the ornament. Pin the small bead to the bottom of the ornament, securing with a dab of hot glue. Prime, then spray paint the ornament in a well-ventilated area. When dry, paint simple snowflakes around the middle. Add a rhinestone to the center of each snowflake. Brush a little

decoupage glue on the top of the ornament and sprinkle with mica flakes. Shake the excess onto the paper plate. For the hanger, hot glue the ends of a chenille stem loop inside the top bead. Make a bunch of these homemade trinkets and fill up the tree!

## Glittered Snowflake Ornament

Instructions are on page 327.

## Jolly Frame Set

- fine-grit sandpaper
- red spray paint
- 5 open-backed frames with glass (5½"x7½" opening)
- clear acrylic spray sealer
- double-sided removable tape
- red cardstock
- craft knife and cutting mat
- ⅛" dia. hole punch
- scrapbook paper
- glue stick
- snowflake punch
- double-sided tape

**1.** For these jolly frames, lightly sand, then spray paint the frames in a well-ventilated area. Lightly sand around the edges for a slightly-worn look. Apply sealer to the frames.

(continued on page 326)

## Girl & Tree Silhouette

Instructions are on page 327.

**Girl & Tree Silhouette**

Holiday Pomander Centerpiece

Cranberry Ice Globes

## Holiday Pomander Centerpiece

*Citrus fruits are studded with whole cloves and other spices to make a naturally aromatic centerpiece.*

- fresh oranges, lemons and limes
- pencil
- round toothpick
- whole cloves
- woven basket
- fresh evergreens
- acorns and pine cones (optional)

**1.** Wash and dry the fruit to be used.

**2.** Choose the desired piece of fruit. With a pencil, mark dots where you want to place the whole cloves. Make patterns such as little stars, lines to form rows or snowflake patterns.

**3.** Use the toothpick to make a hole at each dot. Press the whole clove into the hole pushing in securely. Repeat for the other fruits to be used.

**4.** Arrange the fruits in the woven basket. Add fresh greens, acorns, pinecones, cinnamon sticks or other natural embellishments as desired. This centerpiece will stay fresh for approximately 4 days if kept in a cool place.

## Cranberry Ice Globes

Instructions are on page 327.

Making a Holiday Pomander Centerpiece is so easy and brings a sweet aroma to your holiday home. Cranberry Ice Globes are almost magical! The water and cranberries are frozen together inside a round balloon to form the shape. With fresh fruit, peanut butter and birdseed, you can make Birdie Fruit Ornaments. Your feathered friends will love you!

### Birdie Fruit Ornaments: Birdie Apple Treat, Birdie Orange and Kiwi Cups

- apples
- awl
- table knife
- small star cookie cutter
- peanut butter
- orange
- kiwi
- sharp knife; spoon
- fine twine
- birdseed

1. **For the Birdie Apple Treat,** slice the apple in ¼" slices. Using the cookie cutter, cut the shape from the middle of the apple. Spread peanut butter on the star cutout and the apple slice. Sprinkle with birdseed. Poke a hole at the top of the apple slice using the awl. Thread the twine through the hole to hang on the tree.

2. **For the Orange Cup and Kiwi Cup,** slice the fruit in half and scoop out fruit. Use the awl to poke a hole in each side of cup and tie the twine in the holes. Fill with birdseed and hang on the tree.

Birdie Apple Treat

Birdie Orange Cup

Birdie Kiwi Cup

Country Apple Candles

Snowflakes Under Glass

## Country Apple Candles

*A muffin tin becomes a country candle holder when you add red and green apples that have been carved out to hold votive candles. The apple candle holders rest in each muffin cup.*

- muffin tin
- sharp knife
- apples (red or green)
- small votive candles

**1.** Place the votive candle on top of the apple and mark where to cut for the opening. Use the knife to cut a hole slightly larger than the candle.
**2.** Place the candle into the hole made in the apple. Place the apples in the muffin tin.

## Snowflakes Under Glass
Instructions begin on page 327.

No-Sew Fabric Trims

Twine-Tied Candles

## No-Sew Fabric Trims

*These fabric ornaments look highly embellished but they are actually a no-sew project. The edges of the fabric scraps are pushed into the foam balls and the seams covered with rickrack.*

- tracing paper
- scissors
- pencil
- 3" foam ball, such as Styrofoam
- sharp knife
- scraps of small print fabric
- crafts glue
- scraps of small trims, such as rickrack

(continued on page 328)

Use the beautiful colors of red and green apples to carve out Country Apple Candles for a quick centerpiece. Let the children help cut pretty snowflakes to make Snowflakes Under Glass that everyone will love. Just a little glue and a few scraps of print fabric make special No-Sew Fabric Trims. Twine-Tied Candles come together in minutes and add sparkle to your holiday event.

**Twine-Tied Candles**
Instructions are on page 328.

**Reindeer Wreath**

Want a simple but clever wreath to decorate your door this year? Take a trip to the crafts store and be inspired by the ribbons and supplies available. A Reindeer Wreath sports a reindeer-motif design on the ribbon. Or look in your kitchen drawer to make a Cookie Cutter Wreath by wiring your favorite cutters on the wreath. Have fun wrapping foam balls with white yarn to create little snowmen. Then dress them up for winter to decorate your Happy Snowmen Wreath.

### Reindeer Wreath
- fresh green wreath
- vintage or new small reindeer
- red jingle bells
- ribbon with reindeer motif
- 24-gauge wire

1. Wrap wreath with ribbon securing in the back. Add a ribbon tie at the bottom.
2. Wire jingle bells to the wreath between ribbon.
3. Secure reindeer in the center of the wreath. Add wire for hanging.

### Cookie Cutter Wreath
- fresh green wreath
- vintage or new cookie cutters in desired shapes
- 2" w checked fabric ribbon
- 3" w ribbon for bow
- 24-gauge wire
- small vintage rolling pins

Cookie Cutter Wreath

Happy Snowmen Wreath

**1.** Lay wreath on covered surface. Wind checked ribbon around the wreath.

**2.** Wire cookie cutters and rolling pin onto the wreath. Make a large bow and wire to the top of wreath.

## Happy Snowmen Wreath

- 3" foam balls, such as Styrofoam
- lightweight white cotton batting scraps
- crafts glue
- white cotton yarn
- tracing paper
- pencil
- orange felt scraps for noses
- black glass round 8 mm beads for eyes
- black glass 3 x 4 mm donut beads for mouth
- scraps of felt, fleece or felted wool for hats, scarves
- scraps from discarded knit sweater for ear muffs and long pointed hat
- coordinating colors embroidery floss
- 2 cotton balls for ear muffs
- matching sewing thread

(continued on page 328)

# CHRISTMAS Fun and GAMes

These ideas for decorations and children's toys are sure to be fun for everyone! In fact, lots of grownups will recognize the vintage building toys and board game pieces in this playful collection of tree ornaments. The stuffed toy Horsie and Piggie are simple to sew and will become a child's best pals. Whether you create this Christmas theme for the playroom or the living room, you'll have a wonderful time enjoying the whimsy of the season, right along with the kids!

Fun & Games Tree instructions are on page 329.

Fun & Games Tree

Fun & Games Tree

41

Gift Cubes are colorful and sturdy, and can be used all year for floor pillows or handy ottomans. Too cold to play outside? A few games of Turtle Tic-Tac-Toe Toss will keep youngsters warm and happy indoors.

Gift Cubes

## Gift Cubes
• 22"x22"x4" piece of Nu-Foam® Densified Polyester
• spray adhesive
• ¾ yard each of red and blue baby wale corduroy
• fabric marking pen
• 5 yards of 1½" wide ribbon
• 2" dia. pom-poms (1 red and 1 green)
• craft glue

Match right sides, raw edges and use a ½" seam allowance for all sewing.

**1.** Cut Nu-Foam into four 11"x11"x4" pieces. Stack two pieces together to measure 11"x11"x8"; then, adhere the layers with spray adhesive to make a foam cube. Repeat with the remaining pieces.

**2.** Cut 2 squares 12"x12" and 4 rectangles 12"x9" each from red and blue corduroy. Mark a dot ½" from each corner on the wrong side of each square and rectangle.

(continued on page 331)

## Turtle Tic-Tac-Toe Toss
Instructions begin on page 329.

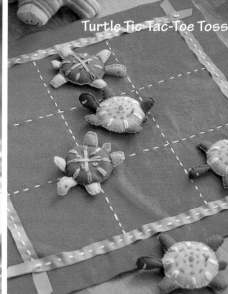

Turtle Tic-Tac-Toe Toss

**Personalized Tree Ornaments**

## Holiday Words Ornaments

- wood letter tiles and trays (we used pieces from a vintage Scrabble® game)
- fine-tooth handsaw
- sandpaper
- acrylic paint and paintbrush
- wood glue
- wood spools (we used vintage Tinkertoys®)
- wood beads (assorted sizes and colors)
- 6-ply multi-colored hemp twine

**1.** Cut the letter trays to fit the desired holiday words. Sand the cut ends and paint the trays.
**2.** Glue letters on the trays.
**3.** For each hanger, thread and glue beads and/or spools to center of a twine length. Glue the hanger ends to either side of the letter trays.

## Personalized Tree Ornaments
## Bead Garland
## Star Ornament/Tree Topper

Instructions are on pages 331 and 373.

**Bead Garland**

**Star Ornament/Tree Topper**

**Holiday Words Ornaments**

43

Piggie
Horsie

## Horsie

- 18"x29" piece of striped knit fabric cut from a gently used T-shirt
- two 20"x24" pieces of green lightweight knit fabric cut from a gently used sweater
- one 17"x28" and two 19"x23" pieces of lightweight fusible interfacing
- fabric marking pen
- paper-backed fusible web
- blue and green felt

- 5 small plastic zipping bags loosely filled with dried beans
- polyester fiberfill
- medium weight yarn (we used green, red, yellow and blue)
- brown and green embroidery floss

(continued on page 329)

## Piggie
Instructions are on page 330.

Spool Family

# Spool Family

scrapbook papers
vintage wooden thread spools (ours range
  from 1⅛" to 1¾" tall)
unfinished wood wheel (same diameter as
  largest spool)
craft glue
low-temp glue gun
wood doll heads (ours are 1", 1¼" and two
  1½" dia.)
acrylic paints
paintbrushes
embroidery floss
fleece scraps
10mm pom-poms
felt scraps
chenille stems

(continued on page 331)

# Hanging Birdfeeder
## and Bag o' Birdseed

Instructions begin on page 373.

Hanging Birdfeeder
and Bag o' Birdseed

Chubby Chirpers are easy
to assemble and decorate
with paint, paper and other
fun items!

## Chubby Chirpers
- acrylic paints
- paintbrushes
- papier-mâché pears (ours are
  3½" to 4" tall)
- clothespins
- low-temp glue gun
- chenille stems (we used bump
  and regular stems)
- tracing paper
- felt and print fabric scraps
- scallop-edged fabric scissors
- fabric glue
- wiggle eyes
- buttons

*A fun and easy craft…let a grown-up
help attach the crest and clothespin
with the glue gun. Use fabric glue
everywhere else.*

**1.** For each bird, refer to Drybrushing
(page 318) to paint a pear and
clothespin using contrasting colors.
Remove the pear stem; then, shape
and glue a chenille stem crest in its
place with the glue gun.
**2.** Using the patterns on page 402,
cut a felt beak and large tail. Cut 2
fabric wings and a small tail. Scallop
the curved edges of the wing and
tail shapes.
**3.** Layer and glue the tail shapes
together at the base. Pinch pleat
the center of the base and glue the
tail to the bird. Glue the wiggle eyes,
beak, pointed wing ends and buttons
to the bird.
**4.** Use the glue gun to attach the
clothespin to the bird.

Chubby Chirpers

**Sweet Sister Dolls**

## Salt Clay Snowflakes

*A simple salt clay recipe yields dozens of snowflakes that are easily decorated with permanent markers. Cookie cutters make cutting the shapes oh-so-easy.*

- one recipe Cornstarch Clay
- snowflake cookie cutter
- rolling pin
- drinking straw
- drying rack or foil
- fine-tip permanent marker in desired color
- narrow ribbon

**1.** Mix up Cornstarch Clay recipe (page 334) and keep in plastic bags until ready to use.
**2.** Roll out the clay onto a smooth surface, rolling to about ¼" thick. Cut out clay shapes using a snowflake cookie cutter or other desired cookie cutter.
**3.** Use a drinking straw to make the hole at the top of the ornament shape for hanging.
**4.** Arrange the cut pieces on a drying rack or foil and allow to dry for about 3 hours or overnight. Turn shapes over halfway through the drying time.

(continued on page 334)

**Sweet Sister Dolls**
**Child's Art Wraps**
Instructions are on pages 332 and 333.

**Child's Art Wraps**

**Salt Clay Snowflakes**

Paper Doll Dress Trims

## Paper Doll Dress Trims

- various fabric scraps
- cardstock or poster board
- crafts glue
- scissors
- tracing or transfer paper
- small buttons, ribbon and rickrack to match fabric
- black permanent marker
- thin fusible interfacing
- iron
- dark lead pencil
- flat paint brush (optional)
- thread for buttons

**1.** Enlarge and trace clothing patterns (page 396) onto poster board using transfer paper or using a copier on card stock; cut out. Using the pencil, trace patterns onto right sides of fabric, excluding the tabs.

**2.** Before cutting out fabric, iron a small square of fusible interfacing onto wrong side of fabric, where the outfit is traced following manufacturer's instructions.

**Note:** There is no need to add interfacing to collars, cuffs, sailor skirt, mittens or front dress facing.

**3.** When the fabric is cooled, cut out all clothing and add any small decorative pieces.

(continued on page 333)

Fold up a hankie, add a touch of paint and you've made a Bandanna Art Trim…perfect for sharing holiday treats. Sweet Candy Ornaments are made by melting colorful hard candy into fun, kid-friendly shapes. Little fingers will love to wear Santa Family Finger Puppets to tell all about their Christmas adventures with Santa Claus.

### Bandanna Art Trim
- purchased bandanna in desired colors
- scissors
- fabric paint pens
- embroidery floss to match bandanna color
- needle
- parchment paper
- cookies or treats to fill trim

(continued on page 334)

### Sweet Candy Ornament
Instructions are on page 334.

Bandanna Art Trim

Sweet Candy Ornament

Child's Art Wrap

Elf Puppets

Santa Family Finger Puppets

## Santa Family Finger Puppets

- tracing paper
- cardstock
- colored pencils or crayons
- scissors
- small scraps of felt
- crafts glue
- pom-poms for hats
- tiny button for collar

**1.** Trace the patterns (page 393). Copy onto cardstock and cut out. Cut out a set of 2 patterns for the Santa Puppets.

**2.** For the Elf Puppets, use colored pencils to color in the areas as desired. Cut out. Cut a slit where marked on the tab. Bend and fasten tab and slide on fingers.

**3.** For the Mr. and Mrs. Claus Puppets, color faces with colored pencils. Cut hat, beard and collar pieces from additional pattern. Draw around the pieces onto felt. Glue felt to colored pieces. Glue pom-poms and button in place. Cut a slit where marked on the tab. Bend and fasten tab and slide on fingers.

50

Ski Pals are sweet little sit-abouts that inspire smiles all season. To add color to a table, make a quick Felted Ball Centerpiece.

## Ski Pals

- acrylic paints
- paintbrushes
- 4½" craft sticks (for skis)
- wood doll pins with flat bottoms
- 1¼" dia. wood doll heads with ⅝" holes
- hot glue gun
- ribbon scraps
- embroidery floss
- tracing paper
- wool felt scraps
- 10mm pom-poms
- chenille stems
- 3½" flat wood sandwich picks or slim craft sticks (for ski poles)

**1.** For each skier, paint 2 skis, a doll pin body and a head. Add face and "button" details.
**2.** Glue the head on the body and a ribbon "belt" around the waist. Glue floss lengths to the head for bangs. For the girl, braid six 7" floss lengths and knot the ends; glue the center of the braid to the top of her head.
**3.** Using the pattern on page 407, cut a wool felt hat. Glue the front to the top of the head. Glue the back edges together and add the pom-pom.
**4.** Glue chenille stem arms at the back of the doll pin. Glue on the skis and ski poles, making sure the poles touch the ground for added support.

Ski Pals

## Cup o' Snow, Man

- white ribbed sweater
- 1" dia. foam ball
- white and black thread
- polyester fiberfill
- orange and black felt scraps
- fabric glue
- one 1½" and six 1" dia. black
  2-hole buttons
- hot glue gun
- heavy-gauge wire
- wire cutters
- two ½" dia. red buttons
- red novelty yarn
- coffee cup (we used a jadite cup)

**1.** Cut a 10" diameter circle from the sweater. To form the snowman's head, center the foam ball on the wrong side of the circle. Wrap the circle around the ball; then, wrap and tie white thread around the sweater circle below the ball.

**2.** For the center of the snowman, work Running Stitches (page 319) around the sweater circle 2" from the outer edge. Stuffing with fiberfill as you go, pull and knot the thread ends to gather the circle at the waist. Working Running Stitches near the outer edge, repeat for the bottom of the snowman.

**3.** Fold a small felt triangle in half for the nose. Glue felt eyes and the nose to the face and add the mouth with Running Stitches. Glue felt "coal" buttons to the belly.

**4.** For the hat, run thread through the large, then small black buttons. Run the thread back through all the buttons; knot and trim the ends. Hot glue the hat to the head.

**5.** Thread a 6" wire length through the center of the snowman for arms. Hot glue the red buttons to the wire ends for mittens. Add a yarn scarf and place the snowman in the cup.

## Glittered Houses

Instructions are on page 369.

Glittered Houses

Cup o' Snow, Man

Delight little ones with a Christmas Bib, appliquéd Tractor Hat and a zany Mitten Puppet.

## Tractor Hat

- child's knit hat
- paper-backed fusible web
- fabric scraps for appliqués and ear flaps
- 5"x4" felt piece to match hat
- clear nylon thread
- embroidery floss
- size 2 snap
- yarn to match hat
- crochet hook

(continued on page 369)

## Mitten Puppet
## Christmas Bib

Instructions are on pages 370 and 372.

**Christmas Bib**

**Tractor Hat**

**Mitten Puppet**

One of the happiest sights of Christmas is surely a Gingerbread Cabin with a chocolate chimney.

## Gingerbread Cabin

*The whole family can help put together this woodsy cabin.*

Gingerbread Cookies dough recipe (page 317)
Royal Icing recipe (make 2, page 317)
2 white mint candies with holes in the middle
9 small red cinnamon candies
3 snack-size milk chocolate candy bars (each section is 1"x½")
2 chocolate-stuffed chocolate rolled cookies (4½" long)
3 1.55-oz. milk chocolate candy bars (each section is 1¼"x⅝")
sliced almonds
6 caramel-flavored hard candies
8-oz. bottle white sparkling sugar sprinkles

    For large cabin pieces, roll out dough to ⅛-inch thickness directly on pieces of parchment paper and then transfer the paper to your baking sheets. Roll out small pieces on a lightly floured surface to ⅛-inch thickness and transfer to ungreased or parchment-covered baking sheets.

(continued on page 370)

**Gingerbread Cabin**

BE KiND TO ★ReiNDeeR★ week·Dec. 19 thru 25

Jazzy Giraffe

You can easily fashion sweet gifts for young ones…and the mom who loves them! The Jazzy Giraffe is made from colorful socks and has shiny button eyes and a yarn mane & tail. Its whimsical striped legs are secured with four bright buttons.

## Jazzy Giraffe
- polka-dot sock (ours is 14" from cuff to toe)
- polyester fiberfill
- pair of striped anklet socks
- four 1" and two ³⁄₁₆" dia. buttons
- embroidery floss
- yarn

*Small objects can be a choking hazard for babies or small children. Make sure they are securely attached.*

**1.** Turn the dotted sock wrong side out. To form the neck, sew 2 seams along the foot of the sock (Fig. 1).

**Fig. 1**

**2.** Trim away the cuff and turn right side out. Stuff the sock and fold the raw edge under. Work Running Stitches (page 319) near the fold; tightly gather the thread and knot the ends.

**3.** Tack the underside of the head (the sock toe) to the neck (the sock foot).
**4.** For each leg, cut a 1½"x6" strip from a striped sock. Matching right sides and long edges, use a ¼" seam allowance to sew along the long edge and one short end. Turn the leg right side out and cut off ¾" from the top; set aside the scrap.
**5.** Stuff the legs. Sew pairs of large buttons and legs to opposite sides of the body, pulling tightly to add shape.
**6.** Sew 2 leg-scrap "ears" and ³⁄₁₆" button eyes to the head.
**7.** For the mane, separate the strands and tie floss lengths together in the middle (we used twelve 2" lengths). Sew the mane to the head. For the tail, braid yarn lengths together (we used six 6" lengths). Tie each end with yarn and sew the tail to the body.

# 'Tis the season to sew

Oh, how time flies when you're stitching these sweet projects! Vintage and reproduction fabrics are "sew" very merry when used to make a Blooming Apron, adorable Hostess Towels, or Stocking Pillows. Give your Christmas décor a fresh look this year by whipping up a whole garden of quick & colorful flower ornaments! They're truly simple to create for the tree, for package decorations and more.

Button Wreath instructions are on page 371.

## Blooming Tree Skirt

- 40"x40" square of fabric
- string
- water-soluble fabric marker
- thumb tack
- 1 yard fabric for ruffle
- 3³⁄₈ yards ball fringe
- large and small gathered fabric ornaments

When sewing, always match right sides and raw edges and use a ¹⁄₂" seam allowance.

**1.** For the skirt, follow Making a Fabric Circle (page 318) and use a 19" string measurement to mark the outer cutting line on the fabric square. Remove the tack and use a 1" string measurement to mark the inner cutting line.

**2.** Cut through all fabric layers along the drawn lines. Unfold the circle. Cut a back opening from the outer edge to the center opening. Press the center opening and the back opening edges ¹⁄₄" to the wrong side twice, clipping as necessary; topstitch.

**3.** Cut a 5"x240" strip for the ruffle, piecing as necessary. Matching the long, raw edges, fold the ruffle in half and sew the ends. Turn right side out and press. Baste along the raw edge at ¹⁄₂" and ¹⁄₄"; pull the basting threads, gathering the ruffle to fit the outer edge of the skirt. Sew the ruffle to the skirt outer edge. Press the seam allowances toward the skirt.

**4.** Sew the fringe over the ruffle seam, turning the ends ¹⁄₂" to the wrong side.

**5.** Pin large and small gathered fabric ornaments to the tree skirt.

**Button Wreath**

**Blooming Tree Skirt**

Who says you can't have a flower garden in December? These fabric flowers are so simple, you can "grow" dozens in a single afternoon! Use your favorite buttons or make covered buttons for quick flower centers. Let the finished flowers blossom on a Christmas tree. You'll find lots of ways to color your holidays with these fast little floral projects, and you don't even need a green thumb!

Felt Flower Ornament

Gathered Fabric Ornament

### Felt Flower Ornament
- fabric and felt scraps
- paper-backed fusible web
- scallop-edged scissors
- $7/8$" dia. self-covered button
- small clothespin
- craft glue

1. Fuse web to the wrong side of a fabric scrap.
2. Enlarge the patterns (page 387) to 200%. Using the enlarged patterns, cut the circle from felt with the scallop-edged scissors and the flower from the web-backed fabric. Fuse the flower to the circle.
3. Cut a 4" diameter fabric circle. Follow Making Yo-Yos (page 318) to make a yo-yo. Cover the button with fabric. Sew the yo-yo and button to the flower center. Glue the clothespin to the flower back.

### Flower Ornament/ Tree Topper Gathered Rickrack Ornament
Instructions begin on pages 334 and 335.

### Gathered Fabric Ornament
- $1\frac{1}{2}$"x22" fabric strip (or a 2"x55" fabric strip for a large ornament)
- matching embroidery floss
- button
- fabric scrap for large ornament center
- felt scrap
- small clothespin
- craft glue

1. For a small ornament, use floss to work Running Stitches (page 319) along 1 long edge of the fabric strip. Pull the thread to tightly gather the strip into a circle; knot the thread. Sew the button to the circle center.
2. Glue the flower to a $1\frac{1}{2}$" diameter felt circle. Glue the clothespin to the flower back.
3. For a large ornament, follow Steps 1-2 using a 2"x55" fabric strip, a $2\frac{3}{4}$" diameter felt circle and Making Yo-Yos (page 318) from a 4" diameter fabric circle for the flower center. Sew the yo-yo and button to the flower.

Flower Ornament/Tree Topper

Gathered Rickrack Ornament

**Basket Liners**

## Basket Liners
• small basket
• fabric to line basket
• cotton yarn
• ribbon for round basket
• Felt Flower or Gathered Fabric Ornament
  (page 58)

### Rectangular Basket
When sewing, always match right sides and raw edges and use a ¼" seam allowance.
**1.** To line a rectangular basket, measure the basket inside bottom width and length; add ½" to each measurement and cut a fabric piece this size. Measure the height of the basket and add 2". Measure around the basket and add 1". Cut a fabric piece this size.
**2.** Matching the short ends, sew the larger fabric piece into a ring. Placing the seam at one corner, sew the ring to the fabric bottom. Press the top raw edge ½" to the wrong side and topstitch. Place the liner in the basket and mark the handles on the liner. Slit the liner open just enough to allow the fabric to fold over the basket top and lie flat. Beginning at each side of the slit, use yarn to work Running Stitches (page 319) near the edge; tie yarn ends in bows and clip on a felt flower ornament.

### Round Basket
When sewing, always match right sides and raw edges and use a ¼" seam allowance.
**1.** To line a round basket with a drawstring-style liner, measure the basket inside bottom diameter; add ½" and cut a fabric circle this size. Measure the height of the basket and add 5". Measure around the basket top and add 1". Cut a fabric piece this size. Cut 2 fabric pieces 2¼"x half the basket top measurement plus 1"; set these 2 pieces aside.
**2.** Matching the short ends, sew the larger rectangular fabric piece into a ring. Sew the ring to the fabric circle. For the casing, press the top raw edge ½" to the wrong side and topstitch. Remove the stitching from side seam above the casing line. Thread a ribbon length through the casing.
**3.** For the basket cuff, press ½" to the wrong side on both ends and 1 long edge of each of the remaining fabric pieces, forming a casing at the bottom; topstitch. Matching the right sides, pin, then stitch the fabric pieces to the basket liner 3½" below the liner top edge. Thread a yarn length through each casing.
**4.** Place the liner in the basket, arrange the cuff around the handle and tie the yarn ends in a bow; clip on a gathered flower.

**Blooming Apron**

## Blooming Apron
Instructions begin on page 335.

Make your Christmas kitchen cozy with Embellished Towels and a Reverse Appliqué Table Runner. Once you know how easy these accessories are to create, you may decide to make extras for gifts!

## Embellished Towels

- white dish towels
- vintage linens
- lacy trim
- rickrack
- clear nylon thread
- velvet ribbon
- cotton ribbon

For each fabric-trimmed towel, cut a linen strip 2½" longer than the width of the towel. Press the long edges of the strip ¼" and the short ends ½" to the wrong side. Adding lacy trim or rickrack along the long edges and wrapping the strip ends to the back, pin the strip near one end of the towel. Zigzag along the long edges of the strip.

For the ribbon-trimmed towel, cut a length of each ribbon 2½" longer than the width of the towel. Sew the velvet ribbon along the center of the cotton ribbon; then, sew a flat velvet ribbon bow at the center of the layered ribbons. Press the ribbon ends ½" to the wrong side. Wrapping the ends to the back, pin the layered ribbon near one end of the towel. Zigzag along the long ribbon edges.

## Reverse Appliqué Table Runner
Instructions are on page 336.

Embellished Towels

## Stocking Pillow
- ⅝ yard of corduroy
- paper-backed fusible web
- 3 coordinating fabric fat quarters
- 3 coordinating scrap fabrics
- contrasting thread or embroidery floss
- 2⅛ yards of ¾"w rickrack
- polyester fiberfill
- skein of yarn

**1.** Cut two 15"x19" corduroy pieces for the pillow front and back.
**2.** Fuse web to the back of each remaining fabric. Enlarge the pattern on page 382 to 334%. Use the pattern and cut a stocking from each of the fat quarters along the outer black lines (we cut one in reverse and made the center stocking ½" longer than the others). Cut 3 cuff, toe and heel appliqué sets (one in reverse) from the scrap fabrics.
**3.** Fuse the stockings to the pillow front. Fuse a cuff, toe and heel to each stocking. Machine or hand Blanket Stitch (page 319) around the edges of the appliqués.
**4.** Using a ⅜" seam allowance, sew rickrack along the edges of the pillow front. Matching right sides and leaving an opening for turning, sew the pillow front and back together. Turn right side out, stuff and sew the opening closed.
**5.** Make four 2" diameter yarn Pom-Poms (page 320) and sew one to each corner.

## Fabric, Felt and Knit Stockings
Instructions are on pages 336-337.

The fun appliqués on the easy-to-make Stocking Pillow are blanket stitched, and the corner pom-poms are also simple to fashion. For more sewing fun, create a Fabric or Felt Stocking for each member of the family. Or treat everyone to their own Knit Stocking… generously sized to hold lots of little gifts!

Fabric Stocking
Felt Stocking
Knit Stocking

63

With handmade gifts, you can be as creative as you like. For instance, the Knit Pillow looks special when embellished with a vintage Christmas hankie. However, it's also festive when topped with an antique red, green & white doily. For a gift that couldn't be more welcome, or simpler to make, add ribbon and yarn fringe to a fleece throw. Everyone in the family will want to curl up in this cozy blanket.

**Knit Pillow and Fringed Throw**
Instructions are on pages 338-339.

Knit Pillow

Fringed Throw

65

Whip up some gifts for the four-legged members of your family! Colorful ribbons and a jingle bell invite your favorite feline to play with a Crocheted Kitty Toy for hours on end. And it's a lucky dog indeed that gets to wear the Knit Doggie Scarf. The happy stripes are finished with a stylish pom-pom closure.

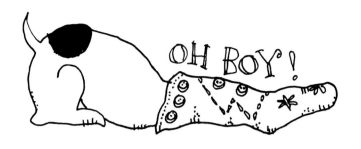

Crocheted Kitty Toy

## Crocheted Kitty Toy
*Read Crochet on pages 322-323 before beginning.*

 ●●□□ **EASY**

### Materials
Light Weight Yarn ⬛ LIGHT 3
    Small amount each of Green, Teal, Purple, Yellow, Ecru
Crochet hook, size F (3.75 mm)
Polyester fiberfill
Tapestry needle
1⅝ yards of one color and one 10" length each of 2 colors of ¼"w ribbon
½" dia. jingle bell
20" length of ¼" dia. dowel, painted with acrylic paint
Fabric glue

Gauge is not of great importance; your cat toy may be a little larger or smaller without changing the overall effect.

### Ball
**Rnd 1:** With Teal, ch 2, 6 sc in second ch from hook; do **not** join, place marker to mark beginning of rnd (see Markers, page 323).
**Rnd 2:** 2 Sc in each sc around: 12 sc.
**Rnd 3:** (Sc in next sc, 2 sc in next sc) around: 18 sc.

(continued on page 339)

# Knit Doggie Scarf

*Read Knit on pages 321-322 before beginning.*

■■□□ **EASY**

## Finished Size

| | |
|---|---|
| Small | 2" (5 cm) wide |
| Medium | 2½" (6.5 cm) wide |
| Large | 3" (7.5 cm) wide |

**Size Note:** Instructions are written for size Small with sizes Medium and Large in braces { }. Instructions will be easier to read if you circle all the numbers pertaining to your dog's size. If only one number is given, it applies to all sizes.

## Materials

Medium Weight Yarn
  Small amount each of Red, Lt Grey, Teal, Lt Green, Dk Grey, Aqua
Straight knitting needles, size 7 (4.5 mm) **or** size needed for gauge
Yarn needle

**Gauge:** In Stockinette Stitch, 20 sts and 28 rows = 4" (10 cm)

## Body

With Red, cast on 22{24-32} sts.

Beginning with a **purl** row and working in Stockinette Stitch (purl one row, knit one row), ★ work 5 rows Red, 3 rows Lt Grey, 5 rows Teal, 3 rows Lt Green, 5 rows Dk Grey, 3 rows Aqua; repeat from ★ until Scarf measures approximately 2{2-3}"/5{5-7.5} cm longer than the dog's neck measurement **or** to desired length and ending by working a **knit** row.

## Loop

**Row 1:** Bind off 9{10-14} sts, purl across: 13{14-18} sts.

**Row 2:** Bind off 9{10-14} sts, knit across: 4 sts.

Beginning with a **purl** row, work in Stockinette Stitch until Loop measures approximately 1½{1½-2}"/4{4-5} cm long, ending by working a **purl** row.

Bind off all sts in **knit**.

Fold Scarf in half and weave seam (Fig. 6, page 322).

With **right** side facing, flatten Scarf with seam in center. Sew cast on end closed; then gather end. Sew bound off end of Loop to center seam.

Make a 1½"/4 cm diameter Pom-Pom (page 320) and sew pom-pom to cast on end.

Knit Doggie Scarf

Every Christmas gift looks more festive with a bow! The Bow-Tied Apron is a snap to sew. It's also easy to add a monogram to a Hostess Towel (don't forget the ribbon bow and buttons). You'll be amazed at how quickly you can sew a Coiled Rag Basket, and it will look so pretty when piled high with bow-topped presents!

## Bow-Tied Apron

- 30"x4" fabric piece for upper band
- 30"x12" fabric piece apron skirt
- 1⅜ yards of fabric for waistband, ties and lining
- 1¾ yards of jumbo rickrack

*Always match right sides and use a ½" seam allowance when sewing.*

1. Cut a 30"x17" fabric piece for the lining, two 5"x44" fabric pieces for the ties and a 30"x3" fabric piece for the waistband.

2. For the apron front, sew the upper band and apron skirt pieces together along one long edge. Cut two 30" lengths of rickrack. Baste a length along the upper band raw edge and near the bottom edge of the apron skirt. Sew the waistband to the upper band.

3. For each tie, sew the long edges and one short end together, angling the end. Clip the corners, turn right side out and press. Matching the raw edges, pin one tie to each side of the waistband. Sew the lining to the apron front, leaving an opening for turning. Clip the corners, turn right side out and press. Sew the opening closed.

Bow-Tied Apron

Coiled Rag Basket

Hostess Towel

### Hostess Towel

Make a quick hostess gift for each holiday party on your calendar. Print or draw a 4" high letter. Transfer the letter to a fabric piece that has been backed with fusible web. Cut out the letter, fuse it to a linen tea towel and zigzag along the raw edges. Use clear nylon thread to sew ribbon along the towel bottom edge. Add buttons and a bow and you're done!

### Coiled Rag Basket

Instructions are on page 340.

## Vintage Handkerchief Pillows

These little pillows can be filled with sachets or just tossed in groups for a festive look.

- one or two vintage Christmas hankies for each pillow
- cotton fabrics for front and/or back of pillows
- matching sewing thread
- polyester fiberfill
- purchased piping or cording and fabric for piping
- buttons, beads, ribbon trims and other embellishments

**1.** Look at handkerchiefs to see what parts can be used and experiment with layouts and combinations of coordinating fabrics before starting.

**Note:** Some handkerchiefs have perfect borders for gathering for a ruffle around a smaller pillow. Others may have worn spots or stains but a center design is good. The pillows shown are 8"-9" in size.

**2.** After deciding the design of the pillow and pieces needed, hand sew parts of hankies onto coordinating cotton fabrics or iron fusible webbing onto the back of designs to cut out and fuse to another piece of handkerchief or coordinating fabric.

**3.** Add small bits of ribbon, old buttons, tiny beads or yo-yos (a 5½" circle makes a finished 2¼" yo-yo) for decoration to pillow front.

**4.** Make piping by covering cording or purchase piping to sew around the outside edge of the pillow or use as a decorative inset trim.

**5.** With right sides together, stitch the pillow front to the pillow back using ¼" seams, leaving an opening for turning.

**6.** Trim across corners and turn. Stuff pillow. Slip stitch opening closed using matching sewing thread.

Vintage Handkerchief Pillows

## Easy Holiday Lamp Shade

- ½ yard green and white stripe fabric
- coordinating sewing thread
- scissors
- one spool (about 30 inches) red pom-pom fringe

**1.** Measure the lamp shade around the bottom edge and add 5" to the width for length measurement. Measure the height of the lamp shade and add 2½" to the height for height measurement. Cut one piece using the measurements width x height.

**2.** Use ¼" seam allowance, unless otherwise instructed, and sew with right sides together. Press seams as you sew.

**3.** Sew the side edges together (the short ends).

**4.** Fold a double ¼" hem on the top edge and sew.

**5.** Fold a ¼" hem, then a 1" hem on the bottom edge and sew.

**6.** Sew a gathering stitch ¾" from the top edge. Start pulling gathers. Place the cover on top of the lamp shade and pull gathers to hold in place so that the lamp shade top and bottom edges do not show. Tie gathering thread. Space gathers evenly and topstitch on top of the gathers to hold in place.

**7.** Pin the pom-pom fringe on the bottom edge and hand or machine sew to the lamp cover. Repeat, sewing the pom-pom fringe at top of shade, covering the gathers.

Motifs from pretty Christmas hankies are stitched and appliquéd to create Vintage Handkerchief Pillows. Add tiny beads to the center of the blooms for some Christmas sparkle. Make reading those favorite holiday stories even more special by creating an Easy Holiday Lamp Shade. A pretty pom-pom edging adds the finishing touch to this simple little accessory.

**Monogram
Wool Stocking**

## Monogram Wool Stocking

*Vintage buttons embellish the toe and heel of this traditional wool pattern stocking.*

- tracing paper
- marking pen
- $\frac{1}{2}$ yard red wool fabric
- $\frac{1}{3}$ yard plaid flannel fabric
- $\frac{1}{8}$ yard gray wool fabric
- $1\frac{3}{4}$ yard of $\frac{1}{4}$" cording
- $\frac{1}{3}$ yard of fusible interfacing
- assorted vintage buttons
- $\frac{1}{8}$" decorative red cording for monogram letters
- matching sewing threads
- light-colored carbon paper

**1.** Enlarge and trace patterns (page 386) onto tracing paper and cut out. From red wool fabric, cut $1\frac{1}{2}$" strips of 45" and 16" lengths to cover cording, cut 2 from stocking pattern for lining, one each from heel and toe patterns and one 2"x 9" strip for hanging loop. From plaid fabric, cut 2 from stocking pattern. From gray fabric, cut 4 from cuff pattern. From interfacing, cut 2 from stocking pattern.

(continued on page 341)

Cozy Mug Wraps

Warm, woolly and waiting to be filled with holiday goodies, our Monogram Wool Stocking is personalized with red cording. Shadow quilting is the technique used to make Cozy Mug Wraps…such a pretty way to dress up winter mugs for holiday entertaining. Don't you just love the bright color of Christmas poinsettias? Create your own holiday blooms by making a Crochet Poinsettia Blossom using bright red yarn.

### Cozy Mug Wraps
- tracing paper
- marking pen
- scissors/pinking shears (optional)
- felt scraps, assorted colors
- matching sewing thread
- 14" of ¼" w ribbon for each wrap

**1.** Enlarge and trace inside and outside wrap patterns (page 380) onto tracing paper and cut out. Trace full-size Christmas motifs (page 380) onto tracing paper and cut figures apart. Cut one each of wrap inside and outside strips from coordinating colors felt. Pinking shears may be used to add interest to cut edges. Cut length of ribbon in half to make two 7" lengths.
**2.** Center inside strip over outside strip and pin in place. Center ribbon and insert between layers at ends.
**3.** Stitch close to cut edges of inside strip, stitching through both layers of felt, back-stitching over ribbon ends. Center motif pattern on back side of wrap and pin in place.
**4.** Using thread to match front inside strip felt color, stitch around lines of motif from the back side of the wrap. On front side cut away front layer of felt where desired to expose back felt layer below. Cut close to stitching lines and remove sections of front layer of felt.
**5.** Place the finished wrap around tumbler or cup and tie in place. Wrap can be used to insulate beverage container or as an identifier for each person's container.

### Crochet Poinsettia Blossom
Instructions are on page 341.

Crochet Poinsettia Blossom

**Striped Pot Holder
Plaid-Trimmed Table Runner**

Stitch up a Bias Tape Birdie Set to use during special holiday get-togethers. The Striped Pot Holder has an outside pocket and simple French-knot details. The Birdie Tea Towel sports pretty winter birds and the Plaid-Trimmed Table Runner is trimmed in overlapped bias tape forming a simple plaid design.

## Bias Tape Birdie Set
*Inspired by a 1920s tea towel, this stitched kitchen set uses colorful bias tape and simple embroidery stitches.*

### Plaid-Trimmed Table Runner
- one white tea towel (approximately 18" x 27")
- 2 5/8 yards red extra wide double fold bias tape
- 2 5/8 yards **each** blue and green single fold bias tape
- matching threads
- gold embroidery floss

1. Stitch bias tapes to towel, starting with green tape placed 1/2" from outside edge of long side of towel. Pin in place, folding cut edge under 1/2" to back of towel.
2. Stitch close to both side edges using matching thread. Repeat process on short ends of towel, crossing tape at corners.

3. Place blue tape 1/4" from edge of green tape and stitch in place. Place wide red tape 1/4" from edge of blue tape and stitch in place.
4. Using 3 strands embroidery floss, make French knots between bias tape rows.

### Birdie Tea Towel
- one white dish towel (approximately 18" x 27")
- four 5" strips of single fold bias tape for birds
- 2 1/2" and 6 1/2" lengths green single fold bias tape for branch
- black embroidery floss
- gold embroidery floss
- matching sewing threads

1. Referring to pattern (page 397), place green bias tape approximately 3 1/2" from bottom edge of towel. Place smaller branch on towel first and pin in place. Hand stitch in place using matching sewing thread. Sew with small stitches through toweling and tape. Fold cut edge under at top edge.
2. Place longer piece of green tape over lower cut edge of short branch. Pin in place and stitch with small hand stitches. Make birds by placing bottom piece of tape in place first, folding under edges

(continued on page 341)

Birdie Tea Towel

**Big, Beautiful Tote**

Someone you know needs an extra bag to carry large projects and necessities. The Big, Beautiful Tote will do the job with flair, and it's a great chance to sew with your favorite fabrics!

### Big, Beautiful Tote
- ⅝ yard brown fabric
- ⅛ yard each of 12 different fabrics for stripes
- ¾ yard fabric for lining
- 1¾ yards lightweight fusible interfacing
- rotary ruler with a 60° line, rotary cutter and cutting mat
- 4½"x13½" piece of cardboard

Always match right sides and use a ½" seam allowance when sewing, unless otherwise indicated.
**1.** From the lining fabric, cut two 19"x17" pieces and two 14½"x5½" pieces. Fuse interfacing to the wrong side of the larger pieces and set aside.
**2.** From the brown fabric, cut two 19"x7¾" bottom pieces, two 24"x4" strap pieces and four 19"x2" top pieces. Center and fuse a 3"x23" interfacing strip to the wrong side of each strap. Fuse interfacing to the wrong side of top pieces; set aside.

(continued on page 342)

## Yo-Yo Sewing Kit

- 14"x14" piece of fabric
- 6"x10" piece of fabric for lining
- 5"x9" piece of fusible interfacing
- thick cardboard
- two $1\frac{1}{8}$" dia. buttons
- $\frac{1}{8}$"w ribbon
- wool felt scrap
- size 2 snap

**1.** Cut a 6"x10" rectangle and two $5\frac{1}{2}$" circles from fabric. Follow Making Yo-Yos (page 318) to make 2 yo-yos, placing a $2\frac{1}{2}$" cardboard circle in the center of each yo-yo before gathering. Sew a button to each yo-yo with ribbon; set aside.

(continued on page 343)

**Yo-Yo Sewing Kit**

Make these day-brightening gifts for all your friends! The Felted Flower Pin and Felted Scarf are pretty presents that are actually made from worn sweaters!

## Felted Flower Pin
- worn wool sweater (with at least 60% wool content)
- tracing paper
- beading needle and thread
- seed beads
- hot glue gun
- pin back

1. Follow Felting (page 320) to felt the sweater.
2. Use the pattern on page 410 and cut 8 petals from the felted sweater. Pinching each petal at the point, sew the points together to form a flower; pull tight and knot the thread ends.
3. Add seed beads and hot glue the pin back to the back of the flower.

Felted Scarf

## Felted Scarf
- 2-color worn wool sweater or 2 different-colored sweaters (with at least 60% wool content)
- rotary cutter, ruler and mat
- seam ripper

*This warm & toasty scarf is designed to be worn with the seam allowances showing for added texture. Match wrong sides and use a 1/4" seam allowance for all sewing.*

1. Follow Felting (page 320) to felt the sweater.
2. Cut 20 strips from the sweater (six 9"x1½" and four 6"x1½" strips from each color).
3. Matching long edges and alternating colors, sew 4 same-size strips together. Repeat to sew the remaining strips together in sets of 4.

4. Matching short ends, sew the 9"-long panels together. Use the seam ripper to make a 2" opening in the center of one of the 9" end panels. Sew across the ends of the opening to secure. Sew a 6" panel to each end panel.
5. Baste across each end of the scarf. Pull to gather; knot the ends.
6. To wear, thread one scarf end through the opening on the opposite end.

## Wrist Corsage Pincushion

• fabric scrap
• polyester fiberfill
• embroidery floss
• ³⁄₈"w elastic
• felt scrap
• pinking shears
• 1 ½" to 2" dia. button (to
  prevent pins from poking
  through the bottom)
• buttons for flower center (ours
  are ⅝" and ¾" dia.)

*Delight a budding seamstress with
this floral-shaped pincushion. To be
extra crafty, measure her wrist ahead
of time without her knowing!*

**1.** Cut two 3¼" diameter fabric
circles. Matching right sides
and leaving an opening for turning,
use a ¼" seam allowance to sew the
pieces together. Clip the curves and
turn right side out. Stuff firmly and
sew the opening closed.
**2.** To form petals, knot the end
of a 6-strand length of floss and
sew through the center of the
pincushion from bottom to top.
Loop the floss over the edge of
the cushion and back up through
the center, pulling the floss tight.
Repeat to make a total of 8 petals.
Knot and trim the floss end.
**3.** Cut elastic to fit snugly around
the wrist with a ½" overlap. Stretch
the elastic and use pinking shears
to cut a ¾"w felt strip this length.
Stretching the elastic as you go,
sew the elastic along the center of
the felt. Overlap and sew the ends
together.
**4.** Sew the elastic loop between
the bottom of the cushion and
the large button. Sew the layered
buttons to the top.

**Wrist Corsage Pincushion**

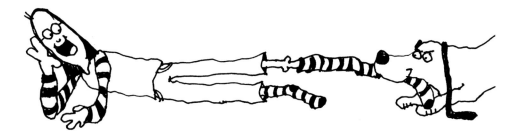

79

Sweater Throw

The happy colors of the Sweater Throw will almost keep you warm all by themselves!
The throw and Tree Sweater Pillow are quick to sew using pieces of gently worn
sweaters. Share your Christmas spirit with the neighbors by displaying a bell-
trimmed Lamp Post Banner.

80

## Tree Sweater Pillow

- two 22"x22" squares of red knit fabric cut from sweaters
- 11"x11" square of green knit fabric cut from a sweater
- green fabric scrap
- brown felt scrap
- red embroidery floss
- 12 assorted red buttons
- red vintage earring
- polyester fiberfill

**1.** Stabilize the red knit squares by zigzagging around the edges, using a medium stitch length and width.

**2.** Enlarge the patterns (page 410) to 200%. Use the circle pattern to cut 12 fabric circles and the trunk pattern to cut a felt trunk. Pin the tree pattern to the green knit fabric and stitch along the pattern edge to stabilize the knit fabric. Cut out the tree 3/4" beyond the stitched line.

**3.** Turning under along the stitched line as you work, hand sew the tree to a red knit square. Work Running Stitches (page 319) with red floss to attach the trunk below the tree.

Use red floss to sew the fabric circles, buttons and earring on the tree.

**4.** Matching the right sides and raw edges and using a 1/2" seam allowance, zigzag the red sweater pieces together, leaving an opening for turning. Turn right side out, stuff with fiberfill and hand sew the opening closed.

## Sweater Throw

Instructions are on pages 342.

Tree Sweater Pillow

# Gifts to Delight

If you're wondering what to do for all the folks on your Christmas list this year, why not make these original gifts? The Country Friends have always believed that the best presents are handmade! Thrill a youngster with a Crochet Toddler Hat. Treat your best friend to a Charm & Button Bracelet. And warm Grandma's heart with a Picture-Perfect Paper Weight. There's something for everyone, even the family pets, in this collection of memorable and merry gifts.

Family Photo Wreath instructions are on page 344.

Family Photo Wreath

Tag sale linens and potholders make oh-so-pretty Hanging Tea Towels, while fabric scraps sew up quickly into a microwaveable Neck Warmer. The JOY Banner is easy layers of fabric and felt.

## Hanging Tea Towels

- vintage linens
- vintage crocheted potholders
- clear nylon thread
- buttons
- ribbons

Rescue vintage linens and turn them into hanging tea towels for your favorite cooks. Cut 16"x18" linen pieces; turn the raw edges ¼" to the wrong side twice and hem. Baste along the top edge. Gathering to fit, pin each towel along the back bottom edges of a potholder. Zigzag using nylon thread. Sew a button to the front of each potholder (for our cherry print towel, we added a button "cherry" with crocheted leaves found in the scrapbooking section of the craft store). Sew a ribbon loop to the back for each hanger.

**Hanging Tea Towels**

## Neck Warmer

## JOY Banner

- water-soluble fabric marker
- white felt
- pinking shears
- red and green print fabrics
- cotton swab
- fabric glue
- ribbon
- jumbo rickrack

Share the JOY this season! Enlarge the patterns on page 394 to 250%; cut out the letters and one of each size circle. Drawing around the patterns with the marker, cut small and large felt circles. Use pinking shears to cut medium circles from red fabric. Cut green fabric circles slightly smaller than the small felt circles. Cut a letter from the center of each small felt circle. Dab away any marker lines with a damp cotton swab. Layer and glue the circles together; add bows at the top. Glue the circles to a rickrack garland.

**JOY Banner**

## Neck Warmer

- fabric scraps (we used 5 fabrics at least 9" long)
- two 10" lengths of 1"w grosgrain ribbon
- flannel for backing
- uncooked rice
- embroidery floss

A cozy gift for cold nights or tired muscles! Match right sides and use a ½" seam allowance unless otherwise noted. Wash and press all fabrics before beginning. Make the warmer as long as you like (the finished size of our neck wrap is 7"x17").

(continued on page 344)

Vintage linens are pretty & practical when you sew them into a Bedside Catchall or a feminine Hankie Blankie.

## Hankie Blankie

- 1⅛ yards of muslin
- 7 vintage hankies (we used 2 more as embellishments)
- clear nylon thread
- one 12½"x12½" square each of 8 vintage-look fabrics (we pieced one square, trimming with rickrack over the seams)
- assorted fabric scraps for yo-yos
- ribbon for leaves
- embroidery floss
- 1⅞ yards of backing fabric (wraps to front for binding)
- baby size cotton batting

*Match right sides and use a ½" seam allowance unless otherwise noted. Our finished blankie is 37"x60".*

(continued on page 344)

## Bedside Catchall

Give an embroidered heirloom that will be enjoyed…and well used! Press the open end of a pillowcase about 10" toward the closed end. Topstitch the side edges together. Sew up the middle of the pillowcase, creating pockets. Sew a button at the top of each line of stitching. Tuck the closed end between the mattress and box springs for a cozy catchall.

Bedside Catchall

Hankie Blankie

Hey Dolly Dolly!

## Keepsake Bracelet

Create a charm bracelet that highlights the life of someone special (we even added a state charm to showcase her birthplace). Start with a vintage bracelet chain and use jump rings and needle-nose jewelry pliers to add a mixture of charms from Mom's jewelry box, flea markets and new charms (see Working with Jump Rings, page 318). Fill tiny frames with dear photos. Earring dangles, beads on eye pins and a silk ribbon bow add plenty of color and personality!

**Keepsake Bracelet**

**Posy Pendant**

## Posy Pendant

- water-soluble fabric marker
- tissue paper
- 5" linen square
- embroidery floss
- white paper for backing
- 1½"x1⅞" photo pendant with top and bottom loops
- ½" and ⅛"w ribbons
- beads
- flower charm
- 1" fancy head pin
- needle-nose jewelry pliers

*Embroider your own or use a small vintage linen remnant to make a very special necklace.*

**1.** Use the pattern on page 390 and follow the Water-Soluble Fabric Marker Method (page 318) to transfer the design to the linen square. Work Stem Stitch (page 319) stems and Lazy Daisy petals and leaves using 2 strands of floss.

**2.** Place the embroidered piece and a paper backing piece between the clear pendant inserts; trim to fit and insert in the pendant. Run the wide ribbon through the top loop of the pendant and tie narrow ribbons to the bottom loop.

**3.** To add the dangle, thread beads and the charm onto the head pin. Curl the end through the bottom pendant loop with pliers.

Picture-Perfect Paperweight

## Picture-Pefect Paperweight

- flat glass candleholder (found at craft stores)
- tracing paper
- scrapbook paper
- poster board
- felt
- spray adhesive
- clear-drying glue
- memorabilia (we used ribbons, photos, a quote, tag, paperclip, chipboard letter, flower charm and button)
- ⅛"w ribbon

**1.** Draw around the base of the candleholder on tracing paper. Use the pattern to cut a piece each from scrapbook paper, poster board and felt.
**2.** Using spray adhesive in a well-ventilated area, sandwich the poster board between the scrapbook paper and felt pieces.
**3.** Arrange and glue memorabilia to the scrapbook paper. Glue the outer edge of the paper to the candleholder bottom. Glue ⅛" ribbon along the bottom side edge to finish.

## Felt Fob

- tracing paper
- water-soluble fabric marker
- fabric scrap
- felt scraps (including cream & blue for backgrounds)
- pinking shears
- embroidery floss
- fabric glue
- key ring
- button

**1.** Trace the patterns on page 387. Refer to the photo and use the patterns to cut the small hill from fabric and the remaining shapes from felt, using pinking shears as desired.
**2.** Pin the flowers on the cream background.
**3.** Refer to the pattern and key and use 6 strands of floss to work Stem Stitch (page 319) stems, Lazy Daisy leaves and Straight Stitch, Backstitch and French Knot flower details. Add Running Stitches around the top and side edges of the cream background piece.
**4.** Glue the hill pieces in place. Fold a ½"x2½" felt tab in half around the key ring. Glue the ends to the back of the cream piece and glue to the blue background piece. Add the button, sewing through all layers.

Felt Fob

**Flap Cap**

You can transform a frame into a Snowbound Tray, or crochet a Flap Cap to keep a special boy warm & toasty.

## Flap Cap
*Read Crochet on pages 322-323 before beginning.*

**Finished Size:** 15" (38 cm) head circumference

### Materials
Medium Weight Yarn
    [3 ounces, 145 yards
    (85 grams, 133 meters) per
    skein]: 1 skein
Crochet hook, size I (5.5 mm) *or* size
    needed for gauge

(continued on page 345)

## Snowbound Tray
- 11"x14" whitewashed wood frame with glass and a sturdy backing
- screwdriver
- drawer pulls
- craft glue
- scrapbook papers
- acid-free marker
- ribbons
- green and black cardstock
- white crayon

(continued on page 345)

**Snowbound Tray**

## Vintage Fabric Scarf

- ¾ yard vintage fabric for scarf
- assorted fabric scraps for mini bundle fringe
- polyester fiberfill
- medium weight yarn [1.75 ounces, 98 yards (50 grams, 90 meters)]
- crochet hook, size F (3.75 mm) or size needed for gauge
  Gauge Swatch:
  5" (12.5 cm) wide
  Work same as Rows 1-3.

*Read Crochet on page 322-323 before beginning. Always match right sides and use a ½" seam allowance when sewing.*

**1.** Cut four 6"x40" pieces of fabric. Sew 2 fabric pieces together along one short end. Repeat with the remaining fabric pieces. Matching the right sides and leaving an opening for turning, sew the fabric pieces together on all sides. Clip the corners, turn right side out and press. Sew the opening closed.

**2.** For the crocheted edgings, work 2 pieces as follows:
Ch 20.
Row 1: Sc in second ch from hook and in each ch across: 19 sc.
Row 2: Ch 1, turn; sc in each sc across.
Row 3: Ch 1, turn; sc in each sc across.
Row 4: Ch 1, turn; sc in first sc, H ch 6, skip 2 sc, sc in next sc; repeat from H to end of row; finish off.

**3.** For each fabric bundle, cut a 2½" fabric circle. Work Running Stitches (page 319) ¼" from the edge and tightly gather the bundle, placing a bit of fiberfill in the center. Wrap the bundle top with the thread and securely knot.

**4.** Sew the edgings to the scarf ends. Sew the fabric bundles to the edging loops.

Vintage Fabric Scarf

Colorful Felt Birds are happy sights to see in a tabletop arrangement or on a Christmas tree. If you're looking for a gift that will be treasured, nestle a Charm & Button Bracelet in a special gift box.

Felt Birds

### Felt Birds
- tissue paper
- coordinating felt colors
- mesh transfer canvas, permanent marker and water-soluble fabric marker (optional)
- coordinating embroidery floss colors
- beading needle
- seed beads
- ⅛"w ribbon
- polyester fiberfill
- ⅜" dia. white buttons for eyes

(continued on page 346)

### Charm & Button Bracelet
Instructions are on page 346.

Charm & Button Bracelet

## Family Platter

*You will need to size the pattern to fit your platter (see Sizing Patterns on page 318). We enlarged our pattern on page 383 to 203%.*

Find a platter (ours is 13¾"x19") at your local do-it-yourself pottery studio. Take the enlarged pattern and graphite transfer paper to the studio to transfer the design. The shop will provide everything you need to complete your platter. For a special family gift, have the kids paint the flower centers with their thumbprints and add names with a liner brush.

The ceramic Family Platter is a wonderful way to serve up cookies and memories for many years to come.

**Family Platter**

Neat!

Personalize gifts for all those special people on your list with a Reverse Painting Ornament and an Initial Bracelet. These one-of-a-kind ornaments are made using a purchased clear glass flat ornament and glass paints, painting in reverse style on the back of the piece. The charming little bracelet is strung on elastic cording. Tiny red and white print fabric makes the binding for purchased towels and creates a clever Dish Towel Apron…just in time for holiday baking. Well-worn jeans are the inspiration for Denim Luggage Tags…a perfect gift for the frequent traveler!

**Reverse Painting Ornament**
**Initial Bracelet**
Instructions are on pages 346 and 347.

**Reverse Painting Ornament**

**Initial Bracelet**

94

## Dish Towel Apron

*Two coordinating towels are folded and trimmed with a printed bias binding to create a favorite apron complete with big pockets.*

- two 18"x28" dish towels
- ½ yard printed cotton fabric (44" w) to make tape and for waistband and belt
- 2"x 36" strip coordinated print cotton fabric for tape to edge pockets
- 1" w bias tape maker tool
- matching sewing thread

(continued on page 347)

## Denim Luggage Tags

instructions are on page 347.

Dish Towel Apron

Denim Luggage Tags

## Country Pot Holders

- vintage 4-square quilt blocks or prepare your own from scraps of fabric (see instructions)
- 7" square of heat-resistant batting
- 7" square cotton fabric for backing
- 1⅞" x 38" cotton fabric for binding
- 20" rickrack (optional)
- 1⅛" plastic ring or 6" rickrack for hanging loop
- matching sewing thread
- perle cotton or embroidery floss if hand quilting the block

**1.** If making your own quilt block, cut four 3½" squares from cotton fabrics and sew together to make a 6½" block. Layer backing fabric, batting and block together.

**2.** Quilt block by hand or machine. Add decorative rickrack to top of block and sew through all layers

(continued on page 347)

Country Pot Holders

Don't know what to do with those favorite vintage fabric scraps? Piece 4-patch style to make them into Country Pot Holders for every cook on your Christmas list! For that special seamstress, whip up some Cupcake Pincushions that are sure to bring a smile!

Cupcake Pincushions

## Cupcake Pincushions

*These clever pincushions celebrate a fascination with cupcakes. Designed using scraps of worn sweaters, the pincushions have embellishments of felt, buttons and yo-yo flowers.*

### For both Cupcake Pincushions:

- tracing paper
- marking pen
- small amount polyester fiberfill
- crushed walnut shells for stuffing
- matching and contrasting sewing threads

### For larger Cupcake:

- 3"x 9" piece ribbing from recycled sweater (ends of sleeves or hem work great or if using a cut edge, turn a 1" hem to the back and use a walking foot to stitch in place)
- 4" square red felt
- 8" x 8" square pink cotton fabric
- 8" x 8" square lightweight iron-on interfacing
- 3" x 11" strip pink fabric
- 3" square red print fabric for yo-yo
- 3" square pink felt for bottom
- 12" piece of jumbo pink rickrack
- ³⁄₈" red button

(continued on page 348)

**Embroidered Baby Bib**

Every little one will love to wear an Embroidered Baby Bib for Christmas dinner! Sewn from tiny print fabrics, the bib has a coordinating collar and special message embroidered in the center. Dress up your little sweetheart with a Crochet Toddler Hat that sports a big happy flower.

### Embroidered Baby Bib

- tracing paper
- marking pen
- fat quarter (18" x 22") cotton fabric for each bib
- 3½" x 1" piece contrasting fabric for band
- scrap fabric for collar
- 11" x 15" piece thin cotton batting
- embroidery floss
- ½ yard of ¼" w lace for girls' bib
- 1½" long section of hook and loop tape
- three 4⅜" buttons
- transfer paper, marking pen
- coordinating threads

**1.** Enlarge and trace patterns (page 377) onto tracing paper and cut out. Seams are ¼" unless otherwise noted. Fold fat quarter of fabric in half and cut 2 bib pattern. Cut one bib pattern from batting.
**2.** Fold collar fabric in half to cut a total of 4 collar pieces. Cut one 3½" x 12" strip from contrasting fabric for the band. Transfer lettering to center of band strip using tracing paper.
**3.** Using 2 or 3 strands of contrasting embroidery floss, stitch around lettering using *Stem Stitch* (page 319). Trim band to 2½" x10½" in size. Fold ¼" back on long edges and iron.

(continued on page 348

# Crochet Toddler Hat

*Crochet abbreviations are on page 322.*

**Skill Level:** Easy

**Sizes:** 1 (2, 3) years. Sizes are written for the smallest size with changes for larger sizes in parentheses. When only one number is given, it applies to all sizes.

**Finished Measurements:**
Circumference: 16 (16 ½, 17) length from first to last rnd: 6 (6 ¼, 6 ½)

- Caron Simply Soft, 100% acrylic yarn, (6oz/170g/315yd/288m) per skein: One skein each of Soft Green (9739) for cap and Plum Wine (9722) for flower.
- Size F/5 (3.75mm) crochet hook or size needed to obtain gauge

**Gauge:**
In sc, 10½ sts and 18 rows = 4"/10cm.
**Take time to check your gauge.**

(continued on page 348)

Crochet Toddler Hat

Crochet Toddler Hat

The simple garter stitch is the only stitch you use to make a Knit Button-Trimmed Clutch. Do you feel like Christmas is coming too fast? You still have time to make an Easy Fleece Hat and Scarf Set because it is a quick-sew project! Warm wool in soft colors makes a beautiful Needle Felted Sewing Case that is sure to become a treasured heirloom.

### Knit Button-Trimmed Clutch

*This little purse is a quick gift to make. It is simply made as a rectangle and then folded for a clutch (with some added interfacing), then finished with a variety of vintage buttons and ribbon for tying.*

**Skill Level:** Beginner

**Size:** Finished bag measures approximately 8" x 6½".

- Hilos La Espiga, No.18, 100% nylon cord: One spool Delft (22)
- Size 3 (3.25 mm) knitting needles or size needed to obtain gauge
- yarn needle
- one yard of 1" w blue satin ribbon
- sewing needle and matching thread
- 7½" x 5½" piece plastic canvas
- 8" x12" piece thin cotton batting
- 8" x12" piece lining fabric
- assorted vintage pearl buttons

(continued on page 349)

Easy Fleece Hat and Scarf Set

### Easy Fleece Hat and Scarf Set
Instructions are on page 350.

100

## Needle Felted Sewing Case

*This darling needle case is the perfect inspiration to settle down to a hand stitching project. A 100% wool felt is the ideal base for decorative needle felting while providing a thick backing for resting needles. The sweet leaf and felt bead berry ties hold the rolled felt in place.*

### Dimensions: 9" w x 5¾" h

- 100% wool felt in white and beige
- 35% wool felt in aqua and pale green
- off-white thread
- two ½" felt beads
- wool roving in brown, beige, aqua, light blue, light green, off-white

(continued on page 349)

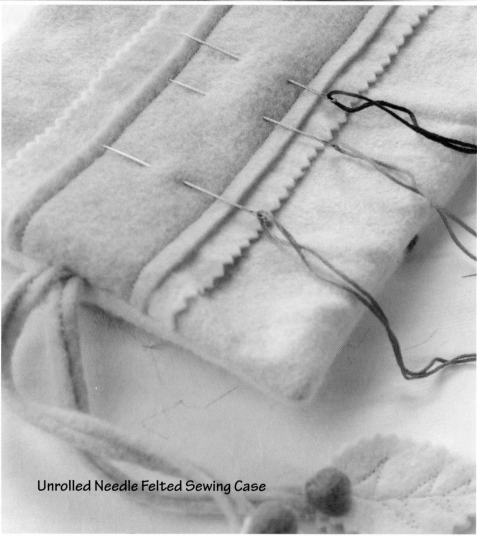

**Unrolled Needle Felted Sewing Case**

Memories are not the key to the past, but to the future. ∽ Corrie ten Boom

## Charming Jewelry

### Necklace

- assorted buttons
- flat charm bases
- E-6000® jewelry and craft adhesive
- wire cutters
- assorted beads
- head pins and eye pins
- needle-nose jewelry pliers
- jump rings
- crocheted or knitted flowers (we found ours in Grandma's attic)
- assorted charms (we used key charms)
- necklace chain (ours is 30" long)
- vintage clip-style earring
- assorted ribbons

**1.** For the button charms, use wire cutters to remove any shanks from buttons and glue to the charm bases.
**2.** For the bead dangles, thread beads onto head pins and eye pins. Follow Shaping Eye Loops (page 320) to connect beads to one another.
**3.** Sew buttons to the flower centers.
**4.** Follow Working with Jump Rings (page 318) to attach the charms, bead dangles and button charms to the necklace chain. Sew the flowers to the necklace and clip a few ribbons to the necklace with the earring.

### Ring

Cut the shank from a vintage button with wire cutters; then, glue the button to an adjustable ring base.

**Charming Jewelry**

**Fanciful Journal Cover**

## Fanciful Journal Cover

- cream felt
- purchased journal (ours is 5"x7")
- tissue paper
- assorted felt and fabric scraps
- embroidery floss
- water-soluble fabric marker
- cotton swab
- buttons and beads

*Read Embroidery Stitches on pages 318-319 before beginning. Use 3 strands of floss.*

**1.** For the cover, cut a cream felt rectangle ¹⁄₂" larger than the open journal on all sides. Cut 2 inside pocket rectangles the same height as the cover and ¹⁄₂" narrower than the journal front.
**2.** Use the patterns on page 399, or cut freeform flowers and leaves from felt and fabric (we cut around a floral motif for one flower). Arrange and pin the shapes on the front cover. Sew the shapes to the cover with freeform stitching lines.
**3.** Use the Tissue Paper Method (page 318) and the embroidery pattern on page 399 to work a Lazy Daisy and French Knot flower.
**4.** Draw swirling stems and leaves with the marker. Sew over each line several times. Remove any marker lines with a damp cotton swab. Sew freeform lines around the edges of the cover. Add buttons and beads to flower centers.
**5.** Match wrong sides and use a ¹⁄₄" seam allowance to sew a pocket rectangle along the outer edges of the cover at each end; insert the journal.

## Sweet Gift Card Holder

- tracing paper
- felt scraps for bird and leaves
- felted wool scraps for wing and holder
- embroidery floss
- hook and loop fastener
- fabric glue
- 14" length of ¹⁄₄"w ribbon
- 2 small wood beads
- alphabet beads

Adjust the size of the holder as you wish (our card is 3³⁄₈"x2¹⁄₈").

(continued on page 350)

**Sweet Gift Card Holder**

# Handy Sewing Tote and Blooming Pincushion

*(Finished size approx. 12" x 12" x 7")*

- ⅝ yard of main color fabric:
  cut two 16" x 20" for body of bag
  cut two 2¼"x 29" for handles
- ⅝ yard each of contrast fabrics:
  cut two 16" x 20" for inside lining (yellow)
  cut one 2¼" x 42" for lining side binding (yellow)
  cut two 5½" x 10½" for front pocket
  cut one 2¼" x 42" for top binding (blue)
  cut two 7½" x 8½" for front pocket (blue)
  cut two 2¼" x 28" for handle lining (pink)
- five 3½" squares assorted fabrics for prairie points
- four 7½" x 9½" pieces for inside pockets from contrast print

## Additional supplies for bag:
- medium to heavyweight iron-on interfacing:
  cut two 16" x 20" for body of bag
  cut two 7" x 9" for inside pockets
  cut one 5" x10" for outside pocket
  cut one 7" x 8" for outside pocket
  cut four 1" x 28" for handles
- ⅛" thick upholstery foam (headliner):
  cut two 12⅜" x 11⅝" for front/back
  cut four 3½" x 11⅝" for sides
  cut one 7⅜" x 12⅜" for bottom
- 1⅛ yard jumbo pink rickrack
- ½ yard ⅝"w ivory lace
- ½ yard single fold gold bias tape
- 5 assorted buttons
- two 28" lengths of yellow tape measure ribbon
- matching sewing threads

## For Pincushion:
- tracing paper
- marking pen
- two 5" squares fabric (pink)
- two 5" squares lightweight interfacing
- 3" square fabric (yellow)
- small amount polyester fiberfill
- 1" square hook and loop tape
- cream-colored embroidery floss

## Directions for Sewing Tote:
**1.** Use ¼" seam allowances for all sewing. Fuse interfacing to back of pockets and outside body pieces of fabric. Stitch the 2 body pieces (16" x 20") together along 20" sides; press seam up.

Stitch the 2 lining pieces together along the 20" sides. Press seam down. Layer the front and lining pieces together with wrong sides together. With a marking pen, mark horizontal lines parallel to joining seam, 3¾" from the seam. Stitch along the lines through both layers of fabric.

**2.** With right sides together, stitch pocket lining pieces to each of the 4 pockets (2 inside bag and 2 on outside front of bag), stitching around all sides for the inside lining pockets and leaving an opening for turning. For the outside pockets, stitch around side and lower edges but not the top edge. Clip corners, turn and press. Center lining pockets 5" from the bottom seam of the lining fabric and edge stitch around side and lower edges.

**3.** Make prairie points from squares of assorted fabrics. See Illustration, below. Arrange points to top edge of shorter front pocket, overlapping, as desired, and baste to top edge. Baste lace over prairie points, having raw edges even. Sew lace to top edge of longer front pocket and stitch on buttons. Stitch gold bias tape to top edges of front pockets. Pin pockets to front of bag, placing them 4" from the bottom joining seam and 4" from side edges of the bag. Edge stitch around side and lower edges of pockets, reinforcing at the top.

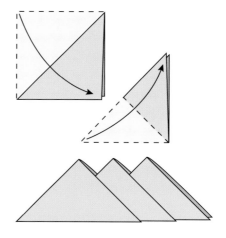

**4.** Insert foam into bottom section of bag. With marking pen, mark vertical lines 3⅝" from the sides of the bag body. Mark four 45 degree lines from bottom horizontal lines up toward the outside cut edge of the bag. Stitch on the vertical and diagonal lines drawn. Slide the large foam pieces between the layers for the front and back of the bag.

**5.** Stitch short handle lining to handle fabric, along the long edge. The strips will be offset ½" at each end. Press seam open. Fuse an interfacing strip close to the stitching line on the wrong side of both the handle fabric and the lining fabric. Pin yellow tape measure ribbon ⅝" from long side edges over interfacing of handle pieces. Fold raw edges over to meet the raw edge of the seam allowance and press. Fold the handle in half lengthwise and press. Stitch through all layers close to both long edges. Repeat to make a second handle. Fold ends under ½" and press.

**6.** Place handles at each end of the bag, placing them 6¼" from each side edge and 1½" from the top cut edge of the bag. Place handles on the inside of the bag and stitch a small rectangle at the ends of the handles through all layers.

**7.** With right sides of bag together and lining to the outside, prepare to stitch side seams by folding bottom of bag up to the inside of the bag, folding along bottom center seam. The bottom part of the side seam now has 4 layers with the inside pleat. Stitch side seams through all layers. Fold the binding strip for the lining in half lengthwise, wrong sides together and press. Stitch lining binding strip to each side seam, allowing an extra ½" to tuck under at the bottom of the bag. Fold binding around to enclose the seam allowance and stitch in place.

**8.** Trim the 4 side panels of foam at a 45 degree angle from bottom corner out to fit in the side slots of the bag. Insert the side foam pieces into the bag. Stitch binding strips for top of bag together to make binding long enough to go around the bag top. Fold binding in half lengthwise, wrong sides together and press. Baste rickrack to top edge of bag. Sew binding over rickrack, with top raw edge even with bag raw edge. Flip binding to back and sew in place over stitching line.

**Blooming Pincushion**
instructions are on page 351.

**Cell Phone Cozy**
• blue wool felt
• water-soluble fabric marker
• assorted felt and fabric scraps
• pinking shears
• cotton swab
• decorative scrapbook brads
• red wool roving
• needle felting tool and mat
• jumbo rickrack
• swivel clasp

Adjust the felt size as needed to fit your phone (the finished size of our cozy is 3¼"x5½"). Use a ¼" seam allowance for all sewing.

(continued on page 350)

Cell Phone Cozy

The Country Friends love to share their ideas for finishing thoughtful Christmas packages. Their newest collection of bags, tags, wraps, cards and package toppers is sure to inspire you. So, gather your favorite holiday wrap and scrapbook papers, fabric and trims. It's time for an evening of creative gift wrapping!

Wrapping Station instructions are on page 351.

Wrapping Station

Greeting Card Trio

When they're made with love, cards and tags can be gifts in themselves! Use copies of family photos to make greeting cards the recipients will cherish. You'll be surprised how quick it is to make these original gift tags.

### Greeting Card Trio

Let the creativity flow! Use double-sided scrapbook papers mixed with red and green cardstock to make one-of-a-kind greeting cards. Glue or machine stitch black & white copies of treasured family photos to cardstock. Embellish any way you *choose* (we used a jingle bell, rickrack, snowflake charm, ribbon, embroidery floss and rubber stamps to personalize our creations). You won't want to stop!

### Five Fun Gift Tags

Gather ribbons, embroidery floss and papercrafting supplies and enjoy making the perfect tags for everyone on your list!

### Joy Tag

Trim the top corners from a cardstock rectangle. Tie on ribbons and a tiny personalized tag (we used a jewelry tag for a pattern and cut it from cardstock). Glue small paper flowers to the tag in a wreath shape (find them in the scrapbook section of your craft store) and add a ribbon bow. Use rub-on letters or write the word "joy" in the center.

108

## Ribbon Tree Tag

Cut a tag from cardstock and trim the corners from the top end (our tag is 3"x6"); punch a hole at the top. On a same-color cardstock piece, glue ribbon loops in the shape of a 4½" tall tree. When dry, trim the edges into a triangle. Glue any loose ribbon edges; then, glue the tree to the tag. Using 3 strands of embroidery floss, work Straight Stitch and French Knot (page 319) snowflakes around the tag. Tie a floss bow and some small vintage ornaments to the tag. So clever, so simple!

## Gingham Tag

• two 1½"w gingham ribbons
• fabric glue
• water-soluble marking pen or tissue paper
• embroidery floss
• cardstock scrap
• wired pom-pom trim
• ¼" dia. hole punch
• ⅛"w ribbon
• mini jingle bells

1. Matching the top short ends, layer the gingham ribbons slightly askew. Fold and glue the top short ends to the back. Trim the bottom ends at an angle.
2. Use the marking pen to freehand an initial on the top ribbon, or print out an initial and trace it onto tissue paper; then, pin the tissue to the tag. Using 3 strands of floss, work Stem Stitches (page 319) along the drawn lines. (Carefully tear away the tissue paper, if using that method.)
3. Glue cardstock to the back of the tag for stability. Tie pom-pom trim through a hole punched in the tag and tack on a ribbon bow and mini jingle bells for added cheer!

**Five Fun Gift Tags**

## Fabric Tag

• fabric scraps
• water-soluble marking pen or tissue paper
• embroidery floss
• fabric glue
• cardstock scrap
• ¼"w ribbon
• ¼" dia. hole punch
• ½" dia. self-covered buttons
• fabric to cover buttons

1. Center and stack 3 different-size fabric circles (ours range from 2" to 2⅜" diameter); pin in place.
2. Follow Step 2 from the Gingham Tag to work a Stem Stitch (page 319) initial on the circles.

3. Glue the fabric circles to a larger cardstock circle (ours is 2¾" diameter). Run ribbon and floss through a hole punched at the top of the tag. Cover the buttons with fabric and sew them to the tag.

## Hole-Punch Tag

The kids will want to help make this sweet tag! Punch different-size holes from light green and white cardstock. Glue the circles in a tree shape to a cardstock tag; add a ribbon bow at the base of the tree. Add ribbons and a tiny personalized tag (we used a jewelry tag for a pattern and cut it from cardstock).

The Invite

Why not make gift wrapping an event you can share with your friends? Have them bring their gifts that need wrapping while you provide the wrapping supplies. Everyone will have such fun visiting and trading ideas for making pretty packages that the gifts will be ready for giving in next-to-no time!

## Soft Wrap

Here's a clever cover-up. Roll up a blanket, sweater or other fabric item and cut a festive fabric piece large enough to wrap around the present with 6" extra on each end. Tie up the ends with ribbon (pinking the fabric edges if you'd like). For the tag, stamp "to:" and "from:" with permanent ink on a folded strip of torn muslin. Pin the tag to the package and tie on a vintage mini ornament with a bit of ribbon.

Wrap-in-a-Snap
Rickrack Wrap
Soft Wrap

## The Invite

• cream and white cardstock
• double-sided tape
• sheer ribbon
• rub-on letters
• oval template (ours is 2" long)
• adhesive foam dots
• striped cardstock

Invite your friends over for a gift-wrapping party! For each invitation, print the party information on cream cardstock and trim to 3"x5". Tape the invite to a slightly larger white piece and tie it up with ribbon. Rub "wrap it up" on a white cardstock oval and adhere it to the invitation with foam dots. Tape the invitation to a 4"x6" striped cardstock piece.

## Wrap-in-a-Snap and Rickrack Wrap
Instructions are on page 351.

Paper Poinsettia Toppers

Buttons and Bows Topper

Christmas Carol Topper

How stripes get on the peppermints

### Paper Poinsettia Topper
- tracing paper
- cardboard box
- 3 colors coordinating cardstock
- 2 patterned papers
- green striped/dot paper for leaves
- circle punches for flower centers
- pearl gems
- foam dots
- tape adhesive

1. Cover box and lid with cardstock using strong tape adhesive. Trim with a narrow strip of cardstock. Cover edge of lid with patterned paper. Layer top of lid with mats of coordinating cardstock/paper.

2. Trace pattern (page 403) onto tracing paper. Cut poinsettias from cardstock and leaves from green striped/dot paper. Adhere the flowers and leaves to lid using foam dots. Punch circles for the center of each flower. Adhere pearl gems to the center of the largest flower.

Paper Poinsettia Topper

### Buttons and Bows Topper
### Christmas Carol Topper
Instructions are on page 352.

Tiny felt sweaters keep pets warm when they become Dressed-Up Doggy Cards. Do you have fabric scraps too pretty to toss? Use those favorite prints to silhouette Christmas motifs for Fabric-Backed Cards.

## Dressed-Up Doggy Cards

- 8½" x 11" sheet of natural cardstock or white cardstock (each sheet will make 2 cards)
- tan, white and brown solid card stock paper scraps
- patterned aqua and off-white dotted scrapbook paper
- small scraps of red and aqua wool felt
- aqua chalk stamp pad
- black stamp pad
- message rubber stamp
- snowflake rubber stamp
- embroidery floss in red and off-white
- crewel needle
- crafts glue and glue stick
- fine point permanent marker
- scissors

*Lady and Fido will love to see themselves on your Christmas cards this year!*

(continued on page 352)

## Fabric-Backed Cards
Instructions begin on page 352.

Poodle Doggy Card

Dachshund Doggy Card

Fabric-Backed Cards

Extra-special packages will delight everyone on your gift list. Toppers such as a beautiful bird, glittered ornament, vintage holiday record and paper snowflakes are all cheery expressions of your affection.

## Well-Rounded Bird Tag

- deckle-edged scissors
- scrapbook papers
- white gift box and lid (ours is 6½"x6½"x2½")
- spray adhesive
- cardstock
- ribbons
- hole punch
- craft glue
- adhesive foam dots
- snap-on paper-crafting fastener (bird's eye)
- twig
- artificial tallow berries
- rub-on alphabets
- glittered snowflake stickers
- decorative chipboard letter
- rickrack

**1.** Cut a deckle-edged scrapbook paper piece to fit the top of the box lid. Using spray adhesive in a well-ventilated area, adhere the paper to the lid.

**2.** Cut and tear a 2¼"x5" cardstock tag and tie ribbons through a hole punched in the top. Layer and glue a 1¾"x3" contrasting cardstock piece near the torn end.

**3.** Enlarge the pattern on page 411 to 125%. Use the pattern and cut a bird, wing and beak from scrapbook papers, clipping the wing and tail feathers as shown on the pattern. To give your bird dimension, shape the bird and wing over your fingers. Adhere the wing with a foam dot and glue the beak on the bird. Add the snap-on fastener for the eye.

**4.** Glue the twig and berries to the tag. Add a rub-on message and stickers. Use foam dots to add the bird and chipboard letter.

**5.** Tie rickrack around the present and add the tag…a "tweet" gift in itself!

## Vintage Vinyl Topper

Childhood memories will come rushing back when your loved one spots this package under the tree. Wrap the gift and tie a big dotted ribbon around it. Add a twill tape "tag" to the ribbon, using rub-on letters to identify the giver. Find a children's Christmas record at a flea market or yard sale, or dig out one you've been saving. Slip the record beneath the ribbon and adhere it to the package with removable double-sided tape. Accent the present with a holiday tag sticker at the ribbon's center. What a magical surprise!

## Snowflake Topper

- white pail with lid (ours is 5" dia.x5"h)
- double-sided removable tape
- red and pink cardstock
- craft knife and cutting mat or small, sharp scissors
- scallop-edged scissors
- scrapbook paper
- double-sided tape
- 1" snowflake punch
- adhesive foam dot
- craft glue
- ¼" dia. hole punch
- embroidery floss
- wired pom-pom trim

1. Enlarge the pattern on page 391 to 168% (for a different size pail, follow Sizing Patterns on page 318 and size the pattern to fit the lid).
2. Tape the pattern to red cardstock with removable tape; cut out the snowflake.
3. Cut a scalloped scrapbook paper circle to fit the pail lid. Tape the circle and snowflake to the lid with double-sided tape; adhere a punched pink cardstock snowflake to the center with a foam dot.

4. Cut a 1¼"x2¼" tag each from red and pink cardstock. Punch a snowflake in the red tag and glue the tags together; punch a hole at the top. Tie the tag to the pail handle with floss and add a trim bow for fun splashes of color.

## Glittered Ornament Topper

For a novel package topper, add a glittered ornament to your bow! To place the design on the glass ornament, trace the pattern on page 391 onto a double-sided adhesive sheet. Cut out the leaves and berries and peel the backing from one side of each shape. Adhere the shapes to the ornament, smoothing the edges. Peel off the remaining backing from each shape. Hold the ornament over a paper plate and sprinkle the design with glitter. Shake off the excess. Tie the ornament to the bow with ribbon.

**Vintage Vinyl Topper**
**Snowflake Topper**
**Glittered Ornament Topper**

Oval Gift Box

## Oval Gift Box

- oval papier-mâché box (ours is 5½"x7")
- red, green and ivory acrylic paints
- paintbrushes
- round foam brush
- sandpaper
- hot glue gun or double-sided tape
- vintage crocheted potholder
- vintage letter squares

Paint the box and lid; then, add polka dots with the round brush. Sand the edges for an aged appearance. Hot glue or tape the vintage potholder to the lid and add a name or initials on top.

## Photo Cards

Giving photo cards will rekindle warm memories. Use double-sided tape to mat a copy of a favorite photo postcard on scrapbook paper. Cut and fold a card from cardstock-backed paper. Adhere rickrack with fabric glue; then, tape the photo in place. Hot glue self-covered buttons and a vintage-look ribbon bow to the card.

For a perfect backdrop to a 3" square photo, fold a 4½"x9" piece of cardstock-backed scrapbook paper in half; unfold. Pierce holes with a sewing needle every ½" along the fold and ½" in from the front edges. Using 6 stands of embroidery floss, work Blanket Stitches (page 319) around the edges. Mount the photo with photo corners. Add the year of the photo and a jeweled brad to a tag; adhere to the card with an adhesive foam dot.

Photo Cards

## Fabric Tree Card

- cardstock
- fabric glue
- mini rickrack
- fabric scrap
- embroidery floss
- tiny buttons with flat-ended shanks
- square button

Make a card to be treasured by your favorite stitcher. Match short ends and fold a 6½"x10" cardstock piece in half. Glue rickrack along the top and bottom of the card front. Glue simple fabric leaves to the card in a tree shape. Tie a floss length through each button. Glue the shank buttons to the tree and the square button "trunk" at the bottom.

## Redbird Collage Card

- white cardstock
- scrapbook papers
- white and colored tissue papers
- disposable foam brush
- decoupage glue
- sharp needle
- embroidery floss
- ribbon

Express yourself with a collage of your favorite papers. Matching short ends, fold a 7"x10" cardstock piece in half. Enlarge the pattern on page 411 to 143%. Using the pattern, cut a scrapbook paper bird. Cut different size leaves and circles from scrapbook and tissue papers. Arrange the shapes on the card front; adhere with a thin layer of glue. Allowing to dry between coats, brush 2 more coats of glue on the card front. Pierce evenly-spaced holes and use 2 strands of floss to work Running Stitches (page 319) along the top of the card. Add a bow at the top.

For gift boxes and greeting cards that are a present in themselves, create these oh-so-thoughtful ideas!

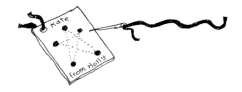

Fabric Tree Card
Redbird Collage Card
Pull-Tab Gift Card Holder

## Pull-Tab Gift Card Holder

- cardstock scraps
- fabric glue
- fabric scraps
- sharp needle
- embroidery floss
- ⅜"w twill tape
- purchased gift card
- jewelry tag

*This clever idea works for any gift card; simply adjust the size of the holder to fit (our card is 2⅛"x3⅜").*

Matching short ends, fold a 3"x8" cardstock piece in half. Glue layered fabric circles and a cardstock "ornament cap" to the front of the holder; unfold. Pierce holes and use 3 strands of floss to work a Running Stitch (page 319) "hanger." Refold the holder and machine stitch ⅛" from the side edges. Tie twill tape around the gift card and add a tiny tag.

117

## Fun-Filled Containers

*These delightful alternatives to gift wrap are as fun to give as they are to receive!*

### Scrapbook Caddy

- ½ yard of 72"w red felt
- pinking shears
- water-soluble fabric marker
- tissue paper (optional)
- embroidery floss
- assorted 2-hole buttons
- scrapbook supplies
- 1⅝ yards of ⅜"w ribbon

*The perfect package for your favorite scrapbooker! Match wrong sides and use a ¼" seam allowance unless otherwise noted.*

1. Cut the following pieces from felt: two 10½"x9" dividers, two 11"x7" bottoms, four 7"x5" sides and four 11"x5" front/back pieces.

2. Enlarge the patterns on page 412 to 222%. Using the divider pattern, cut away the top curve and hole for the handle on both divider pieces. Sew the pieces together along all edges. Pink the top edge.

(continued on page 371)

**Glass Canisters**

**Scrapbook Caddy**

**Personalized Photo Box**

118

For wonderfully whimsical presentations, put gifts in the Scrapbook Caddy and other Fun-Filled Containers. The recipients will know how very special they are to you!

### Glass Canisters

Turn a new glass jar into a treasured memory keeper. Lightly sand, then paint the lid of each square jar (we used red and green acrylic paints). Sand the edges for a vintage look. Fill the jars with cookie cutters and potholders or childhood toys. Tie pre-printed twill tape (ours says "Holiday Hugs") around the cookie cutter jar and add a die-cut label to the front. For the toy jar, hot glue an alphabet block to the top and use adhesive foam dots to add a name to the front with vintage or chipboard letter squares.

### Personalized Photo Box

- sandpaper
- solid color photo box
- wax paper
- thick craft glue
- wood bead garland
- acrylic paint
- paintbrush
- papier-mâché letter (first letter of name)
- patterned cardstock
- pinking shears
- spray adhesive
- decorative chipboard letters (the rest of the name)
- buttons

*A special package for any gift, the photo box is a must-have for a camera buff!*

**1.** Sand the edges of the box and lid for an aged appearance. Place the lid on wax paper. Glue the garland around the lid and allow to dry.

**2.** Paint the top edge and sides of the papier-mâché letter. Trace the letter onto the back of cardstock and cut out with pinking shears. Using spray adhesive in a well-ventilated area, attach the cardstock letter. Glue the remaining letters and buttons in place. Glue the letter to the box lid.

Shiny New Boots

### Shiny New Boots

Like a stocking, only twice the joy! Fill up a new pair of child's wellies with gifts and trinkets. Tuck in small packages and vintage toys along with candy canes and greenery sprigs. Add a mini ornament and Christmas charm to a layered cardstock tag. What fun!

## Stenciled Snowflake Sack

- snowflake template (we used The Crafter's Workshop template TCW-104)
- double-sided removable tape
- brown gift bag (ours is 8"x10½")
- cosmetic sponge wedge
- inkpad (we used brown)
- scrapbook paper
- corrugated cardboard
- T-pin or large sharp needle
- embroidery floss
- emery board or fine-grit sandpaper
- craft glue
- ⅛" and 1/16" dia. hole punches
- 1" snowflake punch
- brown paper lunch bag
- metal bookplate (ours has a 1⅛"w opening) and brads
- rub-on snowflake, holiday message and alphabet
- cardstock tag (we tea-dyed our 1"w tag)
- round tag
- jute twine
- ribbon scrap
- buttons

1. Choose a small snowflake from the template to be stenciled and tape off the nearby holes. Leaving the gift bag closed, press the sponge on the inkpad and stencil the snowflake on the bag. Remove the tape, wash the ink from the template and dry thoroughly. Repeat with other snowflake shapes.

2. Place the template and scrapbook paper on the cardboard. Pierce a hole through the template and paper at the ends of the dashed lines outlining the large snowflake (if your template has a solid outline, just pierce evenly-spaced holes along the line). Cut out the paper snowflake ⅛" larger than the pierced outline.

3. Use 2 strands of floss and work Running Stitches (page 319) through the pierced holes. Cut a scrapbook paper circle slightly smaller than the snowflake center

**Stenciled Snowflake Sack**
**Punched Snowflake Sack**
**Chipboard Snowflake Sack**

and sand the edge. Glue the circle to the stitched snowflake.

4. Stencil small snowflakes on the stitched flake. Punch holes in the branches of the stitched snowflake. Glue on 2 snowflakes punched from the lunch bag.

5. Attach the bookplate to the stitched flake. Rub a snowflake and message on the cardstock tag so a word is centered in the opening when placed in the bookplate. Dot the bottom with glue and insert the tag in the bookplate. Glue the stitched

snowflake to the gift bag.

6. Punch one snowflake each from scrapbook paper and the lunch bag. Personalize the round tag with rubons and add the snowflakes. Tie the tag to the bag handle with twine and add a ribbon tie. Glue buttons on all the punched flakes.

## Punched Snowflake Sack and Chipboard Snowflake Sack

Instructions are on page 353.

With a few scrapbook and craft supplies, you can make ordinary brown bags, kraft paper and newspaper into thoughtful gift wraps! Create a flurry of snowflake gift bags, or cover gift boxes with nature-friendly wraps. Or transform a child's drawing into a template for easy crayon-rubbed wrapping paper!

## Greenery Package

For a natural Christmas feel, tie a layered twill tape and rickrack ribbon around a kraft paper-wrapped package. Paint a pinecone with ivory acrylic paint and while wet, sprinkle with mica flakes. When dry, wire the pinecone to the ribbon and tuck fresh greenery sprigs underneath. Use decorative-edged scissors to cut out a black & white photocopy of a favorite wintry photo. Tie broken sticks together with rusty wire to make a frame. Wire it to the photocopy. Use adhesive foam dots to adhere a vintage tag to the frame and the photocopy to the package.

## Newspaper Package

Recycle a bit of nostalgia with a newspaper-wrapped package. Copy a favorite black & white holiday photo and glue it to red cardstock, trimmed slightly larger than the photocopy...on ours, we added pink to the children's cheeks with chalk and a cotton swab. Cut a slit at each end of the copy a little wider than your ribbon. Thread the ribbon through the slits and tie it around the package. Add a colorful rub-on holiday message to the package.

## Snowman Wrap

Give your child a piece of cardstock and a pencil or crayon and ask for a snowman drawing or other simple holiday design. Outline the drawing with a thick layer of craft glue and allow it to dry. Place kraft paper over the outline and rub with the side of a crayon. Turn the kraft paper and continue making rubbings until the paper is covered. Fill in with drawn snowflakes. Wrap your package and tie it up with red jute twine and a fun tag. The glued outline can be used again & again to make lots of wrapping paper sheets!

Greenery Package
Newspaper Package
Snowman Wrap

Keep the gift a surprise until it's opened! Create a money pad with coordinating box, or secure a piece of jewelry to a card placed in a three-sided box. For unique finishes, top larger boxes with Floral and Necktie Bows.

## Mystery Money Holder
• transfer paper
• 2 double-sided cardstock sheets
• stylist or bone folder
• thin cardboard
• dollar bills
• hot glue gun
• rickrack and jute twine
• embellishments (we used a tag, tag stickers, mini clothespin, ornament and charm)

**1.** For the wrapper, enlarge the pattern on page 376 to 200%. Transfer the pattern to cardstock and cut out. Score, then fold the wrapper along the dashed lines.
**2.** For the money pad, cut a 2⅝"x6¼" piece each from cardstock and cardboard. Cut a 2⅝"x¾" cardstock strip for the top border. Stack the cardboard, cash and large cardstock piece, so they are flush at the top edge. Hot gluing along the top edge, cover the top of the money pad with the cardstock strip (the hot glue will hold the bills in place, but allow them to be removed when desired).
**3.** Add rickrack, a tag and sticker to the front and slip the money pad in the wrapper. Tuck in the flaps; then, tie up the wrapper with rickrack and add embellishments.

## Surprise Jewelry Box
Instructions are on page 353.

Mystery Money Holder

Surprise Jewelry Box

**Floral Bow**

### Floral Bow
- 1½"w ribbon (5⅝ yards for the bow plus extra to tie around the gift)
- fine-gauge wire
- wire cutters
- wrapped gift

*This sweet hand-tied bow will make any girl feel special. The yardage listed will make an 8" diameter floral bow with two 10" streamers. Adjust the amount of ribbon to make a different size bow.*

**1.** For the first streamer, make a light pencil mark on one long edge of the ribbon, 10" from one end. For the loops, measure from this point and lightly mark 9" twenty times along the length of the ribbon.

(continued on page 354)

### Necktie Bow with Photo Tag
- 1⅜"w ribbon (enough to tie around the gift plus 20")
- wrapped gift
- deckle-edged scissors
- embossed white cardstock
- word background stamp
- distressing ink pad
- photo corners
- vintage photo or black & white photocopy
- red cardstock
- silver shank button
- paper clip

*The necktie bow is the perfect way to wrap it up for a great guy! We made a 7" long necktie bow. Adjust the amount of ribbon to make a different size bow.*

(continued on page 354)

**Necktie Bow with Photo Tag**

Stamped Paper Bag

Wraps in Brown Paper

## Woodland Wrap

- paper maché box
- cardstock in 3 shades of green plus white, brown
- snowflakes–felt, punched, die cut or stickers
- small pine cone
- strong tape adhesive
- foam dots
- stapler
- hot-glue gun and glue sticks
- embossing template
- circle punch

(continued on page 356)

## Stamped Paper Bag
## Torn Paper Wrap
Instructions are on page 356.

Woodland Wrap

Torn Paper Wrap

Purchased stickers or die cuts convey sweet holiday messages on Warm Wishes and There's No Place Like Home Cards. Gift-Giving Purses hide little gift cards inside while remaining stylish on the outside. Merry Gift Tags are the perfect way to say, "To you from me!"

## Warm Wishes Snowman Card
- large rectangular snowman image (sticker, die cut, stamp or clip art)
- 3 colors of cardstock to match
- 2 coordinated patterned papers
- tab die or punch
- tulle
- narrow ribbon
- button
- punched snowflake
- self-adhesive jewels
- embossing template
- adhesive–including adhesive dimensional dots
- ink for edging paper
- computer or stamps for inside greeting

**1.** Cut card base from cardstock. Score and fold so that card opens at right side.
**2.** Emboss pattern in the top portion of the card front.
**3.** Ink edges of card; lightly ink embossed pattern.
**4.** Cut strip of patterned paper; ink and adhere across lower portion of card. Cut wider strip of cardstock and adhere just above patterned paper.

(continued on page 355)

## There's No Place Like Home Card
Instructions are on page 355.

Warm Wishes Snowman Card

There's No Place Like Home Card

**Handmade Boxes**

This collection of wraps & tags offers original ways to present special gifts. Tuck a surprise in a gift bag or box, or simply include a one-of-a-kind card that's pretty enough to hang on the tree. With a Box of Tags, you can even make a thoughtful gift of your handcrafted creations.

**Handmade Boxes**
**Menswear Gift Sacks**
Instructions begin on pages 357 and 358.

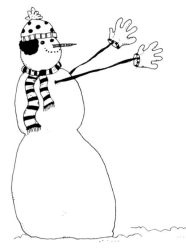

**Menswear Gift Sacks**

Patterned cupcake liners, jingle bells, buttons, toys, sheet music and paper poinsettias are the center of attention when they become Pretty Package Toppers for your holiday gifts.

## Cupcake Liner Topper and Box

*Choose your favorite cupcake liners for inside and out of the box. Stack them for a ruffled bow on the lid, then use them inside as compartments to hold a few of her favorite things!*

- shallow box to fit 4-6 cupcake liners
- cupcake liners in coordinating patterns
- cardstock/patterned paper in colors to match cupcake liners
- ribbon
- stapler
- circle punches in 3 sizes
- adhesive—including tape, foam dots and stapler

### Inside of box:

**1.** Make dividers for box by cutting 2 strips of cardstock the same depth as the box base—one for the width and one for the length of the box.
**2.** Cut a slit in the center of each strip and interlock them.
**3.** Invert the cupcake liners and place in sections of box.

(continued on page 358)

## Toy Topper
## Jingle Bell Topper
Instructions are on pages 358-359.

Jingle Bell Topper/
Cupcake Liner Topper

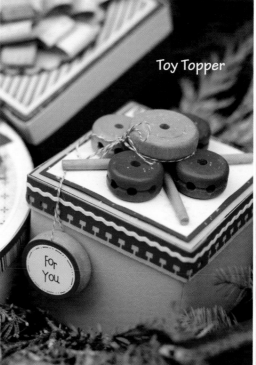

Toy Topper

Cupcake Liner Box

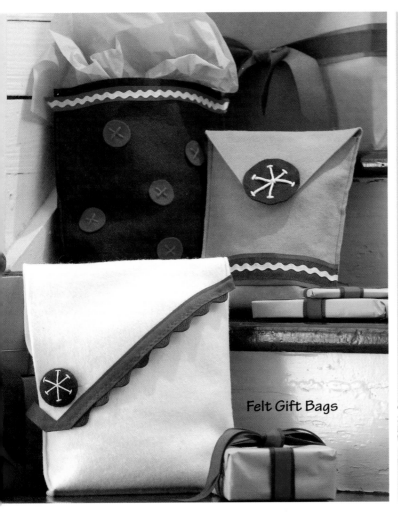

Felt Gift Bags

Blue Bag
Green Pocket Purse

## Felt Gift Bags

- wool felt (¹/₃ yard will make any of the bags)
- clear nylon thread
- trims (we used ribbon, rickrack, yarn, embroidery floss, 1¹/₂" dia. self-covered button and felt scraps)

*Match wrong sides and use a ¹/₄" seam allowance.*

**1.** For the brown bag, cut a 9"x20" felt piece. Attach red felt circles to the top half of the brown felt piece with yarn Cross Stitches (page 319). Layer and sew ribbon and rickrack above the circles. Fold the felt in half and sew the sides together. Pinch the bottom corners and sew across each corner ³/₄" from the points. Trim the excess felt from the corners.

**2.** For the tan bag, cut a 7"x23" felt piece. Mark 2³/₄" from the corners along one short end. Mark 4" from these corners along the long edges. Connect the marks and cut along the drawn lines to form the bag flap. Layer and sew ribbon and rickrack to the felt about 6¹/₂" from the other end. Fold this end up 9" and sew the sides together. Pinch the bottom corners and sew across

each corner ³/₄" from the points. Trim the excess felt from the corners. Using yarn, sew a 2¹/₂" diameter brown felt circle to the flap with a Straight Stitch (page 319) six-point snowflake.

**3.** For the cream bag, cut an 8¹/₂"x30" felt piece. Mark 1¹/₂" in from the left corner along one end; mark 6" down from the right corner of that same end. Connect the marks and cut along the drawn line to form the bag flap. Layer and sew rickrack and ribbon to the flap edge. Fold the opposite short end up 10¹/₂" and sew the sides together. Pinch the bottom corners and sew across each corner ³/₄" from the points. Trim the excess felt from the corners. Work a 1¹/₄" diameter Straight Stitch (page 319) six-point snowflake with floss on a felt scrap; cover the button. Cut a buttonhole in the bag flap; sew the button to the bag under the flap.

## Blue Bag
## Green Pocket Purser

Instructions are on page 332.

Gift Tags

Garland

**Gift Tags and Garland**
Instructions are on page 372.

Special Cards

## Special Cards

So that we may always see Christmas through a child's eyes, add color to photocopies of favorite photos from years past before attaching to simple cardstock cards. A few stickers or some rub-ons create a card that is simply perfect.

For those holiday gift cards or even cash, enlarge the holder patterns (page 410) to 200%. Transfer the pattern to scrapbook paper and cut out. Fold the paper along the dashed lines. Place the gift inside the holder and trim with ribbons, stickers and tags.

## Mailbox Card Holder & Wrappings

For the mailbox, hand sew rickrack to an upholstery webbing length. Secure the webbing around the mailbox. Dress up the card holder with a ribbon and paper tinsel bow, a stamped tag and some jute twine. A button and a bit more rickrack are the final touch for the bow and tag. Brown kraft paper, simple ribbon or twill tape and button-decorated tags combine to wrap the gifts.

## Box of Tags

Purchased shipping tags, backed with patterned cardstock, are the perfect size for Christmas trees fashioned from ribbon and rickrack or vintage wrapping paper. Attach a simple or fancy button topper (add a rub-on holiday message, if you'd like) and a ribbon at the top. Decorate a leftover greeting card box with more ribbon and rickrack and you've got a great hostess or Secret Santa gift.

**Box of Tags**

Gift-Giving Purses

## Pink Patterned Purse Card
- scalloped purse and topper patterns
- heavy double-sided patterned paper
- 2 colors coordinating cardstock
- small hole punch
- button
- floss
- cording for handle
- coordinated ribbon
- adhesive—including fine-tipped adhesive and glue dots
- computer or stamps for inside greeting

(continued on page 355)

## Holly Purse Card
## Tinsel Purse Card
## Merry Gift Tags
Instructions are on pages 355 and 359.

Merry Gift Tags

# Gifts

## from your Christmas Kitchen

Spending time in the kitchen, whipping up Christmas delights …it's a happy way to get ready for the holiday! It's also a fun way to make gifts everyone will love. The recipes in this creative collection aren't just delicious, they're also prettily packaged. Parmesan-flavored Party Mix in colorful take-out boxes, White Chocolate-Cranberry Cookies presented with a mocha beverage, Popcorn balls in an ornament… these and many other special gifts from your kitchen will be welcomed by one and all!

Create a one-of-a-kind gift for a chocolate lover by making easy lollipops and presenting them in a candy-filled bottle. Such a merry treat!

**Candy Tree Lollipops**

We used a lollipop candy mold that makes six 3-inch long trees. We used 4½-inch long lollipop sticks and chocolate candy discs made especially for candy making. Follow package directions to melt the discs. Add oil-based flavorings to the candies, if desired. After the lollipops are removed from the mold, use a hair dryer or heat embossing tool to slightly melt the chocolate and quickly add decorative sprinkles to each tree. All lollipop supplies can be found in the cake and candy decorating section of your favorite craft or specialty store.

**Lollipop Bottle**
instructions are on page 360.

135

## Mom's Applesauce Muffins

*Fill your kitchen with the delectable aroma of apples and cinnamon.*

½ c. butter, softened
1 c. sugar
1 c. applesauce
1 egg, beaten
2 c. all-purpose flour
1 t. baking soda
1 t. cinnamon
½ t. ground cloves
¼ t. salt
1 c. raisins

Combine butter, sugar, apple-sauce and egg. In a separate bowl, combine flour, baking soda, cinnamon, cloves and salt; stir into butter mixture just until moistened. Stir in raisins. Fill paper-lined muffin cups ¾ full; sprinkle with crumb topping. Bake at 350 degrees for 25 to 30 minutes. Makes 12 to 16.

Crumb Topping:
½ c. butter, softened
¾ c. all-purpose flour
¾ c. quick-cooking oats, uncooked
½ c. brown sugar, packed
2 t. cinnamon

Blend all ingredients until crumbly.

*Emily Johnson*
*Pocatello, ID*

**Muffin Tin**
instructions are on page 360.

Honey Popcorn & Cashews in a Party Mix Tin will thrill anyone who likes their snacks sweet & salty.

## Honey Popcorn & Cashews

*This recipe came from a dear neighbor when we first moved to our new home in 1977. My 3 sons just loved it. It is very addictive and always a hit.*

3 qts. popped popcorn
1½ c. cashews
1 c. sugar
½ c. honey
½ c. light corn syrup
1 c. creamy peanut butter
1 t. vanilla extract

Toss together popped popcorn and cashews in a large roaster pan; keep warm in a 250-degree oven.

In a heavy 1½-quart saucepan, combine sugar, honey and corn syrup. Bring mixture to a rapid boil over medium heat, stirring constantly; boil for 2 minutes. Remove from heat; stir in peanut butter and vanilla. Immediately pour over popcorn mixture, stirring to coat thoroughly. Spread on greased aluminum foil to cool. Break into bite-size pieces. Makes 5 quarts.

*Diane Garber*
*Brookville, OH*

Party Mix Tin
instructions begin on page 360.

Honey Popcorn & Cashews
Party Mix Tin

## Carrot Cake Jam

*This is a wonderful jam that tastes just like Grandma's carrot cake!*

1½ c. carrots, peeled and shredded
1½ c. pears, cored, peeled and chopped
14-oz. can crushed pineapple
3 T. lemon juice
1½ t. cinnamon
1 t. nutmeg
1 t. ground cloves
3-oz. pouch liquid pectin
6½ c. sugar
6 ½-pint canning jars and lids, sterilized

Mix all ingredients except pectin and sugar in a large saucepan. Bring to a boil over medium heat. Reduce heat to medium-low; simmer for 20 minutes, stirring occasionally. Add pectin and return to a boil. Stir in sugar; bring to a full rolling boil, stirring constantly. Remove from heat. Pour into hot sterilized jars, leaving ½-inch headspace. Secure with lids. Cool and store in refrigerator up to 3 weeks. Makes 6 jars.

*Teri Johnson
North Ogden, UT*

## Jam Jar

Color photocopy the label on page 394 onto white cardstock; cut out. Use double-sided tape to adhere the label to a vintage-look jar of Carrot Cake Jam. Tie a coordinating ribbon around the lid. What a yummy gift!

Cherry-Chocolate Chip Loaves mix the sweetness of bananas with the zip of dried cherries. It's easy to stamp the Loaf Tin with snowflakes.

## Loaf Tin

- acrylic paints for metal
- white tin with hinged lid (ours is 7"w x 4"d x 5"h)
- foam stamps and round foam brushes
- craft glue
- cardstock
- magnetic photo frame (ours is 3¼"x2¼")
- rub-on letters
- hole punch
- scallop-edged scissors
- 2 plastic-wrapped Cherry-Chocolate Chip Loaves
- ribbons

Using paints, stamp the sides and lid of the tin with foam stamps and brushes. Make a layered cardstock label to fit in the magnetic photo frame using rub-ons and punched cardstock dots (we scalloped the edges of the top cardstock piece). Place the loaves in the tin and tie ribbons around the handle.

Cherry-Chocolate Chip Loaves
Loaf Tin

## Cherry-Chocolate Chip Loaves

*Try substituting sweetened dried cranberries for the cherries…a bit tangy, but just as yummy.*

½ c. butter, softened
1 c. sugar
1 c. ripe banana, mashed
2 eggs, beaten
2 c. all-purpose flour
1 t. baking soda
¼ c. chopped walnuts
¼ c. mini semi-sweet chocolate chips
¼ c. dried cherries, chopped

Blend together butter and sugar in a large bowl. Add banana and eggs; mix well. In a separate bowl, combine flour and baking soda; gradually add to butter mixture. Fold in walnuts, chocolate chips and cherries. Transfer to 4 greased 5½"x3" loaf pans. Bake at 350 degrees for 32 to 37 minutes or until a toothpick inserted near center comes out clean. Cool for 10 minutes before removing from pans to wire racks. Makes 4 mini loaves.

*Vickie*

Caramel-Apple Muffins

## Caramel-Apple Muffins
*An extra-special breakfast treat.*

2 c. all-purpose flour
¾ c. sugar
2½ t. cinnamon
2 t. baking powder
½ t. salt
1 c. milk
¼ c. butter, melted
1 egg, beaten

1½ t. vanilla extract
½ c. apple, cored, peeled and finely diced
12 caramels, unwrapped and diced

Combine flour, sugar, cinnamon, baking powder and salt in a large bowl; set aside.

In a separate large bowl, mix together milk, butter, egg and vanilla; add flour mixture, stirring just until blended. Stir in apples and caramels. Divide batter evenly in 12 paper-lined muffin cups; bake at 350 degrees for 25 minutes or until tops spring back when lightly pressed. Serve warm. Makes one dozen.

*Stephanie White*
*Idabel, OK*

Chocolate-Dipped Crispy Bars look like a gourmet gift in the clear Treat Container.

## Chocolate-Dipped Crispy Bars

*Crunchy and sweet with a taste of peanut butter and chocolate!*

6 c. crispy rice cereal
1 c. sugar
1 c. corn syrup
1 c. creamy peanut butter
12-oz. pkg. dark cocoa-flavored candy wafers, melted
1 c. semi-sweet chocolate chips, melted
1½ c. white chocolate-flavored candy wafers, melted

Place cereal in a large bowl; set aside.

In a heavy medium saucepan, combine sugar and corn syrup over medium-high heat; stir frequently until mixture boils. Allow to boil 30 seconds without stirring. Remove from heat and stir in peanut butter. Pour peanut butter mixture over cereal; stir until well blended. Press mixture into a 13"x9" baking pan; cool. Cut into 4"x1" bars. Combine next 2 ingredients. Dip half of each bar into dark chocolate mixture; place on wax paper until chocolate hardens. Drizzle white chocolate over dark chocolate and return to wax paper to harden. Makes 24.

**Chocolate-Dipped Crispy Bars Treat Container**

## Treat Container

- double-sided holiday scrapbook paper
- clear acrylic container with handle and lid (ours is 6"hx4" dia.)
- wax paper
- Chocolate-Dipped Crispy Bars
- hole punch
- craft glue
- glitter
- jute twine, ribbon and rickrack trims
- rub-on letters
- double-sided tape

**1.** Insert a scrapbook paper piece in the container that fits around the inside and is half the container's height. Line with wax paper and place the bars in the container.
**2.** Cut a motif from scrapbook paper, punch a hole and add glitter; tie to the handle with trims.
**3.** Cut a scrapbook paper circle to fit the container top; add rub-ons and tape the circle to the lid.

## Sugar Cookies

2 18-oz. pkgs. refrigerated sugar cookie dough
Optional: drinking straw
assorted candies and sprinkles

Roll out dough to ¼-inch thickness. Cut out with cookie cutters (for cookie ornaments, before baking, use the straw to make a hole in each cookie for hanging). Place on ungreased baking sheets and bake at 350 degrees for 5 to 7 minutes or until golden. Decorate with Sugar Cookie Frosting, candies and sprinkles. Makes 36 to 40.

Sugar Cookie Frosting:
5 c. powdered sugar
5½ to 6½ T. water
1½ t. almond extract
paste food coloring

Combine powdered sugar, water and almond extract in a medium bowl; beat until smooth. Transfer frosting into small bowls and tint with food coloring. Spread onto cooled cookies.

## Rocky Road Bars

*Brownies with chocolate chips, marshmallows and peanuts... need I say more?*

22½-oz. pkg. brownie mix with chocolate syrup pouch
⅓ c. oil
¼ c. water
2 eggs, beaten
12-oz. pkg. semi-sweet chocolate chips, divided
1½ to 2 c. mini marshmallows
½ c. dry-roasted peanuts, chopped

Grease bottom only of a 13"x9" baking pan; set aside. Combine brownie mix, syrup pouch, oil, water and eggs; stir until well blended. Mix in one cup chocolate chips; spread in baking pan. Bake at 350 degrees for 30 to 35 minutes or until a toothpick inserted 2 inches from side of pan comes out clean. Immediately sprinkle with marshmallows, remaining one cup chocolate chips and peanuts. Cover pan with a baking sheet for 2 to 3 minutes; remove and cool completely. Cut into 4"x2" bars; store tightly covered. Makes one dozen.

*Dale-Harriet Rogovich*
*Madison, WI*

## Paper Trays

instructions begin on page 361.

Sugar Cookies

Rocky Road Bars
Paper Trays

## Banana Supreme Pie

*Shh…don't tell anyone how easy this is to make!*

1 c. sour cream
½ c. milk
3.4-oz. pkg. instant vanilla pudding mix
8-oz. container frozen whipped topping, thawed
¾ c. peanuts, chopped and divided
10-inch graham cracker crust
1 to 2 ripe bananas, sliced

Stir together sour cream, milk and pudding mix. Fold in whipped topping; set aside.

Sprinkle ½ cup peanuts on bottom of pie crust; arrange banana slices on peanuts. Spoon pudding mixture over bananas; sprinkle with remaining ¼ cup peanuts. Cover and chill until ready to serve. Makes 8 servings.

*Regina Kostyu*
*Gooseberry Patch*

## Pie Carrier

- mat board
- craft knife and cutting mat
- 13" dia. papier-mâché plate (ours has a 9½" bottom)
- acrylic paints
- paintbrush
- 2⅜"h chipboard letters (PIE)
- decoupage glue
- disposable foam brush
- assorted Christmas wrapping papers
- glittered star stickers
- mica flakes
- 3½ yards of 1½"w ribbon
- assorted ribbons
- vintage miniature ornaments
- Banana Supreme Pie

(continued on page 363)

To be BUSY is man's only happiness.
—MARK TWAIN—

Banana Supreme Pie
Pie Carrier

Tiny Pecan Tassies, Iced Shortbread Cookies, and Ginger Crinkles are sweet indulgences your friends will adore. Give them on a decorative platter for a festive holiday gift.

Pecan Tassies

## Iced Shortbread Cookies
*Buttery and rich...just like the perfect shortbread should be.*

1 ¼ c. all-purpose flour
3 T. sugar
½ c. butter, softened

Stir together flour and sugar in a mixing bowl; cut in butter with a fork or pastry cutter. Mix until a soft dough forms. Shape cookies into walnut-size balls and place on ungreased baking sheets. Press thumb in the center of each cookie. Bake at 325 degrees for 20 to 25 minutes or until lightly golden; remove to cooling racks. Spread icing in the center of each cookie. Makes about 1 ½ dozen.

Icing:
¼ c. butter
2 c. powdered sugar
1 t. vanilla extract
Optional: food coloring
milk

Melt butter in a saucepan; cook over medium heat until butter is dark golden in color. Combine butter, powdered sugar and vanilla in a mixing bowl; add food coloring, if desired. Add milk, if needed, for spreading consistency.

*Nancy Morris*
*Adams, TN*

## Ginger Crinkles
*These tasty cookies just sparkle from being rolled in sugar.*

2 ¼ c. all-purpose flour
2 t. baking soda
1 t. ground ginger
1 t. cinnamon
½ t. ground cloves
¼ t. salt
1 c. brown sugar, packed
¾ c. oil
¼ c. molasses
1 egg
sugar

Sift together flour, baking soda, spices and salt; set aside. In a mixing bowl, combine brown sugar, oil, molasses and egg; beat well. Add flour mixture to brown sugar mixture; stir until well blended. Shape into one-inch balls; roll in sugar. Arrange on baking sheets and bake at 375 degrees for 10 minutes. Makes 4 dozen.

*Sharon Crider*
*Lebanon, MO*

## Pecan Tassies
*This is a family favorite that can be made ahead.*

½ c. butter or margarine, softened
3-oz. pkg. cream cheese, softened
1 c. all-purpose flour
1 ½ c. brown sugar, packed
2 eggs, lightly beaten
2 T. butter or margarine, melted
1 t. vanilla extract
⅔ c. chopped pecans

Beat softened butter and cream cheese at medium speed with an electric mixer until creamy. Gradually add flour, beating well. Cover and chill 2 hours.
Shape dough into 30 one-inch balls; press balls into lightly greased miniature muffin pans. Set aside.
Combine brown sugar and next 3 ingredients; stir well. Stir in pecans. Spoon 1 tablespoon pecan mixture into each pastry shell. Bake at 350 degrees for 25 minutes. Remove from pans immediately and cool completely on wire racks. Makes 2 ½ dozen.

## Spiced Christmas Cashews

*These well-seasoned cashews are sweet, salty and crunchy...and oh-so
snackable! Everybody raves about them. I often make 10 to 12 batches
for gifts during the holiday season...maybe even more!*

1 egg white
1 T. water
2  9³⁄₄-oz. cans salted cashews
¹⁄₃ c. sugar
1 T. chili powder
2 t. salt
2 t. ground cumin
¹⁄₂ t. cayenne pepper

Whisk together egg white and water in a large bowl.
Add cashews; toss to coat. Transfer to a colander;
drain for 2 minutes. In a separate bowl, combine sugar
and spices; add cashews and toss to coat. Arrange in
a single layer on a greased 15"x10" jelly-roll pan. Bake,
uncovered, at 250 degrees for 1 ¹⁄₄ hours, stirring
once. Cool on a wire rack. Store in an airtight container.
Makes about 3¹⁄₂ cups.

*Paula Marchesi
Lenhartsville, PA*

Spiced Christmas Cashews

Blueberry Cream Coffee Cake
Cake Box

# Blueberry Cream Coffee Cake

*A traditional recipe, but still a favorite of mine!*

$^2/_3$ c. plus 2 T. sugar, divided
$^1/_4$ c. butter, softened
1 egg
$^1/_4$ t. lemon extract
1 c. plus 3 T. all-purpose flour,
    divided
$1^1/_2$ t. baking powder
$^1/_2$ t. salt
$^1/_2$ t. cinnamon, divided
$^1/_2$ c. milk
1 c. blueberries
4 oz. cream cheese, cubed
1 T. cold butter

Blend together $^2/_3$ cup sugar and butter until light and fluffy. Blend in egg and lemon extract. In a separate bowl, combine one cup flour, baking powder, salt and $^1/_4$ teaspoon cinnamon. Add alternately with milk to creamed mixture. Toss blueberries with one tablespoon flour, fold in batter with cream cheese and pour into greased and floured 9" springform pan.

To prepare topping, combine remaining 2 tablespoons sugar, 2 tablespoons flour and $^1/_4$ teaspoon cinnamon. Cut in butter until mixture resembles coarse crumbs. Sprinkle evenly over batter. Bake at 375 degrees for 30 minutes or until cake tests done. Makes 6 servings.

*Stephanie Moon*
*Boise, ID*

## Cake Box

instructions are on page 360.

147

*Cocoa-Cherry Macaroons*
*Macaroons 4 U! Box*

## Macaroons 4 U! Box

- plastic-wrapped Cocoa-Cherry Macaroons
- gift box (ours measures 6"wx4½"hx4½"d)
- pinking shears
- ⅛ yard each of 2 coordinating fabrics
- contrasting thread
- ½"w ribbon
- rub-on letters and number 4
- purchased tag

**1.** Place macaroons in the box.
**2.** Measure around the box and add 8". Use pinking shears to cut one 4"w and one 2½"w fabric strip this length (we cut ours 26" long).
**3.** To make the fabric band, layer the strips and follow Fig. 1 to press pleats at the center of the strips. Use contrasting thread to topstitch the strips together through the center. Matching right sides and short ends, sew the ends together to fit around the box. Turn right side out and slip the band over the box.

**Fig. 1**

1½"    ¾"    1½"

## Cocoa-Cherry Macaroons

*Tuck a dozen of these delights into a candy box for a sweet gift.*

6 c. sweetened flaked coconut
14-oz. can sweetened condensed milk
1 t. vanilla extract
1 c. mini semi-sweet chocolate chips
½ c. maraschino cherries, drained and chopped

Combine coconut, condensed milk and vanilla in a large bowl; mix until coconut is well coated. Stir in chocolate chips and cherries. Drop by heaping teaspoonfuls 2 inches apart on a parchment paper-lined baking sheet. Bake at 350 degrees for 10 to 12 minutes. Makes 3 dozen.

Charity Meyer
Lewisberry, PA

**4.** Tie ribbon around the box. Add the rub-on message to the tag and secure it to the bow.

Rustic Apple Tart
Card

## Rustic Apple Tart

*We like to use a combination of Granny Smith and Rome apples but substitute your favorites, if you'd like.*

1¾ c. all-purpose flour
1 t. salt
⅔ c. shortening, cut into small pieces
½ c. ice water
2 T. unsalted butter, cut into small pieces

Combine flour and salt; cut in shortening with a pastry blender until mixture resembles coarse meal. Sprinkle cold water, one tablespoon at a time, over surface; stir with a fork until dry ingredients are moistened. Press dough into 4-inch circle. Cover and chill at least one hour.

Roll dough into a 12-inch circle on a floured surface. Transfer dough onto a parchment-lined baking sheet. Spoon filling into center of dough and spread to the edges, leaving a 2-inch border. Dot with butter. Fold dough up and over the filling, pleating every 2 inches and leaving the center open. Gently press dough to seal the pleats. Chill 20 minutes.

Bake at 425 degrees on the lower third of the oven for 15 minutes. Reduce heat to 375 degrees and continue to bake 50 minutes or until crust is golden and the fruit is tender. Let tart stand 5 minutes on the baking sheet on a wire rack. Remove from baking sheet to a wire rack to cool completely. Makes 6 to 8 servings.

Filling:
2 c. peeled, cored and sliced Granny Smith apples
2 c. peeled, cored and sliced Rome apples
½ c. sugar
2 to 3 T. all-purpose flour
⅛ t. salt

Combine all ingredients in a large bowl.

Card instructions are on page 361.

good friends good food

149

## Pineapple & Nut Cheese Ball

*This sweet and savory appetizer can be used for 2 gifts…or save one for yourself.*

8-oz. pkg. cream cheese, softened
2 c. chopped pecans, divided
8-oz. can crushed pineapple, drained
¼ c. green pepper, chopped
2 T. onion, chopped
2 t. seasoned salt

Beat cream cheese until smooth. Blend in one cup pecans and remaining ingredients. Shape into 2 balls; roll each ball in remaining pecans. Wrap in plastic wrap. Refrigerate until ready to serve. Makes 2 cheese balls.

*Michelle Camper*
*Peoria, IL*

## Cheese Ball Box

instructions are on page 363.

Pineapple & Nut Cheese Ball
Cheese Ball Box

**Cranberry Scones
Scone Cozy**

## Cranberry Scones

*I've had this recipe for many years; it's a breakfast "must-have!"*

2½ c. all-purpose flour
2½ t. baking powder
½ t. baking soda
¾ c. butter, sliced
1 c. cranberries, chopped
⅔ c. sugar
¾ c. buttermilk

Mix flour, baking powder and baking soda together in a large mixing bowl; cut in butter until mixture resembles coarse crumbs. Stir in cranberries and sugar; add buttermilk, mixing until just blended. Divide dough in half; roll each portion into an 8-inch circle, about ½-inch thick, on a lightly floured surface. Cut each portion into 8 wedges; arrange wedges on ungreased baking sheets.

Bake at 400 degrees for 12 to 15 minutes; remove to a wire rack to cool. Drizzle glaze over the tops. Let stand until glaze is hardened. Wrap loosely in wax paper. Makes 16 servings.

Glaze:
⅔ c. powdered sugar
1 T. warm water
¼ t. vanilla extract

Combine ingredients; mix well, adding additional warm water until desired spreading consistency is achieved.

*Cathy Light
Sedro Woolley, WA*

## Scone Cozy

instructions begin on page 363.

Cranberry Scones, nestled in a festive Scone Cozy, are an irresistible sight. Or create an easy Candy Glass by filling a vintage tumbler with Chocolate Peanut Clusters.

Chocolate-Peanut Clusters
Candy Glass

peanut
JOY
clusters

## Chocolate-Peanut Clusters

*These salty-sweet homemade confections make a large batch to share with many friends.*

16-oz. jar dry-roasted salted
   peanuts
16-oz. jar dry-roasted unsalted
   peanuts

2 lbs. white melting chocolate,
   coarsely chopped
4 oz. sweet baking chocolate,
   coarsely chopped
2 c. semi-sweet chocolate chips

In a 5-quart slow cooker, combine all ingredients. Cover and cook on low setting for 3 hours. Stir and drop candy by heaping tablespoonfuls onto wax paper. Let cool completely. Makes about 3¼ pounds.

## Candy Glass

Instructions are on page 364.

## Parfait Glass Bouquet
- Mint Cookies & Cream Truffle Pops
- parfait glass
- foam cone to fit inverted in the glass
- mica flakes
- ribbons, twill tape and rickrack
- wooden skewers, cut into 6"-8" lengths
- hot glue gun
- rub-on letters
- buttons

**1.** Place the foam in the glass and cover with mica flakes. Insert the pops in the cone.
**2.** For each festive "flag," wrap one or 2 ribbon, rickrack or twill tape 6" lengths around the end of a skewer; glue in place. Fill in between the pops with the flags.
**3.** For a clever tag, glue two 12" twill tape lengths to the end of a skewer. Add a rub-on message near the free end of one length and glue buttons to both pieces. Insert near the front of the glass.

Mint Cookies & Cream
Truffle Pops
Parfait Glass Bouquet

## Mint Cookies & Cream Truffle Pops
*These festive pops will be loved by kids and adults alike.*

8-oz. pkg. cream cheese, softened
4 c. mint chocolate sandwich cookies, crushed
2 c. white chocolate chips
1 T. shortening

Beat cream cheese with a mixer until fluffy; blend in crushed cookies. Refrigerate for 2 hours. Roll dough into one-inch balls. Melt white chocolate chips with shortening in a double boiler over medium heat. Dip balls into mixture to coat. Place on wax paper to set; press ends of 6- to 8-inch wooden skewers into flat sides of balls. Wrap with cellophane and decorate with festive ribbons. Makes 2½ dozen.

## 9-Minute Microwave Peanut Brittle

*This fast recipe makes lots of gifts!*

1 c. sugar
1 c. lightly salted peanuts
½ c. corn syrup
1 t. vanilla extract
1 t. butter, softened
1 t. baking soda

Microwave sugar, peanuts and corn syrup in a large microwave-safe bowl on high for 4 minutes; stir. Reduce power to medium and microwave for 3 minutes. Stir in vanilla and butter. Continue to microwave on medium for 2 minutes. Remove from microwave and stir in baking soda (mixture will foam). Pour onto lightly greased aluminum foil to cool. Break into pieces. Makes ¾ pound.

## Peanut Brittle Boxes

• double-sided cardstock
• double-sided tape
• scallop-edged scissors (optional)
• cellophane bags
• 9-Minute Microwave Peanut
  Brittle
• twist ties
• trims (we used jute twine, wired
  pom-pom trim and mini rickrack)

Enlarge the patterns on page 406 to 166%. For each gift box, use the patterns and cut a front flap and box from cardstock along the solid lines, discarding the window. Fold on the dashed lines. Aligning arrows, tape the front flap to the box bottom. Tape the small tabs to the box sides and tape the side flaps to the box bottom. If you'd like, scallop the front flap.

Fill a bag with peanut brittle; close with a twist tie and a twine bow. Slide the bag in the box. Close the front flap and tie up with trims.

9-Minute Microwave Peanut Brittle
Peanut Brittle Boxes

## White Chocolate-Cranberry Cookies

*Cranberries add a chewy tartness to purchased cookie dough...a tasty treat.*

16-oz. pkg. refrigerated white
  chocolate chip and macadamia
  nut cookie dough
¾ c. sweetened, dried cranberries
½ c. chopped pecans
1 t. orange extract
1 t. vanilla extract

Combine all ingredients and mix well. Drop by tablespoonfuls onto ungreased baking sheets. Bake at 350 degrees for 14 to 17 minutes. Makes about 2 dozen.

*Sandy Bernards*
*Valencia, CA*

## Cookie Holders

Instructions are on page 364.

154

Friends & family will know you care when your homemade goodies look as wonderful as they taste! Package 9-Minute Microwave Peanut Brittle in whimsical window boxes tied with pom-pom trim. When accompanied by a favorite bottled beverage, each White Chocolate-Cranberry Cookie is a complete snack.

**White Chocolate-Cranberry Cookies**
**Cookie Holders**

Mock Cherry Pies
Pie Basket

Cranberries are sweet-tart treats when baked with raisins in Mock Cherry Pies. The liner in the Pie Basket is "oh-sew-simple."

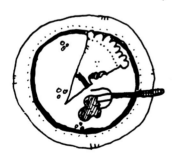

## Mock Cherry Pies

*We suggest serving these miniature pies with a big dollop of vanilla ice cream.*

2 c. cranberries, halved
1 c. raisins, chopped
2 c. sugar
1/4 c. all-purpose flour
2 T. butter, melted
1 t. vanilla extract
1/2 t. almond extract
1 c. boiling water
14.1-oz. pkg. refrigerated pie crusts

Combine all ingredients but pie crusts in a large bowl. Cut each pie crust into two 6 1/2-inch circles, reserving scraps. Place in four 4 1/2-inch pie plates. Divide cranberry mixture evenly over pie crusts in pie plates.

Cut reserved scraps into 1/2-inch wide strips. Lay strips at 1/2-inch intervals; fold back alternate strips as you weave crosswise strips over and under. Trim crusts even with outer rim of pie plates. Dampen edge of crusts with water; fold over strips, seal and crimp. Bake at 375 degrees for 30 minutes or until crust is golden and filling is bubbly. Cool in pans on wire racks. Makes 4 small pies.

## Pie Basket

instructions begin on page 364.

It isn't Christmas without these sweet treats! Fill a Cookie Bucket with Oatmeal-Coconut-Chocolate Chip Cookies and pass out these delicious treats to your neighbors.

## Oatmeal-Coconut-Chocolate Chip Cookies

*These chocolate-studded cookies bake up into crispy bake-shop style treats.*

2 c. brown sugar, packed
2 c. sugar
1 c. shortening
¾ c. butter, softened
4 eggs
2 t. vanilla extract
3 c. all-purpose flour
2 t. salt
2 t. baking soda
3 c. long-cooking oats
2 c. sweetened flaked coconut
1 c. semi-sweet chocolate chips
1 c. chopped pecans

Beat sugars, shortening and butter with an electric mixer until fluffy. Add eggs and vanilla; beat until combined. Combine flour, salt and baking soda; add to sugar mixture, blending well. Stir in remaining ingredients.

Drop dough by 2 tablespoonfuls onto parchment-lined baking sheets. Bake at 350 degrees for 12 to 14 minutes. Let cool 3 minutes on baking sheets; remove cookies to wire racks to cool completely. Makes 6½ dozen.

## Cookie Bucket

- green metal pail (ours is 4¾"h with a 5¾" dia. opening)
- sandpaper
- patterned and solid cardstock
- double-sided tape
- red ribbons and jute twine
- craft glue
- adhesive foam dots
- tag sticker
- patterned food tissue paper
- Oatmeal-Coconut-Chocolate Chip Cookies

**1.** Lightly sand the pail to give it an aged appearance.
**2.** Enlarge the patterns (page 407) to 200%. Use the enlarged patterns to cut the ornament pieces from cardstock.
**3.** Tape ribbon to the top piece; then, tape the ornament pieces and cap together. Glue a twine loop "hanger" to the back and attach the ornament to the pail with foam dots.
**4.** Write a message on a cardstock-backed tag sticker. Fill the pail with cookies nestled in tissue paper.

**Oatmeal-Coconut-Chocolate Chip Cookies Cookie Bucket**

cookies for you!

**Marshmallow Popcorn Balls**
**Ball Ornament**

## Marshmallow Popcorn Balls

*Kids will love to help make these colorful*
*Christmas treats.*

**26 c. popped popcorn**
**1¼ c. dry-roasted salted peanuts**
**½ c. fruit-flavored gumdrops**
**½ c. butter**
**¼ c. canola oil**
**9 c. mini marshmallows**

In a large bowl, combine popcorn, peanuts and gumdrops; toss well. Over low heat, melt together butter, oil and marshmallows; stir until melted. Pour over popcorn mixture to coat. Shape mixture into 16 balls, about 1½ cups each. Makes about 16 balls.

## Ball Ornament

- plastic-wrapped Marshmallow Popcorn Ball
- 4" dia. clear acrylic separating ball ornament
- solid and patterned cardstock
- craft glue
- 1¼" smooth and 1½" scalloped circle punches
- black fine-point permanent pen
- loopy ribbon trims for flowers
- corsage pin
- 2 shank buttons
- ribbons
- hole punch

**1.** Place a popcorn ball in the ornament.
**2.** Trim 2 corners from a 2¼"x4" cardstock tag. Layer and glue smooth and scalloped cardstock circles on the tag; add a holiday message.
**3.** Coil a trim piece into a large round flower on the tag, gluing as you go. Insert the pin in the flower and glue a button to the center.
**4.** Glue a small trim flower and button to the tag. Loop ribbons through a hole punched in the tag and hang from the ornament.

Graham Cracker Fudge
Fudge Box

Treat a favorite chocolate lover with a colorful Fudge Box of Graham Cracker Fudge.

### Graham Cracker Fudge

*My mother wrote down her favorite fudge recipe for me on the first Christmas I was married (over 40 years ago). She saved the original clipping cut from a November 1942 magazine. Now I have both copies...they are yellowed with time, but the fudge is as delicious and chewy as ever.*

2 sqs. unsweetened baking
  chocolate
14-oz. can sweetened condensed
  milk
½ t. vanilla extract
1¾ c. graham crackers, finely
  crushed
1½ c. chopped pecans, walnuts
  or almonds, divided

Melt chocolate in a double boiler over hot water. Add condensed milk and cook, stirring constantly, about 5 minutes or until mixture thickens. Add vanilla, graham cracker crumbs and one cup nuts; mix well. Sprinkle ¼ cup of remaining nuts in the bottom of a buttered 8"x8" baking pan. Use a knife that has been dipped in hot water to spread chocolate mixture in pan. Press remaining ¼ cup nuts into top. Cover and chill overnight. Cut into squares. Makes 16.

*Nancy Otto*
*Indiana, PA*

### Fudge Box
instructions are on page 374.

Let friends & family know how much you prize them with yummy gifts of individual, Prize-Winning Apple Pies. A cinnamon stick holds each name tag in place.

## Prize-Winning Apple Pies

*Smaller than a regular pie, but just as tasty and you have 5 gifts ready to give.*

2  15-oz. pkgs. refrigerated pie crust dough, rolled into 14-inch circles
6 apples, peeled, cored and chopped
½ c. water
2 T. lemon juice
½ c. sugar
2 T. all-purpose flour
1½ t. apple pie spice
milk and sugar
5  2-inch long cinnamon sticks

For each pie, cut a 6-inch and a 7-inch diameter crust. Cut out 2 leaves, scoring "veins" in leaves with a knife. Place the larger crust in a 10-ounce baking dish, pressing dough down into dish. Repeat for remaining dishes. Combine apples, water and lemon juice; set aside. In a large mixing bowl, mix sugar, flour and pie spice. Drain apples and add to sugar mixture, tossing gently to coat. Spoon filling into pie crusts. Place a 6-inch crust on top of each pie and pinch edges of dough together, joining top and bottom crusts. Brush tops with milk and sprinkle with sugar. Insert a cinnamon stick and place 2 leaves on top of each pie to resemble an apple. Bake at 375 degrees for about 25 to 30 minutes or until crust is golden. Makes 5 small pies.

Prize-Winning Apple Pies
Personalized Tags

## Personalized Tags

For extra-special treats, enlarge the pattern on page 407 to 126%. Use the pattern and cut leaf tags from printed cardstock. Age the edges with an emery board. Set an eyelet near one end of each leaf and personalize with a rub-on name. Wrap the leaf tag around your fingers to give it dimension. Use ribbon to tie the tag to the cinnamon stick "apple stem" on each Prize-Winning Apple Pie.

# Cranberry Breakfast Rings

*Our pretty breakfast rings make some yummy gifts for those special friends. Wrap tightly and freeze if making in advance.*

1 pkg. active dry yeast
2 c. all-purpose flour, divided
1/3 c. plus 1/4 c. sugar, divided
1/2 t. salt
1/2 c. milk
2 T. water
1/4 c. butter or margarine
1 egg, beaten

1/2 t. lemon zest, grated
1 c. whole berry cranberry sauce
1/2 c. walnuts, chopped
1 t. cinnamon
6 T. butter or margarine, melted

In a large bowl, combine yeast, 1/2 cup flour, 1/4 cup sugar and salt; set aside.

In a saucepan, combine milk, water and 1/4 cup butter; heat until warm. Add to dry ingredients and beat until smooth. Add egg and 1/2 cup flour, beating again until mixed. Stir in remaining one cup flour and lemon zest.

To make rings, turn dough onto floured surface and divide into 3 pieces. Roll each piece into an 11x5-inch rectangle. Spread 1/3 cup of cranberry sauce over each dough piece. Combine 1/3 cup sugar, nuts and cinnamon; sprinkle 1/3 of mixture over cranberry sauce on each dough piece. Drizzle each with 2 tablespoons melted butter. Beginning with one long side, roll up each piece and seal edges. With seam edge down, place each piece in a circle on a greased baking sheet. Press ends together to seal. Cut slits 2/3 of the way through the ring at one-inch intervals. Cover rings and let rise in a warm place until double in size (about 45 minutes).

Bake at 350 degrees for 15 to 20 minutes or until done. Bread is done when you thump the ring and it makes a hollow sound, not a thud. Cool completely and drizzle with glaze. Makes 3 rings.

Glaze:
1 c. powdered sugar
2 T. milk
1/2 t. vanilla extract

Mix all ingredients until smooth; drizzle over rings.

**Cranberry Breakfast Rings**
**Breakfast Ring Wrap**

*As a thoughtful bonus, present these delicious gifts along with pretty plates.*

**Breakfast Ring Wrap**
instructions are on page 374.

161

# Raspberry-Filled Muffins

*A treat your friends will welcome for breakfast...or anytime!*

2 c. all-purpose flour
2/3 c. plus 2 T. sugar, divided
2 t. baking powder
1/2 t. salt
1 c. milk
1/2 c. butter or margarine, melted
1 egg, slightly beaten
1 t. vanilla extract
1/2 t. almond extract
1/4 c. raspberry preserves
sliced almonds

Line muffin pan with paper muffin cups. Combine flour, 2/3 cup sugar, baking powder and salt in a large bowl. Add milk, butter, egg and extracts. Stir just until dry ingredients are moistened. Fill cups 1/2 full. Spoon one teaspoon preserves into center of each cup. Top with remaining batter. Sprinkle tops with almonds and 2 tablespoons sugar. Bake at 400 degrees for 12 to 17 minutes. Cool 5 minutes. Remove from pan. Makes one dozen.

## Muffin Picks and Box
Instructions are on page 374.

**Raspberry-Filled Muffins
Muffin Picks and Box**

## Cookies & Cream Truffles

*These have become a staple at our house every holiday.*

8-oz. pkg. cream cheese, softened
4 c. chocolate sandwich cookies, crushed
2 c. white chocolate chips
1 T. shortening

Beat cream cheese with a mixer until fluffy; blend in crushed cookies. Chill 2 hours or until firm. Shape into one-inch balls and place on a wax paper-lined baking sheet. Melt white chocolate chips with shortening in a double boiler over medium heat. Dip balls into mixture to coat. Place on wax paper to harden; store covered in refrigerator. Makes 5 dozen.

*Sheila Gwaltney*
*Johnson City, TN*

*A vintage cup filled with fudgy truffles...what delicious gifts for the special people on your list!*

## Peanut Butter-Cocoa Truffles

*Let the kids help roll these in the pecans!*

1 c. peanut butter chips
³/₄ c. butter
¹/₂ c. baking cocoa
14-oz. can sweetened condensed milk
1 T. vanilla extract
1¹/₄ c. pecans, finely chopped

Melt peanut butter chips and butter in a large saucepan over low heat, stirring often. Add cocoa; stir until smooth. Stir in condensed milk. Stir constantly until mixture is thick and glossy, about 4 minutes. Remove from heat; stir in vanilla. Chill 2 hours or until firm. Shape into one-inch balls; roll in pecans. Chill until firm, about one hour. Store covered in refrigerator. Makes about 5¹/₂ dozen.

*Marian Buckley*
*Fontana, CA*

## Mocha Truffles

*So easy to prepare and the taste is unmatched!*

2  12 oz. pkgs. semi-sweet chocolate chips
8-oz. pkg. cream cheese, softened
3 T. instant coffee granules
2 t. water
1 lb. dark melting chocolate

In a microwave-safe bowl, melt chocolate chips. Add cream cheese, coffee and water. Mix well with an electric mixer. Chill until firm. Shape into one-inch balls and place on a wax paper-lined baking sheet. Chill 45 minutes or until firm. Heat melting chocolate in a microwave-safe bowl. Dip balls in chocolate and place on wax paper to harden. Store covered in refrigerator. Makes about 8 dozen.

*Donna Nowicki*
*Stillwater, MN*

## Cupfuls of Truffles

instructions are on page 365.

**Cookies & Cream Truffles**
**Mocha Truffles**
**Peanut Butter-Cocoa Truffles**
**Cupfuls of Truffles**

163

# Creamy Peppermint Brownies

*Delight friends with chocolate and mint in a terrific brownie!*

1½ c. butter, melted
3 c. sugar
5 eggs
1½ T. vanilla extract
2 c. all-purpose flour
1 c. baking cocoa
1 t. baking powder
1 t. salt
24  1½-inch dia. chocolate-covered mint patties

Blend butter and sugar; stir in eggs and vanilla. Add flour, cocoa, baking powder and salt; mix well. Set 2 cups batter aside; spread remaining batter in an ungreased 13"x9" baking pan. Arrange mint patties in a single layer about ½ inch apart on top of the batter; spread with reserved batter. Bake at 350 degrees for 50 to 55 minutes; cool completely before cutting into bars. Makes 3 dozen.

## Brownie Plate

instructions are on page 365.

Creamy Peppermint Brownies
Brownie Plate

Caramel Turtles
Turtle Box

Two tempting sweets! Whether boxed to go or placed on a pedestal of your creation, these treats will disappear in a hurry.

## Caramel Turtles

*Three ingredients make a super treat! Make lots of these for all your co-workers.*

Lightly spray a baking pan with non-stick vegetable spray. Line pan with waffle pretzels and place one chocolate-covered caramel candy on top of each pretzel. Bake at 350 degrees for 3 to 5 minutes. Remove from oven and lightly press one pecan half into each candy. Allow to cool.

## Turtle Box
instructions are on page 365.

Cheddar Cheese Crispies
Cracker Tin

## Cheddar Cheese Crispies

*A quick & easy snack! For a spicier flavor, add a little more cayenne pepper, a little black pepper and a dash of dry mustard.*

8-oz. pkg. shredded sharp Cheddar cheese
1 c. butter, softened
2 c. all-purpose flour
½ t. salt
¼ t. cayenne pepper
2 c. crispy rice cereal

Combine cheese and butter; mix well. Let stand for a few minutes to soften. Add remaining ingredients; mix well. Shape into about 2 dozen balls and flatten slightly to about ¼ to ½-inch thick. Place on ungreased baking sheets. Bake at 350 degrees for 15 to 20 minutes, until lightly browned around the edges. Makes about 2 dozen.

*Lorrie Smith*
*Drummonds, TN*

## Cracker Tin

- metal can with lid
- small pieces of white/solid/patterned cardstock
- adhesive dimensional dots
- stamps, rub-on letters or computer/printer
- ¾" hole punch (to fit magnets)
- small snowflake punch
- ¾" magnets
- glitter glue

**1. For Tag:** Print text onto white cardstock, allowing room for tree at left. Print or stamp border around text. From cardstock or patterned paper, cut a triangle tree and trunk. Adhere to tag using adhesive dimensional dots.
**2. For Magnets:** Punch ¾" circles from cardstock or patterned paper and adhere to magnet fronts. Punch small snowflakes to fit magnets and adhere. Add a dot of glitter glue to each snowflake and allow to dry.
**3.** Secure tag to can with magnets. Add other magnets to the can if desired.

Peggy's Granola

## Peggy's Granola

*When a dear friend put this granola in a gift basket, my husband and I couldn't stop eating it!*

4 c. quick-cooking oats, uncooked
2 c. crispy rice cereal
2 c. sliced almonds
2 T. cinnamon
2 c. brown sugar, packed
$\frac{2}{3}$ c. butter
$\frac{1}{2}$ c. honey
2 c. chopped dried fruit or raisins

Toss oats, cereal, almonds and cinnamon together in a large bowl; set aside. Combine brown sugar, butter and honey in a heavy sauce-pan over medium-high heat. Boil, stirring occasionally, until butter is melted and brown sugar is dissolved. Pour over oat mixture; stir to coat. Spread evenly on an aluminum foil-lined baking sheet. Bake at 350 degrees for 10 minutes; stir well. Bake for an additional 10 minutes. Remove from oven and cool 5 minutes; transfer to a large bowl. Stir in raisins or fruit and cool completely. Store in airtight containers. Makes 14 cups.

*Beth Smith*
*Manchester, MI*

Package Peggy's Granola, so crunchy and honey-sweet, in individual bags and add a patterned tent-style tag.

## Jumbo Fortune Cookies

*Good fortune is sure to smile on you when you give these cookies!*

4 egg whites
1 c. superfine sugar
1 c. all-purpose flour, sifted
⅛ t. salt
¼ c. plus 1 T. butter, melted
3 T. whipping cream
1 t. almond extract
melted white chocolate
red, green and white sugars

Write fortunes on strips of paper about 4" long and ½" wide. Beat together egg whites and sugar; add flour and salt, mixing well. Blend in remaining ingredients except melted chocolate and colored sugars. Pour one table-spoon batter onto half of a baking sheet coated with non-stick vegetable spray; spread with a spoon into a 5-inch circle. Repeat on other half. Bake at 400 degrees for 8 minutes, or until edges turn golden. Working quickly, slice a spatula under cookies; lift and place on a dish towel. Place a fortune on each cookie, close to the middle. Fold cookies in half, pinching at top to form a loose semicircle. Place the folded edge across the rim of a measuring cup and pull the pointed edges down, one on the inside of the cup and one on the outside; allow to harden. Repeat with remaining batter. Dip edges in melted chocolate; immediately dip in colored sugar. Makes 18.

## Fortune Cookie Box
instructions are on page 366.

Jumbo Fortune Cookies
Fortune Cookie Box

Pack spicy Apple-Ginger Chutney into little canning jars...then add a colorful paper topper for a perfect presentation.

## Apple-Ginger Chutney

*When we had Sunday dinner at my grandparents' house, Gran always had extra jars of this fruity, spicy relish for us to take home. It's delicious on roasted or grilled chicken...try it spooned over cream cheese on a cracker too. Yum!*

4 Granny Smith apples, cored,
   peeled and chopped
2 c. onion, minced
1 red pepper, minced
¼ c. fresh ginger, peeled and
   minced
1 c. golden raisins
1½ c. cider vinegar
1½ c. dark brown sugar, packed
¾ t. dry mustard
¾ t. salt
½ t. red pepper flakes
6 ½-pint canning jars and lids,
   sterilized

Combine all ingredients in a large saucepan over medium-high heat. Bring to a boil, stirring frequently. Reduce heat to low. Simmer for 40 minutes, stirring occasionally, until thickened. Spoon chutney into sterilized jars; cool slightly and add lids. Keep refrigerated up to 2 weeks. Makes 6 jars.

Anna McMaster
Portland, OR

## Jar Topper
instructions are on page 366.

Apple-Ginger Chutney
Jar Topper

## Grandma's Zucchini Bread

*Growing up, my favorite harvest memory was getting the chance to go over to my grandma's house. She would let me go out into the yard and pick the zucchini. We'd then use the best ones to make this bread. She would let me set out the ingredients and do the mixing, and afterward, we'd talk and enjoy slices of her delicious zucchini bread.*

3 c. all-purpose flour
1 t. salt
1/4 t. baking powder
1 t. baking soda
1 T. cinnamon
3 eggs
1 c. oil
2 t. vanilla extract
2 1/4 c. sugar
2 zucchini, shredded
1/2 c. chopped walnuts

Sift flour, salt, baking powder, baking soda and cinnamon together; set aside. Beat eggs, oil, vanilla and sugar together; add to flour mixture and blend well. Stir in zucchini and nuts until well combined. Pour batter into 2 lightly greased 8"x 4" loaf pans. Bake at 325 degrees for 55 to 65 minutes. Cool in pans on a wire rack for 20 minutes. Remove from pans and cool. Makes 2 loaves.

*Stefanie Schmidt*
*Las Vegas, NV*

### Apron Tag

- tracing paper
- 2-3 coordinated patterned papers and cardstock
- ribbon
- border punch
- small circle punch
- light tan ink
- embossing template or folder
- stamps, rub-on letters or computer/printer

1. Enlarge and trace pattern (page 407). Cut dress body from patterned paper. Emboss the skirt and lightly ink.
2. Cut small rectangle from coordinating patterned paper and adhere to the center of the dress top. Adhere a strip of narrow ribbon to either side of the dress, leaving length to tie.
3. Print or stamp "Grandma's Zucchini Bread" (or other name) on white cardstock. Cut out and then use border punch along bottom edge.
4. Trim with small punched dots and a strip of patterned paper. Adhere the top of the apron to the dress waist.
5. Cut waistband from coordinating patterned paper and adhere. Knot a short length of coordinating ribbon and adhere to side of apron. Tie to package.

Grandma's Zucchini Bread

Apron Tag

Christmas wouldn't be Christmas without the wonderful flavor of peppermint. Showcase Peppermint Bark Brownies in a red-and-white striped box.

### Peppermint Bark Brownies

*These brownies are welcome at any holiday occasion! Everyone loves chocolate and peppermint at Christmas!*

20-oz. pkg. fudge brownie mix
12-oz. pkg. white chocolate chips
2 t. butter
¾ c. candy canes, crushed

Prepare and bake brownie mix according to package directions, using a greased 13"x9" baking pan. After baking, set aside and cool completely in pan, about one to 2 hours. In a saucepan over very low heat, melt chocolate chips and butter, stirring constantly with a rubber spatula. Spread chocolate mixture over brownies; sprinkle with crushed candy. Let stand for about 30 minutes, until frosting is hardened. Cut into squares. Makes 2 dozen.

Angie Biggin
Lyons, IL

**See-Through Brownie Box** instructions are on page 366.

Peppermint Bark Brownies
See-Through Brownie Box

Country Herb Spread
and Crispy Wheat Crackers
stack up for a savory treat.
Give spicy Pretzels with
Pizzazz in a jar that can be
used after the treats are
gone. Orange-Macadamia
Fudge, nestled in a festive
tin, is the perfect gift for the
sweet-tooth on your list!

## Country Herb Spread

*For variety, omit chives and dill; add one
teaspoon fresh oregano and 1/2 teaspoon
each fresh thyme, basil and marjoram.*

8-oz. pkg. cream cheese, softened
1 T. mayonnaise
1 t. Dijon mustard
1 T. fresh chives, chopped
1 T. fresh dill, chopped
1 clove garlic, pressed
crackers

Combine all ingredients except
crackers; stir until well blended.
Serve with crackers. Makes
1 1/2 cups.

*Cindy Brown*
*Farmington Hills, MI*

## Crispy Wheat Crackers

*So delicious in soups and stews… terrific
topped with cheese too!*

1 3/4 c. whole-wheat flour
1 1/2 c. all-purpose flour
1 t. salt
1/3 c. oil
1 c. water
coarse salt to taste

In a medium bowl, combine
flours and salt. Add oil and water,
mixing until just blended. Roll dough
out on a lightly floured surface to a
thickness no greater than 1/8 inch.
Place dough on an ungreased baking
sheet; score squares with a knife
without cutting through. Prick each
square with a fork several times
and sprinkle with salt. Bake at 350
degrees for 25 to 30 minutes,
until crisp and golden. Allow
crackers to cool on baking sheet.
Remove and break into individual
crackers. Makes 32 servings.

## Country Herb Spread
## Gift Box
instructions are on page 367.

Country Herb Spread
Crispy Wheat Crackers
Gift Box

172

## Pretzels with Pizzazz

*Our family loves to watch sports on television…football, basketball, baseball…we love them all! These spicy pretzels are one of our favorite game-time or anytime snacks.*

24-oz. pkg. mini twist pretzels
1 c. oil
2 T. red pepper flakes
1-oz. pkg. ranch salad dressing mix
2 T. grated Parmesan cheese
2 t. Italian seasoning

Transfer pretzels to a one-gallon container with a tight-fitting lid. Combine remaining ingredients in a bowl. Whisk until well mixed and pour over pretzels. Put lid on container and rotate until well coated, about 2 to 3 minutes. Let stand overnight before serving…if you can wait that long! Makes 20 to 24 servings.

*Beckie Apple*
*Grannis, AR*

Pretzels with Pizzazz
Decorated Pretzel Jar

## Orange-Macadamia Fudge

*A delicious way to let someone know you're thinking of them.*

½ c. butter, melted
1 c. sugar
5-oz. can evaporated milk
2 c. mini marshmallows
1 c. semi-sweet chocolate chips
¾ c. chopped macadamia nuts
1 t. orange extract

Combine butter, sugar and milk in a medium microwave-safe bowl; microwave on high for 5 minutes. Immediately add marshmallows and chocolate chips, stirring until pretzels are melted and smooth. Stir in nuts and orange extract. Pour into an 8"x 8" pan lined with aluminum foil; chill until firm. Remove fudge from pan, peel away foil and cut into squares. Store in refrigerator. Makes about 2 pounds.

## Decorated Pretzel Jar and Candy Tin
instructions are on pages 362 and 367.

Orange-Macadamia Fudge
Candy Tin

Snowy Trail Mix
Candy Sleigh Holder

Maine Maple Candies
Paper Poppers

## Snowy Trail Mix

*So easy and so yummy! I have given it in little cellophane bags tied with a cute ribbon for gifts…everybody loves them.*

3 c. mini pretzel sticks
1½ c. bite-size corn & rice cereal squares
¾ c. pecan halves
½ c. sweetened dried cranberries
½ c. cashew halves
1 c. red and green candy-coated chocolates
12-oz. pkg. white melting chocolate, chopped

In a large microwave-safe bowl, mix together all ingredients except white chocolate; set aside. Place white chocolate in a separate microwave-safe bowl. Microwave chocolate on high for one to 2 minutes; stir until smooth. Slowly pour melted chocolate over pretzel mixture, gently stirring until evenly coated. Scoop out onto wax paper. Let cool 20 minutes; break into bite-size clusters. Makes 10 cups.

Heather Plasterer
Colorado Springs, CO

## Maine Maple Candies

*These arrived as a Christmas surprise from my granny in Maine…what a yummy treat!*

14-oz. can sweetened condensed milk
¼ c. butter, softened
2 T. maple flavoring
1½ c. chopped nuts
32-oz. pkg. powdered sugar
3 8-oz. pkgs. semi-sweet chocolate, chopped

Mix together condensed milk, butter, flavoring and nuts; gradually beat in powdered sugar. Roll into one-inch balls; refrigerate until ready to dip. Melt chocolate in a heavy saucepan over low heat; dip balls into chocolate. Place on wax paper-lined baking sheets until set. Keep refrigerated. Makes about 4½ dozen.

Jennifer Martineau
Delaware, OH

Candy Sleigh Holder and Paper Poppers
instructions are on page 367.

Homemade Graham Crackers
S'mores Container

## Homemade Graham Crackers

*Make a S'mores gift basket and pack these up with chocolate bars and marshmallows…yum!*

1/2 c. butter
3/4 c. brown sugar, packed
1 t. vanilla extract
2 c. whole-wheat flour
1 c. all-purpose flour
1 t. baking powder
1/2 t. baking soda
1/8 t. salt
1/2 c. milk

In a medium bowl, beat together butter and brown sugar with an electric mixer on medium speed; stir in vanilla. In a separate bowl, combine flours, baking powder, baking soda and salt; stir into butter mixture alternating with milk, beating with an electric mixer at medium speed until dough comes together and forms a ball. Divide dough in half and form into 2 discs; wrap tightly and chill one hour.

On a lightly floured surface, roll dough to 1/8-inch thickness; cut into 4-inch by 2-inch rectangles. Place each cracker 1/2 inch apart on parchment-lined baking sheets. Bake at 350 degrees for 12 to 14 minutes, until edges are golden. Remove crackers from baking sheets to cool on wire racks. Makes 30.

## S'mores Container

instructions are on page 362.

A Chip & Dip Mix Container of Baked Pita Chips includes Santa's Zesty Mix for dip.

## Baked Pita Chips
*Chewier and fresher-tasting than bagged chips.*

8 6" round pita breads
2 T. olive oil
1 t. garlic powder

Split pita bread rounds. Brush cut sides with olive oil, then cut into 6 wedges. Sprinkle with garlic powder and bake in a single layer at 350 degrees for 10 to 12 minutes, or until crisp. Store in airtight container. Makes 8 dozen.

## Santa's Zesty Mix
1 T. dried chives
1 t. garlic salt
½ t. dill weed
½ t. paprika
⅛ t. onion powder

Combine ingredients in a small bowl; spoon into a small clear plastic zipping bag. Seal; use within 6 months. Attach instructions.

Instructions: Combine mix with one tablespoon lemon juice, one cup mayonnaise, and one cup sour cream. Refrigerate until chilled. Makes 2 cups.

## Chip & Dip Mix Container
instructions are on page 368.

Add a little spice to a traditional favorite when you make Cinnamon Peanut Brittle. What a treat!

## Cinnamon Peanut Brittle

*I make this simple recipe every year for Christmas, and it's a huge hit...you'll never eat ordinary peanut brittle again!*

1 c. sugar
½ c. light corn syrup
2 c. salted peanuts
1 t. butter
½ t. cinnamon
1 t. baking soda
1 t. vanilla extract

Combine sugar and corn syrup in a 2-quart microwave-safe glass container. Microwave, uncovered, on high for 4 minutes; stir. Heat 3 minutes longer; stir in peanuts, butter and cinnamon. Cook, uncovered, on high for 30 to 60 seconds, until mixture turns a light amber color. Mixture will be very hot. Quickly stir in baking soda and vanilla until light and foamy. Immediately pour onto a greased baking sheet and spread with a metal spatula. Refrigerate for 20 minutes, or until firm; break into pieces. Store in an airtight container. Makes 1¼ pounds.

*Jennifer Oglesby
Brownsville, IN*

Cinnamon Peanut Brittle Candy Pail

## Candy Pail

- clear plastic pail with metal lid/handle
- 2-3 coordinated patterned papers and cardstock
- cardstock border strips
- circle cutter or template
- fine-tipped liquid paint pen
- ball chain
- strong tape adhesive
- small hole punch
- corner rounder
- small tag die or punch
- ribbon and twine
- stamps, rub-on letters or computer/printer

**1.** Adhere a circle cut from patterned paper to the lid. Wrap a cardstock border strip around the middle of the pail and adhere with tape adhesive.

**2.** Print or stamp "Cinnamon Peanut Brittle" on white cardstock, trim to fit inside border and adhere.

**3. For tag:** Cut a rectangle from double-sided patterned paper and fold in half to create a small tag. Round corners and punch a small hole in the top. Die cut a small tag from coordinating cardstock. Print or stamp "Sweets for the Sweet" on white cardstock and adhere to the tag base. Add ribbon and twine to tag. Hang on the pail with ball chain.

## No-Fuss Caramel Corn
*So much tastier than store-bought caramel corn!*

12 c. popped popcorn
1½ c. chopped pecans
1 c. brown sugar, packed
½ c. butter
¼ c. corn syrup
½ t. salt
½ t. baking soda

Place popcorn in a large oven bag; add pecans and set aside. Combine brown sugar, butter, corn syrup and salt in a microwave-safe 2-quart glass bowl. Microwave on high setting for 2 to 3 minutes, stirring after each minute, until mixture comes to a boil. Microwave for 2 additional minutes without stirring. Stir in baking soda (mixture will foam). Pour mixture over popcorn; close bag and shake well. Microwave in bag for 1½ minutes. Shake bag well (be careful, bag is hot) and pour onto greased aluminum foil; stir and cool. Makes about 14 cups.

*Crystal Myers*
*Hillsboro, OH*

No-Fuss Caramel Corn
Caramel Corn Cone

## Caramel Corn Cone
- vintage napkin or hankie (ours is 12"x13")
- double-sided removable tape
- cardstock
- plastic wrap
- liquid starch
- straight pin
- ¼"w ribbon
- cone-shaped icing bag
- No-Fuss Caramel Corn
- vintage ornaments and tag
- embroidery floss

**1.** Fold the napkin once diagonally; then, pull the top center point a few inches to the right so the points don't align (Fig. 1).

**Fig. 1**

**2.** Fold the napkin from right to left, making sure the points don't align (Fig. 2).

**Fig. 2**

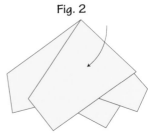

**3.** Roll and tape cardstock into a cone shape; trim the wide end so it will stand when placed upside down. (Our cone is 7½" tall with a 3" diameter...for a different size napkin, adjust the length of the cone so it's a few inches shorter than your folded-up napkin.) Adjust the diameter of the cone if needed so the folded napkin will wrap around it with about 1" overlap. Set the napkin aside and cover the cone with plastic wrap. Place a piece of plastic wrap on the table.
**4.** Dip the folded napkin into a bowl of starch. Squeeze out the excess starch. Overlap and wrap the napkin around the cone. Pin the napkin "seam" together at the top point. Stand the napkin and cone on the plastic wrap with the corners of the napkin draping onto the table; allow to dry overnight. Remove the pin and cone from the stiffened napkin. Sew a ribbon hanger to the cone.
**5.** Fill the icing bag with caramel corn and tie closed with ribbon. Add ornaments and a tag with floss. Place the bag in the cone.

## Fondue Kit

- tissue paper
- water-soluble marking pen (optional)
- $9\frac{1}{2}$"x$10\frac{1}{2}$" cream muslin piece
- brown, blue, red and orange embroidery floss
- $\frac{1}{4}$ yard of red ticking fabric
- fabric glue
- grosgrain ribbon (we used $\frac{3}{8}$"w and $\frac{5}{8}$"w)
- canvas bin (ours measures 13"lx10"wx$7\frac{1}{2}$"h at the top)
- 8 buttons
- cellophane bags of dipping items
- fondue pot and forks
- jar of Mom's Chocolate Fondue
- wood excelsior

*Use 3 strands of floss for all stitching.*

**1.** Follow Transferring Patterns (page 318) to transfer the design on page 412 onto muslin. Work Stem Stitch (page 319) outlines and letters, Straight Stitch snowflakes and French Knot eyes and buttons. Trim the stitched piece to $5\frac{1}{4}$"x$6\frac{1}{4}$". Center and zigzag the stitched piece on a $6\frac{1}{4}$"x$7\frac{1}{4}$" piece of ticking.
**2.** Glue ribbon around the bin and on the handles. Use floss to sew buttons to the handle ends and to catch the corners of the stitched piece on front of the bin.
**3.** Tie strips of ticking around the bags and fondue forks. Use ribbon to tie a square of ticking around the jar lid. Line the bin with excelsior and add the fondue pot with all the trimmings.

**Mom's Chocolate Fondue**
**Fondue Kit**

## Mom's Chocolate Fondue

*What fun to receive a fondue pot and all the fixings to go with it! Keep fondue and fruit in the refrigerator until ready to serve.*

6  1-oz. squares unsweetened baking chocolate
$1\frac{1}{2}$ c. sugar
1 c. half-and-half
$\frac{1}{2}$ c. butter or margarine
$\frac{1}{8}$ t. salt
Optional: 3 T. cocoa cream or orange-flavored liqueur
Items for dipping: marshmallows, pound cake, maraschino cherries, kiwi fruit, strawberries and pineapple

Melt chocolate over low heat. Add sugar, half-and-half, butter and salt. Cook, stirring constantly, about 5 minutes or until thickened. Stir in liqueur, if using. Pour into a jar. To serve, spoon into a fondue pot and keep warm over heat source. Makes $2\frac{3}{4}$ cups.

## Party Mix

*A good combination of flavors!*

¼ c. butter, melted
¼ c. Parmesan cheese
¼ t. oregano
¼ t. garlic powder
Optional: ¼ t. celery salt
22-oz. can mixed nuts
5 cups graham-flavored cereal squares

Combine melted butter, cheese and seasonings in a bowl, stirring in nuts until well coated. Spread nuts on baking sheet; bake at 350 degrees for 15 minutes. Remove from oven and add cereal, mixing well. Cool completely. Makes 9 cups.

## Take-Out Boxes

instructions are on page 368.

Party Mix
Take-Out Boxes

White Confetti Fudge

## White Confetti Fudge

*I like to keep this on hand…just to snack on.*

1 ½ lbs. white baking chocolate
14-oz. can sweetened condensed milk
½ c. red candied cherries, chopped
½ c. green candied cherries, chopped
1 t. vanilla extract
⅛ t. salt

Melt chocolate with milk in a heavy saucepan; stir constantly. Remove from heat; stir in remaining ingredients. Spread evenly in a buttered aluminum foil-lined 8"x8" baking pan; chill about 2 hours or until firm.

Use foil to lift fudge from pan onto a cutting board; remove foil and cut into small squares. Makes 2 dozen.

*Angela Nichols*
*Mt. Airy, NC*

# JUST MIX IT!

For all those times when you wish you had an extra gift on hand, or when company drops by and you need a quick-fix meal or snack…homemade mixes are the answer! These seasonings and sweets are fast to finish by adding a few fresh ingredients, while the Mitten Mix for snacking is ready to serve. Package these recipes for a last-minute present, or simply keep them in your pantry for future enjoyment.

## Italian Soup Mix

*Deliver a jar of soup mix with a loaf of freshly baked bread and all the ingredients (one onion, 3 carrots, 3 celery stalks and canned tomatoes) to make the soup.*

$\frac{1}{2}$ c. dried pinto beans
$\frac{1}{2}$ c. dried pink or red beans
$\frac{1}{2}$ c. dried kidney beans
1 $\frac{1}{2}$ c. small bowtie pasta, uncooked
1 T. dried parsley
1 T. chicken bouillon granules
1 T. salt
1 t. dried oregano
1 t. dried basil
1 t. garlic salt
$\frac{1}{2}$ t. dried, minced garlic
$\frac{1}{4}$ t. red pepper flakes

Layer beans in a 2-cup jar in order listed; secure lid. Place pasta in another 2-cup jar. Combine remaining ingredients; place seasonings in a small plastic zipping bag. Place bag on top of pasta; secure lid. Give with instructions for making soup.

Instructions: Pour beans into a bowl. Rinse with water; drain. Cover beans with water; let soak overnight. Rinse and pour into a 5-quart Dutch oven; add 8 cups water, a 28-ounce can crushed tomatoes, seasoning packet, one cup sliced carrots, one cup sliced celery and one cup chopped onion. Bring to a boil; reduce heat. Simmer, covered, for 2 hours; uncover and boil gently until thickened, about 35 minutes. Stir in pasta; heat until tender, about 20 minutes. Makes about 13 cups.

### Italian Soup Mix
Soup Dinner Kit

### Soup Dinner Kit
instructions are on page 368.

## Bowl o' Bruschetta Blend

*Just like the kind at the family-style Italian restaurants.*

1-lb. pkg. Roma tomatoes,
　　chopped and seeded
1/3 c. sweet onion, diced
1/4 c. olive oil
1/4 c. garlic, minced
2 T. fresh basil, chopped
1/4 t. salt
1/4 t. pepper

Combine all ingredients in a large mixing bowl; whisk well. Pour into an airtight container and refrigerate until ready to serve. Makes 2 to 3 cups.

To serve: Slice one loaf round bread in half horizontally so there are 2, one-inch thick bread circles; cut each into 5 wedges. Brush with garlic-olive oil; broil until golden. Place on a serving dish; spoon bruschetta blend on top. Makes 10 servings.

## Snappy BBQ Seasoning Mix

*Keep this mix on hand for a quick way to add extra spice to your food!*

3 T. onion powder
3 T. garlic powder
2 T. dried parsley
2 T. celery salt
2 T. dry mustard
1 T. pepper

Blend all ingredients together and store in an airtight container. When ready to use, sprinkle on beef, pork or fish while grilling or broiling. Makes about 3/4 cup.

*Lynda Short*
*Janesville, WI*

## Warm-'Em-Up Alphabet Soup Mix

*A fun soup for kids just learning their ABCs!*

1/2 c. pearled barley
1/2 c. dried split peas
1/2 c. instant rice, uncooked
1/2 c. dried lentils
2 T. dried, minced onion
2 T. dried parsley
2 1/2 t. salt
1/2 t. lemon pepper
2 T. beef bouillon granules
1/2 c. alphabet pasta, uncooked
1 c. rotini, uncooked

In a one-quart, wide-mouth jar, layer the ingredients in the order listed. Seal the lid. Makes one quart.

To serve: Add all ingredients to 3 quarts water in a large pot. Add 2 stalks chopped celery, 2 sliced carrots, one cup shredded cabbage and 2 cups diced tomatoes. Cover and cook over medium-low heat for one hour or until vegetables are tender. Makes 10 to 12 servings.

Warm-'Em-Up Alphabet Soup Mix

Mitten Mix

## Mitten Mix

*This is one snack mix no one gets tired of eating!*

6 T. butter, melted
2 T. Worcestershire sauce
1½ t. seasoned salt
¾ t. garlic powder
½ t. onion powder
3 c. bite-size crispy corn cereal squares
3 c. bite-size crispy rice cereal squares
3 c. bite-size crispy wheat cereal squares
1 c. mixed nuts
1 c. pretzels
1 c. garlic-flavored bagel chips

Whisk first 5 ingredients together; set aside. Toss remaining ingredients together in a roasting pan; pour butter mixture over the top. Mix gently until cereal, nuts, pretzels and bagel chips are coated; bake at 325 degrees for 45 minutes, stirring every 10 minutes. Makes 3 quarts.

*Rebekah Neal*
*Springdale, AR*

Always convenient, mixes make thoughtful gifts. Try putting Mitten Mix in plastic bags to tuck into mittens for a quick gift. The dry ingredients for Warm-'Em-Up Alphabet Soup Mix can be layered in quart jars for a pretty presentation.

## Tasty Taco Seasoning Mix

*Use this mix to flavor beef, chicken, soups, meatballs and refried beans.*

¾ c. dried, minced onion
¼ c. salt
¼ c. chili powder
2 T. cumin
2 T. cornstarch
2 T. red pepper flakes
1 T. dried oregano
1 T. garlic powder
1 T. onion salt

Combine ingredients in a large plastic zipping bag; close tightly. Shake to mix well. Makes 2 cups.

To serve: Add 2 tablespoons mix to one pound browned ground beef and ½ cup water; heat through. Serves 4.

## Bacon Dip Spice Packet

*Seal the mix in a small plastic zipping bag and label for a quick & easy dip mix packet.*

2 T. bacon bits
1 T. dried, minced onion
1 t. beef bouillon granules
⅛ t. dried, minced garlic
⅛ t. dried chives

Combine all ingredients; mix well. Place in an airtight container. Makes about ¼ cup.

To serve: Whisk one cup sour cream and spice mix together; cover and refrigerate for at least one hour before serving. Makes one cup.

## Spicy Fruit Tea Mix

*This flavorful treat is great hot or cold.*

20-oz. container orange drink mix
1 c. sugar
1 c. unsweetened instant tea mix
½ c. sweetened lemonade drink mix
¼-oz. pkg. sweetened raspberry-flavored drink mix
2 t. cinnamon
1 t. nutmeg

Combine all ingredients; mix well. Store in an airtight container. Attach instructions. Makes 5½ cups mix.

Instructions on card: Stir 2 tablespoons mix into one cup of hot or cold water. Makes one serving.

### Tea Jar
Instructions are on page 362.

Spicy Fruit Tea Mix
Tea Jar

## Home-Sweet-Home Stroganoff Mix

*Need a quick meal? Just add this mix to cooked beef and serve over noodles...yum!*

2 c. powdered milk
1 c. cornstarch
¼ c. chicken bouillon granules
3 T. dried, minced onion
2 T. dried parsley
1 T. garlic powder
1 t. dried basil
1 t. dried thyme
1 t. pepper

*a sweet treat*

Combine all ingredients; place in an airtight jar or plastic zipping bag. Makes about 3¾ cups.

To serve: Brown one pound ground beef in a 12" skillet; drain. Add 2 cups water, 2 cups uncooked egg noodles and ½ cup stroganoff mix; stir to combine. Bring to a boil; reduce heat and simmer, covered, for 15 to 20 minutes. Top with ½ cup sour cream or plain yogurt; serve warm. Makes 4 servings.

Blonde Brownie Mix

For those times when a snack attack has you searching the kitchen, Blonde Brownie Mix and Peanut Butter Cup Cookie Mix (page 188) come to your rescue. They're also sweet gifts for households with kids!

## Blonde Brownie Mix

*Here's a mix that the kids can do themselves!*

16-oz. pkg. brown sugar
2 c. all-purpose flour
½ c. chopped pecans

Combine all ingredients in a heavy-duty plastic zipping bag. Makes about 5 cups.

To bake: Combine brownie mix with 4 eggs; stir well. Pour into a greased 13"x9" pan. Bake at 350 degrees for 25 to 30 minutes. Makes 2 dozen.

*Kathy Grashoff*
*Ft. Wayne, IN*

## Relaxing Tea Creamer Mix

*Stirred into tea, this mix creates a delightful Chai-like drink...add ¼ teaspoon white pepper for even more spice.*

14-oz. can sweetened condensed milk
1 t. cardamom
1 t. sugar
¾ t. cinnamon
½ t. ground cloves
½ t. nutmeg

Stir all ingredients together; cover and refrigerate for at least 24 hours. Pour into an airtight container. Store in refrigerator. Makes about 2 cups.

To serve: Add 2 teaspoons creamer to a cup of strongly brewed black tea; stir well. Makes one serving.

Peanut Butter Cup Cookie Mix

## Peanut Butter Cup Cookie Mix

*Peanut butter lovers won't be able to resist.*

**20 mini peanut butter cups, chopped**
**1³⁄₄ c. all-purpose flour**
**³⁄₄ c. sugar**
**¹⁄₂ c. brown sugar, packed**
**1 t. baking powder**
**¹⁄₂ t. baking soda**

Place peanut butter cups in a plastic zipping bag. Combine remaining ingredients in another plastic zipping bag. Makes about 3 cups dry mix.

To bake: Place dry mix in a large bowl. Add ¹⁄₂ cup softened butter, one slightly beaten egg and one teaspoon vanilla extract; stir until completely blended (mixture will be crumbly). Stir in peanut butter cups. Shape dough into 1¹⁄₂-inch balls and place on greased baking sheets. Bake at 375 degrees for 12 to 14 minutes; cool 5 minutes before removing cookies to wire racks to cool completely. Makes 2 dozen.

## Mom's Secret Spaghetti Seasoning Mix

*This mix is a quick start to a delicious meal.*

1 T. dried, minced onion
1 T. cornstarch
1 T. dried parsley
2 t. green pepper flakes
1½ t. salt
1 t. sugar
1 t. dried oregano
¾ t. Italian seasonings
¼ t. dried, minced garlic

Combine all ingredients; store in an airtight container. Makes about ⅓ cup.

To serve: Brown one pound ground beef; drain. Add two, 8-oz. cans tomato sauce, a 6-oz. can tomato paste, 2¾ cups tomato juice or water and seasoning mix to the beef; simmer sauce 30 minutes, stirring occasionally. Serve over prepared spaghetti. Makes 4 to 6 servings.

*Vickie*

CHRISTMAS IS FOR SHARING

**Mom's Secret Spaghetti Seasoning Mix**

189

## Snickerdoodle Coffee Mix

*A chocolatey drink all your co-workers will appreciate.*

1 c. sugar
1 c. powdered milk
½ c. vanilla-flavored powdered non-dairy creamer
½ c. baking cocoa
3 T. instant coffee granules
½ t. allspice
¼ t. cinnamon

Combine all ingredients; store in an airtight container. Give with instructions. Makes about 3 cups mix.

Instructions: Add 3 tablespoons mix to ¾ cup boiling water; stir well. Makes one serving.

### Coffee Canister

- plastic zipping bag filled with Snickerdoodle Coffee Mix
- canister (ours is 5"h x 4" dia.)
- pinking shears
- holiday scrapbook papers
- craft knife and cutting mat
- assorted fabric and felt scraps
- large yarn needle
- decorative brad
- ³⁄₈"w ribbon
- jute twine
- chipboard tag with recipient's initial
- rub-on letters
- scrapbook paper label
- double-sided tape

**1.** Place the coffee mix in the canister.
**2.** Use pinking shears to cut a 2½" and a 3½" diameter scrapbook paper circle. Cut a ½"-long slit about 1" in from opposite sides of the larger circle for the ribbon to run through. Cut three 3" diameter circles from fabric and 2 from felt.
**3.** Center the 3" circles between the paper circles. Use the needle to pierce a hole through all layers and join the circles with the brad. Thread the ribbon through the slits in the large paper circle and knot at the bottom of the canister.
**4.** Use twine to tie the initial tag around the brad beneath the fabric.
**5.** Use rub-ons to add individual serving instructions to the label. Tape the label to the canister.

**Snickerdoodle Coffee Mix Coffee Canister**

## Savory Rice Mix

*Altogether, this great gift makes about 16 tasty side-dish servings!*

4 c. long-cooking rice, uncooked
¼ c. dried, minced onion
1 env. from a 2-oz. pkg. onion
    soup mix
1 T. dried parsley
¼ t. garlic salt
¼ t. salt

Combine all ingredients; store in an airtight container for up to 4 months. Give with instructions. Makes about 4 cups mix.

Instructions: Mix one cup mix with 2 cups beef broth in a 2-quart saucepan; add one tablespoon butter. Bring to a rolling boil; reduce heat. Simmer, covered, until liquid is absorbed, about 20 to 25 minutes. Makes 4 servings.

### Rice Mix Jar
instructions are on page 361.

**Savory Rice Mix**
**Rice Mix Jar**

# simply wonderful

To help you during the busy holiday season, the Country Friends gathered these flavor-packed recipes that are quick & easy to make. Kate uses refrigerated ravioli to prepare Pasta with Tomato-Basil Cream. Holly's favorite is Chicken and Rice Casserole, a hearty dish that takes less time to prepare when you use a deli-roasted chicken. A couple of these recipes also make an extra dish for the freezer…Mary Elizabeth likes to keep a pan of Smoked Turkey Tetrazzini on hand for a quick food gift.

## Pasta with Tomato-Basil Cream

*So simple, but so good!*

20-oz. pkg. refrigerated four-cheese ravioli
16-oz. jar sun-dried tomato Alfredo sauce
2 T. white wine or water
14.5-oz. can chopped tomatoes, well drained
½ c. fresh basil, chopped
⅓ c. shredded Parmesan cheese
Garnishes: fresh basil strips, shredded Parmesan
   cheese

Prepare pasta according to package directions; set aside. Pour Alfredo sauce into a medium saucepan. Pour wine or water into sauce jar. Cover tightly and shake well; stir into saucepan. Stir in tomatoes, ½ cup chopped basil and ⅓ cup shredded Parmesan cheese. Cook over medium-low heat 5 minutes or until thoroughly heated; toss with pasta. Garnish, if desired. Makes 4 to 6 servings.

If you like treats with plenty of zip, serve Peppery Molasses Cookies with Spiced Chocolate Coffee.

## Peppery Molasses Cookies

*These are really spicy…the black pepper gives them a kick!*

¾ c. butter, softened
¾ c. sugar
1 egg
¼ c. molasses
2 c. all-purpose flour
2 t. baking soda
1½ t. pepper
1 t. cinnamon
½ t. salt
additional sugar

Beat butter and sugar in a large bowl until fluffy. Beat in egg; add molasses. Combine flour and next 4 ingredients. Gradually add to butter mixture; mix well. Form into one-inch balls and roll in sugar. Arrange 2 inches apart on ungreased baking sheets. Bake at 350 degrees for 12 to 15 minutes. Remove and cool on wire racks. Makes 3½ to 4 dozen.

*Lisa Ashton*
*Aston, PA*

**Peppery Molasses Cookies**
**Spiced Chocolate Coffee**

## Brandied Cranberries

*Family & friends look forward to this spirited cranberry relish at our holiday dinners.*

2 c. sugar
12-oz. pkg. cranberries
½ c. brandy

Combine all ingredients in a lightly greased 1½-quart casserole dish. Cover and bake at 300 degrees for 45 minutes, stirring several times while baking. Refrigerate overnight; serve warm or cold. Serves 5.

*Robin Dennis*
*Vernonia, OR*

## Spiced Chocolate Coffee

*Top with sweetened whipped cream for a special treat.*

8 c. brewed coffee
⅓ c. sugar
¼ c. chocolate syrup
4 4-inch cinnamon sticks, broken
1½ t. whole cloves
Garnish: cinnamon sticks, sweetened whipped cream

Combine first 3 ingredients in a slow cooker; set aside. Wrap spices in a coffee filter or cheesecloth and tie with kitchen string; add to slow cooker. Cover and cook on low setting for 2 to 3 hours. Remove and discard spices. Ladle coffee into mugs. Garnish, if desired. Makes 8¼ cups.

*Regina Vining*
*Warwick, R*

A TINY
TREAT
TO
TAKE
HOME
*good cheer*

Perfect for a tree-trimming party, Nutty Popcorn Snack Mix and Raspberry Cider make are fun munchies while you and your family decorate.

## Nutty Popcorn Snack Mix

*If you're using microwave popcorn, simply pop two 3½-oz. packages.*

16 c. popped popcorn
5 c. mini pretzel twists
1 c. dry-roasted peanuts
2 c. brown sugar, packed
½ c. margarine
½ c. dark corn syrup
¼ t. salt
1 t. vanilla extract
½ t. baking soda
1½ c. mini candy-coated
    chocolate pieces

Combine popcorn, pretzels and peanuts in a large roasting pan; set aside.

Combine brown sugar, margarine, corn syrup and salt in a heavy medium saucepan. Cook over medium heat for 12 to 14 minutes, stirring occasionally, until mixture comes to a full boil. Continue cooking and stirring until mixture reaches the soft-ball stage, or 234 to 240 degrees on a candy thermometer. Remove from heat; stir in vanilla and baking soda. Pour over popcorn mixture in roasting pan; stir until mixture is well coated.

Bake at 250 degrees for 45 minutes, stirring every 15 minutes. Immediately spoon onto wax paper; let cool 10 minutes and sprinkle with chocolate pieces. Cool completely; break into pieces. Store in an airtight container. Makes about 24 cups.

## Raspberry Cider

*Snuggle in with a cup of this fruity cider.*

1 qt. apple cider
2 c. water
1 c. raspberry jelly
1 t. sweetened lemonade drink mix
Garnish: lemon slices

Bring cider and water to a boil in a 3-quart saucepan; add jelly and drink mix. Stir until jelly dissolves; remove from heat. Pour into serving mugs while still warm; garnish with lemon slices. Makes 6 cups.

*Sue Osburn*
*Hot Springs, AR*

Nutty Popcorn Snack Mix
Raspberry Cider

Chicken Piccata

## Chicken Piccata

*As children we always requested our favorite "Flattened Chicken," because Mom used a malle to pound the chicken flat. She always said it was a good recipe to relieve stress! Cooked angel hair pasta or rice goes very well with this*

12 boneless, skinless chicken
    tenderloins
½ t. pepper
½ t. garlic powder
1 egg, beaten
2 T. milk
1 c. dry bread crumbs
1 T. butter
2 T. oil
½ c. water
¼ c. lemon juice
1 t. cornstarch
1 t. chicken bouillon granules
Garnish: chopped fresh parsley and
    lemon wedges

Flatten chicken between 2 layers of plastic wrap with a mallet; sprinkle with pepper and garlic powder. Whisk egg and milk together. Dip chicken in egg mixture; coat with bread crumbs. Melt butter and oil in a skillet over medium heat. Sauté chicken for 4 to 5 minutes on each side, until cooked through. Set aside chicken and keep warm; drain skillet. Whisk together water, juice, cornstarch and bouillon. Add to skillet and simmer until blended; pour over chicken. Garnish, if desired. Serves 6.

A.M. Gilstra
Easley, S

196

Perfect for a holiday evening meal, Deep-Dish Sausage Pizza goes together quickly and will please everyone!

## Deep-Dish Sausage Pizza

*Why go out to a pizza parlor when you can feast on a hot, hearty pizza right from your own kitchen? It's chock-full of the great Italian sausage and sweet pepper flavors that we love.*

16-oz. pkg. frozen bread dough, thawed
1 lb. sweet Italian pork sausage, casings removed
2 1/2 c. shredded mozzarella cheese, divided
1 green pepper, cut into squares
1 red pepper, cut into squares
28-oz. can diced tomatoes, drained
3/4 t. dried oregano
1/2 t. salt
1/4 t. garlic powder
1/2 c. grated Parmesan cheese

Press thawed dough into the bottom and up the sides of a greased 13"x9" baking pan; set aside. In a large skillet, crumble sausage and cook until no longer pink; drain. Sprinkle sausage over dough; top with 2 cups mozzarella cheese. In the same skillet, sauté peppers until slightly tender. Stir in tomatoes and seasonings; spoon over pizza. Sprinkle with Parmesan cheese and remaining 1/2 cup mozzarella cheese. Bake, uncovered, at 350 degrees for 25 to 35 minutes, until crust is golden. Serves 8.

*Kathleen Sturm*
*Corona, CA*

Deep-Dish Sausage Pizza

## Big Eddie's Rigatoni

*This recipe was created by my eighty-four-year-old father who has always been a great cook and is affectionately called "Big Eddie" by family members. It's a delicious and satisfying meal when paired with salad and garlic bread.*

16-oz. pkg. rigatoni pasta, uncooked
1/8 t. salt
2 lbs. lean ground beef
1 1/2-oz. pkg. spaghetti sauce mix
45-oz. jar chunky tomato, garlic and onion pasta sauce
8 slices mozzarella cheese, divided
8 slices provolone cheese, divided
8-oz. container sour cream
Garnish: grated Parmesan cheese

Cook pasta according to package directions; drain, mix in salt and set aside. Meanwhile, in a large, deep skillet over medium heat, brown ground beef; drain. Stir in spaghetti sauce and pasta sauce; heat through. In a greased 13"x9" baking pan, layer half the pasta, 4 slices mozzarella cheese and 4 slices provolone cheese. Spread entire container of sour cream across top. Layer half of ground beef mixture. Repeat layers, except for sour cream, ending with ground beef mixture. Garnish with Parmesan cheese. Bake, uncovered, at 350 degrees for 30 minutes, or until bubbly. Serves 8.

*Mary Beth Laporte*
*Escanaba, MI*

Along with all the fun of gift wrapping, stocking stuffing and cookie baking, Christmas is the perfect time of year to deliver a homemade dinner to friends or neighbors!

## Slow-Cooker Taco Soup

*This soup freezes well and makes enough to share with several friends.*

1 lb. ground beef
1 onion, diced
1 clove garlic, minced
2  15-oz. cans black beans, drained
  and rinsed
2 c. water
15¼-oz. can corn, drained
15-oz. can tomato sauce
12-oz. bottle green taco sauce
4½-oz. can chopped green chiles
1-oz. pkg. taco seasoning mix
Garnishes: sour cream, shredded
  Cheddar cheese

Brown beef, onion and garlic in a large skillet over medium heat; drain. In a slow cooker, combine beef mixture and remaining ingredients except garnishes. Cover and cook on high setting for one hour. Garnish, if desired. Serve with corn chips. Makes 8 to 10 servings.

Susan Ahlstrand
Post Falls, ID

Slow-Cooker Taco Soup

Beef Burgundy Stew

Cut your kitchen time in half…Beef Burgundy Stew can simmer in a slow cooker. Or, celebrate the holidays with Foolproof Pot Roast.

## Beef Burgundy Stew
*This classic recipe works well in a slow cooker.*

6 bacon slices, chopped
2 lbs. beef stew meat
16-oz. pkg. frozen pearl onions, thawed
8-oz. pkg. mushrooms, quartered
6 red potatoes, quartered
2 carrots, cut into 1/2-inch pieces
14-oz. can beef broth
1 c. Burgundy, dry red wine or beef broth
2 T. tomato paste
1 T. fresh thyme leaves
1 t. salt
1/4 t. pepper
3 cloves garlic, minced
2 T. cornstarch
2 t. cold water

Cook bacon in a large skillet over medium-high heat until crisp. Remove bacon, reserving drippings in pan. Set bacon aside.

Brown beef, in batches, in reserved bacon drippings until browned on all sides. Combine reserved bacon, beef, onions and next 10 ingredients in a 5-quart slow cooker. Cover and cook on low setting 7 hours or until beef and vegetables are tender. Whisk together cornstarch and water. Stir into stew. Cover and cook on high setting one hour or until slightly thickened. Makes 9 cups.

## Foolproof Pot Roast
*Fast, easy and tasty…what a great combination!*

16-oz. pkg. fully cooked beef pot roast in gravy
non-stick vegetable spray
1 onion, thinly sliced
1 T. butter
1 t. balsamic vinegar
1/2 t. sugar
1/4 t. salt
1/4 t. pepper

Heat roast according to package directions. Remove roast from package, reserving liquid. Let stand 2 minutes. Cut into 8 pieces.

Coat a large non-stick skillet with non-stick vegetable spray; place over medium-high heat until hot. Add onion and sauté 10 minutes or until browned.

Add reserved liquid, roast, butter and remaining ingredients to pan. Stir well and bring to a boil. Boil 30 seconds or until thoroughly heated. Makes 4 servings.

## Shepherd's Pie

*Thanks to purchased pre-made ingredients, new cooks can get that "made from scatch" taste.*

2 17-oz. pkgs. fully cooked beef tips with gravy
1 c. frozen whole kernel corn, thawed
1 c. frozen sweet peas, thawed
24-oz. pkg. refrigerated mashed potatoes
½ of an 8-oz. pkg. cream cheese, softened
1 T. butter or margarine, softened
1 t. garlic powder
1 c. shredded sharp Cheddar cheese

Cook beef according to package directions. Spoon beef into a lightly greased 11"x7" baking dish. Top with corn and peas; set aside.

Cook potatoes according to package directions; spoon potatoes into a bowl. Add cream cheese, butter and garlic powder; beat at medium speed with an electric mixer until smooth. Spread potato mixture over vegetables; sprinkle with cheese.

Bake, uncovered, at 350 degrees for 15 minutes or until thoroughly heated. Makes 8 servings.

## Smoked Turkey Tetrazzini

12 oz. vermicelli, broken in half
1 T. butter or margarine
1 onion, chopped
8-oz. pkg. sliced mushrooms
1 t. bottled minced garlic
4 c. cubed smoked or honey-roasted turkey (about 1½ lbs.)
1¼ c. shredded Cheddar cheese, divided
¼ c. grated Parmesan cheese
10¾-oz. can cream of mushroom soup
10¾-oz. can cream of celery soup
1 c. sour cream
½ c. chicken broth
½ t. salt
½ t. pepper

Cook vermicelli according to package directions; set aside. Melt butter in a Dutch oven over medium-high heat. Add onion, mushrooms and garlic; sauté 5 minutes or until tender. Stir in turkey, ¾ cup Cheddar cheese and remaining 7 ingredients.

Drain vermicelli and add to turkey mixture; stir well.

Spoon mixture into 2 lightly greased 8"x8" baking dishes; sprinkle with remaining ½ cup Cheddar cheese. Cover each casserole tightly in aluminum foil; freeze up to 2 months.

Remove desired number of casseroles from freezer, leaving foil intact. Bake at 350 degrees for 2 hours; uncover and bake 15 more minutes or until bubbly. Each casserole makes 8 servings.

To bake without freezing: Prepare recipe omitting the covering and freezing process. Bake, uncovered, at 350 degrees for 30 minutes or until bubbly.

To thaw and bake: Let desired number of casseroles thaw overnight in refrigerator. Leave foil cover intact and bake at 350 degrees for one hour and 15 minutes. Uncover and bake 15 more minutes or until bubbly.

Shepherd's Pie

## Chicken and Rice Casserole

*If you are in a hurry, use meat from a deli-roasted chicken.*

6.2-oz. pkg. fast-cooking long-
    grain and wild rice mix
2 T. butter
1 onion, chopped
2 stalks celery, chopped
3 c. cooked chicken, chopped
3 c. shredded Colby-Jack cheese
    blend, divided
10¾-oz. can cream of mushroom
    soup
1 c. sour cream
½ c. milk
½ t. salt
½ t. pepper
1 c. round buttery crackers,
    crushed

Prepare rice mix according to package directions; set aside. Melt butter in a large skillet over medium-high heat; add onion and celery. Sauté 4 minutes or until tender.

Combine rice, sautéed vegetables, chicken, 2 cups cheese and next 5 ingredients; spoon into a lightly greased 5-quart slow cooker. Cover and cook on low setting 4½ hours.

Combine remaining one cup cheese and cracker crumbs; sprinkle over casserole. Cover and cook on low setting 30 more minutes. Makes 6 servings.

## Chicken-and-Black Bean Enchiladas

*Even if you stop at the store for these ingredients, dinner will be ready in no time at all.*

whole deli-roasted chicken (about 3 cups), chopped
15-oz. can black beans, rinsed and drained
10-oz. can diced tomatoes with green chiles
8¾-oz. can no-salt-added corn, drained
8-oz. pkg. shredded Mexican four-cheese blend, divided
8 8-inch whole wheat flour tortillas
non-stick vegetable spray
2 10-oz. cans enchilada sauce
Garnishes: chopped tomatoes, onions and cilantro

Combine first 4 ingredients and 1½ cups cheese in a large bowl. Spoon chicken mixture evenly down the center of each tortilla and roll up. Arrange, seam side down, in a 13"x9" baking dish coated with vegetable spray. Pour enchilada sauce evenly over tortillas and sprinkle evenly with remaining ½ cup cheese. Bake, covered, at 350 degrees for 20 minutes. Remove foil and bake 15 more minutes or until bubbly. Garnish, if desired. Makes 8 servings.

Chicken-and-Black Bean Enchiladas

When dishes are this simple to whip up, you can get out of the kitchen quick! Make Simple Meatloaf ahead of time, so you can make Italian Meatloaf Sandwiches in just minutes. Or, you can warm up a wintry evening with Snowy Day Chili and Broccoli-Cheese Cornbread.

## Simple Meatloaf
*Make two recipes and freeze one for Italian Meatloaf Sandwiches.*

1 1/2 lbs. ground beef
3/4 c. quick-cooking oats, uncooked
1/2 c. milk
1/4 c. onion, chopped
1 egg, lightly beaten
1 t. salt
1/4 t. pepper
1/3 c. ketchup
2 T. brown sugar, packed
1 T. yellow mustard

Combine first 7 ingredients in a large bowl just until blended; place in a lightly greased 8"x4" loaf pan. Stir together ketchup, brown sugar and mustard; pour evenly over meatloaf. Bake at 350 degrees for one hour. Remove from oven; let stand 5 minutes and remove from pan before slicing. Makes 6 servings.

To freeze: Wrap meatloaf in plastic wrap and aluminum foil; freeze up to one month. Thaw in refrigerator.

Italian Meatloaf Sandwich

## Italian Meatloaf Sandwiches
*This great flavor combo also works with leftover roast beef or pot roast.*

14-oz. French bread loaf
4 one-inch-thick cold meatloaf slices
1 c. marinara or spaghetti sauce
8-oz. pkg. shredded Italian cheese blend
1/4 t. dried Italian seasoning

Cut bread into fourths; cut quarters in half horizontally. Place bread quarters, cut sides up, on a baking sheet. Top each bread bottom with one meatloaf slice, 2 tablespoons marinara sauce and 1/4 cup cheese. Top each bread top with 2 tablespoons marinara sauce and 1/4 cup cheese; sprinkle with Italian seasoning.
Bake at 375 degrees for 10 to 15 minutes or until cheese melts and meat is thoroughly heated. Top bread bottoms with bread tops and serve sandwiches immediately. Makes 4 servings.

## Broccoli-Cheese Cornbread

*This recipe, given to me by my Aunt Ora Lee, is one I enjoy toting to potluck dinners at church and at work.*

2 8½-oz. pkgs. cornbread mix
1½ c. cottage cheese
5 eggs, beaten
10-oz. pkg. frozen chopped broccoli, thawed
1 onion, chopped
½ c. margarine, melted
1 c. shredded Cheddar cheese

Mix together all ingredients except Cheddar cheese; spread in a lightly greased 13"x9" baking pan. Bake, uncovered, at 350 degrees for 45 minutes. Sprinkle with cheese and bake for an additional 3 minutes or until cheese is melted. Makes about 12 servings.

*Jane Reynolds*
*Rowlett, TX*

In this WoRLd, We must HeLP one Another.
• JEAN de LA FONTAINE •

Broccoli-Cheese Cornbread
Snowy Day Chili

## Snowy Day Chili

*In Wisconsin snow is inevitable, but shoveling sidewalks isn't so dreaded when there's a pot of chili simmering on the stove!*

2 lbs. ground beef or venison
2 c. chopped onion
4 c. canned or homemade tomato sauce
4 c. water
15-oz. can kidney beans, drained and rinsed
6-oz. can tomato paste
¼ c. Worcestershire sauce
2 T. brown sugar, packed
1 T. seasoned salt
1 T. lemon juice
3 bay leaves
chili powder to taste
Optional: hot pepper sauce to taste
Garnish: shredded Cheddar cheese, chopped onion, sour cream, corn chips

In a large stockpot over medium heat, brown meat; drain. Stir in remaining ingredients except garnish. Reduce heat; simmer for 3 to 4 hours, stirring occasionally.

Garnish if desired. Makes 8 to 10 servings.

*Kathie Poritz*
*Burlington, WI*

203

For a farmhouse style dinner, layer a slice of Texas toast with Make-Ahead Mashed Potatoes and hearty Pepper-Crusted Roast Beef.

## Pepper-Crusted Roast Beef

*A caramelized brown sugar sauce is spooned over tender slices of beef.*

**2 to 3-lb. boneless beef rib roast**
**¼ c. garlic, minced**
**3 T. peppercorns**
**¼ c. Worcestershire sauce**
**2 red onions, thinly sliced**
**1 T. oil**
**1 T. brown sugar, packed**
**2 T. balsamic vinegar**

Rub roast with garlic and coat fat side of roast with peppercorns. Drizzle with Worcestershire sauce. Place in a roaster pan. Roast at 350 degrees for 40 minutes to one hour or until meat thermometer reaches 150 degrees; keep warm.

Cook onions in oil in a small skillet over medium heat until onions are soft. Add brown sugar and vinegar; cook until caramelized, about 8 to 10 minutes.

Slice roast; serve onions over top. Serves 6 to 8.

*Linda Behling*
*Cecil, PA*

Pepper-Crusted Roast Beef
Make-Ahead Mashed Potatoes

## Make-Ahead Mashed Potatoes

*It's impossible not to love the homestyle flavor of these potatoes.*

**6 to 8 potatoes, peeled and quartered**
**¼ c. butter, softened**
**8-oz. pkg. cream cheese, softened**

Boil potatoes until tender; drain. Combine potatoes, butter and cream cheese in a large bowl; let stand 10 minutes or until cream cheese melts. Mash until smooth. Refrigerate until serving time; reheat in a microwave. Serves 6.

*Mary Brown*
*Sayre, PA*

204

Add a little zip to your meal with Guacamole Salad and Slow-Cooker Roast for Tacos.

## Guacamole Salad

*Serve as a salad or an appetizer with corn chips or croutons.*

2 avocados, peeled, pitted and chopped
1 tomato, chopped
1 cucumber, peeled and chopped
2 green onions, chopped
2 T. lime juice
1 clove garlic, minced
1 T. dried parsley
1/4 t. salt
1/2 t. pepper
1/4 t. garlic powder
hot pepper sauce to taste

Toss all ingredients together gently; cover and refrigerate until ready to serve. Serves 4.

*Michael Curry*
*Ardmore, OK*

## Slow-Cooker Roast for Tacos

*Don't forget to offer all the tasty taco toppers...shredded cheese, sour cream, lettuce, tomatoes, onions and salsa. Olé!*

4 to 5-lb. beef chuck roast
1 T. chili powder
1 t. ground cumin
1 t. onion powder
1 t. garlic powder
2  14½-oz. cans Mexican-style stewed tomatoes
taco shells

Place roast in a large slow cooker; sprinkle with spices. Add tomatoes with juice around the roast. Cover and cook on low setting for 8 to 10 hours.
Using 2 forks, shred roast and spoon into taco shells. Makes 10 cups.

*Dana Thompson*
*Gooseberry Patch*

**Guacamole Salad**
**Slow-Cooker Roast for Tacos**

Potato-Corn Chowder

## Potato-Corn Chowder
*Short on time? Use a package of ready-cooked bacon instead.*

2 10³/₄-oz. cans potato soup
2 14³/₄-oz. cans cream-style corn
8 slices bacon, crisply cooked and crumbled
Optional: 1 to 2 T. bacon drippings
¹/₂ to 1 c. milk
salt, pepper and garlic salt to taste
Garnish: fresh parsley, chopped

Combine soup and corn in a 3-quart slow cooker; add bacon and bacon drippings, if desired. Add milk until soup is of desired consistency; add salt, pepper and garlic salt to taste. Cover and cook on low setting for 2 to 3 hours or until hot. Sprinkle with parsley, if desired. Serves 6 to 8.

*Jerry Bostian*
*Oelwein, IA*

Use handy shortcuts such as ready-to-use pizza crust and canned soup to make Barbecue Chicken Pizza and Potato-Corn Chowder.

Barbecue Chicken Pizza

## Barbecue Chicken Pizza

*When you need dinner fast, keep this quick favorite in mind.*

12-inch Italian pizza crust
1 c. barbecue sauce
3 c. cooked chicken, shredded
1 c. shredded mozzarella cheese
1/2 c. shredded Cheddar cheese
Optional: chopped green onion

Place pizza crust on a lightly greased 12" pizza pan. Spread sauce over crust; arrange chicken on top. Sprinkle with cheeses. Bake at 450 degrees for 8 to 10 minutes, or until cheeses melt and crust is crisp. Garnish with green onions, if desired. Serves 4.

*Ginny Bone*
*Saint Peters, MO*

## Apple-Baked Pork Chops

*Add a baked sweet potato for a hearty, comforting meal!*

4 (1/2-inch-thick) boneless pork
    chops
1/4 c. butter
2 red apples, cored and halved
3 T. brown sugar, packed
2 t. cinnamon

Arrange pork chops in a lightly greased 13"x9" baking pan; dot one tablespoon butter over each pork chop. Place one apple half cut-side down onto each pork chop; sprinkle with brown sugar and cinnamon. Bake at 350 degrees for 30 to 45 minutes or until pork chops are no longer pink inside. Serves 4.

*Michelle McCauley*
*Garland, TX*

## Beef Brisket in a Bag

*Pineapple juice and soy sauce are the secret ingredients that make this brisket taste wonderful.*

3 to 4-lb. beef brisket
1/2 t. pepper
1/2 t. paprika
1 T. all-purpose flour
6-oz. can pineapple juice
3 T. soy sauce
1-oz. pkg. onion soup mix

Rub brisket with pepper and paprika. Place brisket, fat-side up, in a large oven bag; add flour to bag, turning to coat. Place bag in a 13"x9" baking pan. Combine pineapple juice, soy sauce and soup mix; pour mixture over brisket. Close bag with nylon tie provided; cut six, 1/2-inch slits in top. Bake at 325 degrees for 3 hours. Remove from oven; place brisket on cutting board and pour remaining bag contents into the baking pan. Slice brisket against the grain; arrange slices over juices in baking pan. Baste with juices; cover pan with aluminum foil and return to oven for an additional 1 1/2 hours or until fork tender, basting occasionally. Serves 8 to 10.

*Meg Venema*
*Kirkland, WA*

Poblano Chowder

Invite the whole gang over for a soup supper and to watch a classic holiday movie! They will be asking for seconds of tangy Poblano Chowder as they cuddle up on the couch.

## Poblano Chowder

*This is wonderful served with toasted Italian or French bread. I usually double the recipe and invite friends over to share it.*

½ c. plus 2 T. butter or oil, divided
2 poblano peppers, diced
1 red onion, diced
8-oz. pkg. sliced mushrooms
½ c. all-purpose flour
4 c. chicken broth
2 to 3 potatoes, peeled and diced
1½ to 2 c. corn
3 tomatoes, diced
1 jalapeño pepper, diced
2 T. salt
1 T. pepper
1 T. garlic powder
2 c. heavy cream
Optional: 1 c. fresh cilantro, finely chopped
Garnish: cooked shrimp, crab, sausage, chicken or beef

Heat ¼ cup butter or oil in a Dutch oven over medium-high heat; add poblano peppers, onion and mushrooms. Cook 6 to 8 minutes, until vegetables are lightly browned. Add in flour, stirring until vegetables are coated. Add remaining ingredients except cilantro and garnish. Bring to a simmer. Reduce heat to low and simmer, uncovered, 20 minutes or until potatoes are tender. Sprinkle with cilantro and garnish, if desired. Serves 10.

*Charlotte Bryant*
*Grayson, GA*

## Henderson Family Gyros

*This recipe marinates the meat for 6 to 12 hours. The result is worth it…meat that's tender and bursting with flavor!*

¼ c. olive oil
¼ c. dry red wine or cranberry
    juice cocktail
Optional: 1 T. vinegar
4 garlic cloves, chopped
1 T. fresh oregano, chopped
2 lbs. pork or turkey tenderloin,
    thinly sliced
6 pita rounds, split
Garnish: baby spinach, red onion
    slices, tomato slices

Combine oil, wine or juice and vinegar (only if using juice), garlic and oregano in a large plastic zipping bag. Add pork or turkey; seal and refrigerate 6 to 12 hours. Line grill surface with a piece of aluminum foil coated with non-stick vegetable spray. Heat grill to medium-high heat. Using a slotted spoon, remove meat mixture from plastic zipping bag and arrange on aluminum foil. Discard marinade. Grill and turn meat slices until browned. Drain and remove from grill. Toast pitas on grill until warmed. Spoon meat into pitas; drizzle with Cucumber Sauce. Top with desired amounts of spinach, onion and tomato. Serves 6.

### Cucumber Sauce:
¼ c. sour cream
¼ c. cucumber, peeled and diced
2 T. red onion, minced
¼ t. lemon pepper
¼ t. dried oregano
⅛ t. garlic powder

Combine all ingredients in a bowl. Chill until ready to serve.

*Jessica Henderson*
*Bloomfield, IA*

## Turkey & Black Bean Quesadillas

*Perfect for those nights when everyone is busy with homework, meetings and rehearsal.*

15-oz. can black beans, rinsed and
    drained
6 oz. Cheddar cheese, cubed
4 oz. thinly sliced, cooked turkey,
    cut into strips
½ c. salsa
8 8-inch flour tortillas
2 T. butter, melted
Garnish: sour cream and salsa

In a large mixing bowl, stir together beans, cheese, turkey and salsa. Brush one side of tortillas with butter. Place buttered side down on an ungreased baking sheet. Spoon about ⅓ cup bean mixture on half of each tortilla; fold in half. Bake at 375 degrees for 10 to 15 minutes, until heated through; let cool for 5 minutes. Cut each quesadilla into 3 wedges. Garnish with sour cream and salsa. Serves 4.

*Jo Ann*

Henderson Family Gyros

## Chicken-Corn Tortilla Soup

*Yummy soup that's ready in a flash!*

3 12½-oz. cans white chicken meat, undrained
4 c. fat-free, less-sodium chicken broth
1 c. salsa
1 c. corn tortilla chips, crushed
½ c. fresh cilantro, chopped
2 t. lime juice
¼ t. pepper
Garnish: shredded Cheddar cheese, sour cream

Shred chicken, using 2 forks, in a large saucepan. Add broth and salsa; bring to a boil over medium-high heat. Add tortilla chips; reduce heat and simmer for 10 minutes. Stir in cilantro, lime juice and pepper. Serve immediately. Garnish, if desired. Serves 8.

Chicken-Corn Tortilla Soup

## Honeyed Raspberry Pork Chops

*aspberry jam pairs up with honey mustard to make
flavorful sauce.*

 boneless pork chops
 T. all-purpose flour
/3 c. honey mustard
/4 c. raspberry jam
 T. cider vinegar
 T. olive oil

Dredge pork chops in flour, shaking off any
xcess. In a small bowl, combine honey mustard,
am and vinegar; set aside.

Heat oil in a large skillet over medium heat.
dd pork chops and sauté until golden on both
ides. Stir in honey mustard mixture; bring to a
oil. Reduce heat and simmer for 10 minutes or
ntil chops are no longer pink inside. Serves 4.

*Elaine Slabinski
Monroe Township, NJ*

## Extra-Cheesy Macaroni & Cheese

*My husband says this is the best
macaroni and cheese he's ever eaten!*

8-oz. pkg. shredded Italian-
    blend cheese
8-oz. pkg. shredded sharp
    Cheddar cheese
2 eggs, beaten
1 2-oz. can evaporated milk
1 1/2 c. milk
1 t. salt
3/4 t. dry mustard
1/2 t. pepper
1/4 t. cayenne pepper
8-oz. pkg. small shell
    macaroni, uncooked

Combine cheeses in a
large bowl; set aside.

Whisk together eggs
and next 6 ingredients in a
large bowl; stir in macaroni
and 3 cups cheese mixture.
Pour macaroni mixture into
a slow cooker; sprinkle with
3/4 cup cheese mixture. Cover
and cook on low setting for
4 hours.

Sprinkle servings with
remaining cheese mixture.
Serves 6 to 8.

*Valarie Dennard
Palatka, FL*

211

## Tropical Chicken Stir-Fry

*This dish is so yummy and cooks up in a jiffy… it's a little taste of the islands! I like to serve scoops of orange sherbet and coconut ice cream for a sweet end to dinner.*

¼ c. soy sauce
2 T. sugar
1 T. cider vinegar
1 T. catsup
1 T. garlic, minced
1 t. cornstarch
½ t. ground ginger
8-oz. can pineapple chunks,
    drained and ¼ c. juice
    reserved
2 T. oil

1 lb. boneless, skinless chicken
    breasts, sliced into strips
16-oz. pkg. frozen stir-fry
    vegetables, thawed
cooked rice
sliced almonds, toasted

In a bowl, mix first 7 ingredients and reserved pineapple juice; set aside. Heat oil in a skillet over medium-high heat. Add chicken; cook and stir for 5 minutes, unti nearly done. Add vegetables; coo and stir for 4 minutes. Stir in pineapple and soy sauce mixture heat through. Serve over cooked rice; sprinkle with almonds. Serves 6.

Vick

Tropical Chicken Stir-Fry

Buffalo Chicken Wing Soup

## Buffalo Chicken Wing Soup

*This spicy, creamy soup warms you up from your toes to your nose on a cold winter day!*

6 c. milk
3 10¾-oz. cans cream of chicken soup
3 c. chicken, cooked and shredded
1 c. sour cream
¼ to ½ c. hot pepper sauce
Garnish: shredded Monterey Jack cheese, chopped green onions

Combine all ingredients except garnish in a 5-quart slow cooker. Cover and cook on low setting for 4 to 5 hours. To serve, garnish with cheese and onions. Serves 8.

Anna McMaster
Portland, OR

## Hearty Kielbasa & Kale Soup

*This flavorful soup is rich and delicious.*

8 oz. Kielbasa sausage, sliced
1 lb. kale, chopped and stems removed
1 onion, chopped
1 potato, cubed
3 cloves garlic, minced
2 14½-oz. cans chicken broth
15-oz. can Great Northern beans, rinsed and drained
1 t. dried thyme
1 t. pepper

In a medium stockpot over medium heat, cook Kielbasa, kale, onion, potato and garlic, stirring frequently until kale begins to wilt and sausage browns. Stir in the next 4 ingredients. Increase heat to high; bring to a boil. Reduce heat to medium; partially cover and simmer for 12 minutes, or until potatoes are tender. Serves 6 to 8.

Kathy Royer
Charlotte, NC

## Grandma Hallie's Spicy Chili

*This recipe is from my Great-Grandma Hallie. I am so glad I actually have one of her recipes written down! She would make the best food and say, "Honey, it's all up here," meaning she memorized all her recipes. This recipe shows what a wonderful cook she was!*

2 lbs. ground beef
1/4 c. dried, minced onion
2 t. salt
2 10³/4-oz. cans tomato soup
2 16-oz. cans kidney beans,
    rinsed and drained
2 1/2 c. water
1 t. Worcestershire sauce
2 T. butter, sliced
3 T. chili powder
Garnish: sour cream, shredded
    Cheddar cheese, sliced green
    onions

Brown beef in a large pot over medium heat; drain. Add remaining ingredients except garnish; reduce heat to medium-low. Simmer for 45 minutes, stirring occasionally. Garnish as desired. Serves 8 to 10.

Ashley Hull
Virden, IL

## Triple-Take Grilled Cheese

*Delicious in winter with a steaming bowl of chili...scrumptious in summer made with produce fresh from the garden!*

1 T. oil
8 slices sourdough bread
1/4 c. butter, softened and divided
4 slices white American cheese
4 slices Muenster cheese
1/2 c. shredded sharp Cheddar
    cheese
Optional: 4 slices red onion,
    4 slices tomato, 1/4 c. chopped
    fresh basil

Heat oil in a skillet over medium heat. Spread 2 bread slices with one tablespoon butter; place one slice butter-side down on skillet. Layer one slice American, one slice Muenster and 2 tablespoons Cheddar cheese on bread. If desired, top each with an onion slice, a tomato slice and one tablespoon basil. Butter 2 slices of bread; add to sandwiches in skillet. Reduce heat to medium-low. Cook until golden on one side, about 3 to 5 minutes; flip and cook until golden on the other side. Repeat with remaining ingredients. Makes 4 sandwiches.

Abigail Smith
Columbus, OH

Grandma Hallie's Spicy Chili
Triple-Take Grilled Cheese

## Down-on-the-Bayou Gumbo

*You can't help but smile with a bowl of gumbo in front of you!*

3 T. all-purpose flour
3 T. oil
½ lb. smoked sausage, sliced ½-inch thick
2 c. frozen okra
14½-oz. can diced tomatoes
1 onion, chopped
1 green pepper, chopped
3 cloves garlic, minced
¼ t. cayenne pepper
¾ lb. cooked medium shrimp, peeled
1½ c. long-cooking rice, cooked

Stir together flour and oil in a small saucepan over medium heat. Cook, stirring constantly, for 5 minutes. Reduce heat and cook, stirring constantly, for about 10 minutes or until mixture turns reddish brown. Spoon mixture into a slow cooker; stir in remaining ingredients except shrimp and rice. Cover and cook on high setting for one hour; then 5 hours on low setting. Twenty minutes before serving, add shrimp to slow cooker; mix well. Cover and cook on low setting. Ladle gumbo over cooked rice in soup bowls. Makes 6 servings.

*Sue Neely*
*Greenville, IL*

Down-on-the-Bayou Gumbo

## Slow-Cooker Lasagna

*Use a mixture of ground beef and ground Italian sausage if you like.*

1 lb. ground beef
1 c. onion, chopped
2 cloves garlic, minced
29-oz. can tomato sauce
6-oz. can tomato paste
1 c. water
1 t. salt
1 t. dried oregano
16-oz. pkg. shredded mozzarella cheese
16-oz. container cottage cheese
½ c. grated Parmesan cheese
10 lasagna noodles, uncooked

Brown beef, onion and garlic in a large skillet; drain. Add tomato sauce, tomato paste, water, salt and oregano; set aside.

In a medium bowl, stir together cheeses. Layer ⅓ meat sauce, ½ uncooked lasagna noodles (broken to fit slow cooker) and ½ cheese mixture in a slow cooker. Repeat layers, finishing with meat sauce. Cover and cook on low setting for 4 to 5 hours. Serves 6 to 8.

*Maria Benedict*
*Stowe, PA*

## Spoon Bread Florentine

*Deliciously different and so simple to make.*

10-oz. pkg. frozen chopped spinach,
    thawed and drained
6 green onions, sliced
1 red pepper, chopped
6-oz. pkg. cornbread mix
4 eggs, beaten
½ c. butter, melted
1 c. cottage cheese
1¼ t. seasoned salt

Combine all ingredients in a large bowl; mix well. Spoon into a lightly greased slow cooker. Cover and cook on low setting 4 to 5 hours or on high setting for 2 to 3 hours. Cook until edges are golden and a knife tip inserted in center comes out clean. Makes 10 servings.

*Jo Ann*

Enjoy the comfort of a home-cooked recipe like Slow-Cooker Lasagna, even when you don't have a lot of time to spend in the kitchen! Or, try some holiday classics like Crockery Sage Dressing or Christmas Morning Muffins.

## Crockery Sage Dressing

*How clever! Make dressing in your slow cooker and free up the oven for other holiday dishes.*

2 c. onion, chopped
2 c. celery, chopped
1 c. butter
2 loaves white bread, torn
1½ t. dried sage
1½ t. salt
1 t. poultry seasoning
½ t. dried thyme
½ t. dried marjoram
½ t. pepper
14-oz. can chicken broth
2 eggs, beaten

Sauté onion and celery in butter in a skillet; set aside.

Place bread in a large mixing bowl; add seasonings and toss well. Add onion mixture and enough broth to moisten bread; toss well. Stir in eggs and mix well. Spoon into a slow cooker. Cook, covered, on low setting for 4 to 5 hours, stirring occasionally and adding more broth as needed. Serves 10 to 12.

*Gina Rongved-Van Wyk*
*Rapid City, SD*

Slow-Cooker Lasagna

216

## Orange Coffee Rolls

1 env. active dry yeast
1/4 c. warm water
1 c. sugar, divided
2 eggs
1/2 c. sour cream
1/4 c. plus 2 T. butter, melted
1 t. salt
2 3/4 to 3 c. all-purpose flour
2 T. butter, melted and divided
1 c. flaked coconut, toasted and
    divided
2 T. orange zest

Combine yeast and warm water (110 to 115 degrees) in a large bowl; let stand 5 minutes. Add 1/4 cup sugar and next 4 ingredients; beat at medium speed with an electric mixer until blended. Gradually stir in enough flour to make a soft dough. Turn dough out onto a well-floured surface; knead until smooth and elastic (about 5 minutes). Place in a well-greased bowl, turning to grease top. Cover and let rise in a warm place (85 degrees), free from drafts, 1 1/2 hours or until doubled in bulk. Punch dough down and divide in half. Roll one portion of dough into a 12-inch circle; brush with one tablespoon melted butter. Combine remaining 3/4 cup sugar, 3/4 cup coconut and orange zest; sprinkle half of coconut mixture over dough. Cut into 12 wedges; roll up each wedge, beginning at wide end. Place in a greased 13"x9" baking pan, point side down. Repeat with remaining dough, butter and coconut mixture. Cover and let rise in a warm place, free from drafts, 45 minutes or until doubled in bulk.

Bake at 350 degrees for 25 to 30 minutes or until golden. (Cover with aluminum foil after 15 minutes to prevent excessive browning, if necessary.) Spoon warm Glaze over warm rolls; sprinkle with remaining 1/4 cup coconut. Makes 2 dozen.

### Glaze:
3/4 c. sugar
1/2 c. sour cream
1/4 c. butter
2 t. orange juice

Combine all ingredients in a small saucepan; bring to a boil. Boil 3 minutes, stirring occasionally. Let cool slightly. Makes 1 1/3 cups.

## Christmas Morning Muffins

*To save time, pour batter into muffin tins the night before, cover with a damp towel and refrigerate until ready to bake.*

2 eggs, beaten
3/4 c. milk
1/2 c. oil
2 c. all-purpose flour
1/3 c. sugar
3 t. baking powder
1 t. salt

Blend eggs, milk and oil together; add remaining ingredients, stirring until just moistened. Fill paper-lined or lightly greased muffin cups 2/3 full; bake at 400 degrees for 20 minutes or until golden. Remove from pan; spread Topping on while warm. Serve at once. Makes 12.

### Topping:
1 c. sugar
1/2 c. butter, melted
2 t. cinnamon

Combine all ingredients; whisk until creamy.

*Mary Jones*
*North Lawrence, OH*

Orange Coffee Rolls

Holiday Morning French Toast will energize your family for a day filled with festivities!

## Holiday Morning French Toast

*A sweet breakfast treat that's sure to have family & friends asking for the recipe.*

1 c. brown sugar, packed
½ c. butter, melted
1 T. cinnamon, divided
3 to 4 Granny Smith apples, peeled, cored and thinly sliced
½ c. raisins
1 loaf French or Italian bread, sliced 1-inch thick
8 to 9 eggs
2 c. milk
1 T. vanilla extract
Optional: syrup

Combine brown sugar, butter and one teaspoon cinnamon in a lightly greased 13"x9" baking pan. Add apples and raisins; toss to coat well. Spread apple mixture evenly over bottom of baking pan. Arrange slices of bread on top; set aside. Blend together eggs, milk, vanilla and remaining 2 teaspoons cinnamon until well mixed. Pour mixture over bread, soaking bread completely. Cover with aluminum foil and refrigerate for 4 to 24 hours.

Bake, covered, at 375 degrees for 40 minutes. Uncover and bake an additional 15 minutes. Let stand 5 minutes. Serve warm with syrup, if desired. Makes 12 servings.

*Coleen Lambert*
*Casco, WI*

## Sausage & Cheddar Grits

*A rich, savory version of a southern favorite…yum!*

4 eggs, beaten
4 c. water
1 t. salt
1 c. quick-cooking grits, uncooked
1 lb. ground pork sausage, browned and drained
1½ c. shredded Cheddar cheese, divided
1 c. milk
¼ c. butter

Place eggs in a small bowl; set aside. Bring water and salt to a boil in large saucepan over medium heat. Stir in grits; cook for 4 to 5 minutes. Remove from heat. Stir a small amount of hot grits mixture into eggs; stir egg mixture back into saucepan. Add sausage, one cup cheese, milk and butter; blend together well. Pour into a greased 13"x9" baking pan. Sprinkle with remaining ½ cup cheese. Bake, uncovered, at 350 degrees for one hour or until cheese is golden. If cheese is getting golden early, cover with aluminum foil. Let cool for about 10 minutes before serving. Serves 6 to 8.

*Sharon Brown*
*Orange Park, FL*

Need a little something sweet? Bake some of Iva's Cinnamon Rolls and you'll find everyone coming to the kitchen!

## Iva's Cinnamon Rolls

*When I first met my husband's Grandma, Iva, she instantly accepted me as her own granddaughter! She showed me how to make these yummy cinnamon rolls…anyone can pass on a recipe, but to watch how a recipe is artfully put together is priceless.*

.75-oz. pkg. active dry yeast
2 c. very warm water, divided
1 c. shortening
2 eggs, beaten
1 c. sugar
1 T. salt
6½ c. all-purpose flour
6 T. butter, softened
½ c. brown sugar, packed
1 T. cinnamon

Dissolve yeast in ¼ cup of very warm water, 110 to 115 degrees. In a separate bowl, combine shortening and remaining water; set aside. Mix together shortening mixture, eggs, sugar and salt. Add yeast mixture to shortening mixture; stir in flour. Turn dough into a greased bowl (dough will be soft); cover with a tea towel. Let rise in a warm place (85 degrees), free from drafts until double in size, about 2 hours; punch down dough. Divide dough into 2 parts. Roll each part into an 18-inch by 13-inch rectangle on a floured surface. Spread butter over surface. Sprinkle evenly with brown sugar and cinnamon, adding more to taste if desired. Roll up, starting on one long side; cut one-inch thick slices. Place into 2 greased 13"x 9" or 10" round baking pans. Cover; let rise for 45 minutes, until double in size. Bake at 375 degrees for about 25 minutes. Cool and spread with Frosting. Makes 2½ dozen.

Frosting:
4 c. powdered sugar
¼ c. butter, softened
1 T. to ¼ c. milk

Combine powdered sugar and butter; add milk to desired consistency. Makes 1¾ cup.

*Bobbi Janssen*
*Lanark, IL*

Iva's Cinnamon Rolls

Gingerbread Pancakes

## Gingerbread Pancakes

*Oh-so scrumptious topped with tangy Lemon Sauce.*

1 ½ c. all-purpose flour
1 t. baking powder
¼ t. baking soda
¼ t. salt
1 t. cinnamon
½ t. ground ginger
1 egg
1 ¼ c. milk
¼ c. molasses
3 T. oil
Garnish: lemon zest strips

Sift together first 6 ingredients in a medium bowl; set aside. In a large bowl, beat egg and milk until well blended; stir in molasses and oil. Add flour mixture to milk mixture, stirring just until moistened. Pour batter by ⅓ cupfuls onto a lightly greased hot griddle. Cook over medium heat until bubbly on top; flip and continue to cook until golden. Serve with Lemon Sauce. Garnish, if desired. Serves 4.

Lemon Sauce:
½ c. sugar
1 T. cornstarch
⅛ t. nutmeg
1 c. water
2 T. butter
½ t. lemon zest
2 T. lemon juice

Stir together sugar, cornstarch and nutmeg in a small saucepan; add water. Cook over medium heat until thick and bubbly; cook and stir for an additional 2 minutes. Remove from heat; add remaining ingredients. Stir just until butter melts. Serve warm.

*Kendall Hale*
*Lynn, MA*

## Grammy's Overnight Pancakes

*Whenever we visit Grammy, these yummy pancakes are on the breakfast table without fail. Usually they're surrounded by sausage or bacon, scrambled eggs and toast with jam. We can't imagine breakfast any other way!*

2 c. long-cooking oats, uncooked
2 c. plus ¼ c. buttermilk, divided
½ c. all-purpose flour
½ c. whole-wheat flour
2 t. sugar
1½ t. baking powder
1½ t. baking soda
1 t. salt
2 eggs
2 T. butter, melted and cooled
oil for frying
Apple Pancake Syrup

Combine oats and 2 cups buttermilk in a bowl; cover and refrigerate overnight.

To prepare pancakes, stir together flours, sugar, baking powder, baking soda and salt. Set aside.

In a large bowl, beat together eggs and butter. Stir into oat mixture. Add flour mixture, stirring well. If batter is too thick, stir in 2 to 4 tablespoons remaining buttermilk. Pour batter by ¼ cupfuls onto a well-greased hot griddle. Cook until bubbles appear on the surface; flip and cook other side until golden. Top with Apple Pancake Syrup. Makes 16.

*Regina Ferrigno*
*Gooseberry Patch*

Grammy's Overnight Pancakes
Apple Pancake Syrup

## Apple Pancake Syrup

*My older sister, Teena, often cooked for my siblings and me. She would make this syrup to serve on our breakfast pancakes and waffles…she could really make something from nothing!*

6-oz. can frozen sugar-free apple
    juice concentrate, thawed
¾ c. water
½ t. lemon juice
1 T. cornstarch
¼ t. cinnamon

Mix all ingredients in a sauce-pan. Cook over medium heat, stirring frequently, until thickened and reduced by half, about 15 minutes. Serves 4 to 6.

*Gail Shepard*
*Missoula, MT*

221

## Smith Family Breakfast Bake

*I created this recipe to duplicate one that I tasted and loved. Now my kids and husband love it too!*

12-oz. tube refrigerated biscuits, baked and torn
1 lb. ground pork sausage, browned and drained
8 eggs, beaten
2 c. milk
1 sprig fresh rosemary, chopped
1 t. Italian seasoning
1 t. dried basil
1 t. dried oregano
1 t. dried thyme
salt and pepper to taste
8-oz. pkg. shredded Cheddar cheese

Arrange torn biscuits in a lightly greased 13"x9" baking pan. Top with sausage; set aside. Blend eggs and milk with seasonings. Pour over sausage; sprinkle with cheese. Bake, uncovered, at 350 degrees for 30 minutes, or until golden. Serves 12.

*Cherylann Smith*
*Efland, NC*

## Winter Fruit Salad

*Perfect to make during the winter months when fresh fruit is not as abundant. It can be made a day ahead for a holiday brunch.*

½ c. sugar
2 T. cornstarch
20-oz. can pineapple chunks, drained and ¾ c. juice reserved
⅓ c. orange juice
1 T. lemon juice
11-oz. can mandarin oranges, drained
3 to 4 red and green apples, cored and chopped
2 to 3 bananas, sliced

In a saucepan, combine sugar and cornstarch. Add reserved pineapple juice, orange juice and lemon juice. Cook and stir over medium heat until thick and bubbly; cook and stir one minute longer. Remove from heat; set aside. In a bowl, combine pineapple, oranges, apples and bananas. Pour warm sauce over fruit; stir gently to coat. Cover and refrigerate before serving. Serves 12.

*Nancy Girard*
*Chesapeake, VA*

Smith Family Breakfast Bake

**Make-Ahead Pumpkin Pie French Toast**

You'll be calm and collected on Christmas morning because you stirred up Make-Ahead Pumpkin Pie French Toast the night before! Using store-bought biscuits makes the Smith Family Breakfast Bake so easy to prepare…just be sure to make plenty!

## Make-Ahead Pumpkin Pie French Toast

*I combined several different French toast recipes to suit my family's tastes. They love anything with pumpkin, so the pumpkin pie spice was a must. It's a great Sunday morning breakfast. Or, it can bake while you get ready for church. It's also super-easy for husbands to whip up so Mom can sleep in just a bit on Saturday morning!*

1 loaf French, Italian, challah
   or Hawaiian bread, cut into
   1-inch slices
3 eggs, beaten
1/2 c. egg substitute
1 c. half-and-half
1 1/2 c. milk
1/4 t. salt
1 t. vanilla extract
1 T. pumpkin pie spice
1/2 c. brown sugar, packed
1 to 2 T. butter, sliced

Arrange bread slices in the bottom of a greased 13"x9" baking pan. Whisk together eggs, egg substitute, half-and-half, milk, salt, vanilla and spice. Stir in brown sugar; pour mixture over bread slices. Refrigerate, covered, overnight. Dot top with butter and bake, uncovered, at 350 degrees for 40 to 45 minutes. Serves 8.

*Jennifer Yandle*
*Indian Trail, NC*

## Creamy Crock Hashbrowns

*I like to serve this yummy side with grilled ham slices. The recipe can easily be halved for a smaller group, but don't underestimate how many people will ask for seconds!*

32-oz. pkg. frozen diced potatoes
16-oz. container sour cream
10 3/4-oz. can cream of celery
   soup
10 3/4-oz. can cream of chicken
   soup
1 onion, chopped
2 T. butter, melted
1/4 t. pepper
2 c. shredded sharp Cheddar
   cheese

Place potatoes in a 5-quart slow cooker. Combine remaining ingredients; pour over potatoes. Stir to mix well. Cover and cook on low setting for 5 to 6 hours. Serves 10 to 12.

*Diane Cohen*
*The Woodlands, TX*

# The Yummy Comfort of Casseroles

When you need to feed a hungry household on a cold day, a warm casserole is hard to beat! Treat your family and holiday guests to individual dishes of Golden Chicken Divan. Fluffy potatoes with parmesan top a mix of savory beef and veggies in Momma's Shepherd's Pie. Cheesy Baked Spaghetti serves a crowd…or a family of pasta lovers who want seconds!

## Golden Chicken Divan

*This casserole is always a crowd-pleaser.*

1 lb. broccoli, chopped
1½ c. cooked chicken, cubed
10¾ oz. can cream of chicken soup
⅓ c. sour cream
½ t. garlic powder
½ t. curry powder
½ t. onion powder
¼ t. seasoned salt
½ c. shredded Cheddar cheese
1 T. butter, melted
¼ c. round buttery crackers, crushed

Cover broccoli with water in a saucepan; bring to a boil over medium heat. Cook 5 minutes or until tender; drain. In a large bowl, combine broccoli, chicken, soup, sour cream, garlic power, curry powder, onion powder and salt. Spread in a greased 8"x8" baking dish; sprinkle with cheese. Mix together melted butter and crackers; sprinkle over cheese. Bake, uncovered, at 450 degrees for 10 minutes or until bubbly and golden. Serves 6.

*Amy Kim*
*Ann Arbor, MI*

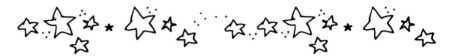

Golden Chicken Divan

The sweet onions in Paula's Corn Casserole make it a side dish that goes well with just about anything else you want to serve. Easy Chicken Enchiladas comes together quickly and contains just 5 ingredients.

Paula's Corn Casserole

## Easy Chicken Enchiladas
*This family-friendly dish is so simple to put together.*

8-oz. can chicken, drained
1 onion, chopped
8-oz. pkg. shredded Monterey
    Jack cheese, divided
2  14-oz. cans enchilada sauce,
    divided
12  6-inch corn tortillas
Garnish: chopped lettuce,
    chopped tomato, sour cream

Combine chicken, onion, one cup cheese and 1/2 cup sauce in a large bowl; set aside. Spoon enough sauce into a lightly greased 13"x9" baking dish to barely cover bottom; set aside. Spoon remaining sauce into a skillet; heat through. Dip both sides of each tortilla into sauce to soften slightly. Spoon chicken mixture evenly down the center of each tortilla and roll up. Arrange, seam sides down, in baking dish; sprinkle with remaining cheese. Bake, uncovered, at 350 degrees for 20 minutes. Garnish, if desired. Serves 6.

*Cindy Shumaker*
*Grottoes, VA*

## Paula's Corn Casserole
*A must-have side dish for any get-together.*

2 sweet onions, thinly sliced
1/2 c. butter
8-oz. container sour cream
1/2 c. milk
1/2 t. dill weed
1/4 t. salt
8-oz. pkg. shredded Cheddar
    cheese, divided
1 egg, beaten
14³/₄ oz. can creamed corn
8¹/₂ oz. pkg. cornbread mix
4 drops hot pepper sauce
Garnish: chopped fresh chives
    and additional sour cream

In a large skillet, sauté onions in butter over medium heat until tender.

Combine sour cream, milk, dill weed and salt in a small bowl; stir in one cup cheese. Add onion mixture; set aside.

Combine egg, creamed corn, cornbread mix and pepper sauce in a large bowl. Spread in a greased 3-quart baking dish; spoon onion mixture over top. Sprinkle with remaining cheese. Bake, uncovered, at 350 degrees for 40 to 45 minutes, or until golden. Let stand 10 minutes before serving. Serves 12 to 15.

*Paula Marches*
*Lenhartsville, P*

Who wouldn't love a gift of Lisa's Best-Ever Lasagna? It's freezer-friendly and so good to have on hand!

Lisa's Best-Ever Lasagna

## Lisa's Best-Ever Lasagna

*If you can assemble this the day before, it's even better.*

2 24-oz. jars spaghetti sauce
14½-oz. can diced tomatoes, drained
10¾-oz. can tomato purée
2 3.8-oz. cans sliced black olives, drained
1 onion, diced
1 red pepper, chopped
1 yellow pepper, chopped
¼ c. sugar
1 clove garlic, minced
1 t. dried oregano
24 oz. shredded mozzarella cheese
12 oz. shredded Monterey Jack cheese
8 oz. provolone cheese, shredded
1 c. grated Parmesan cheese
non-stick vegetable spray
16-oz. pkg. lasagna noodles, cooked

Combine first 10 ingredients in a large stockpot over medium heat. Simmer for one hour. Mix together cheeses; set aside. Spray two 13"x9" baking pans with non-stick vegetable spray. Spread a thin layer of sauce mixture in pans. Layer lasagna noodles, sauce and cheese. Repeat layers for a total of 3 layers. Bake at 350 degrees for 30 to 40 minutes or until golden and bubbly. Each casserole makes 8 to 10 servings.

*Lisa Hill*
*Salinas, CA*

**Momma's Shepherd's Pie**

## Lee's Trim-the-Tree Turkey Tetrazzini

*This heart-warming casserole can be made ahead and refrigerated. Just be sure to let it stand 1 hour at room temperature before baking.*

½ c. butter, divided
¼ c. all-purpose flour
1 c. evaporated milk
1 c. milk
2 c. turkey or chicken broth
⅓ c. dry sherry
3 4 oz. cans mushrooms, drained
1 t. oil
1 lb. thin spaghetti (broken into 3" to 4" pieces), cooked
4 c. cooked turkey, cubed
1 c. grated Cheddar cheese
½ c. bread crumbs

In a large skillet, melt ¼ cup butter over medium heat. Stir in flour. Add evaporated milk, whole milk and turkey broth; cook, stirring constantly, until sauce is thickened. Remove pan from heat; stir in sherry.

Sauté mushrooms in oil and 1 teaspoon butter in a Dutch oven over medium heat until tender. Fold in cooked spaghetti, cream sauce, and turkey and place in a buttered 4-quart or two 2-quart baking dishes. Combine cheese, bread crumbs and remaining butter; sprinkle cheese mixture over top of noodle mixture. Bake, covered, at 425 degrees for 15 minutes. Uncover and bake 15 to 20 more minutes or until golden and bubbly.

*Lee Charrier*

## Momma's Shepherd's Pie

*This recipe is very quick to prepare, looks delicious and tastes even better...my family loves it!*

24-oz. pkg. refrigerated mashed potatoes
1½ lbs. ground beef, browned and drained
10¾ oz. can cream of mushroom soup
14½ oz. can green beans, drained
15¼ oz. can corn, drained
2 eggs, beaten
½ c. grated Parmesan cheese
1½ c. shredded sharp Cheddar cheese
½ c. Colby cheese, shredded

Cook mashed potatoes according to package directions; set aside.

Stir together ground beef, soup, green beans and corn; spread in an ungreased 11"x7" baking dish. Set aside.

Combine mashed potatoes, eggs and Parmesan cheese; spread over meat mixture. Top with shredded cheeses. Bake, uncovered, at 375 degrees for 45 minutes. Let stand 10 minutes before serving. Serves 4.

*Barb Scott*
*Bowling Green, IN*

## Mom's Famous Macaroni & Cheese

*This recipe is the best macaroni & cheese I have ever eaten! The recipe was given to me by my mother, Bessie Wilson, who has been preparing this dish for 60 years. It is always a must-have for her children, grandchildren and great-grandchildren.*

8-oz. pkg. elbow macaroni, cooked
6 T. butter, softened
5-oz. can evaporated milk
1 c. milk
2 eggs, beaten
12-oz. pkg. shredded Cheddar cheese, divided

Combine macaroni, butter, milks, eggs and 2 cups shredded cheese; mix well. Spoon into a greased 13"x9" baking dish; top with remaining cheese. Bake, uncovered, at 350 degrees for 30 minutes or until golden. Makes 8 to 10 servings.

*Sonja Wilsey*
*Alachua, FL*

Crispy Pecan-Chicken Casserole

## Crispy Pecan-Chicken Casserole

*This creamy casserole is fast and fantastic!*

2 c. cooked chicken, chopped
1/2 c. chopped pecans
2 T. onion, finely chopped
3/4 c. celery, sliced
1 c. mayonnaise
1/2 c. sour cream
10 3/4-oz. can cream of chicken
   soup
2 t. lemon juice
1 c. potato chips, crushed
1 c. shredded Cheddar cheese

Mix together all ingredients except chips and cheese. Place in a lightly greased 3-quart casserole dish. Combine chips and cheese; sprinkle on top. Bake, uncovered, at 375 degrees for 30 to 35 minutes, until golden and bubbly. Serves 6.

*Michelle Greeley*
*Hayes, VA*

## Cheesy Baked Spaghetti

*This will easily become a potluck favorite.*

16-oz. pkg. spaghetti noodles, cooked
2  24-oz. jars spaghetti sauce
1 lb. ground beef, browned
1 lb. ground Italian pork sausage, browned
¼ c. butter
¼ c. all-purpose flour
¼ c. grated Parmesan cheese
2 t. salt
½ t. garlic powder
12-oz. can evaporated milk
3 c. shredded Italian cheese blend, divided
Garnish: chopped fresh parsley

Combine spaghetti noodles, spaghetti sauce, ground beef and sausage in a large bowl; set aside. Melt butter in a saucepan over medium heat; add flour, Parmesan cheese, salt and garlic powder, stirring constantly until smooth and bubbly. Add evaporated milk and one cup Italian cheese blend; stir until thickened.

Pour half of spaghetti noodle mixture into a greased 13"x9" casserole dish and pour cheese mixture over top. Pour remaining noodle mixture into dish; top with remaining 2 cups Italian cheese blend. Bake, uncovered, at 350 degrees for 25 to 30 minutes. Sprinkle with parsley, if desired. Makes 12 to 18 servings.

## Early-Riser Breakfast Casserole

*This has become a tradition at Easter and Christmas because it's so easy to prepare the night before and everyone loves it!*

8 slices bread, cubed
1 c. shredded Cheddar cheese
1 c. shredded Monterey Jack cheese
1½ lbs. ground pork sausage, browned
4 eggs, beaten
3 c. milk, divided
10¾ oz. can cream of mushroom soup
¾ t. dry mustard

Arrange bread cubes in the bottom of an ungreased 13"X9" baking dish; sprinkle with cheeses and sausage. Set aside.

Beat together eggs and 2½ cups milk; pour over bread. Cover with aluminum foil, refrigerate overnight.

Combine remaining ½ cup milk, cream of mushroom soup and mustard; pour over bread mixture. Bake, uncovered, at 300 degrees for 1½ hours or until golden and cheese bubbles. Serves 8.

*Patty Laughery*
*Moses Lake, WA*

**Cheesy Baked Spaghetti**

## Ham, Cheddar & Chive Wraps

*I love these handy wraps…they're so easy to make and as yummy as a classic ham & cheese omelet.*

1 T. butter
4 eggs, beaten
1¼ c. cooked ham, diced
½ c. Cheddar cheese, cubed
2 T. fresh chives, snipped
pepper to taste
4 flour tortillas, warmed

Melt butter in a medium skillet; pour in eggs. Add remaining ingredients except tortillas. Scramble until eggs are desired consistency; remove from heat. Place egg mixture in tortillas and wrap tightly. Secure with toothpicks and serve warm. Makes 4.

*Jackie Smulski*
*Lyons, IL*

## Company Breakfast Casserole

*For a Southwest flair, replace the mushrooms with a small can of sliced olives, add Monterey Jack cheese instead of Cheddar and serve with spicy salsa on the side.*

16-oz. pkg. shredded frozen
 hashbrowns, thawed and
 divided
1 onion, chopped and divided
1 lb. ground pork sausage,
 browned and drained
1 green pepper, chopped
4-oz. can sliced mushrooms,
 drained
½ to 1 c. shredded Cheddar
 cheese, divided
1 doz. eggs, beaten
1½ c. milk
salt and pepper to taste
Optional: garlic salt to taste

Company Breakfast Casserole

Spread half of the hashbrowns in a lightly greased 13"x9" baking pan. Layer ingredients as follows: half the onion, sausage, remaining onion, green pepper, mushrooms and half the cheese. In a separate bowl, whisk together eggs, milk and seasonings. Pour egg mixture over casserole; top with remaining hashbrowns and remaining cheese. Cover with aluminum foil and refrigerate overnight.

Bake, covered, at 350 degrees for 45 to 60 minutes. Uncover and bake an additional 20 minutes or until a knife inserted in center comes out clean. Serves 8 to 10.

*Jena Buckler*
*Bloomington Springs, TN*

231

# Country Chicken Pot Pies

*Just the perfect single serving size.*

1 c. onion, chopped
1 c. celery, chopped
1 c. carrot, chopped
⅓ c. butter or margarine
½ c. all-purpose flour
2 c. chicken broth
1 c. half-and-half
4 c. cooked chicken, chopped
1 c. frozen peas, thawed
1 t. salt
¼ t. pepper
1 egg, beaten

Sauté first 3 ingredients in butter in a skillet until tender. Add flour; stir until smooth. Cook one minute, stirring constantly.

Add chicken broth and half-and-half; cook, stirring constantly, until thickened and bubbly. Stir in chicken, peas, salt and pepper.

Divide Basic Pastry into 8 equal portions. Roll 4 portions of pastry into 10-inch circles on a floured surface. Place in four 6-inch ceramic pie plates. Divide chicken mixture evenly over pastries in pie plates. Roll remaining 4 portions of pastry into 7-inch circles on a floured surface. Place pastry circles over filling; fold edges under and flute. Cut slits in tops to allow steam to escape. Brush with beaten egg. Bake at 400 degrees for 35 to 40 minutes or until crust is golden. Makes 4 servings.

To store: Tightly cover and freeze unbaked pies up to one month. Let stand at room temperature 30 minutes. Bake, uncovered, at 400 degrees for one hour or until crust is golden.

## Basic Pastry:
4 c. all-purpose flour
2 t. salt
1½ c. plus 1 T. shortening
⅓ to ½ c. cold water

Combine flour and salt; cut in shortening with a pastry blender until mixture resembles coarse meal. Sprinkle cold water, one tablespoon at a time, over surface; stir with a fork until dry ingredients are moistened.

**Country Chicken Pot Pies**

## Layered Ravioli Florentine

*This delicious, cheesy dish is similar to lasagna, but goes together quickly using frozen ravioli.*

10-oz. pkg. frozen chopped
    spinach, thawed and drained
15-oz. container ricotta cheese
1 c. shredded mozzarella cheese,
    divided
1 c. shredded Parmesan cheese,
    divided
1 egg, beaten
1 t. Italian seasoning
16-oz. jar marinara sauce,
    divided
25-oz. pkg. frozen 4-cheese
    ravioli, divided

Combine spinach, ricotta cheese, ½ cup mozzarella cheese, ½ cup Parmesan cheese, egg and seasoning; set aside. Spread half of sauce in the bottom of a lightly greased 9"x 9" baking pan. Arrange half of frozen ravioli in a single layer on top of sauce. Top with all of spinach mixture and remaining ravioli, sauce and mozzarella cheese. Bake, covered, at 400 degrees for 30 minutes. Remove from oven. Sprinkle with remaining Parmesan cheese; let stand about 15 minutes before serving. Serves 6.

*Michelle Campen*
*Peoria, IL*

**Layered Ravioli Florentine**

## Struffoli

*Struffoli has been made by our family for generations. Every year between Christmas and New Year's, my children and I spend a day rolling, cutting and frying. The time we spend cooking and talking is priceless.*

2 c. all-purpose flour
¼ t. salt
3 eggs
1 t. vanilla extract
oil for frying
1 c. honey
1 T. sugar
Optional: sprinkles

In a large bowl, whisk together flour and salt. Add eggs, one at a time, mixing well by hand. Stir in vanilla. Turn dough out onto a lightly floured surface and knead, 5 minutes, until smooth. Divide dough in half and roll out each half to form a ¼-inch thick rectangle.

Cut rectangle into ¼-inch wide strips and roll each strip into a pencil shape, about 7 inches long. Slice each pencil-shaped roll into ¼ to ½-inch pieces. Add enough oil to a deep skillet to equal 2 inches. Over medium-high heat, fry several pieces of dough at a time until golden. Drain on paper towels; place in a large bowl. Repeat with remaining dough. In a small skillet over low heat, cook honey and sugar together for 5 minutes. Remove from heat and drizzle over fried pieces; stir gently to coat. Remove from bowl with a slotted spoon; arrange on a large platter. Decorate with sprinkles, if desired. Refrigerate until ready to serve. Serves 12.

*Pam Little*
*Pleasant View, TN*

Mandy's Easy Cheesy
Chicken Casserole

## Ravioli Taco Bake

*I was looking for something easy and different to take to our church potluck suppers so I came up with this recipe. Not only was it a hit…I came home with an empty dish and over 50 people wanting the recipe!*

1½ lbs. ground beef
¾ c. water
1¼-oz. pkg. taco seasoning mix
40-oz. can meat-filled ravioli
8-oz. pkg. shredded Cheddar
   cheese
Garnish: sliced black olives

Brown ground beef in a large skillet over medium heat; drain. Stir in water and seasoning mix. Reduce heat; simmer for 8 to 10 minutes. Place ravioli in a lightly greased 13"x9" baking pan; spoon beef mixture over top. Sprinkle with cheese. Bake, uncovered, at 350 degrees for 25 to 30 minutes or until cheese is melted and bubbly. If desired, sprinkle with olives before serving. Serves 6 to 8.

*Margie Kirkman*
*High Point, NC*

## Mandy's Easy Cheesy Chicken Casserole

*This is a recipe that I created by combining a few different recipes. My husband loves it and it is always a hit at reunions and potlucks.*

3 to 4 cooked chicken breasts,
   chopped
16-oz. pkg. wide egg noodles,
   cooked
24-oz. container sour cream
2 10¾-oz. cans cream of
   chicken soup
8-oz. pkg. shredded Cheddar
   cheese
8-oz. pkg. shredded mozzarella
   cheese
1 sleeve round buttery
   crackers, crushed
¼ c. margarine, melted
2 T. poppy seed

Combine chicken, noodles, sour cream, soup and cheeses in a large bowl. Pour into a lightly greased 13"x9" baking dish. Mix together cracker crumbs and margarine; sprinkle over top. Sprinkle poppy seed over cracker crumbs. Bake at 350 degrees for 25 to 30 minutes or until crackers are crispy and golden and cheese is melted. Serves 8 to 10.

*Mandy Wheeler*
*Ashland, KY*

234

## Sausage & Chicken Cassoulet

*This traditional French casserole is full of wonderful flavors. Serve it with some hearty bread to sop up the tasty juices.*

1 lb. ground hot Italian pork sausage
1 c. carrots, peeled and thinly sliced
1 onion, diced
2 t. garlic, minced
1 c. red wine or beef broth
1 T. tomato paste
1 bay leaf
1 t. fresh thyme leaves
1 t. chopped fresh rosemary
salt and pepper to taste
2 c. cooked chicken, diced
2  15-oz. cans Great Northern beans, undrained
Garnishes: fresh thyme leaves and chopped fresh rosemary

Brown sausage in an oven-safe Dutch oven; drain. Add carrots, onion and garlic. Sauté for 3 minutes; drain. Add wine or broth, tomato paste, bay leaf, thyme, rosemary, salt and pepper; bring to a boil. Remove pan from heat; stir in chicken and beans. Bake, covered, at 350 degrees for 45 minutes or until bubbly. Discard bay leaf before serving. Garnish with fresh herbs, if desired. Serves 4 to 6.

*Diane Stout*
*Zeeland, MI*

If your gang likes to work up an appetite playing in the great outdoors, fill them up with hearty Sausage & Chicken Cassoulet. Need a quick meal? Chicken & Wild Rice Casserole is simple to make, leaving you more time to wrap gifts or trim the tree!

## Chicken & Wild Rice Casserole

*The ultimate comfort food casserole! Try with leftover turkey too, when you have Thanksgiving leftovers and houseguests to feed.*

¼ c. butter
1 onion, chopped
4 stalks celery, chopped
8-oz. can sliced water chestnuts, drained
2  6-oz. pkgs. long-grain and wild rice, cooked
5 c. cooked chicken, chopped
16-oz. pkg. shredded Cheddar cheese, divided
2  10¾ oz. cans cream of mushroom soup
16-oz. container sour cream
1 c. milk
½ t. salt
½ c. bread crumbs

In a large skillet, melt butter over medium heat. Add onion, celery and water chestnuts; sauté 10 minutes, or until tender. Stir in rice, chicken, 3 cups cheese, soup, sour cream, milk and salt. Spread in a lightly greased 13"x9" baking pan; sprinkle with bread crumbs. Bake, uncovered, at 350 degrees for 30 minutes. Sprinkle with remaining cheese and bake for an additional 5 minutes. Serves 8.

*Karen Lehmann*
*New Braunfels, TX*

Sausage & Chicken Cassoulet

# Holiday Open House

One of the best things about Christmas is the chance to celebrate the spirit of the season with family & friends! This collection of finger foods and desserts offers something delicious for every taste. From Crispy Chicken Fingers to Key Lime-White Chocolate Chippers, you'll find everything you need for hosting a casual open house gathering…and most of these recipes can be prepared ahead of time!

## Crispy Chicken Fingers

*Look for frozen chicken strips for an even speedier appetizer!*

4 boneless, skinless chicken
   breasts
1 c. all-purpose flour
1 t. salt
1/4 t. pepper
3/4 c. milk
vegetable oil

Cut chicken into 2½-inch strips; set aside. Combine flour, salt and pepper in a large plastic zipping bag; set aside.

Dip chicken strips in milk. Place chicken in flour mixture; seal bag and shake to coat. Fry coated chicken strips in 350-degree deep oil for 3 minutes on each side or until golden. Place on paper towels to drain. Serve with Honey-Mustard Sauce. Makes about 2 dozen.

Honey-Mustard Sauce:
1/2 c. honey
1/4 c. Dijon mustard
2 T. yellow mustard

Combine ingredients and mix well. Keep refrigerated up to one or 2 days. Makes one cup.

*Vickie*

Crispy Chicken Fingers

## Dreamy Hot Chocolate
*So creamy and rich.*

14-oz. can sweetened condensed
   milk
$1/3$ c. baking cocoa
2 t. vanilla extract
6 c. boiling water, divided
Garnishes: whipped cream,
   cinnamon

Combine condensed milk and
cocoa in a saucepan; stir over low
heat until smooth and warm. Add
vanilla and one cup boiling water;
mix well. Stir in remaining water.
Top each serving with garnishes, if
desired. Makes 6 to 8 servings.

*Patty Fosnight*
*Baytown, TX*

## Friendship Sip Mix
*This fruity drink really takes the chill off a cold
winter's day.*

2 c. orange drink mix
1 c. lemonade drink mix
$1 1/3$ c. sugar
$1 1/2$ t. cinnamon
$1/2$ t. ground cloves
Garnish: orange slices

Mix all ingredients together;
store in an airtight container. For
each serving, stir 2 tablespoons mix
into one cup boiling water. Garnish,
if desired. Makes 4 cups mix and
32 servings.

## Dainty Turkey Sandwiches
*Garnish half of these finger sandwiches for the
grown-ups at your party, leaving the other half
plain for the little ones.*

$1/2$ lb. smoked turkey breast, cut
   into 1-inch cubes
$1/2$ c. unsalted butter, cut into
   pieces and softened
1 T. orange marmalade
2 t. honey mustard
2 t. lemon juice
$1/4$ c. fresh parsley, chopped
3 T. fresh chives, chopped
$1/4$ t. salt
16 firm white bread slices
Garnishes: fresh whole chives or
   $1/4$ c. unsalted soft butter
   and $1/4$ c. fresh chopped parsley

Process turkey in a food
processor until chopped. Add
$1/2$ cup butter and next 3 ingredients; process until almost
smooth, stopping to scrape down
sides. Transfer turkey spread to a
medium bowl. Stir in $1/4$ cup parsley,
3 tablespoons chives and salt.
Trim crusts from bread, using a
serrated or an electric knife.

Spread about $1/4$ cup turkey
spread on each of 8 bread slices.
Top with remaining 8 bread slices.
Cut each sandwich into 4 fingers.

To garnish, tie a whole chive
around each finger sandwich and
knot, or spread cut sides of sandwiches with $1/4$ cup softened butter
and dip lightly into $1/4$ cup chopped
parsley, if desired. Arrange on a
serving platter.

Note: You can make sandwiches
up to one day ahead. Just lay a
damp paper towel over sandwiches
before covering with plastic wrap.
Store in refrigerator. Makes 32.

**Friendship Sip Mix**

Yum! What could be better than enjoying a mug of Caramel Hot Chocolate and a plate of Fluffy Marshmallows?

## Caramel Hot Chocolate

*So rich and thick, you could almost eat it with a spoon!*

4 c. half-and-half
3 6.8-oz. dark chocolate bars, chopped
½ c. caramel sauce
Toppings: sweetened whipped cream, warm caramel sauce

Heat half-and-half until hot, but not boiling, in a medium saucepan. Whisk in chocolate until smooth; stir in ½ cup caramel sauce. Serve hot in mugs with a dollop of Sweetened Whipped Cream drizzled with warm caramel sauce. Makes 4 servings.

**Sweetened Whipped Cream:**
2 c. whipping cream
¼ c. powdered sugar

Beat whipping cream until soft peaks form. Gradually adding powdered sugar, beat until stiff peaks form.

## Fluffy Marshmallows

*A special treat for your little ones…and big people, too!*

⅔ c. powdered sugar
2 t. cornstarch
1 c. cold water, divided
2 pkgs. unflavored gelatin
2¼ c. sugar
1 t. vanilla extract

Line an 8"x8" pan with aluminum foil, extending foil over sides of pan; grease foil. In a small bowl, combine powdered sugar and cornstarch; set aside.

In a large bowl, combine ½ cup water and gelatin; set aside. In a heavy medium saucepan, combine remaining ½ cup water and sugar over medium-high heat. Stirring constantly, bring mixture to a boil and boil 2 minutes. Whisk hot sugar mixture into gelatin mixture, blending well. Chill 10 minutes. Beat at highest speed with an electric mixer about 5 minutes or until mixture turns white and becomes thick like meringue. Beat in vanilla. Pour into prepared pan. Chill about one hour or until set.

Use ends of foil to lift marshmallows from pan. Use a sharp knife dipped in hot water to cut into 2½-inch squares; coat with powdered sugar mixture. Store in an airtight container. Makes 9.

Caramel Hot Chocolate
Fluffy Marshmallows

## Turkey-Watercress-&-Cranberry Sandwiches

*A good combination of flavors.*

2½ c. cooked turkey, diced
¾ c. sweetened, dried cranberries, chopped
1 bunch fresh watercress, torn
8-oz. pkg. cream cheese, softened
½ t. seasoned salt
¼ t. pepper
96 party pumpernickel bread slices, crusts trimmed
Garnish: fresh parsley leaves

Stir first 6 ingredients together. Spread about one tablespoon filling on each of 48 bread slices. Top each with another bread slice.

Garnish, if desired. Store sandwiches covered with a damp paper towel in an airtight container in the refrigerator. Makes 4 dozen.

## Vegetable Canapés

*The pretty toppings are cut using a mandoline.*

3-oz. pkg. cream cheese, softened
3 T. frozen minced chives
3 T. sour cream
1 t. dried dillweed
¼ t. garlic salt
⅛ t. white pepper
16 thin white bread slices
16 thin whole wheat bread slices
Toppings: thinly sliced cucumber, squash or radishes, shredded carrots, sliced cherry tomatoes, fresh parsley, dill sprigs

Beat cream cheese at medium speed with an electric mixer until fluffy. Stir in chives and next 4 ingredients; set aside. Cut a 2-inch round from each bread slice. Keep rounds covered with damp paper towels before assembling to prevent drying out.

Spread each round with one teaspoon cream cheese mixture. Top with assorted vegetables, as desired. Add parsley or dill sprigs just before serving. Makes 32.

Sherried Shrimp Sandwiches (page 248)
Turkey-Watercress-&-Cranberry Sandwiches
Vegetable Canapés

Fill the air with the heavenly smell of Holiday Wassail! The fruit-and-cinnamon drink will warm everyone's heart with a classic flavor of Christmas.

## Artichoke-Cheese Squares

*You can make these ahead and freeze until you need them. Enjoy hot or cold.*

2 6-oz. jars artichoke hearts
1/2 red onion, finely chopped
1/4 c. dry bread crumbs
1/8 t. pepper
1/8 t. dried oregano
1/8 t. hot pepper sauce
1 1/2 c. grated Cheddar cheese
1/2 c. grated Parmesan cheese
2 T. fresh parsley, chopped
4 eggs, beaten

Drain artichokes, reserving liquid from jar. Slice artichokes; set aside. Sauté onion in artichoke liquid for about 3 minutes or until tender. Combine bread crumbs and remaining ingredients in a large bowl. Stir in artichokes and onion mixture. Pour into a greased 13"x9" baking pan. Bake at 325 degrees for 30 minutes. Let cool in dish 15 minutes; cut into squares.

★ tree trio ★

## Holiday Wassail

*We have had this recipe in our family for years. The sweet aromas of nutmeg and cinnamon will fill the house with holiday cheer.*

64-oz. can apple juice
64-oz. can pineapple juice
1/3 c. lemon juice
1/4 c. honey
1/4 t. nutmeg
4-inch cinnamon stick
Garnishes: lemon slices and cinnamon sticks, optional

Combine all ingredients in a large stockpot over medium-low heat. Bring to a boil. Simmer uncovered 15 minutes. Garnish, if desired. Makes one gallon.

Lori Downing
Bradenton, FL

Holiday Wassail

## Antipasto Kabobs

*Easy-to-pick-up party food! Enjoy any time of year by adding some crunchy bread sticks for a light meal during warmer months.*

1/3 c. olive oil
1/3 c. balsamic vinegar
1 T. fresh thyme, minced
1 clove garlic, minced
1 t. sugar
9-oz. pkg. refrigerated cheese
    tortellini, cooked
5-oz. pkg. thinly sliced salami
12-oz. jar artichoke hearts,
    drained and quartered
5³⁄₄-oz. jar green olives with
    pimentos, drained
16-oz. jar whole banana peppers,
    drained
1 pt. cherry tomatoes
16 6-inch skewers
Garnish: fresh basil leaves

Combine oil, vinegar, thyme, garlic and sugar; set aside. Thread remaining ingredients onto skewers alternately in order given. Arrange skewers in a single layer in a glass or plastic container; drizzle with marinade. Cover and refrigerate for 2 to 3 hours, turning occasionally. Drain and discard marinade before serving. Garnish with fresh basil leaves. Makes 16 skewers.

## Citrus-Mint Orzo Salad

*This recipe is a family favorite from my late mom. It is a much-requested dish for gathering with family & friends.*

16-oz. pkg. orzo pasta, uncooked
1 c. olive oil & vinegar salad
    dressing
1/2 c. frozen orange juice
    concentrate, thawed
1/2 c. fresh mint, minced
1/2 c. dried apricots, chopped
1 c. currants
1 c. slivered almonds, toasted
1 c. sun-dried tomatoes, chopped
1 green pepper, diced
1 c. red onion, minced
Optional: 1 c. goat cheese, cubed,
    salt and pepper to taste
Garnish: thin orange slices, fresh
    mint sprigs

Cook orzo according to package directions; drain and rinse with cold water. Measure out 3 cups cooked orzo into a large serving bowl; reserve remaining orzo for another recipe. In a separate bowl, whisk together salad dressing, orange juice and mint. Drizzle dressing over orzo and mix well. Add remaining ingredients except garnish; toss gently. Garnish as desired. Serves 6 to 8.

*JoAlice Welton*
*Lawrenceville, GA*

**Antipasto Kabobs**

**Ham & Swiss Rolls**

Ham & Swiss Rolls

Be sure to buy dinner rolls that come in foil pans.

¼ c. Dijon mustard
1 onion, minced
1 c. butter, melted
4 oz. Swiss cheese, grated
2 T. poppy seed
1 T. Worcestershire sauce
1 lb. shaved deli ham
4 pkgs. small dinner rolls

Combine mustard, onion, butter, cheese, poppy seed and Worcestershire sauce in a small bowl. Using a serrated knife, slice an entire package of rolls in half, horizontally. Spread the bottom half with ¼ of the mustard mixture, top with ¼ lb. ham and replace the top half. Repeat with remaining rolls, mustard mixture, and ham. Return rolls to foil pans. Bake at 325 degrees for 20 to 30 minutes, or until thoroughly heated.

*Charmaine Hahl*

**Easy Sweet-and-Sour Meatballs**

*A quick and easy appetizer for guests and potlucks…keep it warm by serving right from the slow cooker.*

2-lb. pkg. frozen meatballs, thawed
2 8-oz cans pineapple tidbits
1 8-oz. bottle barbecue sauce
1 onion, diced
1 green pepper, diced
Optional: ¼ c. chopped fresh parsley

Combine all ingredients except parsley in a 4-quart slow cooker. Cover and cook on low setting 2 hours or until heated through. Stir in parsley just before serving, if desired.

*Lynn Fazz*
*Yuma, AZ*

Easy Sweet-and-Sour Meatballs

Checkerboard Cheese Sandwiches are the perfect snack for the cheese lovers in your crowd, while oven-fresh Poppy Seed Mini Muffins will tempt everyone to enjoy two...or three!

## Checkerboard Cheese Sandwiches

*You can also serve this cheesy filling as a dip with fresh veggies and crackers.*

10-oz. block extra-sharp Cheddar cheese, shredded
10-oz. block Swiss cheese, shredded
1¼ c. mayonnaise
4-oz. jar diced pimiento, drained
1 t. dried, minced onion
¼ t. pepper
20 thin white bread slices, crusts trimmed
20 thin wheat bread slices, crusts trimmed

Stir first 6 ingredients together. Spread half of mixture evenly on half of white bread slices; top with remaining half of white bread slices. Spread remaining half of mixture evenly on half of wheat bread slices; top with remaining half of wheat bread slices.

Cut each sandwich into 4 squares. Arrange, stacked in pairs, on a serving plate in a checkerboard pattern, alternating white and wheat. Makes 40.

## Poppy Seed Mini Muffins

*Split and top with a tiny scoop of ice cream for the children.*

2 c. all-purpose flour
1 T. brown sugar, packed
1½ t. baking powder
⅛ t. salt
¼ c. butter, softened
8-oz. pkg. shredded Cheddar cheese
1 c. buttermilk
1 egg, beaten
1 T. poppy seed

Sift first 4 ingredients together. Mix in butter; stir in cheese. Add buttermilk and egg; mix just until moistened. Stir in poppy seed. Spoon into greased miniature muffin cups to ¾ full. Bake at 400 degrees for 12 to 16 minutes or until tops are golden. Makes about 3 dozen.

*Donna Rasheed*
*Greer, SC*

## Lemon Tea Loaf

*The lemon flavor is so refreshing with your favorite beverage.*

½ c. butter, softened
¾ c. sugar
2 eggs
1 c. buttermilk
¼ t. lemon extract
2 c. all-purpose flour
½ t. baking soda
½ t. salt
2 T. frozen lemonade concentrate, thawed

Beat butter and sugar until fluffy; add eggs and beat well. Beat in buttermilk and lemon extract. Combine next 3 ingredients; stir into buttermilk mixture. Pour in a greased and floured 8"x4" loaf pan. Bake at 350 degrees for 60 to 65 minutes or until lightly golden. Remove from oven and brush lightly with lemonade concentrate; cool. Makes 6 to 8 servings.

Checkerboard Cheese Sandwic

## Crabby Artichoke Spread

*Your guests will just love this creamy, spicy dip!*

1 jalapeño pepper, seeded and chopped
1 t. oil
14-oz. can artichokes, drained and chopped
2 6-oz. cans crabmeat, drained
1 c. mayonnaise
½ red pepper, chopped
¼ c. grated Parmesan cheese
2 green onions, chopped
2 t. lemon juice
2 t. Worcestershire sauce
½ t. celery seed
toasted bread rounds or crackers

Sauté jalapeño in oil until tender. Combine jalapeño and remaining ingredients except bread rounds in a slow cooker. Cover and cook on low setting for 4 hours. Serve with bread rounds or crackers. Makes 3 to 4 cups.

*Kathy Grashoff*
*Fort Wayne, IN*

## Jumbo Quiche Muffins

*These oversized muffins are always a breakfast hit.*

16.3-oz. tube refrigerated flaky buttermilk
   biscuits
1/2 c. cream cheese, softened
4 eggs, beaten
1/4 t. seasoned salt
1/4 t. pepper
6 slices bacon, crisply cooked and crumbled
1/2 c. shredded Cheddar cheese

Place each biscuit into a greased jumbo muffin cup; press to form a well. Combine cream cheese, eggs, salt and pepper. Spoon 3 tablespoons egg mixture into each biscuit well; sprinkle with bacon and top with cheese. Bake at 375 degrees for 15 minutes. Serves 8.

*Debra Alf*
*Robbinsdale, MN*

Jumbo Quiche Muffins

Mini Spinach & Bacon Quiches

## Mini Spinach & Bacon Quiches

*An elegant addition to a holiday brunch buffet that can be assembled the night before and refrigerated.*

1/4 c. onion, diced
3 slices bacon, crisply cooked and crumbled,
   drippings reserved
10-oz. pkg. frozen chopped spinach, thawed and
   drained
1/8 t. salt
1/2 t. pepper
1/8 t. nutmeg
15-oz. container ricotta cheese
8-oz. pkg. shredded mozzarella cheese
1 c. grated Parmesan cheese
3 eggs, beaten

In a skillet over medium heat, cook onion in reserved drippings until tender. Add spinach and seasonings; stir over medium heat about 3 minutes or until liquid evaporates. Remove from heat; stir in bacon and cool.

Combine cheeses in a large bowl. Add eggs; stir until well blended. Add cooled spinach mixture; stir until well blended. Divide mixture evenly among 12 lightly greased muffin cups. Bake at 350 degrees for 40 minutes or until filling is set. Let stand 10 minutes; run a thin knife around edges to release. Serve warm. Makes 12.

*Vickie*

You can feed a crowd in a hurry with hearty Jumbo Quiche Muffins and Mini Spinach & Bacon Quiches, and Loaded Potato Rounds. Turn your get-together into a real fiesta by setting out generous dishes of Zesty Corn Salsa and Spicy Guacamole!

## Zesty Corn Salsa

*This simple salsa is even better when made the day before.*

2 c. frozen corn, thawed
1/4 c. red pepper, chopped
2 green onions, sliced
1 jalapeño pepper, seeded and
    chopped
1 T. fresh cilantro, chopped
2 T. lime juice
1 T. oil
1/2 t. salt
corn chips

Gently stir together first 8 ingredients; cover and refrigerate at least one hour before serving. Serve with corn chips. Makes 2 1/2 cups.

*Connie Fortune*
*Covington, OH*

## Spicy Guacamole

*Serve this festive dip with your favorite tortilla chips and veggies.*

4 avocados, pitted, peeled and
    chopped
1 clove garlic, minced
2 T. lemon juice
1 t. pepper
1 tomato, diced
1/2 t. salt
1/8 t. cayenne pepper

Mash avocados with a fork; stir in remaining ingredients. Makes about 2 cups.

*Sharon Reagan*
*Concord, NH*

## Loaded Potato Rounds

*An amazing combination of flavors…you'll love these!*

2 baking potatoes
olive oil
1 c. shredded Colby Jack cheese
6 slices bacon, crisply cooked and
    crumbled
1/3 c. green onion, sliced
1/4 c. barbecue sauce

Cut unpeeled potatoes into 1/4-inch-thick rounds. Brush both sides with oil; arrange in one layer on an ungreased baking sheet. Bake at 450 degrees for 20 minutes, or until tender and golden.

Combine cheese, bacon and onion in a small bowl; set aside. Brush baked potato rounds with barbecue sauce; sprinkle with cheese mixture. Bake an additional 3 to 5 minutes, or until cheese is melted. Makes 2 1/2 dozen.

*Claudine King*
*Fremont, MI*

247

Your guests will feel oh-so special while enjoying these dainty hors d'oeuvres. Pecan-Stuffed Dates with Bacon are yummy and truly easy to make.

## Pecan-Stuffed Dates with Bacon
*Super quick and easy to make!*

15 pecan halves
15 seedless dates
15 slices precooked packaged bacon

Heat pecan halves in a small non-stick skillet over medium-low heat, stirring often, 2 or 3 minutes or until toasted. Cut a lengthwise slit down the center of dates. Stuff one pecan half in each date, and wrap each with one slice of bacon. Bake at 425 degrees for 8 minutes or until bacon is crisp. Makes 15.

## Sherried Shrimp Sandwiches
*Yummy sandwiches for a tea.*

1 1/2 lbs. unpeeled, small fresh shrimp
3-oz. pkg. shrimp, crawfish and crab boil
4-oz. pkg. crumbled blue cheese, softened
4 oz. cream cheese (1/2 of an 8-oz. pkg.), softened
Optional: 1/4 c. sherry
5 green onions, minced
1/2 c. celery, diced
1/2 c. walnuts, finely chopped and toasted
1/2 t. seasoned salt
1/4 t. red pepper
112 party pumpernickel bread slices
Garnish: fresh dill sprigs

Cook shrimp using seafood boil according to package directions; drain. Peel shrimp and devein, if desired. Chop shrimp.

Stir together shrimp, blue cheese and next 7 ingredients. Spread about one tablespoon filling on each of 56 bread slices. Top each with another bread slice. Cut sandwiches in half diagonally.

Garnish, if desired. Store sandwiches covered with a damp paper towel in an airtight container in refrigerator. Makes 56 servings.

248

**Cobb Sandwiches**

Everyone loves sandwiches! In no time you can make layered Cobb Sandwiches for everyone to enjoy! Or put together Red Pepper & Chicken Bagels... they are sure to ask for more!

## Cobb Sandwiches

*If you don't have time to fry bacon, mix bacon bits with the blue cheese dressing.*

2 T. blue cheese salad dressing
3 slices bread, toasted
4-oz. grilled boneless, skinless
     chicken breast
1 leaf green leaf lettuce
2 slices tomato
3 slices avocado
1 slice red onion
3 slices bacon, crisply cooked

Spread blue cheese dressing on one side of each slice of toasted bread. On the first slice of bread, place chicken breast on dressing; top with a second bread slice. Layer on lettuce, tomato, avocado, onion and bacon; top with remaining bread slice. Cut sandwich in quarters, securing each section with a toothpick. Makes 4 sandwich wedges.

*Joyce Chizauskie*
*Vacaville, CA*

## Red Pepper & Chicken Bagels

*This is a quick recipe that's perfect whenever time is short.*

2 boneless, skinless chicken
     breasts
1/8 t. salt
1/8 t. pepper
1/4 c. balsamic vinegar
3 T. Worcestershire sauce
2 bagels, split
2 slices fresh mozzarella cheese
2 slices roasted red pepper

Place chicken between 2 pieces of wax paper; pound until thin. Sprinkle with salt and pepper. In a bowl, combine vinegar and Worcestershire sauce; marinate chicken 10 to 15 minutes. Drain and discard marinade. Place chicken on a lightly greased grill or in a skillet over medium heat. Cook and turn chicken until golden and juices run clear, about 20 minutes. Place chicken on bagel halves; top with cheese, pepper slices and remaining bagel halves. Arrange on an ungreased baking sheet and bake at 350 degrees until cheese is melted, about 5 to 10 minutes. Serves 2.

*Janice Pigga*
*Bethlehem, PA*

249

**Cranberry-Buttermilk Scones**
*Homemade Devonshire Cream*

## Cranberry-Buttermilk Scones
*Best enjoyed warm from the oven topped with butter or Devonshire cream.*

2 c. all-purpose flour
⅓ c. sugar
1½ t. baking powder
½ t. baking soda
¼ t. salt
6 T. butter, softened
½ c. buttermilk
1 egg
1½ t. vanilla extract
⅔ c. sweetened, dried cranberries

Stir first 5 ingredients together; cut in butter with a pastry blender. Combine remaining ingredients except cranberries; mix into flour mixture until just moistened. Add cranberries; drop by ¼ cupfuls onto a greased baking sheet. Bake at 375 degrees for 15 to 19 minutes or until golden. Makes 10.

*Jenny Sisson*
*Broomfield, CO*

## Homemade Devonshire Cream
*A must for scones.*

1 c. whipping cream
½ c. sour cream
2 t. powdered sugar

Beat whipping cream until soft peaks form. Blend in sour cream and powdered sugar. Chill and serve. (Will keep no longer than 4 to 6 hours in refrigerator.) Makes 2¾ cups.

## Norwegian Rice Pudding

*Take this creamy treat to your Christmas potluck.*

4 c. milk
¾ c. long-cooking rice, uncooked
1 egg, beaten
½ c. whipping cream
¾ c. sugar
1 t. salt
1 t. all-purpose flour
Garnish: sliced almonds, cinnamon

Heat milk to just boiling in a medium saucepan; set aside.

Rinse rice with hot water. In a double boiler, combine hot milk and rice. Cover and cook over medium heat for one hour, or until rice is tender and milk is almost absorbed, stirring occasionally; let cool.

Combine egg, whipping cream, sugar, salt and flour. Stir egg mixture into cooled cooked rice. Pour into a one-quart ovenproof serving bowl or baking dish. Bake at 325 degrees for 30 minutes or until custard is set and edges begin to turn golden. Garnish pudding, if desired. Makes 10 to 12 servings.

Norwegian Rice Pudding

We couldn't celebrate the goodness of citrus without including grapefruit! Honey-Grapefruit Granita is simple to make, pretty to serve, and just plain delicious.

## Honey-Grapefruit Granita

*Here's a new way to highlight one of the season's best citrus fruits. It's so refreshing!*

2 c. sugar
2 c. water
4 c. fresh pink grapefruit juice
1/3 c. honey, warmed

Combine sugar and water in a large saucepan; bring to a boil. Cook until sugar dissolves, stirring constantly; cool. Combine sugar mixture, grapefruit juice and honey; stir well. Pour into a 13"x9" baking dish. Cover with plastic wrap; place in freezer. Freeze 8 hours, scraping occasionally, until frozen. Makes 6 cups.

*Tiffany Brinkley*
*Broomfield, CO*

**Honey-Grapefruit Granita**

## Key Lime-White Chocolate Chippers

*These tasty cookies taste just like Key lime pie. Leave a plateful for Santa as a special treat.*

1/2 c. butter, softened
1 c. sugar
1 egg
1 egg yolk
2 c. all-purpose flour
1 t. baking powder
1/2 t. salt
1/4 c. lime juice
1 1/2 t. lime zest
3/4 c. white chocolate chips

In a large bowl, beat butter, sugar, egg and egg yolk at medium speed with an electric mixer. Add flour, baking powder, salt, lime juice and lime zest. Stir in chocolate chips. Roll dough into walnut-size balls. Place 2 inches apart on lightly greased baking sheets. Bake at 350 degrees for 8 to 10 minutes. Makes 2 1/2 dozen.

*Cora Baker*
*La Rue, OH*

252

Winter fun calls for special ways to keep toasty! Spicy Cake Donuts and Hot Caramel Apple Cider will keep young folks warm on the inside.

## Hot Caramel Apple Cider

*Fill a slow cooker before going out for a shopping trip...the spicy aroma will fill the house!*

1/2 gal. apple cider
3/4 c. brown sugar, packed
1 1/2 t. cider vinegar
1 t. vanilla extract
4-inch cinnamon stick
6 whole cloves
1 orange, sliced
1/3 c. caramel ice cream topping

Combine all ingredients except topping in a slow cooker. Cover; cook on low setting for 5 to 6 hours. Strain; discard spices and orange. Serve in mugs, drizzling a teaspoonful of topping into each mug. Makes 7 1/2 cups.

*Kimberly Hancock*
*Murrieta, CA*

## Spicy Cake Donuts

*After ice skating or sledding, enjoy these donuts served with warm apple cider, cocoa or cinnamon tea.*

3 1/4 c. all-purpose flour
2 t. baking powder
1 1/2 t. cinnamon, divided
1/2 t. salt
2 eggs
1 1/3 c. sugar, divided
1 t. vanilla extract
2/3 c. whipping cream
1/4 c. butter, melted

Combine flour, baking powder, one teaspoon cinnamon and salt. Beat together eggs, 2/3 cup sugar and vanilla until thick and lemon colored. Combine cream and butter. Alternately add dry ingredients and cream mixture to egg mixture. Beat each time until just blended. Chill dough for 2 hours.

Combine remaining 2/3 cup sugar and remaining 1/2 teaspoon cinnamon in a resealable plastic freezer bag; set aside. Roll out dough 3/8-inch thick on a floured surface. Cut with donut cutter. Fry in 375-degree oil, turning once; allow about one minute per side. Drain on paper towels. Shake warm donuts in bag with sugar and cinnamon. Makes about 17 donuts and holes.

*Liz Roundtree*
*Petersburg, AK*

Hot Caramel Apple Cider
Spicy Cake Donuts

# CHRISTMAS DINNER ♥ CLASSICS

These are the dishes we remember from years gone by! Each one is full of old-fashioned flavor. Roast your turkey with savory butter, serve up a yummy Sweet Onion Casserole and bake melt-in-your mouth Popovers. From Rosemary Pork Roast with Tangerine-Cranberry Relish to Maple-Pecan Pie, these recipes were sent to the Country Friends from *good cooks all over the country*. See how many delicious memories you can find in these pages. Christmas dinner should always taste this good!

Cranberry-Glazed Ham

## Cranberry-Glazed Ham

*Serve slices topped with a generous spoonful of the brown sugar-cranberry glaze...wonderful!*

5 to 6-lb. ham
16-oz. can jellied cranberry sauce
1 c. brown sugar, packed
¼ c. orange juice
½ t. ground cloves
¼ t. cinnamon
¼ t. allspice

Bake ham at 350 degrees for 18 to 20 minutes per pound or until meat thermometer registers 160 degrees. While ham is baking, combine remaining ingredients in a saucepan; heat slowly, whisking until smooth. Spoon half the glaze mixture over the ham 30 minutes before removing it from the oven; continue baking for 30 minutes. Serve with remaining glaze. Serves 8 to 10.

*Beverly Smith*
*Malin, OR*

## Roast Turkey with Sage Butter

*An All-American dish that's perfect for your holiday table.*

1 c. butter, softened
3 T. fresh sage, chopped
8 slices bacon, crisply cooked and
    crumbled
salt and pepper to taste
16-lb. turkey, thawed if frozen
3 c. leeks, chopped
8 sprigs fresh sage
3 bay leaves, crumbled
4 c. chicken broth, divided
Garnishes: fresh sage sprigs,
    parsley sprigs, fresh cherries,
    plums and grapes

Combine butter, sage and bacon; sprinkle with salt and pepper. Set aside.

Remove giblets and neck from turkey; reserve for another use. Rinse turkey and pat dry. Sprinkle inside of turkey with salt and pepper; add leeks, sage and bay leaves. Loosen skin and spread ⅓ cup butter mixture over breast meat under skin. Place turkey on rack of a large broiler pan. Rub 2 tablespoons butter mixture over turkey. Set aside ⅓ cup mixture for gravy; reserve remainder for basting. Pour ⅓ cup broth over turkey.

Bake turkey at 350 degrees for about 2½ hours, or until a meat thermometer inserted into thickest part of inner thigh registers 170 degrees, shielding to prevent overbrowning. Baste every 30 minutes with ⅓ cup broth brush occasionally with remaining butter mixture. Transfer turkey to a platter; keep warm.

For gravy, pour juices and bits from pan into large measuring cup. Spoon off fat and discard. Bring juices and 2 cups broth to a boil in a large saucepan; boil until liquid is reduced to 2 cups, about 6 minutes. Whisk in reserved ⅓ cup butter mixture. Season with pepper. Garnish, if desired. Serve turkey with gravy. Serves 12.

*Kendall Hal*
*Lynn, M*

Roast Turkey with Sage Butter

# Rosemary Pork Roast with Tangerine-Cranberry Relish

*Arrange pork slices over mashed potatoes for a farm-style meal that's so hearty and filling.*

3 cloves garlic, minced
1 T. dried rosemary
salt and pepper to taste
2-lb. boneless pork loin roast
2 T. olive oil
1/2 c. white wine or chicken broth

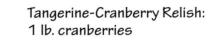

Tangerine-Cranberry Relish:
1 lb. cranberries
4 tangerines
1 1/2 to 2 c. sugar
2 c. seedless raisins or nuts, coarsely
    chopped

Crush garlic with rosemary, salt and pepper. Pierce pork with a sharp knife tip in several places and press half the garlic mixture into openings. Rub pork with remaining garlic mixture and olive oil. Place pork in a lightly greased 13"x9" baking pan.

Bake, uncovered, at 350 degrees for 1 hour and 15 minutes or until a meat thermometer inserted into thickest portion registers 155 degrees. Let stand, covered, 10 minutes or until thermometer registers 160 degrees. Remove to a serving platter; slice and keep warm. Add wine or broth to pan, stirring to loosen browned bits. Spoon pan drippings over pork and serve with Tangerine-Cranberry Relish. Serves 8.

*Tiffany Brinkley*
*Broomfield, CO*

Wash cranberries (do not thaw berries if frozen) and put into a food processor; pulse until chopped. Set aside.

Wash tangerines and remove peel. Put the peel into food processor; pulse until finely chopped.

Remove seeds from tangerines and cut sections into smaller pieces. Combine cranberries, tangerine peel and pieces and sugar in a medium saucepan; add raisins or nuts. Cook 15 minutes over medium heat, stirring occasionally until thickened. Serve warm or pour into jelly glasses. Relish may be stored in refrigerator for 2 to 4 weeks. Makes 2 1/2 pints.

Rosemary Pork Roast with
Tangerine-Cranberry Relish

Ham with Cumberland Sauce

## Ham with Cumberland Sauce

*It's the fruity sauce that makes this ham special. Named after the Duke of Cumberland, the sauce was actually created in Germany... you're going to love it!*

9 to 10-lb. fully-cooked
    bone-in ham
½ c. brown sugar, packed
1 t. dry mustard
1 to 2 t. whole cloves
Garnish: fresh currants, fresh
    thyme and sage

Using a sharp knife, score ham in diamond shapes. In a medium bowl, combine brown sugar and mustard; spread over ham. Insert a whole clove in center of each diamond. Place ham in a large roaster with a rack. Bake, uncovered, at 325 degrees for 20 to 22 minutes per pound, about one hour and 40 minutes, or until ham is heated through and meat thermometer reads 140 degrees. Garnish with fresh currants, thyme and sage. Serve with Cumberland Sauce. Serves 8 to 10.

Cumberland Sauce:
12-oz. jar red currant or apple
    jelly
¼ c. orange juice
¼ c. lemon juice
¼ c. red wine or apple juice
2 T. honey
1 T. cornstarch

Combine ingredients in a medium saucepan. Cook over medium heat until sauce thickens, stirring often. Makes 1¾ cups.

*Geneva Rogers*
*Gillette, WY*

258

A Southern favorite, Cornbread Stuffing with Sage & Sausage is a hearty side dish your family will love.

## Caramelized Brussels Sprouts

These go great with a golden turkey and all the trimmings. My friend Lisa and I usually eat any leftovers before we can put them away!

lbs. Brussels sprouts, halved
1/2 c. butter
onions, halved and thinly sliced
1/4 c. red wine vinegar, divided
T. sugar
salt and pepper to taste
Optional: 1/2 c. pistachio nuts, chopped

Place Brussels sprouts and 2" water in a Dutch oven; bring to a boil. Cover and steam 8 to 10 minutes, or until just crisp-tender.
Meanwhile, melt butter in a large skillet. Add onions and 3 tablespoons vinegar; cook until golden. Add Brussels sprouts, sugar and remaining vinegar. Sauté over medium heat until Brussels sprouts are lightly caramelized. Sprinkle with salt, pepper and nuts, if desired. Serves 8.

*Beth Schlieper*
*Lakewood, CO*

## Sweet Onion Casserole

sweet onions, sliced into thin rings
c. butter, softened
24 round buttery crackers, crushed
1/2 c. grated Parmesan cheese
Optional: 2 T. milk

Sauté onions in melted butter in a skillet over medium heat, 15 minutes or until tender. Spoon half of onions into a 1 1/2 quart baking dish. Sprinkle half of cracker crumbs and half of cheese over onions; repeat layers. Bake, uncovered, at 325 degrees for 25 to 30 minutes. Add milk if crackers have absorbed too much liquid. Serves 6 to 8.

*Virginia King-Hugill*
*Woodinville, WA*

**Cornbread Stuffing with Sage & Sausage**

## Cornbread Stuffing with Sage & Sausage

*Use mild sausage and thyme, if you prefer.*

8" square day-old cornbread, cut into 1/2-inch cubes
1 lb. sweet Italian ground pork sausage
2 small onions, finely chopped
6 stalks celery, finely chopped
2 cloves garlic, minced
1 T. dried sage
Optional: 1/2 c. pine nuts, toasted
1 c. chicken broth
1/4 c. butter, melted
salt and pepper to taste

Spread cornbread evenly on a baking sheet. Bake at 350 degrees for 20 minutes, or until golden brown.
Brown sausage in a large skillet over medium-high heat; drain, reserving one teaspoon of drippings in pan. Add onion, celery and garlic to drippings in pan. Sauté over medium heat until tender.
Combine sausage, onion mixture, cornbread, sage and pine nuts, if desired, in a large bowl and mix well. Add chicken broth and melted butter and toss to combine. Season with salt and pepper to taste. Transfer to a greased 13"x9" baking dish. Bake, uncovered, at 350 degrees for 1 hour or until golden. Makes 8 to 10 servings.

259

## Scalloped Potato Duo
(shown on page 265)

*Two types of potato, nutty Gruyère cheese and salty ham give this dish unusual appeal.*

1 onion, chopped
1 T. vegetable oil
3 cloves garlic, minced
2 sweet potatoes (about 1½ lbs.), peeled and cut into ¼-inch slices
2 baking potatoes (about 1½ lbs.), peeled and cut into ¼-inch slices
½ c. all-purpose flour
1 t. salt
¼ t. pepper
2 c. ham, chopped
8 oz. Gruyère cheese, shredded and divided
1½ c. whipping cream
2 T. butter, cut into pieces

Sauté onion in oil over medium-high heat 5 minutes. Add garlic; cook 30 seconds. Remove pan from heat; set aside.

Place potatoes in a large bowl. Combine flour, salt and pepper; sprinkle over potatoes, tossing to coat. Arrange half of potato mixture in a greased 13"x9" baking dish or 3-quart gratin dish. Top with onion mixture, ham and one cup cheese. Top with remaining potato mixture. Pour cream over potato mixture. Dot with butter and cover with aluminum foil. Bake at 400 degrees for 50 minutes. Uncover, top with remaining one cup cheese and bake 20 more minutes or until potatoes are tender and cheese is browned. Let stand 10 minutes before serving. Makes 6 servings.

## Whole Wheat Spirals
*Delicious and has a little different look.*

2 pkgs. active dry yeast
1¾ c. warm water
½ c. sugar
2 t. salt
½ c. butter or margarine, melted and divided
1 egg, lightly beaten
2¼ c. whole wheat flour
2¼ to 2½ c. all-purpose flour

Combine yeast and warm water in a 2-cup liquid measuring cup; let stand 5 minutes.

Combine yeast mixture, sugar, salt, ¼ cup melted butter, egg and whole wheat flour in a large mixing bowl; beat until well blended. Gradually stir in enough all-purpose flour to make a soft dough.

Turn dough out onto a well-floured surface and knead until smooth and elastic (about 5 minutes). Place in a well-greased bowl, turning to grease top. Cover and let rise in a warm place (85 degrees), free from drafts, 30 minutes or until double in bulk.

Punch dough down and divide in half; shape each portion into a 14x7-inch rectangle. Cut each rectangle into twelve 7x1-inch strips. Roll each strip into a spiral and place in well-greased muffin pans. Cover and let rise in a warm place, free from drafts, 20 minutes or until double in bulk.

Bake at 350 degrees for 20 to 25 minutes or until golden. Remove from pans and cool on wire racks. Brush with remaining ¼ cup melted butter. Makes 2 dozen.

Whole Wheat Spirals

You can keep your hungry crowd from raiding the kitchen before dinner by letting them snack on Hot Smoky Pecans. There's a surprise ingredient in the cheesy Scalloped Potato Duo…sweet potatoes! Whole Wheat Spirals are almost too pretty to eat, but no one will be able to resist their fresh-baked fragrance. Once the dinner plates are cleared away, it's time for a serving of Christmas Ambrosia.

Hot Smoky Pecans

## Hot Smoky Pecans
*Here's a little something to munch on before dinner.*

1/4 c. butter or margarine, melted
2 T. soy sauce
1 T. Worcestershire sauce
1/2 t. hot sauce
2 c. pecan halves

Stir together all ingredients; spread pecans in a single layer in a 15"x10" jellyroll pan. Bake at 300 degrees for 25 minutes or until toasted, stirring 3 times. Makes 2 cups.

## Christmas Ambrosia

*What is Christmas without ambrosia? In Greek mythology it was the food of the gods on Mt. Olympus!*

Peel and section oranges, catching juice in a large nonmetal bowl. Add orange sections, pineapple and coconut to juice; toss gently. Cover and chill thoroughly. Makes 6 to 8 servings.

12 navel oranges
20-oz. can crushed pineapple, undrained
2 c. fresh coconut, grated

Christmas Ambrosia

Add a fresh flavor twist when you serve Bruschetta with Cranberry Relish, and create Christmas memories with this 3-ingredient ambrosia.

### Bruschetta with Cranberry Relish

*Serve these crisp, savory slices at your next holiday feast…you may just start a new tradition!*

1 French baguette loaf, sliced ¼-inch thick
1 to 2 T. olive oil
1 t. orange zest
1 t. lemon zest
½ c. chopped pecans
½ c. crumbled blue cheese

Brush baguette slices lightly with oil. Arrange on a broiler pan; toast lightly under broiler. Turn slices over; spread with Cranberry Relish. Sprinkle with zests, pecans and blue cheese. Place under broiler just until cheese begins to melt. Makes 18 to 20 appetizer servings.

Cranberry Relish:
16-oz. can whole-berry cranberry sauce
6-oz. pkg. sweetened dried cranberries
½ c. sugar
1 t. rum extract
1 c. chopped pecans

Stir all ingredients together.
*Rhonda Johnson*
*Studio City, CA*

Bruschetta with Cranberry Relish

Roasted Brussels Sprouts

## Roasted Brussels Sprouts

*Orange zest and juice give these Brussels sprouts a pleasing hint of citrus.*

1 T. orange juice
2 t. olive oil
1 t. grated orange zest
1 lb. Brussels sprouts, halved
non-stick vegetable spray
½ t. salt
¼ t. pepper
Garnish: orange zest strips

Combine orange juice, olive oil and orange zest in a small bowl. Place Brussels sprouts on a jelly-roll pan coated with vegetable spray; drizzle orange juice mixture over sprouts and toss gently to coat. Sprinkle with salt and pepper. Bake at 450 degrees for 15 to 20 minutes or until edges of sprouts look lightly browned and crisp. Garnish, if desired. Makes 4 servings.

## Grandma's Holiday Stuffing

*Apples keep this stuffing moist.*

1 large loaf day-old bread, torn
Optional: 4 day-old corn muffins,
   broken up
1/2 c. butter
1 onion, diced
3 stalks celery, diced
1/2 c. sliced mushrooms
2 tart apples, cored and diced
1/2 c. walnuts, coarsely chopped
1/2 c. raisins
3/4 c. water or chicken broth
1/2 to 1 T. poultry seasoning
2 t. dried parsley
salt and pepper to taste

Place torn bread in a large baking dish; mix in muffins, if using (you should have about 12 cups of the bread and muffin mixture). Bake at 250 degrees for about 30 minutes or until dried out; set aside.

Melt butter over low heat in a large skillet; sauté onion, celery and mushrooms until tender. Add apples, walnuts and raisins; stir to coat with butter. Mix in water or chicken broth and seasonings; pour over bread and toss to moisten. Add a little more water or chicken broth if bread is very dry. Spread stuffing in a lightly greased 13"x9" baking pan and bake at 350 degrees for 30 to 40 minutes. (Or use to stuff a 12- to 15-pound turkey before roasting; do not overstuff.) Makes 10 to 12 servings.

*Wendy Lee Paffenroth*
*Pine Island, NY*

265

Garlicky Green Beans, Prize-Winning Pineapple-Cheddar Bake and Parmesan Pull-Aparts are the perfect accompaniments for Cranberry-Glazed Ham (page 255). Start the meal with tangy Spinach & Clementine Salad (page 270).

## Garlicky Green Beans
*Crispy-tender green beans cooked with the flavor of garlic...a wonderful side dish.*

**3 lbs. green beans**
**¹/₂ c. olive oil**
**9 cloves garlic, crushed**
**¹/₂ c. fresh parsley, chopped**
**1 c. dry bread crumbs**
**³/₄ c. grated Romano cheese**

Steam green beans until crisp-tender; drain and set aside.

Heat oil in a large skillet; add garlic and parsley. Cook until garlic is lightly golden; add beans and cook, stirring, for 2 minutes. Remove from heat; discard garlic. Combine bread crumbs and cheese; sprinkle over beans. Serves 8 to 10.

*Melanie Lowe*
*Dover, DE*

## Prize-Winning Pineapple-Cheddar Bake
*This recipe has been in my family for a very long time and I even won 2nd place when I entered it in a Dairy Council contest.*

**2  20-oz. cans pineapple tidbits**
**8-oz. pkg. shredded Cheddar cheese**
**1 c. sugar**
**³/₄ c. all-purpose flour**
**1 sleeve round buttery crackers, crushed**
**¹/₄ c. margarine, melted**

Mix together pineapple, cheese, sugar and flour; spread into a greased 2-quart casserole. Combine cracker crumbs and margarine; sprinkle over pineapple mixture. Bake, covered, at 350 degrees for 30 minutes. Serve hot or cold. Makes 8 servings.

*Marta May*
*Anderson, IN*

## Praline-Topped Butternut Squash

*When we're invited to a family gathering I'm always asked to bring this dish.*

3 12-oz. pkgs. frozen butternut
    squash purée
7 T. butter, divided
1/2 t. salt
1/8 t. pepper
2 eggs, beaten
1/2 t. cinnamon
1/2 c. brown sugar, packed
1/8 t. nutmeg
1/2 c. chopped pecans

Heat squash according to microwave package directions; stir in 1/4 cup butter, salt and pepper. Add eggs, mixing well. Spoon mixture into a greased one-quart baking dish; set aside.

Combine cinnamon, brown sugar, remaining butter, nutmeg and pecans; sprinkle over squash mixture. Bake, uncovered, at 350 degrees for 30 minutes. Serves 8.

*Nancy Kowalski*
*Southbury, CT*

**Praline-Topped Butternut Squash**

## Herb-Seasoned Beans

*These are also great in the summer when you can find fresh green beans at the farmer's market.*

1 c. water
8 c. fresh green beans, trimmed
1/2 c. butter, melted
1/2 c. seasoned bread crumbs
4 t. fresh parsley, chopped

In a Dutch oven, cover green beans with water. Simmer 15 minutes or until crisp-tender; drain.

Combine butter and remaining ingredients. Add green beans, mixing well. Serves 10.

*Debbie Cummons-Parker*
*Lakeview, OH*

## Crunchy Salad Almondine

*Very pretty for a special holiday luncheon or buffet table!*

1/4 c. butter
1/2 c. slivered almonds
1 head lettuce, chopped
2 c. celery, chopped
2 T. fresh parsley, chopped
2 c. green onions, chopped
2 11-oz. cans mandarin oranges,
    drained
1/2 c. oil
1/2 t. hot pepper sauce
1/4 c. sugar
1 t. salt
1/8 t. pepper
1/4 c. tarragon vinegar

Melt butter in a small skillet. Add almonds and sauté 2 minutes or until toasted; set aside to cool.

In a large serving bowl, combine lettuce, celery, parsley, green onions, mandarin oranges and almonds; refrigerate until ready to serve.

Whisk together oil, hot pepper sauce, sugar, salt, pepper and tarragon vinegar, until thoroughly mixed. Pour dressing over salad just before serving.

*Jackie Crough*
*Salina, KS*

Roasted Walnut & Pear Salad

### Roasted Walnut & Pear Salad

*This is wonderful for a formal dinner or a casual warm family gathering. Be sure to use fresh pears for the best flavor.*

1 head romaine lettuce, torn
2 c. pears, thinly sliced
2 Roma tomatoes, chopped
1 c. walnuts
2 T. butter
¼ c. brown sugar, packed
4-oz. pkg. crumbled blue cheese
8-oz. bottle raspberry white wine
    salad dressing

Place lettuce in a large serving bowl; lay pears on top and add tomatoes. In a medium skillet, toast walnuts in butter until golden; add brown sugar and stir over low heat until walnuts are hardened with glaze. Add walnuts to salad, sprinkle blue cheese and toss with desired amount of vinegar dressing. Serves 6 to 8.

*Laurie Johnson*
*Rosenberg, TX*

268

With raisins, walnuts, bacon and cabbage in the mix, Cranberry Broccoli Salad offers a world of flavor in every bite.

## Old-Fashioned Yeast Rolls

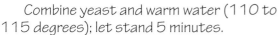

2 pkgs. active dry yeast
1/3 c. warm water
1 c. butter
1 1/2 c. milk
4 1/2 to 5 c. all-purpose flour
1/2 c. sugar
1 t. salt
2 eggs, beaten

Combine yeast and warm water (110 to 115 degrees); let stand 5 minutes.

Combine butter and milk in a small saucepan; cook over low heat until melted. Let stand until mixture reaches a temperature between 110 and 115 degrees. Add yeast mixture and stir until blended.

Meanwhile, combine 4 1/2 cups flour, sugar and salt in a large mixing bowl. Add milk mixture and eggs; beat at medium speed with an electric mixer until well blended.

Turn dough out onto a floured surface, and knead in enough of remaining flour to make a soft dough. Knead until smooth and elastic (about 10 minutes). Place in a well-greased bowl, turning to grease top.

Cover dough with plastic wrap, and let rise in a warm place (85 degrees), free from drafts, until dough doubles in bulk.

Punch dough down; turn out onto a lightly floured surface and knead lightly 4 or 5 times. Shape into rolls and arrange in a buttered and floured 13"X9" baking pan. Cover and let dough double in bulk. Bake at 400 degrees for 15 to 20 minutes or until golden. Makes 3 dozen.

## Cranberry-Broccoli Salad

*Colorful, crunchy and refreshing.*

1 1/4 c. cranberries, halved
2 c. broccoli flowerets
4 c. cabbage, shredded
1 c. walnuts, coarsely chopped
1/2 c. raisins
1 small onion, finely chopped
8 slices bacon, crisply cooked and
    crumbled
1 c. mayonnaise
1/3 c. sugar
2 T. cider vinegar

Combine first 7 ingredients; toss well. Combine remaining ingredients, stirring well with a whisk. Drizzle mayonnaise mixture over cranberry mixture and toss to coat. Cover and refrigerate for up to 24 hours. Makes 6 to 8 servings.

Cranberry Broccoli Salad
Old-Fashioned Yeast Rolls

## Parmesan Pull-Aparts

*Three kinds of savory seeds really dress up ordinary biscuits.*

3 T. margarine
1 T. onion, minced
2 t. dill seed
1 t. poppy seed
¼ t. celery seed
12-oz. tube refrigerated biscuits, quartered
¼ c. grated Parmesan cheese

Melt margarine in a 9" round cake pan. Sprinkle onion, dill, poppy and celery seed over margarine. Sprinkle quartered biscuits with cheese and arrange in pan. Bake at 400 degrees for 15 to 18 minutes. To serve, invert pan over a serving platter and turn out biscuits. Makes 10 servings.

*Diane Cohen*
*Kennesaw, GA*

## Old-Fashioned Corn Pudding

*It wouldn't be Christmas without this dish on our table…I usually double the recipe!*

2 eggs, beaten
¼ to ½ c. sugar
2 slices bread, crusts trimmed
14¾-oz. can creamed corn
½ c. evaporated milk
1 t. vanilla extract

Mix together eggs and sugar; cube bread and add to mixture. Stir in corn, milk and vanilla. Pour mixture into a buttered 1½-quart casserole dish. Bake at 350 degrees for one hour. Serves 4 to 6.

*Jodi King*
*Friendship, MD*

MAKE A TOAST WITH HOT CHOCOLATE IN WINE GLASSES!

## Spinach & Clementine Salad

*This fresh, crunchy salad is a perfect way to use a Christmas gift box of clementines.*

2 lbs. clementines, peeled and sectioned
2 lbs. baby spinach
4 stalks celery, thinly sliced
1 c. red onion, thinly sliced
½ c. pine nuts or walnuts, toasted
¼ c. dried cherries
¼ c. olive oil
2 T. red wine vinegar
1 clove garlic, minced
1 t. Dijon mustard
⅛ t. sugar
salt and pepper to taste

Place clementines in a large salad bowl with spinach, celery, onion, nuts and cherries. Toss to mix well. Whisk together remaining ingredients in a small bowl; drizzle over salad. Serve immediately. Makes 8 servings.

*Sharon Jones*
*Oklahoma City, OK*

Welcome
SET UP A SWEET CANDY BAR!

Spinach & Clementine Salad

## Pear-Walnut Salad

*The natural sweetness of the pears plays off the tang of the blue cheese perfectly.*

4 c. mixed salad greens, torn and tightly packed
2 ripe red pears, cored and sliced
1½ c. walnut halves, toasted
2 oz. crumbled blue cheese

Combine all ingredients in a large bowl; toss gently. Pour dressing over salad mixture just before serving; toss. Makes 5 servings.

**Dressing:**
½ c. olive oil
¼ c. sugar
3 T. white vinegar
½ t. celery seed
¼ t. salt

Combine all ingredients in a jar; cover and shake vigorously. Makes one cup.

271

You can't spread it on too thick! Not when you are serving Almond-Bacon Spread...sure to become everyone's asked-for cracker topper. Oh-so-gooey and yummy,

### Almond-Bacon Spread

*This is a very old recipe that I've used for many years.*

1/4 c. roasted almonds, finely
    chopped
2 slices bacon, crisply cooked and
    crumbled
1 c. shredded American or sharp
    Cheddar cheese
1 T. green onion, chopped
1/2 c. mayonnaise
1/8 t. salt
crackers or sliced party rye

Stir together all ingredients except crackers or bread in a bowl until thoroughly combined. Serve with crackers or sliced party rye. Serves 6.

*Joan Clark
Cortland, OH*

**Almond-Bacon Spread**

Slow-Cooked Brown Sugar Apples

## Slow-Cooked Brown Sugar Apples

*Nothing says comfort like the aroma of these apples cooking…unless, of course, it's sitting down to enjoy them.*

6 apples, cored
¾ c. orange juice
½ c. apple cider
½ c. brown sugar, packed
¼ t. cinnamon
Optional: frozen whipped topping, thawed

Peel a strip around the top of each apple to help prevent cracking. Arrange apples in a slow cooker. In a large bowl, combine remaining ingredients except whipped topping; mix to blend. Spoon over apples. Cover and cook on low setting for 3 to 4 hours or until apples are tender. Cool slightly and serve warm with whipped topping, if desired. Makes 6 servings.

*Lynn Williams*
*Muncie, IN*

Panzanella Salad

## Panzanella Salad

*Enjoy this farm-fresh salad any time of year.*
*If you can't find heirloom tomatoes, large red*
*tomatoes will be just as good.*

2 lbs. heirloom tomatoes, diced
¼ c. red onion, minced
2 t. garlic, minced
½ c. olive oil
2 T. lemon juice
2 T. fresh basil, chopped
1 T. fresh tarragon, chopped
1 t. salt
pepper to taste
2 c. arugula leaves
Garnish: grated Parmesan cheese

Place tomatoes in a colander to allow liquid to drain; set aside. Combine remaining ingredients except arugula and garnish. Top with Homemade Croutons and toss well. Divide tomato mixture among 4 serving plates. Top each serving with arugula; garnish with cheese. Serves 4.

Homemade Croutons:
¼ c. butter
1 T. garlic, minced
6 slices day-old bread, crusts
    trimmed, cubed
salt and pepper to taste
6 T. grated Parmesan cheese

Melt butter in a large skillet over medium heat. Cook until butter foams. Add garlic and cook 30 seconds to one minute. Add bread cubes and toss to coat. Season with salt and pepper. Transfer to a baking sheet and bake at 375 degrees for about 15 minutes, until lightly golden. Sprinkle with cheese and toss until cheese melts. Serves 6 to 8.

*Kelly Anderso.*
*Erie, P.*

274

# Popovers

*Mom's beef stew wasn't complete without a batch of popovers straight from the oven. As kids we'd peel the tops off and use them to sop up the leftover stew in the bottom of our bowls. We'd butter the bottom and eat them while the steam was still escaping.*

1 c. milk
1 T. butter, melted
1 c. all-purpose flour
¼ t. salt
2 eggs

Let all ingredients come to room temperature. Stir together milk, butter, flour and salt in a large mixing bowl. Add eggs, one at a time, beating until blended; do not over beat.

Pour batter into large buttered muffin pans, filling ¾ full. Bake at 450 degrees for 15 minutes. Reduce heat to 350 degrees and bake 20 more minutes or until edges of rolls are firm.

*Kara Allison*
*Dublin, OH*

Old-fashioned Popovers are so easy to make, you'll wonder why you don't serve them all the time.

Popovers

Teri's Butternut Squash Soup

## Cajun Spiced Pecans

*Fill small ribbon-tied bags with these delightful nuts to send home with dinner guests as party favors.*

16-oz. pkg. pecan halves
1/4 c. butter, melted
1 T. chili powder
1 t. dried basil
1 t. dried oregano
1 t. dried thyme
1 t. salt
1/2 t. onion powder
1/4 t. garlic powder
1/4 t. cayenne pepper

Combine all ingredients in a slow cooker. Cover and cook on high setting for 15 minutes. Turn to low setting and cook, uncovered, for 2 hours, stirring occasionally. Transfer nuts to a baking sheet; cool completely. Store in an airtight container. Serves 12 to 16.

*Kerry Mayer*
*Dunham Springs, LA*

## Teri's Butternut Squash Soup

*We tried a delicious squash soup at a local restaurant. This recipe is my own version and it's so good! We find it's also wonderful served chilled with sliced green onions on top.*

1 T. olive oil
1 T. butter
2 2-lb. butternut squash, peeled and
    cubed
1 onion, chopped
1 clove garlic, minced
1/2 t. allspice
2 14 1/2-oz. cans chicken broth
Garnish: sour cream, allspice

Combine oil and butter in a large saucepan over medium heat. Add squash, onion and garlic. Cook for about 5 minutes, stirring occasionally, until crisp-tender. Add allspice; cook just a minute more. Add broth. Bring to a boil; cover. Reduce heat to low; simmer for 15 minutes or until squash is tender. Process in a food processor until smooth. Return to saucepan; heat until hot. If a thinner soup is preferred, add a little more broth or water. Ladle soup into soup bowls. Garnish, if desired. Serve with crackers. Serves 8.

*Teri Johnson*
*North Ogden, UT*

LIGHT THE CANDLES and WELCOME YOUR GUESTS!

Harvest Vegetables

## Harvest Vegetables

*Roasted and slightly garlicky in flavor, these vegetables are everyone's favorites!*

2 lbs. butternut squash, halved,
    seeded and cut into
    1 1/2-inch cubes
2 lbs. redskin potatoes, quartered
2 to 3 red onions, quartered
16-oz. pkg. baby carrots
4 to 6 cloves garlic, crushed
3 T. olive oil, divided
2 t. coarse salt, divided
1/4 t. pepper, divided

Combine vegetables and garlic; spread evenly onto 2 lightly greased baking sheets. Toss with oil, salt and pepper. Bake at 450 degrees for 40 to 50 minutes, tossing vegetables and rotating sheets from top to bottom of oven halfway through. Serve hot or at room temperature. Serves 8.

*Jo Ann*

## Creamy Bacon & Herb Succotash

*You'll love this deluxe version of an old harvest-time favorite...I do!*

1/4 lb. bacon, chopped
1 onion, diced
10-oz. pkg. frozen lima beans
1/2 c. water
salt and pepper to taste
10-oz. pkg. frozen corn
1/2 c. whipping cream
1 1/2 t. fresh thyme, minced
Garnish: 2 t. fresh chives, snipped

In a Dutch oven over medium-high heat, cook bacon until crisp. Remove bacon, reserving 2 tablespoons drippings in Dutch oven. Add onion; sauté until tender, about 5 minutes. Add beans, water, salt and pepper; bring to a boil. Reduce heat; cover and simmer for 5 minutes. Stir in corn, cream and thyme; return to a simmer. Cook until vegetables are tender, about 5 minutes. Toss with reserved bacon and chives before serving. Serves 6.

*Vickie*

Quick-cooking oats and brown sugar are the secret to Cloverleaf Oat Rolls... just add a pat of butter and enjoy!

Cloverleaf Oat Rolls

## Cloverleaf Oat Rolls

*It wouldn't be dinner at Grandma's without a basket of her delicious homemade rolls on the dinner table!*

1 c. quick-cooking oats, uncooked
1/3 c. brown sugar, packed
1 t. salt
1/3 c. shortening
1 1/2 c. boiling water, divided
1 env. active dry yeast
4 c. all-purpose flour, divided
1 egg, beaten

Place oats, brown sugar, salt and shortening in a large bowl; pour 1 1/4 cups boiling water over all. Let stand until lukewarm. In a separate small bowl, let remaining water cool slightly (110 to 115 degrees); sprinkle with yeast and stir until dissolved. Add yeast mixture to oat mixture along with 2 cups flour and egg. Beat until well blended. Add remaining flour, a little at a time, to make a soft dough. Turn onto a lightly floured surface; knead until smooth and elastic. Place dough in a greased bowl; turn so top is greased. Cover with a tea towel; let rise in a warm place until double in bulk, about 1 1/2 hours. Punch down; let rise again until double, about 30 minutes. Form into one-inch balls; place 3 balls in each cup of greased muffin tins. Let rise again until double, 20 to 30 minutes. Bake at 375 degrees for about 25 minutes, until golden. Makes about 2 1/2 dozen.

*Sharon Cinder*
*Junction City, KS*

## Spinach Soufflé

*Use Swiss cheese instead of Cheddar if you like.*

10-oz. pkg. frozen, chopped spinach, thawed
3 T. all-purpose flour
3 eggs, beaten
1/2 t. salt
12-oz. carton cottage cheese
1/2 c. shredded Cheddar cheese
1/4 c. butter, melted

In a large mixing bowl, combine spinach and flour; add eggs, salt, cottage cheese, Cheddar cheese and butter. Place in a greased 13" x 9" baking dish. Bake, covered, at 375 degrees for 45 minutes. Uncover and bake an additional 15 minutes. Serves 6.

*Gloria Robertson*
*Midland, TX*

# ELF stockings

Smothered Green Beans pack all the rich flavor of bacon and tomatoes. Everyone's heard of sausage stuffing, but Stuffed Turkey Roll offers an updated version with spinach and garlic.

## Smothered Green Beans
(shown on page 265)
*Lots of wonderful flavors in these beans.*

1 lb. green beans
6 bacon slices
3 stalks celery, chopped
1 onion, chopped
1 red pepper, chopped
3 plum tomatoes, seeded and chopped
2 cloves garlic, minced
1½ t. salt
½ t. dried thyme
½ t. dried basil
½ t. paprika
¼ t. pepper

Cook green beans in boiling water to cover for 6 to 8 minutes or until crisp-tender. Drain and place in ice water to stop the cooking process. (This can be done 2 days ahead of time.)

Cook bacon in a large skillet until crisp; remove bacon and drain on paper towels, reserving 2 tablespoons drippings in skillet. Crumble bacon and set aside. Cook celery, onion and red pepper in hot drippings in skillet over medium-high heat for 5 minutes. Add green beans and remaining ingredients; cook, stirring often, until heated through. Sprinkle bacon on top. Makes 6 to 8 servings.

## Stuffed Turkey Roll
(shown on page 265)
*This gives turkey a whole new look!*

12 oz. ground pork
10-oz. pkg. frozen chopped spinach, thawed and well drained
½ c. soft breadcrumbs
⅓ c. onion, minced
1 egg, beaten
2 cloves garlic, minced
¾ t. dried thyme
¾ t. dried rosemary, crushed
1½ t. salt, divided
1 t. pepper, divided
3-lb. boneless turkey breast
2 T. butter or margarine
2 T. vegetable oil

Combine first 8 ingredients. Stir in ½ teaspoon salt and ½ teaspoon pepper; set aside.

Lay turkey breast flat on wax paper, skin side down. Trim fat, keeping skin intact. From center, slice horizontally (parallel with skin) through thickest part of each side of breast almost to outer edge; flip cut piece and breast fillets over to enlarge breast. Pound breast to flatten and to form a more even thickness.

Spoon stuffing mixture in center of width of turkey breast, leaving a 2-inch border at sides. Fold in sides of turkey breast over filling; roll up turkey breast over filling, starting from bottom. (Roll should be 12 to 14 inches long.) Tie turkey breast roll securely in several places with heavy string. Sprinkle with remaining one teaspoon salt and ½ teaspoon pepper. Brown turkey in large roasting pan in butter and oil over medium-high heat, turning frequently, for 10 minutes or until browned. Insert meat thermometer, making sure tip touches meat of turkey. Bake at 375 degrees for 50 to 55 minutes or until thermometer registers 165 degrees, basting often. Let stand 10 minutes before slicing. Makes 10 servings.

Smothered Green Beans

# Blue Ribbon Cakes

Served with ice cream, topped with fruit, or just enjoyed as-is... cake is a dessert everyone loves! Try the Strawberry Cake for a flavor of springtime in December. Or slice into the ooey-gooey, marshmallow goodness of Chocolate & Marshmallow Cupcakes. Know someone who's nutty for bananas? Surprise them with a Banana-Walnut Upside Down Cake!

The moist layers of cake, filling and frosting in Triple Chocolate Ecstasy are oh-so good with the spicy flavor of Cheery Christmas Coffee.

Cheery Christmas Coffee
Triple Chocolate Ecstasy

## Triple Chocolate Ecstasy
*This cake will satisfy the chocolate lovers in your family.*

4 1-oz. sqs. semi-sweet baking
    chocolate
½ c. butter or margarine
1 c. pecans, finely chopped
2 c. sugar
2 eggs, lightly beaten
1½ c. all-purpose flour
1 t. baking powder
½ t. salt
1½ c. milk
1 t. vanilla extract

Grease two 9" round cake pans; line with wax paper. Grease wax paper; set aside.

Combine chocolate and butter in top of a double boiler; bring water to a boil. Reduce heat to low; cook until chocolate melts. Add pecans; stir well. Remove from heat.

Combine sugar and eggs. Stir in chocolate mixture. Combine flour, baking powder and salt; add to chocolate mixture alternately with milk, beginning and ending with flour mixture. Stir in vanilla. Pour batter into prepared pans. Bake at 350 degrees for 45 to 48 minutes or until a wooden pick inserted in center comes out clean. Cool in pans on wire racks 5 minutes; remove from pans and let cool completely on wire racks.

Spread filling between layers of cake. Spread frosting on top and sides of cake. Makes 12 servings.

**Chocolate Filling:**
4 1-oz. sqs. semi-sweet baking
    chocolate
¼ c. butter or margarine
½ c. powdered sugar, sifted
⅓ c. milk

Combine chocolate and butter in top of a double boiler; bring water to a boil. Reduce heat to low; cook until chocolate melts. Gradually add powdered sugar alternately with milk, beginning and ending with powdered sugar; stir until smooth. Cover and chill 30 minutes or until spreading consistency.

**Chocolate Frosting:**
2 c. whipping cream
1 c. powdered sugar, sifted
⅔ c. baking cocoa, sifted
1 t. vanilla extract

Combine all ingredients in a bowl; beat at high speed with a mixer until stiff peaks form. Chill 30 minutes.

## Cheery Christmas Coffee
*Spiced coffee with a surprising orange twist!*

⅓ c. ground coffee
½ t. cinnamon
⅛ t. ground cloves
¼ c. orange marmalade
3 c. water
Optional: sugar

Place coffee, cinnamon and cloves in filter in brew basket of coffee maker. Place marmalade in empty coffee pot. Brew coffee as usual with water. When brewing is complete, mix well. Pour into coffee mugs; serve with sugar, if desired. Makes 6 servings.

*Kay Marone*
*Des Moines, IA*

## Pumpkin Cheesecake with Ginger Cream Topping

*This one will become a "must-have-every-year" recipe.*

¾ c. sugar, divided
¾ c. brown sugar, firmly packed and divided
¾ c. graham cracker crumbs
½ c. pecans, finely chopped
¼ c. butter or margarine, melted
16-oz. can pumpkin
1 t. vanilla extract
1 T. all-purpose flour
1½ t. cinnamon
½ t. ground ginger
½ t. nutmeg
¼ t. salt
3  8-oz. pkgs. cream cheese, softened
3 eggs
Garnish: chopped pecans

Combine ¼ cup sugar, ¼ cup brown sugar, graham cracker crumbs, ½ cup pecans and butter; press in bottom and one inch up sides of a lightly greased 9" springform pan. Cover and chill one hour.

Combine remaining ½ cup sugar, ½ cup brown sugar, pumpkin, vanilla and next 5 ingredients; set aside.

Beat cream cheese at medium speed until creamy. Add pumpkin mixture, beating well. Add eggs, one at a time, beating after each addition. Pour mixture into prepared crust. Bake at 350 degrees for 55 minutes. Cool completely in pan on a wire rack.

Spoon topping over cheesecake. Cover and chill at least 8 hours. To serve, carefully remove sides of springform pan; garnish cheesecake, if desired. Makes 16 servings.

Ginger Cream Topping:
1 c. whipping cream
1 c. sour cream
2 T. sugar
¼ c. crystallized ginger, minced
3 T. dark rum or 1 t. rum extract
½ t. vanilla extract

Combine first 3 ingredients in a bowl; beat at high speed until soft peaks form. Fold in ginger, rum and vanilla.

Pumpkin Cheesecake with Ginger Cream Topping

Victorian Jam Cake

## Victorian Jam Cake

*A favorite of Queen Victoria (and Kate)!*

1 ½ c. all-purpose flour
1 ½ t. baking powder
2 to 3 t. lemon zest, finely grated
½ t. salt
¾ c. butter or margarine, softened
¾ c. sugar
3 eggs
¾ c. seedless strawberry jam
powdered sugar
Garnish: fresh strawberry

Combine flour, baking powder, lemon zest and salt; set aside.

Blend butter and sugar together until light and fluffy. Add eggs, one at a time, beating well after each addition.

Stir in flour mixture. Spread batter evenly into 2 greased 8" round cake pans. Bake at 350 degrees for 18 to 20 minutes. (Cake should spring back when touched lightly.)

Cool in pans for 10 minutes, then invert onto wire racks to cool completely. Assemble cake on serving plate by putting layers together with strawberry jam in between. Sprinkle with powdered sugar. Garnish, if desired. Makes 8 servings.

When company shows up, treat them to their choice of these oh-so-good desserts. Chocolate, spices and cream cheese are all such welcome Christmas flavors!

## Rich Spice Cake

*A family favorite from one of my Grandmother's oldest cookbooks dated 1928.*

2 c. plus 1 T. all-purpose flour,
    divided
2 t. cinnamon
1 t. ground cloves
1 t. allspice
$\frac{1}{2}$ t. nutmeg
1 t. baking soda
1 c. milk
2 T. vinegar
$\frac{1}{2}$ c. shortening
2 c. brown sugar, packed
3 egg yolks
2 egg whites, stiffly beaten
1 c. raisins

Sift 2 cups flour, cinnamon, cloves, allspice, nutmeg and baking soda together; set aside. Stir milk and vinegar together; set aside. Beat shortening, brown sugar and egg yolks together in a large mixing bowl. Gradually beat in flour mixture alternately with milk; fold in egg whites.

Toss raisins with remaining one tablespoon flour; fold into batter. Pour into 2 greased and floured 8" round baking pans; bake at 350 degrees for 28 minutes or until a toothpick inserted into center comes out clean. Cool; frost with caramel icing. Makes 8 to 12 servings.

Caramel Icing:
3 c. brown sugar, packed
1$\frac{1}{2}$ c. whipping cream
1$\frac{1}{2}$ T. butter
1$\frac{1}{2}$ t. vanilla extract

Heat brown sugar and cream together in a heavy saucepan until soft-ball stage or 234 degrees on a candy thermometer. Stir in butter and vanilla; remove from heat. Stir until desired spreading consistency is reached.

*Naomi Cycak*
*Ligonier, PA*

Rich Spice Cake

## Black Bottom Cupcakes

*Chocolate and cream cheese...what a scrumptious combination!*

2 8-oz. pkgs. cream cheese, softened
2 eggs, beaten
2⅔ c. sugar, divided
1¼ t. salt, divided
1½ c. semi-sweet chocolate chips
3 c. all-purpose flour

½ c. baking cocoa
2 t. baking soda
2 c. water
⅔ c. oil
2 T. vinegar
2 t. vanilla extract

Combine cream cheese, eggs, ⅔ cup sugar, ¼ teaspoon salt and chocolate chips; mix well and set aside.

Combine remaining 2 cups sugar, remainng one teaspoon salt and last 7 ingredients in a large bowl; fill paper-lined muffin cups ¾ full with chocolate batter. Top each with ¼ cup cream cheese mixture. Bake at 350 degrees for 25 or 30 minutes. Makes 2 dozen.

*Gretchen Brown*
*Forest Grove, OR*

## Cookie Dough Cheesecake

*Who can resist cookie dough? Indulge in this!*

1¾ c. chocolate chip cookie crumbs
1½ c. sugar, divided
½ c. butter, melted and divided
3 8-oz. pkgs. cream cheese, softened
3 eggs
1 c. sour cream
1½ t. vanilla extract, divided
¼ c. brown sugar, packed
½ c. all-purpose flour
1½ c. mini semi-sweet chocolate chips, divided

In a small bowl, combine cookie crumbs and ¼ cup sugar; stir in ¼ cup butter. Press into bottom and slightly up the sides of a greased 9" springform pan; set aside.

In a mixing bowl, beat cream cheese and one cup sugar until smooth. Add eggs; beat on low speed just until combined. Add sour cream and ½ teaspoon vanilla; beat just until blended. Pour over crust; set aside.

In a separate mixing bowl, beat remaining ¼ cup butter, remaining ¼ cup sugar and brown sugar on medium speed; add remaining one teaspoon vanilla. Gradually add flour and stir in one cup chocolate chips. Drop by teaspoonfuls over filling, gently pushing dough below surface. Bake at 350 degrees for 50 to 55 minutes or until center is almost set. Cool on a wire rack for 10 minutes. Carefully run a knife around the edge of pan to loosen; cool one hour longer. Refrigerate overnight, then remove sides of pan and sprinkle with remaining ½ cup chips. Makes 8 servings.

*Valarie Dobbins
Edmond, OK*

286

# Chocolate & Marshmallow Cupcakes

*Super for the kids' Christmas parties!*

8-oz. pkg. unsweetened dark baking chocolate,
    chopped
1 c. butter, softened
4 eggs
1 c. sugar
3/4 c. all-purpose flour
1 t. salt
1/2 c. mini semi-sweet chocolate chips
Garnish: 1/2 c. mini marshmallows

Place chocolate and butter together in a microwave-safe bowl; heat on high setting just until melted. Cool until just warm. Blend together eggs and sugar until light and foamy. Add flour and salt; mix well. Pour in chocolate mixture; blend until smooth. Spoon batter into 12 paper-lined muffin cups; sprinkle chocolate chips evenly over tops.

Bake at 350 degrees for 15 minutes or until toothpick tests clean. Remove from oven; arrange several marshmallows on top of each cupcake. Broil just until marshmallows turn golden. Remove from oven and let stand 5 minutes to cool slightly. Makes one dozen.

*Kathy Grashoff*
*Fort Wayne, IN*

Chocolate & Marshmallow Cupcakes

## Chocolate-Cappuccino Cheesecake

*This makes an absolutely delicious gift…if you can bear to give it away!*

1½ c. pecans, finely chopped
1½ c. chocolate wafer cookies, crushed
⅓ c. butter, melted
½ c. semi-sweet chocolate chips, melted

Mix pecans, cookies and butter together; press into the bottom and up the sides of a greased 9" springform pan. Drizzle with chocolate; chill until chocolate is firm.

Pour Filling into crust; bake at 300 degrees for one hour and 10 minutes. Cool completely. Cover and chill 8 hours. Spread Topping over cake. Remove sides of pan. Makes 12 servings.

**Filling:**
2 8-oz. pkgs. cream cheese, softened
1½ c. semi-sweet chocolate chips, melted and cooled
1 c. brown sugar, packed
4 eggs
1 c. sour cream
⅓ c. cold coffee
2 t. vanilla extract

Combine all ingredients; blend until smooth.

**Topping:**
⅔ c. whipping cream
¼ c. sugar
½ c. semi-sweet chocolate chips

Heat whipping cream and sugar over low heat, whisking constantly. Add chocolate chips, whisking until smooth.

*Sandy Stacy*
*Medway, OH*

**Chocolate-Cappuccino Cheesecake**

*The richness of Red Velvet Cake will become a delicious tradition at your house!*

Red Velvet Cake

## Red Velvet Cake

*My grandma and aunt make this wonderful cake for my birthday and again for Christmas. The homemade frosting is scrumptious...well worth the time!*

18¼-oz. pkg. fudge marble
    cake mix
1 t. baking soda
1½ c. buttermilk
2 eggs, beaten
1-oz. bottle red food coloring
1 t. vanilla extract

Combine dry cake mix, fudge marble packet and baking soda in a medium bowl; add remaining ingredients. Blend with an electric mixer on low speed until moistened.

Beat on high speed for 2 minutes. Pour batter into 2 greased and floured 9" round cake pans. Bake at 350 degrees for 30 to 35 minutes or until cake tests done. Cool in pans for 10 minutes; turn out onto a wire rack. Cool completely; if desired, freeze layers overnight to make cake easier to frost. Spread Vanilla Frosting between layers and on top and sides of cake. Makes 10 to 12 servings.

**Vanilla Frosting:**
5 T. all-purpose flour
1 c. milk
1 c. butter, softened
1 c. sugar
2 t. vanilla extract

Whisk flour and milk in a saucepan over medium-low heat until smooth. Bring to a boil; cook and stir for 2 minutes or until thickened. Cover and refrigerate until chilled.

In a medium bowl, blend butter and sugar; add chilled milk mixture. Beat for 8 minutes or until fluffy; stir in vanilla.

*Angela Miller*
*Jefferson City, MO*

Tangy Cranberry Breakfast Cake

## Tangy Cranberry Breakfast Cake

*Three heavenly layers!*

2 c. all-purpose flour
1⅓ c. sugar, divided
1½ t. baking powder
½ t. baking soda
¼ t. salt
2 eggs, divided
¾ c. orange juice
¼ c. butter, melted
2 t. vanilla extract, divided
2 c. cranberries, coarsely chopped
Optional: 1 T. orange zest
8-oz. pkg. cream cheese, softened

Combine flour, one cup sugar, baking powder, baking soda and salt in a large bowl; mix well and set aside. Combine one egg, orange juice, butter and one teaspoon vanilla in a small bowl; mix well and stir into flour mixture until well combined. Fold in cranberries and zest, if using. Pour into a greased 9" round springform pan and set aside.

Beat together cream cheese and remaining ⅓ cup sugar in a small bowl until smooth. Add remaining egg and one teaspoon vanilla; mix well. Spread over batter; sprinkle with topping. Place pan on a baking sheet; bake at 350 degrees for 1¼ hours or until golden. Let cool on wire rack for 15 minutes before removing sides of pan. Serves 12.

Topping:
6 T. all-purpose flour
¼ c. sugar
2 T. butter

Combine flour and sugar in a small bowl. Cut in butter with a fork until mixture resembles coarse crumbs.

*Linda Hendrix*
*Moundville, MO*

Hot Fudge Spoon Cake

## Hot Fudge Spoon Cake

*Heavenly!*

1 c. all-purpose flour
1¾ c. brown sugar, packed and divided
¼ c. plus 3 T. baking cocoa, divided
2 t. baking powder
¼ t. salt
½ c. milk
2 T. butter, melted
½ t. vanilla extract
1¾ c. hot water
Optional: vanilla ice cream

Combine flour, one cup brown sugar, 3 tablespoons cocoa, baking powder and salt in a medium bowl. Whisk in milk, butter and vanilla. Spread evenly in a slow cooker. Mix together remaining ¾ cup brown sugar and ¼ cup cocoa; sprinkle evenly over top of batter. Pour in hot water; do not stir. Cover and cook on high setting for 2 hours or until a toothpick inserted one inch deep comes out clean. Spoon warm cake into bowls; top with vanilla ice cream, if desired. Makes 6 servings.

*Sara Plott*
*Monument, CO*

Not a pineapple in sight…it's the sweet flavor of bananas and the crunch of walnuts in maple syrup that make Banana-Walnut Upside Down Cake so special. So indulgent!

## Banana-Walnut Upside Down Cake

*Here's a twist on an old-time favorite that was popular in the 1950s.*

1 c. brown sugar, packed
½ c. plus 2 T. butter, divided
3 T. pure maple syrup
¼ c. walnuts, coarsely chopped
    and toasted
4 ripe bananas, peeled and sliced
¾ c. sugar
1 egg
½ t. vanilla extract
1 c. all-purpose flour
2 t. baking powder
½ t. cinnamon
¼ t. salt
6 T. milk
Garnish: sweetened whipped cream

Combine brown sugar and ¼ cup butter in a saucepan; cook over low heat until butter melts and mixture is well blended. Pour in a 9" round cake pan, spreading to coat bottom of pan. Pour maple syrup over sugar mixture and sprinkle evenly with walnuts. Place banana slices in concentric circles over nuts, overlapping slightly and covering bottom.

Blend together sugar and remaining 6 tablespoons butter until fluffy in a large mixing bowl; add egg and vanilla, beating until well blended. Combine flour, baking powder, cinnamon and salt; gradually add to creamed mixture alternately with milk, beginning and ending with flour mixture. Spoon batter over bananas and bake at 325 degrees for 55 minutes or until a toothpick inserted in center comes out clean. Carefully run a knife around the edge of pan to loosen. Cool in pan on a wire rack 30 minutes; invert cake onto a serving platter. Let stand 3 minutes; remove cake from pan. Serve warm with whipped cream.

*Judy Clark*
*Jacksonville, FL*

**Banana-Walnut Upside Down Cake**

**Maple Nut Twist**

## Maple-Nut Twist

*Cinnamon and maple syrup mixed with chopped walnuts make the perfect pairing in this beautifully braided bread.*

1/2 c. milk
1/2 c. butter, divided
1 pkg. active dry yeast
1/4 c. warm water
1/3 c. plus 3 T. sugar, divided
1 1/2 t. salt
2 eggs, beaten
3 1/4 to 3 1/2 c. plus 2 T. all-purpose
　flour, divided
1/2 c. brown sugar, packed
1/2 c. chopped walnuts
1/4 c. maple syrup
1/2 t. cinnamon

1/2 t. maple extract
1 c. powdered sugar
1 to 2 T. water

In a saucepan, heat milk and 1/4 cup butter until butter is melted.

In a large bowl, dissolve yeast in warm water (110 to 115 degrees); add 3 tablespoons sugar, salt, eggs and 2 cups flour; beat until smooth. Blend in milk mixture. Add 1 1/4 to 1 1/2 cups flour until dough forms; knead until smooth. Cover and let rise in a warm place (85 degrees), away from drafts, 2 hours or until doubled in bulk. In a medium bowl, combine brown sugar, walnuts, remaining sugar, maple syrup, 1/4 cup softened butter, remaining 2 tablespoons flour and cinnamon; set aside. Punch dough down and divide in half; roll out each half into a 14"x8" rectangle. Spread walnut filling over each rectangle. Starting at long side, roll up dough jelly-roll style. With a sharp knife, cut down the center of the jelly-roll lengthwise; twist 2 pieces together to form a rope braid. Turn ends under and shape braid into a ring. Place dough in a greased 9" pie plate and let rise in a warm place one hour or until doubled in bulk. Bake at 350 degrees for 30 minutes or until golden. Mix together remaining ingredients; drizzle glaze over warm bread. Makes 16 to 20 servings.

## Cherry Nut Cake

*This moist and tender cake can be served for dessert or as a breakfast treat on Christmas morning.*

1¾ c. cake flour
1½ t. baking powder
¼ t. baking soda
½ t. salt
½ c. butter, softened
1 c. sugar
1 egg
1 egg white
¾ c. orange juice
¾ c. chopped pecans
½ c. cherries canned in water, drained and liquid reserved

Sift flour, baking powder, baking soda and salt together; set aside. Beat butter and sugar until fluffy; add egg and egg white and beat well. Gradually add flour mixture alternately with orange juice. Fold in pecans and cherries.

Pour into a greased and floured 6-cup Bundt® pan. Bake at 350 degrees for 45 to 50 minutes or until a toothpick inserted in center comes out clean. Cool on a wire rack for 5 minutes. Carefully run a knife around the edge of pan to loosen; cool completely on wire rack. Spoon Cherry Sauce over cake.

Cherry Sauce:
Juice from 14½-oz. can cherries in water
1 T. cornstarch
1 T. butter
21-oz. can cherry pie filling

Combine first 3 ingredients in a medium saucepan; heat over medium heat 3 minutes or until thickened. Stir in pie filling; cook one minute or until heated through.

*Lucille Pulliam*
*Fort Smith, AR*

A tangy sauce made with pie filling is the perfect topper for Cherry Nut Cake! Coconut lovers will delight in this rich and delicious Double-Coconut Cake.

Cherry Nut Cake

## Double-Coconut Cake

*A snowy white cake that is just as delicious as it is pretty.*

2¼ c. cake flour
2¼ t. baking powder
½ t. salt
1⅔ c. sugar
⅓ c. butter, softened
2 eggs
1 T. vanilla extract
14-oz. can coconut milk
⅔ c. sweetened flaked coconut, divided

Stir together first 3 ingredients in a medium bowl. Beat sugar and butter at medium speed with an electric mixer until fluffy. Add eggs, one at a time, beating after each addition. Stir in vanilla.

Add coconut milk alternately with flour mixture, beginning and ending with flour mixture. Pour batter into 2 greased and floured 9" round cake pans; bake at 350 degrees for 30 minutes or until a toothpick inserted in center comes out clean. Cool in pans on a wire rack for 10 minutes; remove from pans. Cool completely on wire racks.

Spread one cup Fluffy Coconut Frosting in between layers; sprinkle with ⅓ cup coconut. Spread remaining frosting on top and sides of cake. Sprinkle with remaining coconut; refrigerate until chilled. Serves 14.

### Fluffy Coconut Frosting:
4 egg whites
½ t. cream of tartar
⅛ t. salt
½ t. vanilla extract
¼ t. coconut extract
1 c. sugar
¼ c. water

Beat egg whites, cream of tartar, salt and extracts at high speed with an electric mixer until soft peaks form. Set aside. Combine sugar and water in a saucepan. Stir to dissolve sugar, then bring to a boil. Continue to boil, without stirring, until mixture reaches the soft-ball stage, or 234 to 243 degrees on a candy thermometer. Remove from heat and pour in a thin stream over egg white mixture. Blend until fluffy. Makes 5 cups.

*Debby Phillips*
*Lamar, IN*

**Double-Coconut Cake**

Easiest Pumpkin Cupcakes

## Easiest Pumpkin Cupcakes

*Short on time? Whip up these cupcakes in the blink of an eye using a spice cake mix.*

18¼-oz. pkg. spice cake mix
15-oz. can pumpkin
3 eggs
⅓ c. oil
⅓ c. water
16-oz. container cream cheese frosting

Combine cake mix, pumpkin, eggs, oil and water in a large bowl. Blend with an electric mixer on medium speed for 2 minutes. Spoon batter into 24 paper-lined muffin cups, filling each ¾ full. Bake at 350 degrees for 18 to 22 minutes or until toothpick tests clean. Cool in pans for 10 minutes; remove to wire racks. Cool completely. Spread cupcakes with frosting. Makes 2 dozen.

# Raspberry Truffle Cheesecake

*Garnish with whipped cream, raspberries and mint leaves for a beautiful presentation.*

1½ c. chocolate sandwich cookies, crushed (about 18 cookies)
2 T. butter, melted
4  8-oz. pkgs. cream cheese, softened, divided
1¼ c. sugar
3 eggs
1 c. sour cream
1 t. almond extract
2 6-oz. pkgs. chocolate chips
⅓ c. seedless raspberry jam
¼ c. whipping cream

In a small bowl, mix together cookies and butter. Press into bottom of a 9" springform pan; set aside.

In a mixing bowl, beat 3 packages of cream cheese and sugar at medium speed with an electric mixer until smooth. Add eggs, one at a time, beating at low speed just until combined. Add sour cream and almond extract; beat just until blended. Pour over crust; set aside.

Place one package of chocolate chips in a medium microwave-safe bowl; microwave 30 seconds to one minute or until melted. Add remaining package of cream cheese and jam to melted chocolate; blend until smooth. Drop chocolate mixture by rounded tablespoonfuls onto batter in pan; do not swirl. Bake at 325 degrees for one hour and 20 minutes. Remove from oven and run knife around sides of pan to remove sides. Cool completely in pan on a wire rack. Remove from pan and place on a serving platter or cake plate.

In a medium saucepan, heat remaining chocolate chips and whipping cream over low heat; stir until smooth. Spread over cheesecake. Cover and chill 8 hours. Serves 12 to 14.

*Deborah Hilton*
*Oswego, NY*

**Raspberry Truffle Cheesecake**

## Strawberry Cake

*Be gentle with the frosting so that it doesn't become too runny.*

18¼-oz. pkg. white cake mix
3-oz. pkg. strawberry gelatin mix
4 eggs
¾ c. oil
½ c. frozen strawberries, thawed
    and undrained
½ c. water

Combine all ingredients in a large mixing bowl. Beat at medium speed with an electric mixer until well blended. Pour into a greased and floured 13"x9" baking pan and bake at 350 degrees for 33 to 35 minutes; cool. Spread Frosting over cooled cake. Makes 12 to 15 servings.

**Frosting:**
¼ c. butter, softened
½ c. fresh strawberries, chopped,
    divided
16-oz. pkg. powdered sugar,
    divided

Beat butter at medium speed with an electric mixer until light and fluffy. Add ¼ cup strawberries and about ⅓ of sugar, beating until blended. Gradually add remaining sugar, beating until creamy. Fold in remaining ¼ cup strawberries. Makes 2½ cups.

*Melanie Wallace*
*Corinth, TX*

Strawberry Cake

Use a cake mix and strawberry gelatin to save time when you bake a Strawberry Cake.

## Sweet Potato Pound Cake

*This old-fashioned dessert will scent your kitchen with the aroma of cinnamon and spice as it bakes.*

1 c. butter, softened
1½ c. sugar
¼ c. brown sugar, packed
2½ c. sweet potatoes, peeled,
    cooked and mashed
4 eggs
1 T. vanilla extract
3 c. all-purpose flour
2 t. baking powder
1 t. baking soda
1 t. salt
1½ t. cinnamon
¼ t. nutmeg
¼ t. mace

In a bowl, beat butter and sugars until fluffy. Add sweet potatoes; beat thoroughly. Add eggs, one at a time, beating well after each addition; stir in vanilla. Whisk together remaining ingredients. Gradually add to butter mixture, beating at low speed until blended. Pour batter into a lightly greased and floured 10" tube pan. Bake at 350 degrees for one hour, or until cake tests done. Serves 10 to 12.

*Cindy Spears*
*Keithville, LA*

## Eggnog Pound Cake

*This is a cake that reminds me of sweet Christmases and favorite family gatherings.*

1 c. butter, softened
1 c. shortening
3 c. sugar
6 eggs
3 c. all-purpose flour
1 c. eggnog
1 t. lemon extract
1 t. vanilla extract
1 t. coconut extract
1 c. sweetened flaked coconut
Garnish: edible glitter, red berry
    sprinkles

Blend together butter and shortening using an electric mixer on medium speed. Gradually add sugar; beat until fluffy. Add eggs, one at a time, beating well after each addition. Use a spoon to stir in flour alternately with eggnog. Blend in extracts and coconut.

Pour into a greased and floured 10" Bundt® pan. Bake at 325 degrees for 1½ hours; cool for 10 minutes before removing from pan. Cool completely before spreading with Spice Frosting. Garnish with edible glitter and red berry sprinkles. Serves 12 to 14.

Spice Frosting:
2 T. butter, softened
2 oz. cream cheese, softened
2 c. powdered sugar
3 T. milk
⅛ t. cinnamon
pinch nutmeg

Blend together butter and cream cheese until smooth. Gradually add sugar alternately with milk; beat until smooth. Blend in cinnamon and nutmeg.

*Nancy Cohrs*
*Donna, TX*

## Tennessee Fudge Pie

*My mama has always made this pie for holiday meals ... people request it for church socials, parties and family suppers. It's a chocolate lover's dream!*

2 eggs, beaten
½ c. butter, melted and cooled
¼ c. baking cocoa
¼ c. all-purpose flour
1 c. sugar
2 t. vanilla extract
⅓ c. semi-sweet chocolate chips
⅓ c. chopped pecans
9-inch pie crust

Beat together eggs and butter in a large bowl. Add remaining ingredients except pie crust; mix well. Pour into pie crust. Bake at 350 degrees for 25 minutes, or until center is firm. Serves 8.

*Dusty Jones*
*Paxton, IL*

Eggnog Pound Cake

## Sour Cream Streusel Coffee Cake

*This sweet, nutty coffee cake can be made a day ahead…what a time saver for busy hostesses! Cool completely, then wrap in aluminum foil and store at room temperature.*

1 ¼ c. walnuts, coarsely chopped
1 ¼ c. brown sugar, packed
4 ½ t. cinnamon
4 ½ t. baking cocoa
3 c. cake flour
1 ½ t. baking powder
1 ½ t. baking soda
¾ t. salt
¾ c. butter, softened
1 ½ c. sugar
3 eggs
1 T. vanilla extract
6-oz. container sour cream
1 c. powdered sugar
1 T. milk

Mix walnuts, brown sugar, cinnamon and cocoa in a small bowl; set aside. Sift flour, baking powder, baking soda and salt into a medium bowl; set aside. With an electric mixer on medium speed, beat butter and sugar in a large bowl. Beat in eggs, one at a time; mix in vanilla. Add flour mixture and sour cream alternately into butter mixture in 3 additions; beat on high speed for one minute. Pour ⅓ of batter into a buttered 12-cup Bundt® pan; sprinkle with half of nut mixture. Spoon remaining batter over top. Bake at 350 degrees until a toothpick inserted near center comes out clean, about one hour. Cool cake in pan on a wire rack for 10 minutes; run a knife around pan sides to loosen. Turn cake out onto rack and cool for one hour. Transfer to a serving platter. Whisk powdered sugar and milk together in a small bowl and drizzle over cake. May be served warm or at room temperature. Serves 8 to 10.

*Kathy Terry*
*Delaware, OH*

# Tiny Turtle Cupcakes

*I give these little chocolate bites to my kids' soccer coaches for an end-of-the-season gift...and keep some for myself, too!*

2 1/2-oz. pkg. brownie mix
1/2 c. pecans, chopped
16-oz. container chocolate
    frosting
1/2 c. pecans, toasted and
    coarsely chopped

Prepare brownie batter according to package directions. Stir in chopped pecans. Fill paper-lined mini muffin cups 2/3 full. Bake at 350 degrees for 18 minutes, or until a toothpick tests clean. Cool cupcakes in tins on wire racks 5 minutes. Remove from tins; cool completely. Frost cupcakes; top with toasted pecans. Spoon Caramel Sauce evenly over cupcakes. Store in refrigerator. Makes 4 1/2 dozen.

**Caramel Sauce:**
12 caramels, unwrapped
1 to 2 T. whipping cream

Combine caramels and one tablespoon cream in a small saucepan; cook and stir over low heat until smooth. Add remaining cream as needed for desired consistency.

*Teresa Podracky*
*Solon, OH*

**Tiny Turtle Cupcakes**

# Delightful Desserts

If you think dessert should always taste as good as it looks, then you'll find plenty to love about this recipe collection! Chocolate is the theme for the tempting Chocolate-Covered Cherry Cups, Chocolate Chess Pie and Winslow Woopie Pies. For cinnamon lovers, Gingerbread with Lemon Sauce and Oatmeal Scotchies are sure to become new favorites. Remember, it's always better to make extras at Christmastime!

## Cheesecake Cranberry Bars

*These pebbly-topped holiday bars will disappear in a flash.*

2 c. all-purpose flour
1½ c. long-cooking oats, uncooked
¼ c. brown sugar, packed
1 c. butter, softened
12-oz. pkg. white chocolate chips
8-oz. pkg. cream cheese,
    softened
14-oz. can sweetened
    condensed milk
¼ c. lemon juice
1 t. vanilla extract
14-oz. can whole-berry
    cranberry sauce
2 T. cornstarch

In a large bowl, combine flour, oats and brown sugar; cut in butter until coarse crumbs form. Stir in chocolate chips; reserve 2½ cups of crumb mixture for topping. With floured fingers, press remaining mixture into a greased 13"x9" baking pan; set aside.

Beat cream cheese in a large bowl until creamy. Add condensed milk, lemon juice and vanilla; mix until smooth. Pour cream cheese mixture over crust. Combine cranberry sauce and cornstarch; spoon over cream cheese mixture. Sprinkle reserved crumb mixture over top. Bake at 375 degrees for 35 to 40 minutes, or until golden. Let cool and cut into bars. Makes 2 dozen.

*Linda Galvin*
*Ames, IA*

## Chocolate Fondue

*A fun dessert the whole family will love. Experiment with your favorite candy bars for a new twist.*

2  8-oz. chocolate candy bars with
    almonds
2 to 4 T. light cream
Optional: 1 t. cherry brandy or
    peppermint liqueur
Items for dipping: marshmallows,
    bananas and pineapple,
    maraschino cherries, pound
    cake, shortbread cookies

Melt chocolate over low heat. Add cream. Cook, stirring constantly, about 5 minutes or until thickened. Stir in liqueur, if using. To serve, spoon into a fondue pot and keep warm over heat source.

*Echo Renner*
*Meeteetse, WY*

303

## Chocolate-Covered Cherry Cups

*I created this simpler version of a more difficult recipe and I think they are wonderful. My grandchildren like to push the cherries in for me.*

20-oz. pkg. brownie mix
16-oz. jar maraschino cherries, drained, ½ c. juice
    reserved and divided
6-oz. pkg. semi-sweet chocolate chips
½ c. sweetened condensed milk

Prepare brownie mix according to package directions, using ¼ cup cherry juice plus water needed to equal amount of water called for in directions. Place paper liners in mini muffin cups; fill about ½ full of brownie batter. Push a cherry into each cup; bake at 350 degrees for 15 to 20 minutes. Remove baked cups in liners from muffin cups; let cool.

Combine chocolate chips and condensed milk in a small saucepan; stir over low heat until melted. Remove from heat; stir in remaining ¼ cup cherry juice as needed for frosting consistency. Place a dollop of warm frosting on each cherry cup; let cool. Makes 3 dozen.

*Robin Healy*
*Honeoye, NY*

Chocolate-Covered Cherry Cups

## Christmas Cherry-Berry Pie

*The cranberry sauce adds a special flavor to the all-time favorite cherry pie.*

21-oz. can cherry pie filling
16-oz. can whole-berry cranberry
    sauce
¼ c. sugar
3 T. quick-cooking tapioca,
    uncooked
1 t. lemon juice
¼ t. cinnamon
2 T. butter
2 T. milk

Combine all ingredients except butter and milk; let stand 15 minutes. Divide pastry in half; set one half aside. Roll half the dough out and line a 9" pie plate; add filling mixture. Dot with butter. Roll remaining dough into a 12-inch circle; cut into ¾-inch wide strips. Lay strips on pie at one-inch intervals; fold back alternate strips as you weave crosswise strips over and under. Trim crust even with outer rim of pie plate. Dampen edge of crust with water; fold over strips, seal and crimp. Brush lattice with milk. Bake at 400 degrees for 40 to 45 minutes, covering edge of crust with aluminum foil after 15 minutes to prevent browning. Serves 8.

Flaky Pastry:
3 c. all-purpose flour
1 c. plus 1 T. shortening
⅓ c. cold water
1 egg, beaten
1 T. vinegar
½ t. salt

Blend together flour and shortening. Add remaining ingredients; blend with an electric mixer on low speed.

*Joyce LaMure*
*Reno, NV*

Christmas Cherry-Berry Pie

## Sugar Cookie Pops

*You'll want to buy several containers of colored sugars and jimmies so you'll have plenty for coating these cookie balls.*

½ c. butter, softened
½ c. shortening
1 c. sugar
1 c. powdered sugar
2 eggs
¾ c. vegetable oil
2 t. vanilla extract
4 c. all-purpose flour
1 t. baking soda
1 t. salt
1 t. cream of tartar
Colored sugars, sparkling sugars
    and multicolored jimmies
4" white lollipop sticks

Beat butter and shortening at medium speed with an electric mixer until fluffy; add sugars, beating well. Add eggs, oil and vanilla, beating until blended.

Combine flour and next 3 ingredients; add to butter mixture, blending well. Cover and chill dough 2 hours or overnight.

Shape dough into 1½-inch balls. Roll each ball in colored sugar or jimmies in individual bowls, pressing gently, if necessary, to coat balls. Place 2 inches apart on ungreased baking sheets. Insert sticks about one inch into each cookie to resemble a lollipop.

Bake at 350 degrees for 10 to 11 minutes or until set. Let cool 2 minutes on baking sheets; remove cookie pops to wire racks to cool completely. Makes 4½ dozen.

## Grandma Mary's Shortbread

*I received this wonderful recipe 20 years ago from a dear friend who was like a grandmother to me.*

1 c. butter, softened
2 c. all-purpose flour
1/2 c. superfine sugar
2 T. cornstarch

Combine all ingredients in a medium bowl and knead to form a smooth dough. Roll out on a floured surface to 1/4-inch thick. Cut out with a cookie or biscuit cutter. Transfer to ungreased baking sheets. Bake at 275 degrees for 45 minutes; cool. Frost with Cream Cheese Frosting. Refrigerate until set or ready to serve. Makes about 3 dozen.

**Cream Cheese Frosting:**
4 oz. cream cheese, softened
1/4 c. butter, softened
1 t. vanilla extract
2 1/4 c. powdered sugar

With an electric mixer on medium speed, beat cream cheese and butter together. Add vanilla and mix well. On low speed, add powdered sugar until mixed. Beat on high speed for one minute.

*Kerry McNeil*
*Anacortes, WA*

Grandma Mary's Shortbread

## Velvety Lime Squares

*This frosty treat can be made ahead and is guaranteed to be a hit.*

3-oz. can flaked coconut, divided
2 c. vanilla wafer crumbs
¼ c. butter, melted
2 T. sugar
2 3-oz. pkgs. lime gelatin mix
2 c. boiling water
6-oz. can frozen limeade
    concentrate
3 pts. vanilla ice cream, softened
⅛ t. salt
3 drops green food coloring
Optional: chopped pecans

Spread ½ cup coconut on a baking sheet; toast at 375 degrees until lightly golden, about 5 minutes; set aside.

Blend together remaining coconut, vanilla wafer crumbs, butter and sugar; press into an 11"x7" baking pan. Bake at 375 degrees for 6 to 7 minutes; cool.

Stir together gelatin and boiling water; mix until gelatin dissolves. Add limeade, ice cream, salt and food coloring, stirring until smooth. Pour over crust; sprinkle with reserved toasted coconut and pecans, if desired. Cover and freeze until firm. Let stand at room temperature a few minutes before serving. Makes 15 servings.

*Kathy Unruh*
*Fresno, CA*

Velvety Lime Squares

## Orange-Ginger Biscotti

*These crispy cookies are perfect for dipping in tea. Wrap a handful in cellophane bags and give as gifts.*

⅔ c. almonds
2 c. all-purpose flour
2 t. ground ginger
2 t. baking powder
¼ c. butter, softened
½ c. brown sugar, packed
6 T. plus 2 t. sugar
2 T. orange zest
2 eggs, divided and beaten
½ t. vanilla extract
⅔ c. pistachios, chopped

Finely grind almonds, flour, ginger and baking powder in a food processor; set aside.

Beat butter in a large bowl at medium speed with an electric mixer until creamy; gradually add brown sugar and 6 tablespoons sugar, beating until light and fluffy. Add zest, one egg yolk and vanilla; beat until smooth. Gradually add almond mixture, beating until blended. Stir in pistachios.

Divide dough in half. Using floured hands, roll each half on a lightly floured surface into a ½-inch thick log. Arrange logs 4 inches apart on a greased and floured baking sheet. Cover with plastic wrap; refrigerate for one hour.

Brush dough with remaining egg yolk; sprinkle with remaining sugar. Bake at 350 degrees for 30 minutes or until golden and firm to the touch. Let cool for 10 minutes. Using a serrated knife, cut logs crosswise into ½-inch thick slices. Arrange slices cut-sides down on baking sheet. Bake at 300 degrees until golden on top, about 12 minutes. Turn over; bake an additional 12 minutes or until golden brown. Transfer biscotti to a wire rack; cool completely. Store in an airtight container at room temperature. Makes 1½ dozen.

*Carrie O'Shea*
*Marina Del Ray, CA*

Orange Meringue Pie

## Orange Meringue Pie

*Here's a twist on the traditional Lemon Meringue Pie.*

**9-inch pie crust**
**1 c. orange juice**
**1 c. orange sections**
**1 T. orange zest**
**1 c. plus 6 T. sugar, divided**
**¼ t. salt**
**5 T. cornstarch**
**3 egg yolks, beaten**
**2 T. lemon juice**
**2 T. butter**
**4 egg whites, room temperature**
**½ t. vanilla extract**

Place pie crust into a 9" pie plate. Fold edges under and flute. Prick bottom and sides with a fork. Bake at 450 degrees until golden. Remove from oven and let cool on a wire rack. Reduce oven temperature to 325 degrees.

Whisk together orange juice, orange sections, orange zest, one cup sugar, salt and cornstarch in a medium saucepan. Cook over medium-low heat, whisking constantly until thickened. Place egg yolks in a small bowl; gradually add half of orange mixture to egg yolks, whisking constantly. Return egg yolk mixture to remaining orange mixture in pan; cook over medium

heat 5 minutes or until thickened, stirring constantly. Remove from heat and stir in lemon juice and butter. Keep warm.

Beat egg whites and vanilla at high speed with an electric mixer until foamy. Beat in remaining sugar, one tablespoon at a time, until stiff peaks form. Set aside.

Pour orange filling into warm pie crust. Dollop meringue onto filling. Lightly spread dollops together in decorative swirls, completely sealing meringue to pie crust. Bake at 325 degrees for 22 to 25 minutes or until golden. Cool completely on a wire rack. Serves 8.

*Patricia Wesso*
*Westminster, C*

308

# Gingerbread with Lemon Sauce

*Nothing tastes like the holiday season more than homemade gingerbread!*

1 c. molasses
1 c. hot water
1/2 c. brown sugar, packed
1/2 c. shortening
1 egg
2 1/2 c. all-purpose flour
1 t. ground ginger
1 t. ground cloves
1 t. cinnamon
1 1/2 t. baking soda
1 1/2 t. baking powder
Garnish: whipped cream and
    lemon zest

Mix together molasses and hot water; set aside. Beat brown sugar and shortening in a large mixing bowl at medium speed with an electric mixer until fluffy. Add egg and beat until incorporated. Combine flour and remaining ingredients; add to brown sugar mixture alternately with molasses mixture, beginning and ending with flour mixture. Beat just until blended after each addition. Pour batter into a greased 9-inch square pan. Bake at 350 degrees for 35 to 45 minutes or until cake springs back when gently touched. Cut cake into squares and garnish, if desired; serve with Lemon Sauce. Makes 10 to 12 servings.

Lemon Sauce:
1/2 c. sugar
2 T. cornstarch
1 c. water
2 T. butter
1 T. lemon zest
1 T. lemon juice

Combine sugar and cornstarch in a medium saucepan; gradually stir in water. Bring to a boil over medium heat. Cook, stirring constantly, one minute or until thickened. Remove from heat; stir in remaining ingredients. Let cool until warm.

*Kathie Williams*
*Oakland City, IN*

**Gingerbread with Lemon Sauce**

## Chocolate Chess Pie

*My favorite winter recipe...Mom always made it at Christmas.*

½ c. butter
1½ 1-oz. sqs. unsweetened baking chocolate, chopped
1 c. brown sugar, packed
½ c. sugar
2 eggs, beaten
1 T. milk
1 t. all-purpose flour
1 t. vanilla extract
9-inch pie crust
Garnish: whipped cream

Melt butter and chocolate in a small saucepan over low heat; set aside. Combine sugars, eggs, milk, flour and vanilla in a medium bowl. Gradually add chocolate mixture, beating constantly. Pour into unbaked pie crust; bake at 325 degrees for 40 to 45 minutes. Let cool before serving. Garnish, if desired. Serves 6 to 8.

*Heidi Jo McManaman*
*Grand Rapids, MI*

## Apple-Gingerbread Cobbler

*My new favorite dessert...the flavors are scrumptious!*

14-oz. pkg. gingerbread cake mix, divided
¾ c. water
¼ c. brown sugar, packed
½ c. butter, softened and divided
½ c. chopped pecans
2 21-oz. cans apple pie filling
Optional: vanilla ice cream

Mix together 2 cups gingerbread cake mix and water until smooth; set aside.
Stir together remaining gingerbread cake mix and brown sugar; cut in ¼ cup butter until mixture is crumbly. Stir in pecans; set aside.
Combine pie filling and remaining ¼ cup butter in a large saucepan; cook, stirring often, for 5 minutes over medium heat or until thoroughly heated. Spoon apple mixture evenly into a lightly greased 11"x7" baking pan. Spoon gingerbread mixture over apple mixture; sprinkle with pecan mixture. Bake at 375 degrees for 30 to 35 minutes or until set. Serve with scoops of ice cream, if desired. Serves 8.

*Wendy Jacobs*
*Idaho Falls, ID*

Chocolate Chess Pie

Sugar Cookie Mittens

## Sugar Cookie Mittens

*Everybody needs a dependable cut-out cookie recipe for Christmas…this is mine! I collect cookie cutters and this works so well with them.*

2 c. butter, softened
1⅓ c. sugar
2 eggs, beaten
2 t. vanilla extract
5 c. all-purpose flour

Blend butter and sugar together; stir in eggs and vanilla. Add flour; mix until well blended. Shape into a ball; cover and chill for 4 hours to overnight. Roll out dough ¼-inch thick on a lightly floured surface; cut out with cookie cutters as desired. Arrange cookies on lightly greased baking sheets. Bake at 350 degrees for 8 to 10 minutes, until golden. Frost cookies when cool. Makes 4 dozen.

Frosting:
4½ c. powdered sugar
6 T. butter, melted
6 T. milk
2 T. vanilla extract
1 T. lemon juice
Optional: few drops food coloring

Combine all ingredients in a medium bowl. Beat with an electric mixer on low speed until smooth.

*Tina Knotts*
*Cable, OH*

311

Grab the kids, frosting and colorful sprinkles and have some family fun creating Emily's Gingerbread Cookies. Each little member of the gingerbread family will have his or her own personality! Little bits of red cherries make Santa's Whiskers a sweet cookie that everyone will love.

## Emily's Gingerbread Cookies

*This came from my daughter Emily's elementary class assignment. She unscrambled words to uncover the recipe… she wrote "flower" instead of "flour." I still have the paper and treasure it!*

Emily's Gingerbread Cookies

1/3 c. brown sugar, packed
1/3 c. shortening
2/3 c. molasses
1 egg, beaten
3 c. all-purpose flour
1 T. baking powder
1 1/2 t. ground ginger
1/2 t. salt
Garnish: Frosting (page 311)

Blend together brown sugar and shortening until light and fluffy. Beat in molasses. Add egg, beating well. In a separate bowl, sift together flour, baking powder, ginger and salt. Add flour mixture to sugar mixture; mix well. Cover and refrigerate for 2 hours. Divide dough into fourths. Roll out to 1/4-inch thickness. Cut with cookie cutters. Place on greased baking sheets. Bake at 350 degrees for 5 to 7 minutes, until dark golden. Cool slightly on pans before removing to wire racks to cool completely. Decorate as desired. Makes 2 dozen.

*Vickie*

## Oatmeal Scotchies

*These chewy, delicious cookies are favorites of my family. I used to bake them for my stepson before he went to college…he could almost eat the entire batch by himself!*

3/4 c. butter, softened
3/4 c. sugar
3/4 c. brown sugar, packed
2 eggs, beaten
1 t. vanilla extract
1 1/4 c. all-purpose flour
1 t. baking soda
1/2 t. salt
1/2 t. cinnamon
3 c. long-cooking oats, uncooked
11-oz. pkg. butterscotch chips

Beat together butter and sugars until light and fluffy. Add eggs and vanilla; beat well. In a separate bowl, combine flour, baking soda, salt and cinnamon. Gradually add flour mixture to butter mixture, beating until well blended. Stir in remaining ingredients; mix well. Drop by heaping teaspoonfuls 2 inches apart onto ungreased baking sheets. Bake at 375 degrees for 8 to 10 minutes, until golden. Cool slightly on baking sheets; remove to a wire rack to cool completely. Makes 4 dozen.

*Abigail Smith*
*Columbus, OH*

## Santa's Whiskers

*In years gone by, I always made dozens of Christmas cookies to share with family & friends. This recipe is one of my son's favorites…he just loves the maraschino cherries!*

1 c. butter, softened
1 c. sugar
2 T. milk
1 t. vanilla extract
2½ c. all-purpose flour
¾ c. maraschino cherries, drained and finely chopped
½ c. pecans, finely chopped
¾ c. sweetened flaked coconut

Blend together butter and sugar; mix in milk and vanilla. Stir in flour, cherries and pecans. Form dough into 2 logs, each 8 inches long. Roll logs in coconut to coat dough. Wrap in wax paper or plastic wrap; chill dough for several hours to overnight. Slice ¼-inch thick; place on ungreased baking sheets. Bake at 375 degrees until edges are golden, about 12 minutes. Makes 5 dozen.

*Kendra Walker*
*Hamilton, OH*

Santa's Whiskers

## Georgia Tea Cakes

*The perfect "company is coming" goodie! These are so easy to bake up in a jiffy…you probably already have all the ingredients in your kitchen. Yummy with tea or coffee and conversation.*

1 c. sugar
½ c. butter, softened
1 t. vanilla extract
1 egg, beaten
½ c. milk
2 to 2½ c. self-rising flour
Garnish: colored sugar

Mix together sugar, butter, vanilla, egg and milk. Stir in enough flour to make a stiff dough. Drop by teaspoonfuls onto greased baking sheets; sprinkle with colored sugar. Bake at 375 degrees for 9 to 10 minutes. Center should be soft when cooled. Makes about one dozen.

*Denise Jones*
*Fountain, FL*

NOEL

JOY

MERRY CHRISTMAS

313

**Winslow Whoopie Pies**

**Marshmallow Filling:**
2 c. powdered sugar
1/3 c. shortening
1/3 c. butter, softened
2 T. milk
6 T. marshmallow creme
1 t. vanilla extract

Combine all ingredients; stir until smooth.

*Carissa Ellerd*
*Thomaston, ME*

## Maple-Pecan Pie
*Great anytime, but seems to be just about perfect when served warm on a chilly day.*

4 eggs, lightly beaten
2/3 c. sugar
1/2 t. salt
6 T. butter, melted
1 c. maple syrup
1 1/2 c. pecan halves
9-inch unbaked pie crust
Garnish: whipped topping

Combine first 5 ingredients in a large bowl; stir well with a wire whisk until blended. Sprinkle pecan halves into pie crust; pour syrup mixture over pecans. Bake at 375 degrees for 15 minutes; lower oven temperature to 350 degrees and bake 25 more minutes or until center is set. Cover with aluminum foil after 25 minutes to prevent excessive browning, if necessary. Cool completely on a wire rack. Serve with whipped topping, if desired. Makes 8 servings.

*Peggy Bowman*
*Palisade, CO*

## Winslow Whoopie Pies
*This yummy and often-requested family recipe is a huge hit at any social gathering. I like to tint the filling with food coloring to match the occasion!*

1/3 c. baking cocoa
1 c. sugar
1 egg, beaten
1/3 c. oil
3/4 c. milk
2 c. all-purpose flour
1 t. baking soda
1/8 t. salt
1 t. vanilla extract
Optional: Christmas sprinkles, crushed peppermint candies

In a bowl, combine cocoa and sugar. In another bowl, beat egg and oil; add to cocoa mixture and stir in remaining ingredients except sprinkles and candies. Drop by rounded tablespoonfuls onto lightly greased baking sheets. Bake at 350 degrees for 15 minutes. Let cool. Frost the flat sides of half the cookies with Marshmallow Filling; top with remaining cookies. Roll edges in sprinkles or candies, if using. Makes one dozen.

Tiramisu

## Tiramisu

*No wonder this fabulous dessert is popular in many Italian restaurants!*

¾ c. sugar
2 c. milk, divided
6 egg yolks
¼ c. all-purpose flour
4 T. unsalted butter, cut into pieces
¼ c. light rum
2 t. pure vanilla extract
¾ c. mascarpone cheese
3 3-oz. pkgs. soft ladyfingers
2 c. espresso or very strong, freshly brewed coffee
Garnish: whipped cream, cocoa and chocolate curls

In a heavy saucepan over medium heat, combine sugar and all but 2 tablespoons of milk. Cook just until boiling and until sugar dissolves completely.

In a bowl, beat the egg yolks with reserved 2 tablespoons of milk and flour. Gradually add hot milk mixture to the egg mixture, stirring constantly with a wire whisk. Return mixture to saucepan. Cook over medium heat until mixture comes to a boil, whisking constantly. Boil 2 minutes or until thickened. Remove from the heat and strain into a clean bowl. Whisk in the butter, rum and vanilla. Cover the surface of custard with plastic wrap; refrigerate 2 hours or until completely cooled.

Place mascarpone cheese into a medium bowl, stirring to soften. Gradually fold in the cooled custard. Brush ladyfingers with espresso. Arrange ⅓ of ladyfingers on the bottom and sides of a trifle dish. Top with ⅓ of custard. Repeat layers twice. Refrigerate for at least one hour. Garnish with whipped cream, sifted cocoa and chocolate curls, if desired.

Individual Tiramisus:
Prepare recipe up to layering step. Divide mixture among 6 to 8 individual custard cups or small trifle dishes, repeating same layering method as above.

Maple Pecan Pie

## Blueberry Linzer Tarts

*Any flavor of preserves will work in these divine cookies!*

1 ¼ c. butter, softened
⅔ c. sugar
1 ½ c. almonds, ground
⅛ t. cinnamon
2 c. all-purpose flour
6 T. blueberry preserves
powdered sugar

Blend butter and sugar until light and fluffy. Stir in almonds, cinnamon and flour, ½ cup at a time. Cover and refrigerate for about one hour. On a lightly floured surface, roll out half of dough ⅛-inch thick. Cut out 24 circles with a ½-inch mini cookie cutter; leave remaining 12 circles uncut. Arrange one inch apart on ungreased baking sheets. Bake at 325 degrees for 10 to 12 minutes, until golden. Cool completely on a wire rack. Thinly spread preserves over solid circles; sprinkle cut-out cookies with powdered sugar. Carefully sandwich solid and cut-out cookies together. Spoon a little of remaining jam into cut-outs. Makes one dozen.

*Cathy Hillier*
*Salt Lake City, UT*

Add your own special decorating touch to Gingerbread Cookies. Pretty little holiday shapes let the preserves peek through, making Blueberry Linzer Tarts a fancy cookie treat.

**Blueberry Linzer Tarts**

## Gingerbread Cookies

*Just the smell of these cookies baking will get you in the Christmas spirit!*

½ c. butter, softened
½ c. brown sugar, packed
½ c. molasses
1 egg
3 c. all-purpose flour
1½ t. cinnamon
1 t. ground ginger
½ t. baking soda
½ t. salt
¼ t. baking powder

Beat butter and brown sugar until fluffy in a large bowl. Beat in molasses and egg. Combine remaining ingredients in another large bowl. Stir dry ingredients into butter mixture. Wrap dough in plastic wrap; chill one hour.

Roll out dough on a lightly floured surface to ⅛-inch thickness. Use cookie cutters to cut out 8 each of gingerbread men, stars and trees. Transfer to an ungreased baking sheet and bake at 350 degrees for 10 to 12 minutes. Transfer cookies to a wire rack to cool. Decorate with Royal Icing. Makes 2 dozen.

Royal Icing:
2 c. powdered sugar
3 T. warm water
1½ t. meringue powder

Beat powdered sugar, water and meringue powder in a medium bowl at high speed with an electric mixer 7 to 10 minutes or until stiff. Spoon icing into a pastry bag fitted with a small, round #3 decorating tip (refill bag as necessary). Keep icing tightly covered when not using to prevent drying.

# General Instructions

## Making Patterns

Place tracing or tissue paper over the pattern and draw over the lines. For a more durable pattern, use a permanent marker to draw over the pattern on stencil plastic.

## Sizing Patterns

**1.** To change the size of the pattern, divide the desired height or width of the pattern (whichever is greater) by the actual height or width of the pattern. Multiply the result by 100 and photocopy the pattern at this percentage.

**For example:** You want your pattern to be 8"h, but the pattern on the page is 6"h. So 8÷6=1.33x100=133%. Copy the pattern at 133%.

**2.** If your copier doesn't enlarge to the size you need, enlarge the pattern to the maximum percentage on the copier. Then repeat step 1, dividing the desired size by the size of the enlarged pattern. Multiply this result by 100 and photocopy the enlarged pattern at the new percentage. (For very large projects, you'll need to enlarge the design in sections onto separate sheets of paper.) Repeat as needed to reach the desired size and tape the pattern pieces together.

## Transferring Patterns to Fabric

*Pick the transfer method that works best with the fabric and project you've chosen. If you choose the method using a water-soluble fabric marker, check first on a scrap piece to make sure the floss colors won't bleed when you remove the marker lines.*

## TISSUE PAPER METHOD

Trace the pattern onto tissue paper. Pin the tissue paper to the felt or fabric and stitch through the paper. Carefully tear the tissue paper away.

## WATER-SOLUBLE FABRIC MARKER METHOD

Trace the pattern onto tissue paper or photocopy the design. Tape the pattern and fabric to a sunny window or light box; then, trace the pattern onto the fabric with the marker. After embroidering, lightly spritz the finished design with water to remove any visible markings.

## MESH TRANSFER CANVAS METHOD

Trace the pattern onto tissue paper and place mesh transfer canvas over the pattern. Using a permanent marker, trace the pattern onto the canvas. Place the marked canvas on the felt or fabric and draw over the pattern with a water-soluble marking pen, leaving a dashed line on the felt or fabric. After needle felting, stitching or cutting out the design, dampen any areas where the marking pen shows with a cotton or paper towel or a cotton swab to remove the marks.

## Drybrushing

Use this painting technique for an aged appearance. Without dipping in water, dip an old paintbrush in paint; wipe most of the paint off onto a dry paper towel. Lightly rub the brush across the surface and repeat for desired coverage.

## Making a Fabric Circle

Matching right sides, fold the fabric square in half from top to bottom and again from left to right. Tie one end of a length of string to a water-soluble fabric marker; insert a thumbtack through the string at the length indicated in the project instructions. Insert the thumbtack through the folded corner of the fabric. Holding the tack in place and keeping the string taut, mark the cutting line (Fig. 1).

**Fig. 1**

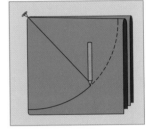

## Making Yo-Yos

To make each yo-yo, cut a circle as indicated in the project instructions. Press the circle edge ¼" to the wrong side and sew Running Stitches (page 319) around the edge with a doubled strand of thread. Pull the thread tightly to gather. Knot and trim the thread ends. Flatten the yo-yo with the small opening at the center of the circle.

## Working with Jump Rings

To open a jump ring without putting too much stress on the ring, use 2 pairs of needle-nose jewelry pliers to grasp each side of the ring near the opening. Pull one set of pliers toward you and push the other away to open the ring. Work the pliers in the opposite direction to close the ring.

## Embroidery Stitches
### BACKSTITCH

Bring the needle up at 1, go down at 2, come up at 3 and go down at 4. Continue working as shown in Fig. 1.

## Fig. 1

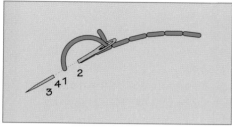

### BLANKET STITCH

Referring to Fig. 2, bring the needle up at 1. Keeping the thread below the point of the needle, go down at 2 and come up at 3. Continue working as shown (Fig. 3).

## Fig. 2

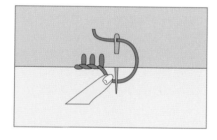

## Fig. 3

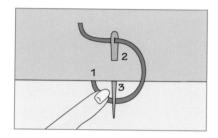

### CROSS STITCH

Bring the needle up at 1 and go down at 2. Come up at 3 and go down at 4 (Fig. 4).

## Fig. 4

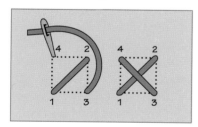

For horizontal rows, work the stitches in 2 journeys (Fig. 5).

## Fig. 5

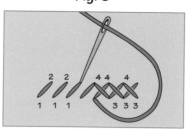

### FRENCH KNOT

Referring to Fig. 4, bring the needle up at 1. Wrap the floss once around the needle and insert the needle at 2, holding the floss end with non-stitching fingers. Tighten the knot; then, pull the needle through the fabric, holding the floss until it must be released. For a larger knot, use more strands; wrap only once.

## Fig. 4

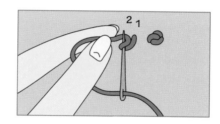

### LAZY DAISY

Bring the needle up at 1; take the needle down at 2 to form a loop and bring the needle up at 3. Keeping the loop below the point of the needle (Fig. 5), take the needle down at 4 to anchor the loop.

## Fig. 5

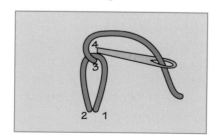

### RUNNING STITCH

Referring to Fig. 6, make a series of straight stitches with the stitch length equal to the space between stitches.

## Fig. 6

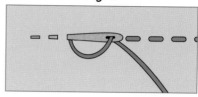

### SATIN STITCH

Referring to Fig. 7, come up at odd numbers and go down at even numbers with the stitches touching but not overlapping.

## Fig. 7

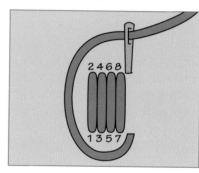

### STEM STITCH

Referring to Fig. 8, come up at 1. Keeping the thread below the stitching line, go down at 2 and come up at 3. Go down at 4 and come up at 5.

## Fig. 8

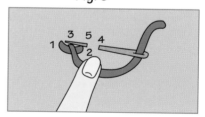

### STRAIGHT STITCH

Referring to Fig. 9, come up at 1 and go down at 2.

## Fig. 9

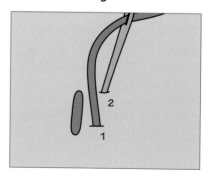

319

## Felted Wool Balls

Pour 6 cups of hot water in a plastic basin; mix in 4 tablespoons of liquid dishwashing detergent. Tear roving into 4" to 5" long sections.

**For a foam-based ball**, dip a foam ball in the soapy water (wearing rubber gloves if desired). Use dry fingers to tightly wrap a piece of roving around the wet ball. Roll the ball in your hands for a few minutes to help the fibers interlock. Dip the ball in the water again and add more roving, wrapping in a different direction. Repeat until the ball is well covered (some shrinkage will occur as it dries). Allow the ball to dry overnight.

**For an all-wool ball**, squeeze a fist-sized piece of roving into a tight ball. Dip the ball in the soapy water (wearing rubber gloves if desired) and squeeze several times to shape the ball. Add one new length of dry roving at a time, wrapping in a different direction. Roll the ball in your hands for a few minutes between each added layer to help the fibers interlock. This ball will shrink quite a bit more than a foam-based ball, so make it larger than your desired finished size. Allow the ball to dry overnight.

## Needle Felting

*Visit leisurearts.com to view a short needle felting Webcast.*

Apply wool felt appliqués, yarn or roving to background fabric using a needle felting tool and mat (Fig. 1). Lightly punch the needles to interlock the fibers and join the pieces without sewing or gluing (Fig. 2). The brush-like mat allows the needles to easily pierce the fibers. We used the Clover Felting Needle Tool to make our projects...it has a locking plastic shield that provides protection from the sharp needles. Felt, wool and woven cotton fabrics all work well as background fabrics.

**Fig. 1**

**Fig. 2**

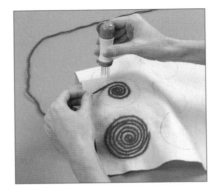

## Felting

*For the felting process to work, choose an item with wool content of 60% or higher.*

**1.** Set your top-loading washing machine for a HOT wash cycle and a COLD rinse cycle. Add about a tablespoon of laundry detergent.
**2.** Place the item in a tight-mesh lingerie or sweater bag and toss into the machine. Check every 2-3 minutes during the agitation part of the wash cycle to keep an eye on the amount of felting and the final size. A properly felted item has shrunk to the desired size and the stitches are no longer easy to see. You may want to wear rubber gloves for this, as the water can be very hot.
**3.** Once the item has felted to your satisfaction, remove it from the washer, spin out the wash water and then run the item through the cold rinse part of the cycle. To avoid setting permanent creases, don't let the item go through the spin portion of the cycle.

**4.** While wet, shape the item, stretching it to the finished size. Let the item air dry, which may take a day or two depending on the weather.

## Shaping Eye Loops

Bend the end of a wire length or head pin to a 90° angle (Fig. 1). Repositioning the round nose pliers as needed, bend the wire end into a small loop (Fig. 2). Cut off any excess wire (Fig. 3). To open an eye loop, follow the instructions for opening a jump ring.

**Fig. 1**

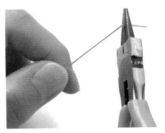

**Fig. 2**

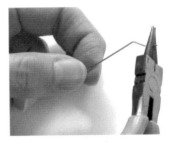

**Fig. 3**

## Pom-Poms

Cut a 4"-long cardboard strip half the diameter of the pom-pom you want to make. Place an 8" piece of yarn along one long edge of the strip. Follow Fig. 1 to wrap yarn around and around the strip and yarn piece (the more you wrap, the fluffier the pom-pom). Tie the wound yarn together tightly with the 8" piece. Leaving the tie ends long to attach the pom-pom, cut the loops opposite the tie; then, fluff and trim the pom-pom into a smooth ball.

### Fig. 1

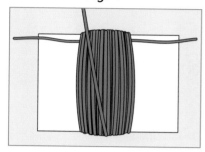

## Knit

### ABBREVIATIONS

| | |
|---|---|
| cm | centimeters |
| K | knit |
| mm | millimeters |
| P | purl |
| PSSO | pass slipped stitch over |
| st(s) | stitch(es) |
| tog | together |
| YO | yarn over |

★ — work instructions following ★ as many **more** times as indicated in addition to the first time.
( ) or [ ] — work enclosed instructions **as many** times as specified by the number immediately following **or** work all enclosed instructions in the stitch or space indicated **or** contains explanatory remarks.
colon (:) — the number(s) given after a colon at the end of a row denote(s) the number of stitches you should have on that row.

### GAUGE

Exact gauge is **essential** for proper size. Before beginning your project, make the sample swatch given in the individual instructions in the yarn and needle specified. After completing the swatch, measure it, counting your stitches and rows carefully. If your swatch is larger or smaller than specified, make another, changing needle size to get the correct gauge. Keep trying until you find the size needles that will give you the specified gauge.

### CHANGING COLORS

When changing colors, always pick up the new color yarn from **beneath** the dropped yarn and keep the color which has just been worked to the left (Fig. 1). This will prevent holes in the finished piece.

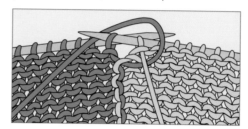

### MARKERS

As a convenience to you, we have used markers to help distinguish a pattern. Place markers as instructed. You may use purchased markers or tie a length of contrasting color yarn around the needle. When you reach a marker on each row, slip it from the left needle to the right needle; remove it when no longer needed.

### INCREASE

Knit the next stitch but do **not** slip the old stitch off the left needle (Fig. 1a). Insert the right needle into the **back** loop of the **same** stitch and knit it (Fig. 1b), then slip the old stitch off the left needle.

### Fig. 1a and Fig. 1b

### YARN OVERS
**After a knit stitch, before a purl stitch**
Bring yarn forward **between** the needles, then back **over** the top of the right hand needle and forward **between** the needles again, so that it is now in position to purl the next stitch (Fig. 2a).

### Fig. 2a

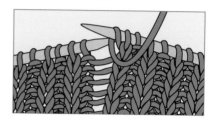

**After a purl stitch, before a knit stitch**
Take yarn **over** right hand needle to the back, so that it is now in position to knit the next stitch (Fig. 2b).

### Fig. 2b

### KNIT 2 TOGETHER
(abbreviated K2 tog)
Insert the right needle into the **front** of the first two stitches on the left needle as if to **knit** (Fig. 3); then, **knit** them together as if they were one stitch.

### Fig. 3

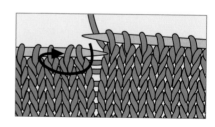

(continued on next page)

## PURL 2 TOGETHER
(abbreviated P2 tog)

Insert the right needle into the **front** of the first two stitches on the left needle as if to **purl** (Fig. 4); then, **purl** them together as if they were one stitch.

**Fig. 4**

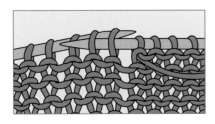

## SLIP 1, KNIT 1, PASS SLIPPED STITCH OVER
(abbreviated slip 1, K1, PSSO)

Slip one stitch as if to **knit** (Fig. 5a). Knit the next stitch. With the left needle, bring the slipped stitch over the knit stitch (Fig. 5b) and off the needle.

**Fig. 5a**

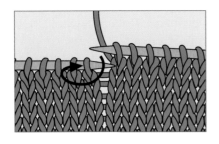

**Fig. 5b**

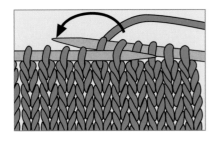

## PICKING UP STITCHES

When instructed to pick up stitches, insert the needle from the **front** to the **back** under two strands at the edge of the worked piece (Fig. 6). Put the yarn around the needle as if to **knit**; then, bring the needle with the yarn back through the stitch to the right side, resulting in a stitch on the needle. Repeat this along the edge, picking up the required number of stitches. A crochet hook may be helpful to pull the yarn through.

**Fig. 6**

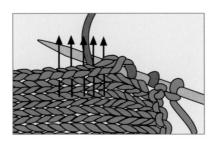

## WEAVING SEAMS

With the **right** side of both pieces facing you and edges even, sew through both sides once to secure the seam. Insert the needle under the bar **between** the first and second stitches on the row and pull the yarn through (Fig. 7). Insert the needle under the next bar on the second side. Repeat from side to side, being careful to match rows. If the edges are different lengths, it may be necessary to insert the needle under two bars at one edge.

**Fig. 7**

# Crochet
## ABBREVIATIONS

| | |
|---|---|
| ch(s) | chain(s) |
| cm | centimeters |
| dc | double crochet(s) |
| FP | Front Post |
| FPdc | Front Post double crochet(s) |
| mm | millimeters |
| Rnd(s) | Round(s) |
| sc | single crochet(s) |
| sp(s) | space(s) |
| st(s) | stitch(es) |
| YO | yarn over |

★ — work instructions following ★ as many **more** times as indicated in addition to the first time.

† to † — work all instructions from first † to second † **as many** times as specified.

( ) or [ ] — work enclosed instructions **as many** times as specified by the number immediately following **or** work all enclosed instructions in the stitch or space indicated **or** contains explanatory remarks.

**colon (:)** — the number(s) given after a colon at the end of a row or round denote(s) the number of stitches you should have on that row or round.

## GAUGE

Exact gauge is **essential** for proper size. Before beginning your project, make the sample swatch given in the individual instructions in the yarn and hook specified. After completing the swatch, measure it, counting your stitches and rows or rounds carefully. If your swatch is larger or smaller than specified, make another, changing hook size to get the correct gauge. Keep trying until you find the size hook that will give you the specified gauge.

## MARKERS

Markers are used to help distinguish the beginning of each round being worked. Place a 2" (5 cm) scrap piece of yarn before the first stitch of each round, moving marker after each round is complete.

## JOINING WITH Sc

When instructed to join with sc, begin with a slip knot on the hook. Insert the hook in the stitch or space indicated, YO and pull up a loop, YO and draw through both loops on the hook.

## BACK RIDGE

Work only in loops indicated by arrows (Fig. 1).

### Fig. 1

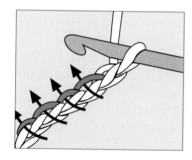

## FREE LOOPS OF BEGINNING CHAIN

When instructed to work in free loops of a chain, work in loop indicated by arrow (Fig. 2).

### Fig. 2

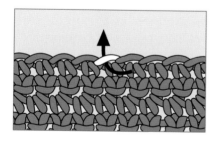

## FRONT POST STITCH

Work around post of stitch indicated, inserting hook in direction of arrow (Fig. 3).

### Fig. 3

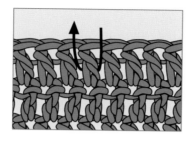

## REVERSE SINGLE CROCHET

(abbreviated reverse sc)

Working from left to **right**, ★ insert hook in st to **right** of hook (Fig. 4a), YO and draw through, under and to left of loop on hook (2 loops on hook) (Fig. 4b), YO and draw through both loops on hook (Fig. 4c) **(reverse sc made,** Fig. 4d**)**; repeat from ★ around.

### Fig. 4a

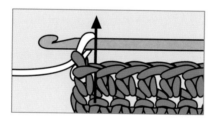

### Fig. 4b

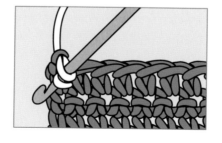

### Fig. 4c

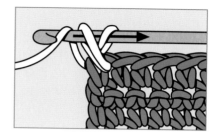

### Fig. 4d

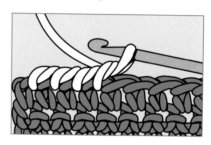

## WHIPSTITCH

Place two Strips with **wrong** sides together. Sew through both pieces once to secure the beginning of the seam, leaving an ample yarn end to weave in later. Insert the needle from **front** to **back** through **both** loops on **both** pieces (Fig. 5). Bring the needle around and insert it from **front** to **back** through next loops of both pieces. Continue in this manner across, keeping the sewing yarn fairly loose.

### Fig. 5

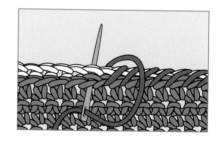

GOING HOME FOR THE HOLIDAYS IS GOOD FOR THE HEART ★ SURPRISE SOMEBODY SPECIAL!

# Project Instructions

## Dapper Doorman
(also shown on page 9)
- party balloons (inflated to 9" dia. for the head, two 12" elongated for the arms and four 33" elongated for the body)
- masking tape
- foam brush
- matte decoupage glue
- newspaper
- serrated knife
- white spray primer
- pink, red, black and white acrylic paints
- paintbrushes
- clear acrylic spray sealer
- mica flakes
- 2" dia. foam ball, cut in half for the nose
- air-drying clay (we used Creative Paperclay®)
- hot glue gun
- 14" dia. wooden charger
- drill with ³/₈" bit
- two 22" lengths of ³/₈" dia. dowel
- two ³/₄" dia. black snaps for eyes
- five ³/₈" dia. black snaps for mouth
- felt hat
- scarf
- medium-gauge wire
- wire cutters
- mini tinsel tree
- child's snow shovel

Keep this warm-hearted snowman on a covered porch for protection from snow or rain. Use decoupage glue for all gluing unless otherwise noted. Use primer and sealer in a well-ventilated area and allow to dry after each application.

1. Tape the 4 body balloons together (Fig. 1). To papier-mâché the body, brush glue on both sides of torn newspaper strips; overlapping the edges, cover all but the bottom end of the body with the strips. Allow to dry; then, apply one or 2 more layers. Let dry completely.

2. To add the head, cut away a 6" diameter hole at the top of the body. Tape the head balloon in place and cover the head with papier-mâché, overlapping strips onto the body to join at the neck (Fig. 2). Add papier-mâché arms in the same manner, positioning each arm as desired and joining to the body at the shoulder (Fig. 3). Allow to dry; then, apply one or 2 more layers to the head and arms.

3. When completely dry, trim the bottom edge of the snowman with the knife. Prime the snowman; then, paint the cheeks pink. Spray with several coats of sealer and while the last coat is still wet, sprinkle with mica flakes. Shake the excess onto newspaper.

4. Follow manufacturer's instructions to cover the foam nose with clay; allow to dry. Paint, then seal the nose. Hot glue the nose to the snowman.

5. For the base, paint the charger black; apply sealer. Invert the charger and drill 2 holes near the center, 4" apart. Insert the dowels. Brush a little glue on the charger and sprinkle with mica flakes. Place the snowman over the dowels.

6. Glue on the snap eyes and mouth. Add the hat and scarf (we brushed a little white paint on the hat and while wet, sprinkled it with mica flakes). Wire the tree to one arm and prop the shovel against the other.

**Fig. 1**    **Fig. 2**    **Fig. 3**

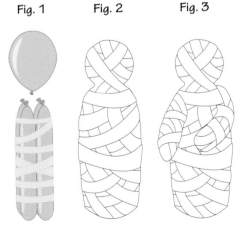

## Snowman Trio
(also shown on page 20)
- serrated knife
- foam cones (we used three 6" tall cones)
- hot glue gun
- foam balls (we used four 1½" dia. balls)
- air-drying clay (we used Creative Paperclay®)
- tinsel chenille stems
- cream, red, black and orange acrylic paints
- paintbrushes
- flannel scraps
- decoupage glue
- small foam brush
- ³/₁₆" dia. black buttons
- ⅛"w ribbon
- clear glitter
- mica flakes (optional)
- paper plate
- plates (ours are 7¼" dia.)
- miniature marshmallows, air-dried
- bell jars (ours are 10"h)

These simple snowmen are sure to make you smile!

1. For each snowman, trim away the pointed end of the cone and hot glue a ball on top. Follow manufacturer's instructions to cover the snowman with clay, adding a carrot-shaped nose and smoothing the neck seam with your finger. Poke holes and insert chenille stem arms; allow to dry completely.

2. For the "knit" hat, form a cone shape with clay, press it onto the head and bend it into a hat shape. Allow the hat to dry.

3. For the top hat, cut a cylinder shape from a foam ball and hollow out the bottom. Mold clay around the top and sides of the cylinder. For the brim, press a flat clay circle to the bottom and cut a hole in the center. Slice one sliver at a time from the head until the hat fits well. Allow the hat to dry.

4. Paint the snowmen cream; then, paint the hats and face details. Tie a strip of flannel around a neck for a scarf. Glue buttons to a belly and a ribbon band around the top hat.

5. Brush glue on the snowmen, including the scarves and hats; while wet, sprinkle with glitter (we added mica flakes to the brim of the top hat). Shake the excess onto the paper plate.

6. Place each snowman on a plate surrounded by marshmallows. Cover with a bell jar.

## Felted Ball Wreath

(continued from page 13)

2. Using 6 strands of floss, run the needle through the bottom of a large ball (Fig. 1) and tie it to the 2 center wires of the wreath form. Repeat with the remaining large balls.

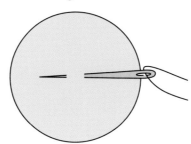

**Fig. 1**

3. Attach each medium ball to the outer wire and each small ball to the inner wire. Spot glue the balls to each other for stability.

4. Add a ribbon bow and streamers to the outer wire at the top of the wreath form. Attach a ring to the back for the hanger.

## Bell Mini-Banner Ornament

(also shown on page 17)
- red vinyl
- apple green felt
- pinking shears
- ivory acrylic paint and round paintbrush
- three 25mm green jingle bells
- 1½" D-ring
- fabric glue
- 15mm silver jingle bell
- twill tape

1. Use pinking shears to cut a ¼"x6¼" felt piece and the long edges of a 2"x12" vinyl piece.

2. Matching the short ends, fold the vinyl in half. Slide the felt piece between the vinyl layers and trim the upper corners of the felt and vinyl. Paint dots on the vinyl. Sew the green jingle bells to the top vinyl layer.

3. Slip the D-ring between the vinyl and felt layers. Glue the layers together. Knot the silver bell to the D-ring with twill tape.

## Fabric Christmas Cookie Ornaments

(continued from page 24)

1. Trace patterns (page 375) onto tracing paper. For each ornament, use pinking shears to cut 2 pattern pieces from muslin fabric, having wrong sides together and cutting just outside of the outside lines on the pattern. Cut 2 layers of batting, making shapes about ⅜" smaller on all edges than pattern shapes so that batting fits inside the outside running stitch lines.

2. Using washable marking pen, mark stitching lines on fabric front. For ornaments with smaller felted wool pieces, apply to center of fabric with fusible webbing and then embroider and embellish. If adding seed beads, sew on using invisible nylon thread. Sew on buttons, as desired.

3. After fronts are embellished, layer backing fabric, batting hanging loop and decorated front, with wrong sides together. Pin in place. Stitch around outside edges, ⅛" from outside edges, using 2 strands embroidery floss to make Running Stitches (page 319). Start and stop at the top where the hanger is inserted between fabric layers, stitching over and through hanging ribbon to reinforce loop securely.

## Gingerbread House Garland

(continued from page 25)

4. Flatten the paper garland. Cut the small pieces for the doors and windows from the tissue paper. Glue behind the openings in the houses. Let dry.

5. Referring to the lines on the patterns, add details using the fabric paint. Let dry. Glue or tape the finished pieces together as needed to make the length desired.

## Jolly Frame Set

(continued from page 33)

2. Use your computer to print 5" tall J, O, L, L, Y letters in a cute font. Use removable tape to adhere the letter patterns to cardstock. Cut out the letters with the craft knife. Remove the patterns.

3. Cut and punch scrapbook paper highlights for each letter. Glue the highlights to the letters. Punch several scrapbook paper snowflakes.

4. Use double-sided tape to adhere the letters and snowflakes to the bottom glass pieces. Add the top pieces and replace the glass in the frames.

## Counting the Days Calendar

(also shown on page 30)

Paint a 12"x12" square wood plaque; glue a ribbon border around the edges. Adhere letter stickers, spelling "Merry Christmas," on 1¼" punched cardstock circles. Paint and then decorate a 4"x4" wood square with scrapbook paper, burlap and stickers. Glue the letters and wood square to the plaque. Attach layered cardstock backgrounds using long nails to the left of the square. Hang number tags (use stickers for the numbers and trims) on the nails to count down the days to Christmas.

## Matchbox Garland

(also shown on page 30)

Use decorative papers, ribbons, 3-D embellishments and number stickers to decorate small matchboxes. Place a Christmas treat in each box and glue a twill tape hanger to the inside back of the box cover. Attach each hanger to a ribbon garland with a small brad. We also mixed in a few vintage children's nursery rhyme rubber stamps. Bells, charms and tiny ornaments tied on with floss top off each hanger.

## Mini Gift Sacks

(also shown on page 31)

Matching short ends and right sides, fold a 4"x9½" fabric piece in half. Use a ¼" seam allowance to sew the side seams, catching a piece of twill tape in one side seam. Turn the sack right side out and press the top edge ¾" to the inside. Leaving a long tail at the beginning and end, start at one seam and work embroidery floss Running Stitches (page 319) around the top edge; trim and knot the ends together to complete the drawstring. Use an office-type date stamp, small charms, mini safety pins, embroidery stitches, ornaments and buttons to decorate the twill tape labels.

## Tree Stocking

(also shown on page 29)
- two 14"x23" pieces of green felt
- pinking shears
- vintage tablecloth with large motif
- fabric glue
- assorted rickrack
- assorted buttons
- clear nylon thread

326

1. Enlarge the Poinsettias Stocking pattern (page 390, ignoring the poinsettia design) to 206%. Use the enlarged pattern and pinking shears to cut 2 green felt stocking pieces. For the hanger, cut a 1"x5" felt piece; set aside.

2. Trim ½" from all edges of the pattern. Using the trimmed pattern, decide placement of the motif and cut the tablecloth stocking piece. Glue the rickrack to the toe and cuff areas. Sew buttons on the cuff and tree.

3. Centering the tablecloth piece on top, stack the stocking pieces and use clear thread to zigzag all 3 layers together, leaving the top edge open. Glue the top edge of the tablecloth stocking in place. Sew a button and the hanger to the upper right corner.

## Glittered Snowflake Ornament

(also shown on page 32)
• hot glue gun
• ⅝", ½" and ¼" dia. wooden beads (we used 6 of each size)
• ¾" dia. wooden bead
• sandpaper
• spray primer
• spray paint
• small foam brush
• decoupage glue
• glitter to match paint color
• paper plate
• ⅛"w ribbon

Make snowflake ornaments any color you like! Hot glue the ⅝" beads around the large bead, with the holes radiating away from the center. Glue the ½" beads next, then the small beads, placing one with the

hole turned sideways (for the ribbon hanger to go through). Fill in the outer holes with hot glue; sand any rough edges. Prime, then spray paint the ornament in a well-ventilated area; allow to dry. Brush decoupage glue over one side of the snowflake and sprinkle with glitter. Shake the excess onto the paper plate. Repeat to glitter the other side. Tie a ribbon hanger on the ornament.

## Girl & Tree Silhouette

(also shown on page 33)
• fine-grit sandpaper
• red spray paint
• unfinished wood frame (5"x7" opening)
• clear acrylic spray sealer
• double-sided removable tape
• red cardstock
• craft knife and cutting mat
• spray adhesive
• scrapbook papers
• ⅜"w green striped ribbon
• jingle bells
• hot glue gun
• snowflake punch

*Use spray paint, sealer and spray adhesive in a well-ventilated area.*

1. Lightly sand, then spray paint the frame. Apply sealer to the frame.

2. Enlarge the pattern on page 378 to 142%. Tape the pattern to cardstock. Cut out the image with the craft knife. Remove the pattern.

3. Using spray adhesive, adhere scrapbook paper to the frame backing; trim. Place the backing in the frame and adhere the image to the paper.

4. Wrap ribbon around the frame, add bells and tie a bow. Hot glue the ribbon to the frame back. Using spray adhesive, adhere punched scrapbook paper snowflakes to the frame.

## Cranberry Ice Globes

(also shown on page 34)
• round balloons
• birdseed, orange peel
• dried cranberries or other dried fruit
• funnel (optional)
• water; freezer

1. Drop the birdseed, dried fruit and orange peel into the empty balloon. (Use a funnel if necessary.) Fill the balloon with water and tie a knot at the top.

2. Place in the freezer, turning the balloon every 20 minutes until frozen. Remove from freezer and peel off balloon. Set outside in cold weather for the birds.

## Snowflakes Under Glass

(also shown on page 36)
• lightweight paper in desired color
• sharp scissors

(continued on next page)

- pencil
- charger, or underneath plate, in desired color
- one clear glass plate smaller than the charger plate

1. Use the patterns (page 378) or make your own snowflake patterns to measure the size desired for the plates you are using. Fold the paper as shown and with a pencil mark the areas to be cut out.
2. Use scissors to cut out the shapes. Unfold snowflake and press if desired using a cool iron. Place snowflake between plates.

## Twine-Tied Candles

(also shown on page 37)

- purchased candles in desired sizes
- twine in variegated colors
- paper embellishments, buttons or charms
- short straight pins

1. Starting at the back of the candle, pin the twine to the candle. Begin wrapping the candle until desired width.
2. Thread a button or other embellishment on another piece of twine and wrap and pin in place. Tie a bow and pin to the front of candle if desired.

**Never leave a burning candle unattended.**

## No-Sew Fabric Trims

(continued from page 37)

1. Trace pattern (page 396) onto tracing paper and cut out. Cut shapes desired from cotton fabric, being generous in cutting shapes to cover the area desired. Lay first piece of fabric over plastic foam ball. Press paring knife blade at outside cut edge to work raw edges into ball.
2. Place adjoining fabric slightly over the pressed edge of previous fabric piece and press knife edge over raw edge to work it into the ball. Cut a length of trim and fold it in half to make loop. Poke cut ends of loop into ball at top and glue in place. Glue lengths of trim over edges of fabric.

## Happy Snowmen Wreath

(also shown on page 39)

1. Enlarge and trace patterns (page 413) onto tracing paper and cut out. Lay pattern for ball wrappings onto cotton batting and cut out. Wrap balls in cotton batting and pull edges together to completely cover plastic foam balls. Glue edges in place. Wrap white cotton yarn around balls,

crossing yarns until ball is mostly covered. Some fleece pieces will show through.
2. Cut embellishments from scraps of felt, felted wool or fleece. **For Nordic hat,** cut one of pattern from felted wool. Place onto smaller ball and gather together top point about 1" from the end. Wrap length of embroidery floss tightly around end and knot at the back. Clip small pieces from the end of the point toward the wrapped string to make fringe. Chain stitch a length of thread from the ear points of the hat about 1½" down. Loop contrasting floss through the ends of the chained length and cut to make hat fringe.
3. **For ear muffs,** cut two circles from pattern. Roll cotton balls to make balls about 1" in size. Wrap fabric circles around balls and gather together at the back by stitching running stitches along the outside edges and pulling up thread tightly. Cut a thin strip of felted wool about 4½" long for the center of the ear muffs. Lay the strip over the ball at the top and pin in place, pushing straight pins through foam ball. Position muff circles over center band and tack in place by taking a couple hand stitches using matching sewing thread.
4. **For pointy stocking cap,** cut one of hat pattern from fabric desired. With right sides together, sew long slanted side seam using ¼" seam. Turn right side out. Slip over top of larger ball and fold up bottom for a little cuff. At end point, sew loops of embroidery thread and clip to make tassel.
5. **For hoodie,** cut one piece 3½" x 9" from desired fabric. Fold long edge under ½" to inside. Fold in half with short ends together and sew ¼" seam. Turn right side out and place over smaller ball. Cut a narrow strip of fabric about 9" long to tie into a bow. Stitch bow to bottom of hood with a few hand stitches.
6. Make scarves out of 1" wide strips of fabric, cutting ends in narrow pieces to make fringe. Loop around balls and knot in place. **For head band,** use 1" strip of felted wool and wrap around ball, tacking in place with a couple of hand stitches.
7. Make noses by cutting triangle-shaped patterns from orange felt. Fold in half and hand stitch close to edge to make a tube. Glue noses to balls. Glue beads to make

eyes and mouth on each ball. If using as ornaments, sew a length of embroidery floss to the top as a hanger and knot in place.

## Turtle Tic-Tac-Toe Toss
(also shown on page 42)
*Supplies and instructions are for six turtles and one game mat*

- 12"x18" sheet each of green and light green felt
- green and light green embroidery floss
- polyester fiberfill
- yellow, blue, light green and coral medium weight yarn
- dried beans
- 24"x24" square of red felt
- 3 yards of 1"w blue ribbon
- fabric marking pen

**1.** To make the Turtles, enlarge the patterns (page 391) to 200%. Using the enlarged patterns, cut 6 heads, 6 shells, 3 tails and 24 legs each from green and light green felt.
**2.** Matching the raw edges and working ⅛" from edges, use green floss and Running Stitches (page 319) to sew 2 green legs together leaving the straight edge open; stuff with fiberfill. Make 12 green legs. Repeat with light green floss and legs.
**3.** Repeat Step 2 to make 3 green and 3 light green heads. For eyes, thread a needle with light green or blue yarn; knot one yarn end and sew straight through the head. Knot the yarn close to the opposite side of the head; cut the yarn.
**4.** Leaving the beginning knot on the right side, use blue yarn to work 2 Running Stitch

circles and a Satin Stitch (page 319) dot in the centers of 3 light green shells. Use yellow yarn to work 8 Lazy Daisies (page 319) around each larger circle.
**5.** In the center of 3 green shells, work a large "X" using 2 strands of light green yarn; tack the "X" center to the shell with a Straight Stitch (page 319). Work 4 Lazy Daisies with light green yarn. Leaving the beginning knots on the right side, work 4 coral Lazy Daisies on the shell.
**6.** Fold tail as shown in Fig. 1; pin.

**Fig. 1**

**7.** Matching the wrong sides and raw edges, layer 1 light green plain shell and 1 light green embroidered shell. Pin 4 green legs, 1 green head and 1 green tail between the shells. Using green floss and leaving an opening for inserting beans, whipstitch the shells together, catching the head, legs, and tail in the stitching. Fill the shell with beans and sew the opening closed. Make 3 turtles with light green shells and 3 turtles with green shells.
**8.** To make the game mat, cut ribbon into four 24" lengths. Leaving the beginning knots on the right side, work yellow yarn Running Stitches to attach the ribbons 2½" from the red felt square edges; trim each ribbon end at an angle. Draw a nine-block grid of 6½" squares (Fig. 2). Work yellow yarn Running Stitches over the drawn lines.

**Fig. 2**

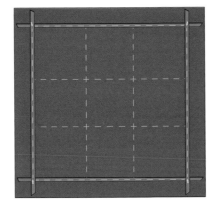

## Fun & Games Tree
(also shown on page 41)

Add a cheery touch to the children's playroom with a child-size tree decorated with ornaments made from vintage toys and displayed in a brightly colored wagon. Red corduroy fabric tucked around the tree base serves as a tree skirt. Fill the wagon with packages to create a movable holiday decoration for children of all ages.

## Horsie
(continued from page 44)

*Match right sides, raw edges and use a ½" seam allowance for all sewing.*
**1.** Center and fuse the interfacing to the wrong sides of the T-shirt and sweater pieces.

(continued on next page)

**2.** Enlarge the patterns (pages 387 and 388) to 250%. Using the enlarged gusset pattern, cut 1 gusset from the T-shirt piece. Using the enlarged body pattern, cut 2 bodies from the sweater pieces. Transfer the pattern markings to the wrong sides of the pieces.

**3.** Fuse web to the remaining T-shirt scraps. Using the enlarged pattern, cut 2 ears from the striped knit. Fuse the ears to the green felt and cut out about 1/2" beyond the striped ears.

**4.** For the back seam, sew the bodies together from the nose dot to the tail dot. To shape the nose, fold and stitch across a small triangle of fabric where the face curves (Fig. 1).

**Fig. 1**

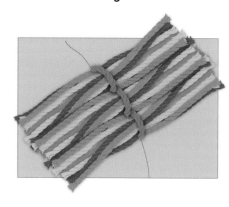

**5.** Matching the dots, pin the gusset and body pieces together. Leaving an opening for turning between one set of stars, sew the gusset to the body. Clip the curves and turn right side out.

**6.** Place a bag of beans in each foot and in the tummy area; stuff tightly with fiberfill. Hand sew the opening closed.

**7.** For the eyes, cut 2 5/8" circles from the blue felt. Pin the eyes in place. Using yellow yarn and leaving the beginning knot on the surface, run the needle through the center of one eye, through the head and come out in the opposite eye center. Knot the yarn close to the surface and trim. Work a Stem Stitch (page 319) mouth and Straight Stitch (page 319) eyelashes with brown floss.

**8.** For the tail, cut 28 18" yarn lengths; tie together at the center with another yarn piece. Place the bundle over the body/gusset intersection; tack in place and trim yarn ends.

**9.** For the mane, cut 180 9" yarn lengths. Separate yarn into 20 bundles of 9 lengths each. Beginning at the square on

the forehead, place a bundle center over the seam. Use green floss to work a few Backstitches (page 319) over the bundle (Fig. 4). Place a second bundle next to the first; work Backstitches over the second bundle. Continue attaching the remaining bundles. Trim the yarn ends.

**Fig. 4**

**10.** Pleat the bottom straight edge of each ear. Use green embroidery floss to sew the ears to the head.

## Piggie
(also shown on page 44)

- two 13"x16" pieces of striped knit fabric cut from a gently used sweater
- 14"x16" rectangle of cotton print fabric
- two 12"x15" rectangles of lightweight fusible interfacing
- fabric marking pen
- paper-backed fusible web
- pink and light green felt
- 5 small plastic zipping bags loosely filled with dried beans
- 9" of 1/4" wide pink ribbon
- brown embroidery floss
- blue yarn
- polyester fiberfill

*Match right sides, raw edges and use a 1/2" seam allowance for all sewing.*

**1.** Center and fuse the interfacing to the wrong sides of the sweater pieces.

**2.** Enlarge the patterns (pages 388 and 389) to 146%. Using the enlarged gusset pattern, cut a gusset from the cotton piece. Using the enlarged body pattern, cut 2 bodies from the sweater pieces. Transfer the pattern markings to the wrong sides of the pieces.

**3.** Fuse the web to the remaining cotton scraps. Using the enlarged patterns, cut 2 ears from cotton. Fuse the ears to the pink felt and cut out about 1/4" beyond the cotton ears.

**4.** For the back seam, sew the bodies together from the snout dot to the tail dot.

**5.** Matching the dots, pin the gusset and body pieces together. Leaving an opening for turning between one set of stars, sew the gusset to the body. Clip the curves and turn right side out.

**6.** Press under 1/2" on the nose. Pin the nose over the snout opening and slipstitch in place.

**7.** Place a bag of beans in each foot and in the tummy area; stuff tightly with fiberfill. Hand sew the opening closed.

**8.** For the eyes, cut 2 1/2" circles from the green felt. Pin the eyes in place. Using blue yarn and leaving the beginning knot on the surface, run the needle through the center of one eye, through the head and come out in the opposite eye. Knot the yarn close to surface and trim. Work a Stem Stitch (page 319) mouth and Straight Stitch (page 319) nostrils and eyelashes with brown floss.

**9.** For the tail, tie a knot at each end of the pink ribbon; tack the tail at the body/gusset intersection.

**10.** Pleat the bottom straight edge of each ear. Use pink embroidery floss to sew ears to the head.

## Gift Cubes
(continued from page 42)

**3.** Matching the short ends and beginning and ending at the dots, refer to Fig. 1 to sew the red rectangles and squares together.

### Fig. 1

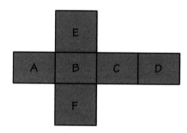

**4.** To form the cube, sew A and E, then A and F together. Sew E and C, then F and C together to make a box with one open side. Press the raw edges of D ½" to the wrong side. Insert a foam cube into the box. Fold D over the opening and slipstitch in place.
**5.** Overlapping and gluing the ends at the top center, wrap the cube with a 40" ribbon length. Loop an 18" ribbon length into a bow and stack on a 24" long streamer. Wrap a 6" ribbon length around the bow center and glue the ends together. Glue the bow and a pom-pom to the cube.
**6.** Repeat Steps 2-5 with blue corduroy, remaining foam cube, ribbon and pom-pom.

## Personalized Tree Ornaments
(also shown on page 43)

• wood logs and slats (we used vintage Lincoln Logs™)
• wood spools (we used vintage Tinkertoys®)
• wood glue
• fine-tooth handsaw
• sandpaper
• green acrylic paint and paintbrush
• wood letter tiles (we used pieces from a vintage Scrabble® game)
• assorted sizes and colors wood beads
• 6-ply multi-colored hemp twine

**1.** For the tree trunk, glue a wood log to the flat side of a spool (we used 4½" long logs, but you can adjust the length of the logs to fit the desired name).
**2.** For the branches, cut slats into 2", 3" and 4" long pieces (for taller trees cut more braches, increasing the length in 1" increments). Sand and drybrush (page 318) the ends with green paint. Spacing the branches one letter tile height apart, glue the branches to the trunk. Glue the letter tiles on and between the branches.
**3.** Glue beads to the branches and tree top.
**4.** For the hangers, knot the ends of a twine length together. Glue the ends in the top bead hole.

## Spool Family
(continued from page 45)

*Make a spool person for each member of your family! Ask a grown-up for help with the glue gun. Use craft glue unless otherwise noted.*

**1.** For each doll, cut scrapbook paper to fit around a spool; glue in place. Use the glue gun to attach a doll head to the spool. Paint a simple face. Glue floss lengths to the head for bangs.
**2.** Use the glue gun to attach the wheel to the bottom of Papa's spool.
**3.** Enlarge the patterns on page 402 to 125%. Using the patterns, cut a fleece hat to fit the doll head (large for Papa and Mama, medium for the Child and small for Baby). Using the glue gun, glue the short edges of the hat together, attach the hat to the head and add a pom-pom to the point.
**4.** For Papa, Mama and the Child, use the enlarged patterns and cut felt feet; glue in place. Use the glue gun to add chenille stem arms at the back of the spools.

## Felt Gift Bags
(also shown on page 128)

For both Gift Bags, you'll need:
• felt
• ruler
• embroidery floss
• assorted buttons
• fabric glue

For the Blue Bag, you'll also need:
• water-soluble fabric marker
• cotton swab

Our blue bag is 5"x7" and the green pocket purse is 5"x4". Adjust the size of your bag to fit the gift you tuck inside. Read Embroidery Stitches on page 318 before you begin and use 3 strands of floss.

### Blue Bag
1. Matching short ends, fold a 5"x14" blue felt piece in half.
2. On the bag front, draw a 5" tall line for the tree trunk. Draw 4 branches (1" apart) with the shortest branch at the top and the longest at the bottom.
3. Work Running Stitches along the trunk and branch lines. Remove any visible markings with a damp cotton swab. Sew button "ornaments" below the branches.
4. Add a Straight Stitch star at the top. Sew the sides together with Blanket Stitches (shown) or Running Stitches, catching the folded ends of a 1"x10" felt strip handle in the stitching (or simply fold and glue the ends inside the bag).

### Green Pocket Purse

1. Cut a 5"x10½" green felt piece and fold the short bottom end up 4" to form a pocket. Work Running Stitches along the sides of the pocket and flap. Fold the flap over the pocket.
2. For a cute closure, stack 2 felt circles and 2 buttons from largest to smallest and sew them together. Repeat and glue one set to the flap and the other to the pocket.
3. Work French Knots around each closure set.
4. Glue one end of a 6" floss length between the larger button and top felt circle on the flap. Wrap the loose end around the buttons on the pocket to close.

### Sweet Sister Dolls
(also shown on page 47)

• one pair of white, finely-woven cotton or cotton blend socks for each doll
• tea bags, if dying is preferred (optional)
• tracing paper
• pencil
• 14½" square of blanket fabric and soft lining fabric (for baby doll)
• 2¼" buttons for eyes for each doll
• pink embroidery floss
• red colored pencil

• white quilting thread
• ¾ yard small print fabric (for toddler dress)
• two 2" x 5" strips pink gingham fabric (for toddler dress sleeve ruffles)
• one 2" x 22" strip pink gingham fabric (for toddler dress skirt)
• polyester fiberfill
• yellow curly yarn for hair
• small red button (for toddler doll's dress)
• black crafts paint
• 8" of ¼" w black satin ribbon (for toddler doll shoes)
• 16" of 1" w satin ribbon (for toddler's skirt)
• 16" of 1" w ribbon (for baby's blanket)
• scrap of cotton (for bloomers)

1. Tea dye sock if desired to obtain a softer color. Let dry. Referring to the diagram, below, cut sock as shown for the arms and legs for the baby doll. For the toddler doll body, trace pattern (page 392). Lay sock on pattern and cut with toe of sock at top of pattern. Mark all pattern line indications using a pencil.

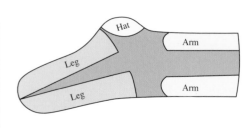

2. Trace clothing patterns (pages 392 and 393) onto tracing paper and cut out. Draw around clothing pattern pieces on fabric and cut out. Cut a 9" x 22" piece from small print fabric for toddler skirt. Set aside.
3. To make the bodies, stitch with right sides together using a ¼" seam. Turn. Stuff body firmly but do not stretch sock.
4. Whipstitch the bottom of the sock closed using quilting thread. For the toddler, sew straight across. For the baby, follow stitching line on pattern.
5. Move the batting around until the desired face shape is achieved. Using the quilting thread, sew a running stitch on the pencil line. Pull slightly, secure and make a knot. Make 2 pencil dots for the eyes.

6. Using the quilting thread, sew the 2 buttons in place, pulling the thread slightly and knot thread. For the nose, stitch 2 short stitches about ⅛" apart; sew a tiny stitch at the bottom of the stitches, forming a U shape. Pull thread to make nose using tip of needle to pull and shape nose.

7. For the mouth, sew a straight line of pink embroidery thread. With the needle tip, pull the top lip over the thread and pull tight then pull out the bottom lip to make a smile. Color cheeks, tip of nose and bottom lip with a red colored pencil.

8. Cut the heel end of the sock for the hat. Using a sewing machine, pull the edge taut as you are sewing and zigzag the edge with coordinating thread to match the blanket or dress, for a ruffled edge.

9. **For toddler's hair,** cut ten 12" lengths of golden yellow yarn and 12" of ¼" w pink satin ribbon. Align lengths of yarn and mark center. Pin to center of forehead. Hand stitch down center line, stitching through head to attach. Tack at sides where ears would be by stitching through yarns and stuffed head. Cut ribbon in half and tie where hair is attached to sides of head.

10. **For baby's hair,** cut five 2½" lengths golden yellow yarn. Coil lengths of yarn at top of head to make curls. Couch (below) onto stuffed head using matching sewing thread.

### COUCHING STITCH

Referring to Fig. 1, lay the thread to be couched on the fabric; bring the needle up at 1 and go down at 2. Continue until entire thread length is couched.

### Fig. 1

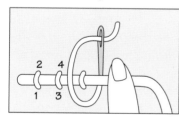

11. Pull hats tightly over dolls heads and fasten using small stitches.

12. **For baby doll,** sew the front and back pieces of the blanket with right sides together leaving about 3" open. Turn with right sides out and press seams. Top stitch edges of blanket, turning in edges of opening and stitch closed. Fold blanket over baby doll body and tie with satin ribbon.

13. **For the toddler doll body,** stuff arms and legs firmly using polyester fiberfill and whip stitch arms to body of doll. For the legs, paint shoes using the black crafts paint. When dry, cut black ribbon in half and sew on each side of foot. Tie in bows and trim ends. Sew legs to body of doll. **For bodice top,** sew edge of collar under. With right sides of fabric together, sew under arm seam. Turn right side out. For sleeve ruffles, stitch short ends together in ¼" seam. Fold lengths in half with wrong sides together. Baste ¼" along long unfinished edge to gather. Pin underneath sleeve edge and stitch along stitching line to attach to sleeve. Sew button to bodice front. Put bodice on doll and overlap at back. Stitch to doll body. **For skirt,** narrow hem side and bottom edges of skirt. Gather top to fit waist of doll. Center and sew white satin ribbon over gathers. Make skirt ruffle by narrowly hemming sides and lower edge of gingham strip. Baste ¼" along long unfinished edge to gather. Stitch ruffle to top of skirt along lower edge of white ribbon. Stitch pink satin ribbon over unfinished edge of ruffle at waist, folding in ends of pink ribbon at sides. **For bloomers,** stitch raw edges of hem. With right sides together, sew crotch seam. Turn under small hem on waist and sew a running stitch with quilting thread. Put bloomers on doll. Gather and pull the stitch tight; knot. Put the skirt over the shirt and bloomers and tie in back.

**Note:** Dolls have small parts and are not intended for children under 3 years old.

### Child's Art Wraps
(also shown on pages 47 and 49)

- white craft paper
- crayons or markers
- ribbons to coordinate with crayon colors
- scissors
- clear tape

1. Unroll the craft paper and lay out on a flat surface. Have the children draw and color on the white paper using crayons or markers.
2. Lay package to be wrapped on the paper. Cut enough to wrap the package. Secure with tape. Add desired ribbon.

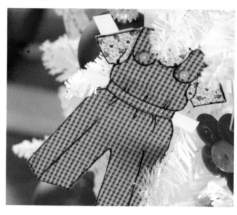

### Paper Doll Dress Trims
(continued from page 48)

4. Using a flat paintbrush or even a straight side of poster board, make sure the glue is applied in a thin layer. Lay fabric clothing onto the poster board clothing and press firmly, making sure there are no bubbles under the fabric. When the glue is no longer tacky, glue on the decorative pieces, collars, cuffs, sailor skirt, mittens, ribbons, rickrack or front dress facing. For the buttons, sew thread into button holes with thread and glue on buttons.
5. When all desired fabric trims are applied, turn clothing over and trim any excess fabric with scissors. Using transfer paper, copy lines of fabric folds onto fabric and then trace over lines with the black permanent marker. Add ribbon or floss for hanging.

## Bandanna Art Trim
(continued from page 49)

1. Cut the bandanna in half making 2 triangles. Referring to diagram 1, below, fold up long bottom edge along fold line. Turn over. Referring to diagram 2, below, fold along outside dotted line. Referring to diagram 3, below, fold on inside dotted line. Whipstitch where the two sides meet. Use paint pen to make dots or other designs on the bandanna. Let dry.

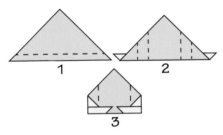

2. Fold tissue paper to fit opening and fill with cookies or candy. Use a needle threaded with floss to make a hanger for the Trim.

## Sweet Candy Ornament
(also shown on page 49)

• 6 hard candies, such as Life Savers in desired colors

• baking sheet
• aluminum foil
• oven
• string

1. Arrange 5 candies in a circle with one on top on an aluminum foil-lined baking sheet. Be sure all of the candies are touching.
2. Bake at 250 degrees for about 5 minutes until candies have just started to melt together. Watch carefully because oven temperatures vary. Remove from oven and let cool on baking sheet.
3. Remove from sheet and thread the string through the top hole for hanging.

## Salt Clay Snowflakes
(continued from page 47)

5. Use the markers to make shapes and doodles on the dry clay shapes. Thread a narrow ribbon through the hole for hanging.

### Cornstarch Clay

Stir together 2 cups baking soda and one cup cornstarch in a medium saucepan. Slowly add 1 1/4 cups cold water. Stir until dissolved. Cook over medium heat stirring constantly until the mixture looks like mashed potatoes (about 10-15 minutes). Carefully place clay onto a large piece of foil and cover with a damp cloth. Allow to cool. Keep in plastic bag until ready to use.

## Flower Ornament/Tree Topper
(also shown on page 58)

• 1/4 yard fabric for flower petals
• fabric scraps for leaf and flower center
• felt scrap
• button
• craft glue
• clothespin

1. For petals, cut six 5"x5" pieces of petal fabric. Matching the wrong sides, fold a fabric square in half diagonally, fold the side points to the center and finally, fold the corner Point A's to the back (Figs. 1-3). Use Running Stitches (page 319) to baste along the raw edge (Fig. 3). Tightly gather the basting thread and securely knot. Repeat with the remaining fabric squares.

**Fig. 1**

**Fig. 2**

Point A          Point A

**Fig. 3**

Point A

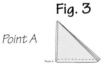

2. Cut a 2" diameter felt circle and 1½" diameter fabric circle. Glue the petals to the felt circle. Sew the fabric circle and button to the flower center.

3. For the leaf, fold and slit a 5"x5" fabric square as shown in Fig. 4. Whipstitch through the slit, cinching the leaf. Glue the leaf to the flower back. Glue the clothespin to the leaf.

## Fig. 4

4. For the tree topper, follow Steps 1-3 using 7"x7" fabric squares for the petals, a 2½" diameter felt circle, a 1¾" diameter fabric circle and a 6"x6" fabric square for the leaf.

## Gathered Rickrack Ornament
(also shown on page 58)
- 58" length of jumbo rickrack
- matching embroidery floss
- button
- felt scrap
- small clothespin
- craft glue

1. Use floss to work Running Stitches (page 319) along 1 long edge of the rickrack (Fig. 1). Pull the thread to tightly gather the rickrack, forming a flower; tack the rickrack together on the back and securely knot the thread. Glue as necessary on the flower wrong side to maintain the shape. Sew the button to the flower center.

## Fig. 1

2. Enlarge the leaf pattern (page 392) to 200%. Use the enlarged pattern to cut a felt leaf. Glue the leaf and the clothespin to the flower back.

## Blooming Apron
(also shown on page 59)
- 1¼ yards of fabric for ties, waistband and ruffle
- 14"x12" fabric piece for bib
- 28"x16" fabric piece for skirt
- fabric scrap for bib trim
- pinking shears
- ½ yard fabric for lining
- 3½ yards rickrack
- vintage hankie
- 3¾ yards 1"w ribbon
- green felt scrap
- light green acrylic paint
- liner paintbrush
- twill tape
- Gathered Fabric Ornament (page 58) without clothespin

*Match right sides and use a ½" seam allowance for all sewing unless otherwise indicated.*
1. Cut two 4"x87" waistband/tie strips (these will have to be pieced) and a 6½"x70" ruffle strip (this will have to be pieced) and two 22"x4" straps. Set the waistband/tie and ruffle strips aside.

2. Matching the long edges, fold each strap in half and sew the long edge and 1 short end together. Turn right side out and press. Matching the raw edges, pin the straps to 1 long edge of the bib, placing the straps 1" from the side edges.

3. Use pinking shears to trim the fabric scrap to a 5"x5" square. Turn diagonally and center the square on the bib top edge; baste in place and trim excess fabric. Cut a 14"x12" lining piece for the bib. Leaving the bottom edge open, sew the bib pieces together. Turn right side out and press.

4. Sew rickrack to 2 hankie edges. Fold the hankie in half diagonally. Pin the hankie to the bib with the fold 1" below the top edge. Raise the top layer of the hankie and topstitch the hankie along the top edge of the bib.

5. For the skirt ruffle, match the long edges and fold the ruffle fabric piece in half. Sew the side seams. Turn right side out and press. Baste along the raw edge at ½" and ¼"; pull the basting threads, gathering the ruffle to 27". Center and sew the ruffle to the skirt bottom edge.

6. Cut a 28"x16" lining piece for the skirt. Leaving the top edge open, sew the skirt pieces together. Turn right side out and press.

7. Matching the raw edges, center, pin, and then sew the bib to a waistband/tie strip. Repeat to sew the skirt to the bottom of the strip. Matching right sides, pin the remaining waistband/tie strip to the first strip. Leaving the skirt and bib areas unstitched, sew along the long edges and short ends of the ties. Clip the corners, turn right side out and press, turning the raw edges of the waistband under ½". Pin, then topstitch the waistband area.

8. Pin, then sew ribbon and rickrack to the center of the waistband/ties, turning the ends ½" to the wrong side.

9. Turning the ends ½" to the wrong side and whipstitching in place, twist and tack the remaining ribbon over the ruffle seam.

10. Enlarge the holly leaf pattern (page 379) to 200%. Use the enlarged pattern to cut 2 felt holly leaves. Paint the leaf veins. Sew the leaves, a twill tape bow and the gathered fabric ornament to the bib.

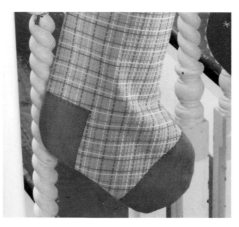

## Reverse Appliqué Table Runner

(also shown on page 61)

- ½ yard of 72"w red felt
- ⅜ yard of 36"w white felt
- mesh transfer canvas
- water-soluble marking pen
- small sharp scissors
- cotton towel
- fabric glue
- white embroidery floss
- white buttons

1. Cut a 14"x72" red felt piece for the table runner and two 14"x12" white felt pieces for the appliqués.
2. Enlarge the pattern on page 391 to 200%. Use the Mesh Transfer Canvas Method (page 318) to transfer the pattern onto each appliqué piece. Carefully cut out the designs. Using the pattern, scallop the ends of the runner. Spritz the pieces with water and blot dry to remove any remaining pen marks.
3. Glue an appliqué piece 1½" from each end of the runner. Sew buttons to the flower centers and use 6 strands of floss to work Running Stitches (page 319) on the runner along the appliqué scallops.

## Fabric Stocking

(also shown on page 63)

- ⅓ yard of stocking fabric
- ¼ yard of solid fabric
- paper-backed fusible web
- ½ yard of pom-pom fringe
- ¼ yard of ⅝"w ribbon for hanger

*Match right sides and use a ½" seam allowance unless otherwise indicated.*

1. Cut two 5½"x15" cuff pieces from solid fabric. Fuse web to the back of the remaining solid fabric. Enlarge the patterns on page 382 to 328%. Use the patterns and cut 2 stockings, 2 toes and 2 heels from fabrics, cutting one set in reverse.
2. Fuse the heel and toe pieces to the stocking pieces. Machine or hand Blanket Stitch (page 319) around the inside edges of the heel and toe pieces.
3. Sew the stocking front and back together, leaving the top edge open.
4. Baste the fringe to one long edge of one cuff piece. Sew the cuff pieces together along this edge; open out flat. Sew the short ends together to form a tube. Press the seam allowances open. Match wrong sides with the fringe at the bottom; press.
5. Matching the cuff seam to the heel-side seam, place the cuff inside the stocking. Matching raw edges, place the hanger between the cuff and stocking at the heel-side seam. Sew the pieces together along the top edge. Turn the cuff to the outside.

## Felt Stocking

(also shown on page 63)

- ⅓ yard felt
- felt scraps for ornaments
- fabric glue
- embroidery floss
- rickrack

1. Enlarge the patterns on page 382 to 335%. Use the patterns and cut 2 stockings and 3 ornaments from felt. Cut desired ornament details from felt scraps.
2. Glue the ornament details to the ornaments; let dry.
3. Embellish by working French Knots, Running Stitches, Stem Stitches and Cross Stitches (page 319) as desired on each ornament. Work Stem Stitch hangers on the stocking front. Glue the ornaments to the stocking front. Add some Straight Stitch snowflakes.
4. Sew rickrack along the side and bottom edges of the stocking front.
5. Matching right sides, sew the stocking front and back together along the previously sewn line; turn right side out.
6. Glue rickrack along the top edge of the stocking. Glue a rickrack hanger to the inside of the stocking.

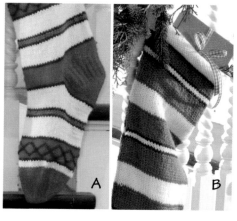

# Knit Stockings

(also shown on page 63)

*Read Knit on pages 321-322 before beginning.*

Finished Size: 7" x 27" (18 cm x 68.5 cm)

Medium Weight Yarn
[3 ounces, 197 yards (85 grams,
    180 meters) per skein]:

Colorway A
    Red - 1 skein
    Ecru - 1 skein
    Green - 1 skein
    Dk Green - 1 skein
    Brown - 1 skein
Colorway B
    Green - 1 skein
    Ecru - 1 skein
    Red - 1 skein
    Dk Green - 1 skein
Straight knitting needles, size 8 (5 mm)
    or size needed for gauge
3 stitch holders
Yarn needle

Gauge: In Stockinette Stitch,
18 sts and 24 rows = 4" (10 cm)

Note: Instructions are written for Colorway
A with Colorway B in braces { }.Instructions
will be easier to read if you circle all the
colors pertaining to your colorway. If
only one color is given, it applies to both
colorways.

## Leg
### Cuff
With Red {Ecru}, cast on 66 sts.
Row 1: Purl across.
Row 2: Knit across.
Rows 3-20: Repeat Rows 1 and 2,
9 times. Cut yarn.

### Body
Row 1: With Ecru {Green}, purl across.
Row 2 (Right side): Knit across.
Row 3: Purl across.
Rows 4-7: Repeat Rows 2 and 3 twice.
Cut yarn.
Row 8: With Dk Green, knit across;
drop yarn.
Row 9: With Green {Ecru}, purl across.
Row 10: Knit across; cut yarn.
Row 11: With Dk Green, purl across;
cut yarn.
Row 12: With Ecru {Green}, knit across.
Row 13: Purl across.
Row 14: Knit across.
Rows 15-20: Repeat Rows 13 and 14,
3 times. Cut yarn.
Row 21: With Brown {Red}, purl across; cut
yarn.
Row 22: With Red {Ecru}, knit across.
Row 23: Purl across.
Row 24: Knit across.
Rows 25-30: Repeat Rows 23 and 24,
3 times. Cut yarn.
Row 31: With Brown {Red}, purl across; cut
yarn.
Row 32: With Ecru {Green}, knit across.
Row 33: Purl across.
Row 34: Knit across.
Rows 35-40: Repeat Rows 13 and 14,
3 times. Cut yarn.
Row 41: With Dk Green, purl across;
drop yarn.
Row 42: With Green {Ecru}, knit across.
Row 43: Purl across; cut yarn.
Row 44: With Dk Green, knit across;
cut yarn.
Row 45: With Ecru {Green}, purl across.
Row 46: Knit across.
Row 47: Purl across.
Rows 48-53: Repeat Rows 46 and 47,
3 times. Cut yarn.
Row 54: With Brown {Red}, knit across;
cut yarn.

Row 55: With Red {Ecru}, purl across.
Row 56: Knit across.
Row 57: Purl across.
Rows 58-63: Repeat Rows 56 and 57,
3 times. Cut yarn.
Row 64: With Brown {Red}, knit across; cut
yarn.
Row 65: With Ecru {Green}, purl across.
Row 66: Knit across.
Row 67: Purl across.
Rows 68-73: Repeat Rows 66 and 67,
3 times.
Rows 74-90: Repeat Rows 8-24.
Rows 91-93: Repeat Rows 23 and 24
once, then repeat Row 23 once more.
Cut yarn.

## Heel Option 1 as shown on Colorway A
### Left Heel
Note: When instructed to slip a stitch,
always slip as if to purl, unless otherwise
instructed.
Row 1: Slip 18 sts onto st holder (Right
Heel), slip next 30 sts onto second st
holder (Top of Foot), with Red, knit across:
18 sts.
Row 2: Purl across.
Row 3: Slip 1, knit across.
Rows 4-17: Repeat Rows 2 and 3, 7 times.
Heel Turning: P1, P2 tog (Fig. 3, page 321),
P1, turn; slip 1, K2, turn; P2, P2 tog, P1,
turn; slip 1, K3, turn; P3, P2 tog, P1, turn;
slip 1, K4, turn; P4, P2 tog, P1, turn; slip 1,
K5, turn; P5, P2 tog, P1, turn; slip 1, K6,
turn; P6, P2 tog, P1, turn; slip 1, K7, turn;
P7, P2 tog, P1, turn; slip 1, K8, turn; P8,
P2 tog, P1: 10 sts.
Slip remaining sts onto st holder; cut yarn.

### Right Heel
With right side facing, slip 18 sts from
Right Heel st holder onto empty needle.
Row 1: With Red, knit across.
Row 2: Slip 1, purl across.
Row 3: Knit across.
Rows 4-16: Repeat Rows 2 and 3, 6 times;
then repeat Row 2 once more.
Heel Turning: K1, K2 tog (Fig. 2, page 321),
K1, turn; slip 1, P2, turn; K2, K2 tog, K1,
turn; slip 1, P3, turn; K3, K2 tog, K1, turn;
slip 1, P4, turn; K4, K2 tog, K1, turn; slip 1,
P5, turn; K5, K2 tog, K1, turn; slip 1, P6,

turn; K6, K2 tog, K1, turn; slip 1, P7, turn; K7, K2 tog, K1, turn; slip 1, P8, turn; K8, K2 tog, K1; do not cut yarn: 10 sts.

## Heel Option 2 as shown on Colorway B
### Left Heel
Note: When instructed to slip a stitch, always slip as if to purl, unless otherwise instructed.

Row 1: Slip 18 sts onto st holder (Right Heel), slip next 30 sts onto second st holder (Top of Foot), with Ecru, knit across: 18 sts.
Row 2: Purl across.
Row 3: (Slip 1, K1) across.
Rows 4-17: Repeat Rows 2 and 3, 7 times.
Heel Turning: P1, P2 tog (Fig. 3, page 321), P1, turn; slip 1, K2, turn; P2, P2 tog, P1, turn; slip 1, K3, turn; P3, P2 tog, P1, turn; slip 1, K4, turn; P4, P2 tog, P1, turn; slip 1, K5, turn; P5, P2 tog, P1, turn; slip 1, K6, turn; P6, P2 tog, P1, turn; slip 1, K7, turn; P7, P2 tog, P1, turn; slip 1, K8, turn; P8, P2 tog, P1: 10 sts.
Slip remaining sts onto st holder; cut yarn.

### Right Heel
With right side facing, slip 18 sts from Right Heel st holder onto empty needle.
Row 1: With Ecru, knit across.
Row 2: (Slip 1, P1) across.
Row 3: Knit across.
Rows 4-16: Repeat Rows 2 and 3, 6 times; then repeat Row 2 once more.
Heel Turning: K1, K2 tog (Fig. 2, page 321), K1, turn; slip 1, P2, turn; K2, K2 tog, K1, turn; slip 1, P3, turn; K3, K2 tog, K1, turn; slip 1, P4, turn; K4, K2 tog, K1, turn; slip 1, P5, turn; K5, K2 tog, K1, turn; slip 1, P6, turn; K6, K2 tog, K1, turn; slip 1, P7, turn; K7, K2 tog, K1, turn; slip 1, P8, turn; K8, K2 tog, K1; do not cut yarn: 10 sts.

### Gusset and Instep
Row 1: With right side facing, pick up 8 sts along side of Right Heel (Fig. 5, page 322), slip 30 sts from Top of Foot st holder onto an empty needle and knit across, pick up 8 sts along side of Left Heel, knit 10 sts from Left Heel st holder: 66 sts.
Row 2: Purl across.

Row 3: K 16, K2 tog, K 30, slip 1 as if to knit, K1, PSSO tog (Fig. 4, page 322), K 16; cut yarn: 64 sts.
Row 4: With Brown {Red}, purl across; cut yarn.
Row 5: With Ecru {Green}, K 15, K2 tog, K 30, slip 1 as if to knit, K1, PSSO, K 15: 62 sts.
Row 6: Purl across.
Row 7: K 14, K2 tog, K 30, slip 1 as if to knit, K1, PSSO, K 14: 60 sts.
Row 8: Purl across.
Row 9: K 13, K2 tog, K 30, slip 1 as if to knit, K1, PSSO, K 13: 58 sts.
Row 10: Purl across.
Row 11: K 12, K2 tog, K 30, slip 1 as if to knit, K1, PSSO, K 12: 56 sts.
Row 12: Purl across.
Row 13: K 11, K2 tog, K 30, slip 1 as if to knit, K1, PSSO, K 11; cut yarn: 54 sts.
Row 14: With Dk Green, purl across; drop yarn.
Row 15: With Green {Ecru}, K 10, K2 tog, K 30, slip 1 as if to knit, K1, PSSO, K 10: 52 sts.
Row 16: Purl across; cut yarn.
Row 17: With Dk Green, knit across; cut yarn.
Row 18: With Ecru {Green}, purl across.
Row 19: Knit across.
Row 20: Purl across.
Rows 21-26: Repeat Rows 19 and 20, 3 times. Cut yarn.
Row 27: With Brown {Red}, knit across; cut yarn.
Row 28: With Red {Ecru}, purl across.
Row 29: Knit across.
Row 30: Purl across.
Rows 31-36: Repeat Rows 29 and 30, 3 times. Cut yarn.
Row 37: With Brown {Red}, knit across; cut yarn.
Row 38: With Ecru {Green}, purl across.
Row 39: Knit across.
Row 40: Purl across; cut yarn.

### Toe Shaping
Row 1: With Red {Ecru}, K 10, K2 tog, K1, place marker, K1, slip 1 as if to knit, K1, PSSO, K 20, K2 tog, K1, place marker, K1, slip 1 as if to knit, K1, PSSO, K 10: 48 sts.
Row 2: Purl across.
Row 3 (Decrease row): ★ Knit across to

within 3 sts of marker, K2 tog, K2, slip 1 as if to knit, K1, PSSO; repeat from ★ once more, knit across 44 sts.
Row 4: Purl across.
Rows 5-18: Repeat Rows 3 and 4, 7 times: 16 sts.
Bind off all sts in knit.

### Finishing
Using photos as a guide, work Straight Stitch (page 319) accent lines as desired. With right sides together and beginning at Toe, weave seam to 1³⁄₄" (4.5 cm) from top (Fig. 6, page 322); with wrong sides together, weave remaining seam. Roll Cuff to right side.

**Hanging Loop:** With Red {Ecru}, cast on 24 sts. Bind off all sts in knit. Sew Hanging Loop to inside of Cuff at seam.

## Knit Pillow  EAS
(also shown on page 64)
*Read Knit on pages 321-322 before beginning.*

Finished Size: 14" (35.5 cm) square

Medium Weight Yarn
[3 ounces, 185 yards (85 grams, 170 meters) per skein]:
     Lt Green - 3 skeins
     Green - 1 skein
Straight knitting needles, size 7 (4.5 mm) or size needed for gauge
3 bobbins
14" (35.5 cm) square pillow form
Yarn needle
Felt scrap
Pinking shears
Sewing needle and thread

Holiday napkin (ours is 8"x8½"/
20.5 cm x 21.5 cm)
4 assorted vintage buttons
Purchased crocheted doily (ours is
6¼"/16 cm dia.)

Gauge: In Stockinette Stitch,
20 sts and 28 rows = 4" (10 cm)

### Front
### Bottom Border
With Lt Green, cast on 78 sts.
Row 1: (K1, P1) across.
Row 2: (P1, K1) across.
Rows 3-22: Repeat Rows 1 and 2,
10 times.

### Center
Wind a small amount of Green onto one
bobbin and a small amount of Lt Green onto
2 bobbins. Wind more yarn onto bobbins as
needed.
Row 1 (Right side): (K1, P1) 8 times, with
Green K 46 (see Changing Colors, page
321), with Lt Green (K1, P1) across.
Row 2: (P1, K1) 8 times, with Green P 46,
with Lt Green (P1, K1) across.
Rows 3 and 4: Repeat Rows 1 and 2.
Row 5: (K1, P1) 8 times, with Green K3,
with Lt Green K 40, with Green K3, with Lt
Green (K1, P1) across.
Row 6: (P1, K1) 8 times, with Green P3,
with Lt Green P 40, with Green P3, with Lt
Green (P1, K1) across.
Rows 7-60: Repeat Rows 5 and 6,
27 times.
Cut center Lt Green and left side Green.
Rows 61-64: Repeat Rows 1 and 2 twice.
Cut Green and left side Lt Green.
Row 65: (K1, P1) 8 times, K 46,
(K1, P1) across.
Top Border
Row 1: (P1, K1) across.
Row 2: (K1, P1) across.
Rows 3-21: Repeat Rows 1 and 2, 9 times;
then repeat Row 1 once more.
Bind off all sts in pattern.

### Back
Work same as Front.

Sew 3 sides of the Front and Back

together. Insert the pillow form and sew
the remaining side closed.

Cut four 1½" (4 cm) diameter felt circles
with pinking shears. Sew the holiday napkin,
felt circles and buttons to the Front. Sew
the doily to the Back.

## Fringed Throw
(also shown on page 65)

• fleece throw
• 1"w grosgrain ribbon
• yarns (we chose 7 colors)
• ⅛"w silk ribbon (we chose
2 colors)

**1.** For the fringe base, cut grosgrain ribbon
the width of the throw plus 1".
**2.** Cut a 2-yard length of each yarn and silk
ribbon. Hold the lengths together and fold
them in half.
**3.** Beginning ½" from one end of the base
ribbon, zigzag the yarn/ribbon bundle to the
base ribbon, so the loose (fringe) ends of
the bundle extend about 6" beyond the long
edge of the base (Fig. 1).

### Fig. 1

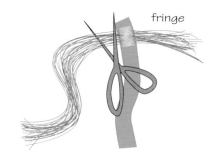

fringe

**4.** Leaving the needle in the ribbon, trim the
bundle along the top long edge of
the base.
**5.** Align the new bundle ends beside the
sewn fringe ends and zigzag this next
section to the base. Trim along the top long
edge.
**6.** Continue sewing fringe to the base,
cutting new 2-yard long bundles as needed,
and stopping ½" from the remaining base
end.
**7.** Folding the base ribbon ends to the
wrong side, pin, then zigzag the ribbon side
of the fringe to one end of the throw. Trim
the fringe.

## Crocheted Kitty Toy
(continued from page 66)

Rnd 4: (2 Sc in next sc, sc in next 2 sc)
around: 24 sc.
Rnd 5: (Sc in next 3 sc, 2 sc in next sc)
around: 30 sc.
Rnd 6: (2 Sc in next sc, sc in next 4 sc)
around: 36 sc.
Rnd 7: (Sc in next 5 sc, 2 sc in next sc)
around: 42 sc.
Rnd 8: Sc in each sc around.
Rnd 9: Sc in each sc around; slip st in next
st, finish off; do not remove marker.
Rnd 10: With right side facing, join Ecru
with sc in same st as joining (see Joining
with Sc, page 323); sc in each sc around;
slip st in next st, finish off; do not remove
marker.
Rnd 11: With right side facing, join Purple
with sc in same st as joining; sc in each sc
around.
Rnd 12: Sc in each sc around.

(continued on next page)

Rnd 13: Sc in each sc around; slip st in next st, finish off; do not remove marker.

Rnd 14: With right side facing, join Ecru with sc in same st as joining; sc in each sc around; slip st in next st, finish off; do not remove marker.

Rnd 15: With right side facing, join Green with sc in same st as joining; sc in each sc around.

Rnd 16: Sc in each sc around.

Rnd 17: Sc in each sc around; slip st in next st, finish off; do not remove marker.

Rnd 18: With right side facing, join Ecru with sc in same st as joining; sc in each sc around; slip st in next st, finish off; do not remove marker.

Rnd 19: With right side facing, join Yellow with sc in same st as joining; sc in each sc around.

Rnd 20: Sc in each sc around.

To work sc decrease (uses next 2 sc), pull up a loop in next 2 sc, YO and draw through all 3 loops on hook.

Rnd 21: (Sc in next 5 sc, sc decrease) around: 36 sc.

Rnd 22: (Sc decrease, sc in next 4 sc) around: 30 sc.

Rnd 23: (Sc in next 3 sc, sc decrease) around: 24 sc.

Rnd 24: (Sc decrease, sc in next 2 sc) around: 18 sc.

Stuff Ball with polyester fiberfill.

Rnd 25: (Sc in next sc, sc decrease) around: 12 sc.

Rnd 26: Sc decrease around; slip st in next sc, finish off leaving a long end for sewing: 6 sc.

Thread needle with long end, weave needle through sts on Rnd 26, gather tightly and secure end.

Finishing

Leaving a 4" tail at the bottom, run the two 10" ribbons through the ball. Run the top ends back into the ball to secure and knot each bottom end.

Leaving a 4" tail at the bottom, run the 1⅝-yard ribbon through the ball. Tie a knot at the bottom end and knot the ribbons together just below the ball. Thread the bell

on the ribbon above the ball. Glue the loose ribbon end to one end of the dowel. Wrap the ribbon around the dowel to the opposite end and knot the ribbon to itself, securing it to the dowel.

## Coiled Rag Basket
(also shown on page 69)

• ³/₁₆" dia. poly-reinforced cotton clothesline (two 50-foot packages)
• 2 yards total of assorted fabrics (we used 8 different fabrics)
• 2 large spools of sewing thread (we used white for a "rag" look)
• rotary cutter, rotary ruler and cutting mat
• size 90/14 sharp sewing machine needle

1. Use the rotary cutter, ruler and mat to cut fabrics into ½" wide strips, cutting selvage to selvage.

2. Wrap one clothesline cord end with a fabric strip and stitch, catching the cord in the stitching (Fig. 1).

**Fig. 1**

3. Wrap the fabric strip around the cord, angling the fabric as you wrap toward your body. When you get to the end of the fabric strip, pin the loose fabric end in place.

4. Fold about 6" of the cord down to the left and place the fold under the presser foot. Using a wide stitch width and short stitch length, zigzag the folded area (Fig. 2).

**Fig. 2**

5. When you reach the end of the folded cord, stop with the needle in the cord, pivot the work and continue zigzagging the cord together (Fig. 3).

**Fig. 3**

6. To add a new fabric strip, slip the new strip between the cord and the old strip (Fig. 4); continue wrapping, zigzagging and pivoting until the base is about 7½"x12½".

**Fig. 4**

7. To add height to the basket, hold the base at an angle to the sewing machine

(Fig. 5). Continue wrapping and zigzagging around the base until the basket is about 5½" high.

## Fig. 5

**8.** Cut the cord and fabric strip, leaving a 4" length of fabric. Wrap the cord end with the fabric, zigzag over the cord end, backstitch, and trim the excess fabric.

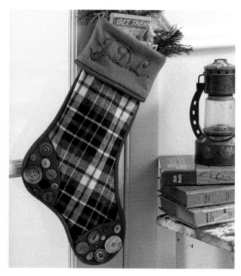

## Monogram Wool Stocking
(continued from page 72)

**2.** Apply interfacing to wrong sides of plaid stocking pieces. On red heel and toe pieces, turn under inside curved edges ¼" and press. Pin to plaid stocking front and stitch close to folded edges of heel and toe pieces. Baste outside edges to stocking. Arrange the buttons on the heel and toe pieces and stitch in place.

**3.** Wrap long strips of red wool fabric around cording and baste close to cording. Stitch cording around stocking front, with raw edges even and using a ¼" seam. With right sides together, stitch stocking front to stocking back, using ¼" seam. Clip curves, turn right side out and press. With

right sides together stitch red lining pieces together using ¼" seam. Clip curves. Slip lining inside plaid stocking, with lining wrong side facing stocking wrong side. Baste around top edges.

**4.** Print out letters to be used for monogram. On right side of one gray cuff piece, center letters to be used. Slide carbon paper underneath letters and trace letters onto cuff front. Pin red cording over traced lines and Couch on cording using matching sewing thread. With right sides together, stitch cuff front to cuff back at side seams using ¼" seam. Repeat for cuff lining. On cuff front, stitch red piping to lower edge, stitching close to cording. With right sides together, stitch cuff to cuff lining at lower edge, using ¼" seam. Turn and press. Baste top edges together.

**5.** For hanging loop, fold strip of red fabric in half and stitch down long side in ¼" seam. Turn right side out and press. Fold loop in half and place raw edges of loop at side edge of stocking, having loop extend down toward center of stocking. Pin at top side edge. Place cuff inside stocking, with right side of cuff next to the right side of the red stocking lining fabric, with monogrammed lettering to the front button edge of stocking. Pin in place and stitch around top edge in ½" seam allowance. Edge stitch close to seam line on lining fabric. Flip cuff over to outside of stocking and press.

## Crochet Poinsettia Blossom
(also shown on page 73)
**Skill Level:** Easy **Size:** About 7" wide

- Caron Simply Soft, 100% acrylic yarn, (6oz/170g/315yd/288m) per skein:

One skein of Red #9729
- size E/4 (3.5mm) crochet hook or size needed to obtain gauge
- six ¼" diameter dark yellow buttons
- black sewing thread

**Gauge:** First leaf measures 3" long and 2" across widest portion.
**Take time to check your gauge.**

### Foundation:
Ch 5; join with sl st in first ch to form a ring.

### Leaf
**1.** Leaving a 10" tail, ch 15. Sc in 2nd ch from hook; * working 1 st into each ch work 1 hdc, 3 dc, 4 tr, 3 dc, 1 hdc **, 1 sc. Working 1 st into each ch along opposite edge, sc in first ch then rep from * to ** again, 3 sc in last ch. Sc in each of 29 sts, 2 sc in next st. Sl st in 15 sc then sl st in ring.
**2.** Make 4 more leaves as est. After 5th leaf, leave a 10" tail, fasten off. Take tails to WS and tie into an overhand knot.

### Finishing
Sew tiny buttons to center of flower using black thread. Tie off ends.

## Bias Tape Birdie Set
(continued from page 74)

of tape at bottom ends for tail. Pin in place and stitch with small hand stitches. Curve top pieces of bias tape over bottom pieces for bird bodies, tucking under both cut ends. Pin in place and stitch.

**3.** Using 3 strands black embroidery floss, make French Knots (page 319) for eyes and Stem Stitch (page 319) to make feet. Using 3 strands gold embroidery floss, make Stem Stitch in small triangular shapes for beaks.

## Striped Pot Holder

- one white dish towel (approximately 18" x 27")
- 10" lengths each of red extra wide double fold bias tape, blue and green single fold bias tapes
- 9" blue double fold bias tape
- gold embroidery floss
- matching sewing threads
- marking pencil
- 10" x 26" piece of heat-resistant batting

**1.** From towel, cut two 10" squares. Cut two 6" x 10" pieces, having both pieces with one 10" side using hemmed edge of towel. From batting, cut one 10" square and two 6" x 10" pieces.

**2.** On one 6" x 10" piece of toweling, place red bias tape 1/2" from hemmed long side. Pin and stitch in place using matching sewing thread. Place blue tape 1/4" from edge of red tape and sew in place using matching sewing thread. Place green tape 1/4" from edge of blue tape and sew in place using matching sewing thread. Make French Knots using 3 strands gold embroidery thread. Layer the remaining 6"x10" piece of toweling, 6"x10" piece of batting and decorated piece of 6"x10" toweling, having towel hemmed edges together for pocket top. Baste around outside edges and stitch close to hemmed edges through all layers.

**3.** Place batting on back of both 10" toweling squares. With marking pencil, mark stitching lines to quilt layers together. Stitch through toweling and batting. Sew close to side edge of blue bias tape using matching sewing thread. Fold loop in half and place at top right corner of one 10" toweling square, having raw edges even at corner and loop hanging to inside of square. Place pocket over this same square, aligning bottom edges. Baste around outside edges.

**4.** With right sides together, pin potholder front to back. Stitch around outside edges in a 1/2" seam, leaving an opening for turning. Trim batting close to seam line and clip corners. Turn right side out and sew opening closed with matching sewing thread.

## Sweater Throw
(also shown on page 80)

- assorted red and green knit sweaters (we used 9 different sweaters)
- red flannel for backing and binding (we used 3¼ yards of 43"w flannel for our 45"x60" throw)
- red embroidery floss

*Match right sides and use a 1/2" seam allowance when sewing unless otherwise indicated.*

**1.** Cut the sleeves from the sweaters and cut open the sleeve seams. Trim all the knit pieces to the same width. Stabilize the knit pieces by zigzagging around the edges, using a medium stitch length and width.

**2.** Arrange the knit pieces in horizontal rows. Zigzag the pieces together (along the short ends) one row at a time. Trim the rows to the same length; then, zigzag the rows together to complete the top.

**3.** Cut a flannel piece the same size as the top, piecing as necessary. Matching the wrong sides, baste the top to the flannel backing along the outer edges. Use floss lengths to tie the top and backing together.

**4.** For the binding, cut a 3½"w flannel strip the same length as 1 long edge of the throw. Press 1/2" to the wrong side along 1 long edge. Matching right sides, sew the long raw edge of the binding to the throw edge. Fold the pressed edge to the throw wrong side and slipstitch the binding to the backing. Repeat for the remaining long edge.

**5.** Cut a 3½"w flannel strip the length of 1 short end of the throw, plus 1". Press 1/2" to the wrong side along 1 long edge and both ends. Matching right sides, sew the long raw edge of the binding to the throw edge. Fold the pressed edge to the throw wrong side and slipstitch the binding to the backing. Repeat for the remaining short end.

## Big, Beautiful Tote
(continued from page 76)

**3.** From each fabric for stripes, cut six 2"x7" fabric strips. Arranging the fabrics in random order and offsetting the strips by 1", use a 1/4" seam allowance to sew the long edges of 4 fabric strips together (Fig. 1). Repeat to make 17 more strip sets.

### Fig. 1

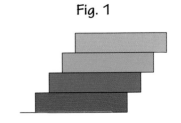

**4.** Align the 60° line on the rotary ruler with the bottom edge of one strip set and trim the fabric right edge with the rotary cutter (Fig. 2).

### Fig. 2

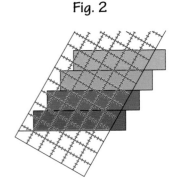

**5.** Rotate the trimmed strip set so that the trimmed edge is on the left. Aligning the 60° line on the ruler with the bottom edge again, place the ruler on the strip set so that the 4¼" mark on the ruler is aligned with the trimmed edge (Fig. 3). Cut on the right side on the ruler. Repeat Steps 4 and 5 with the remaining strip sets.

**Fig. 3**

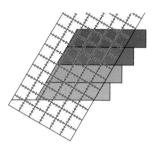

**6.** Using a ¼" seam allowance, sew 3 strip sets together (Fig. 4). Repeat to make 6 striped bands.

**7.** For the front striped panel, refer to Fig. 5 and sew 3 striped bands together, slightly offsetting the seams. Trim the striped panel to 19"w. Repeat for the back striped panel.

**Fig. 4**

**Fig. 5**

19"

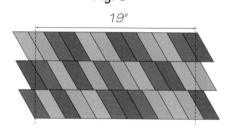

**8.** Mark the brown bottom pieces at 1⅝" and 2¾" from the top (Fig. 6). Fold the fabric along these marks and topstitch close to the fold, creating pintucks.

**Fig. 6**

1⅝"
2¾"          1⅝"
            2¾"

**9.** For the tote front, sew a brown top, the front striped panel and a brown bottom together (Fig. 7). Repeat for the tote back with the back striped panel.

**Fig. 7**

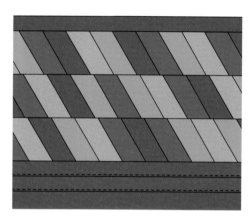

**10.** Sew the tote front and back together along the sides and bottom. Flatten and match the side seams to the bottom seam and sew across each corner 2¼" from the point (Fig. 8). Turn right side out.

**Fig. 8**

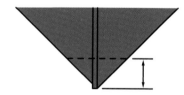

**11.** For each strap, press the long edges ½" to the wrong side. Matching the wrong sides, fold the strap in half lengthwise and press; topstitch along both long edges. Matching the raw edges and leaving 4½" between the strap ends, center and pin the straps on the tote front and back.

**12.** Sew the remaining brown top pieces to the larger lining pieces. Repeat Step 10 with the larger lining pieces, leaving an opening along the bottom for turning. Do not turn the lining right side out.

**13.** Matching the right sides, insert the tote in the lining. Sew the tote and lining together along the top edge. Turn right side out and sew the opening closed. Tuck the lining in the tote. Topstitch close to the seam between the top brown pieces and the striped panels of the tote.

**14.** Sew the remaining lining pieces together along the long edges and one short end. Turn right side out and insert the cardboard. Fold the fabric raw edges to the inside and sew the opening closed. Insert the covered cardboard in the tote. Slipstitch to the lining if desired.

## Yo-Yo Sewing Kit
(continued from page 77)

**2.** Center and fuse the interfacing to the wrong side of the lining fabric. Cut a 2¾"x2" rectangle and two ¾" diameter circles from the felt. Referring to Fig. 1, use Running Stitches (page 319) to sew one long edge of the felt rectangle to the lining fabric. Use long Straight Stitches to sew a felt circle and one snap piece near the top.

**Fig. 1**

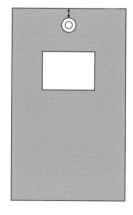

(continued on next page)

**3.** Sew the remaining felt circle and snap piece to the right side of the lining fabric rectangle (Fig. 2).

**Fig. 2**

**4.** Matching the right sides, using a ¹⁄₂" seam allowance and leaving an opening for turning, sew the lining and rectangle together. Clip the corners, turn right side out and press. Sew the opening closed.

**5.** Slipstitch the lined fabric piece to the yo-yos, leaving about 2¹⁄₄" of each yo-yo unstitched.

## Family Photo Wreath
(also shown on page 83)

- floral and craft ring (our wooden ring is 12" dia.)
- fine-grit sandpaper
- acrylic paint
- paintbrush
- unfinished wood discs (ours are 1¹⁄₂", 2³⁄₈", 3" and 3³⁄₄" dia.)
- spray adhesive
- black & white photographs (or photocopies)

- scrapbook papers
- circle templates (ours are 1¹⁄₄", 2¹⁄₈", 2³⁄₄" and 3¹⁄₂" dia.)
- extra-strength craft glue
- mica flakes
- fine-point permanent pen
- jewelry tags
- ¹⁄₈"w and 2¹⁄₈"w ribbons
- medium-gauge wire
- wire cutters
- adhesive foam dots
- jeweled snowflake embellishments

**1.** Sand, then paint the discs. Using spray adhesive in a well-ventilated area, adhere photos to a few of the discs and scrapbook paper circles to the rest. Glue mica flakes around the edge of some of the circles.

**2.** For each photo disc, write the year of the photo on a jewelry tag. Knot narrow ribbon through the hole in the tag and glue to the disc.

**3.** Tie a wire hanger around the ring. Beginning with the largest, arrange the discs on the ring. (If you like, take a digital photo to show placement before removing the discs for gluing.) Overlapping as desired and using foam dots as needed to support unglued areas, glue the discs in place. Add snowflake embellishments to a few of the discs.

**4.** Glue a wide-ribbon bow to the front of the wreath.

## Neck Warmer
(continued from page 85)

**1.** For the front of the warmer, cut each fabric piece in different-width strips at least 9" long…they shouldn't be perfect rectangles, so cut each strip a little narrower on one end, but at least 2" wide (Fig. 1).

**Fig. 1**

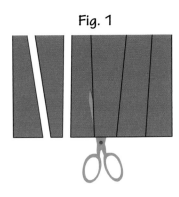

**2.** Matching long edges and mixing fabrics, sew strips together. Trim the edges into the desired neck warmer size, plus 1" (we trimmed ours to an 8"x18" rectangle). Press the seam allowances open.

**3.** Matching raw edges, baste the ends of each ribbon "handle" to the short ends of the front piece about 2" from the top and bottom.

**4.** Cut the flannel backing the same size as the front. Leaving an opening for turning, sew the backing to the front; trim corners and turn right side out. Fill with rice so the warmer is a little floppy and sew the opening closed. Evenly distribute the rice and pin across the warmer to divide it into sections (ours has 3 sections). Use 6 strands of floss and work Running Stitch (page 319) section dividers and Blanket Stitch around the outer edges.

**5.** Include instructions for use: Heat the neck warmer in a microwave on high for 2 minutes.

## Hankie Blankie
(continued from page 86)

**1.** Cut seven 12¹⁄₂"x12¹⁄₂" muslin squares. Center a hankie on each muslin square and zigzag in place using nylon thread.

2. Arrange the hankie and fabric squares and sew the squares into 5 rows of 3 squares each. Sew the rows together.

3. Follow Making Yo-Yos (page 318) and add yo-yo flowers with looped ribbon leaves to some of the squares (we cut 3½", 4½" and 5½" fabric circles for our yo-yos). Use floss to sew folded or rolled hankies and rickrack to other squares as desired.

4. Cut a 37"x60" batting piece. Cut a 40½"x63½" backing piece; press the edges ½" to the wrong side. With the backing wrong side up, center the batting and pieced top (right side up) on the backing; pin the layers together.

5. Fold and pin the sides of the backing to the front to form the binding; topstitch. Repeat for the top and bottom binding. Using 6 strands of floss, sew through all thicknesses at the center of each block. Tie the ends together and trim.

## Snowbound Tray
(continued from page 90)

1. Turn a picture frame into a captivating tray in no time. Attach drawer pulls to the sides of the frame to use as handles.

2. Glue pieced scrapbook papers to the backing to form the sky. Tear papers for snow-dusted hills and drifts.

3. Enlarge the patterns on page 394 to 182%. Use the patterns (sometimes in reverse) and cut scrapbook paper snowmen, birds and a tree. Layer and glue the shapes to the background. Draw the eyes, mouths, arms and birds' legs. Replace the backing in the tray and use ribbons to tie a layered cardstock tag to one handle.

## Flap Cap
(continued from page 90)

**Gauge Swatch:** 4" (10 cm) diameter
Work same as Rnds 1-7 of Crown.

### Stitch Guide
**Beginning Decrease**
(uses first 2 sc)
Pull up a loop in first 2 sc, YO and draw through all 3 loops on hook (**counts as one sc**).

**Decrease** (uses next 2 sc)
Pull up a loop in next 2 sc, YO and draw through all 3 loops on hook (**counts as one sc**).

### Crown
**Rnd 1** (Right side): Ch 2, 7 sc in second ch from hook; do **not** join, place marker to mark beginning of rnd (see Markers, page 321).

**Note**: Loop a short piece of yarn around any sc to mark Rnd 1 as **right** side.

**Rnd 2:** 2 Sc in each sc around: 14 sc.
**Rnd 3:** (Sc in next sc, 2 sc in next sc) around: 21 sc.
**Rnd 4:** (Sc in next 2 sc, 2 sc in next sc) around: 28 sc.
**Rnd 5:** (Sc in next 3 sc, 2 sc in next sc) around: 35 sc.
**Rnd 6:** (Sc in next 4 sc, 2 sc in next sc) around: 42 sc.
**Rnd 7:** (Sc in next 5 sc, 2 sc in next sc) around, do **not** finish off: 49 sc.

### Body
**Rnds 1-13:** Sc in each sc around.

### Left Flap
**Row 1:** Slip st in next sc, remove marker, ch 1, sc in same st and in next 9 sc, leaving remaining sc unworked: 10 sc.
**Rows 2-8:** Ch 1, turn; sc in each sc across.
**Row 9:** Ch 1, turn; work beginning decrease, sc in next 6 sc, decrease: 8 sc.
**Row 10:** Ch 1, turn; sc in each sc across.
**Row 11:** Ch 1, turn; work beginning decrease, sc in next 4 sc, decrease: 6 sc.
**Rows 12 and 13:** Ch 1, turn; sc in each sc across.

Finish off.

### Right Flap
**Row 1:** With **right** side facing, skip 15 sc from Left Flap and join yarn with sc in next sc (see Joining With Sc, page 323); sc in next 9 sc, leave remaining sc unworked: 10 sc.
**Rows 2-13:** Work same as Left Flap; at end of Row 13, do **not** finish off: 6 sc.

### Edging
**Rnd 1:** Ch 1, do not turn; working in end of rows, skip first row, sc in next 12 rows, skip next sc, sc in next 12 sc, † skip next sc, sc in next 12 rows, skip last row, 2 sc in next sc, sc in next 2 sc, place marker in last sc made for st placement, sc in next 2 sc, 2 sc in next sc †, skip first row, sc in next 12 rows, skip next sc, sc in next 13 sc, repeat from † to † once; join with slip st to first sc: 89 sc.

**Rnd 2:** Ch 1, working from **left** to **right**, work reverse sc in next sc and in each sc across to first marked sc (Figs. 4a-d, page 323), † ch 25, working in back ridge of chs (Fig. 1, page 323), slip st in each ch across (Tie made), skip marked sc †, work reverse sc in next sc and in each sc across to next marked sc, repeat from † to † once, work reverse sc in next sc and in each sc around; join with slip st to first st, finish off.

Make a 1½" (4 cm) diameter Pom-Pom (page 320); attach to the top of the Crown.

## Felt Birds
(continued from page 92)

*Use a ¼" seam allowance.*

1. For each bird, use the patterns on page 395 and cut 2 birds and one of each remaining pattern piece from felt.
2. Follow Transferring Patterns to Fabric (page 318) to transfer the design to each wing. Use 2 strands of floss and work Stem Stitch (page 319) flowers and stems. Sew beads to the flower centers.
3. Accordion-fold the straight edge of the tail and baste to secure. Sew beads along the scalloped edge. With the folds at the top, sew the basted edge of the tail to the end of one bird piece; fold and sew the beak to the head (Fig. 1).

### Fig. 1

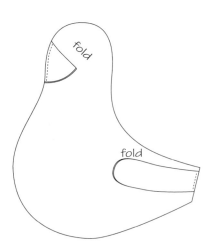

4. Loop a 6" ribbon and knot the ends together. Matching raw edges, sew the loop to the top back of the bird.
5. Matching right sides, sew the bird pieces together, leaving an opening for turning. Turn right side out, stuff and sew the opening closed. Sew the wings and button eyes to the bird.

## Charm & Button Bracelet
(also shown on page 92)

- 5mm jump rings
- needle- and round-nose pliers
- vintage shank buttons
- assorted charms
- link bracelet
- assorted beads
- 2" headpins
- wire cutters
- craft glue
- scrapbook papers
- flip-top box with window lid (ours is 6⅜"x6⅜"x1½")
- large-eye needle
- 22-gauge white plastic-coated wire
- tag punch (optional)
- ¼"w silk ribbon
- ⅛" dia. hole punch
- hot glue gun
- adhesive foam dot

*Read Working with Jump Rings on page 318 before beginning.*

Use jump rings to attach buttons and charms to the bracelet. Thread one or more beads on each headpin; trim the pin ¼" from the last bead and tightly loop the pin end onto the bracelet with round-nose pliers.

Layer and glue scrapbook papers together to fit in the box. Using the needle to pierce holes in the paper, secure the bracelet to the center of the paper with wire. Place the paper in the box.

Punch or cut a tag from scrapbook paper. Thread silk ribbon through a hole punched at one end. Hot glue buttons and a charm to the tag; then, secure it to the box lid with a foam dot.

## Reverse Painting Ornament
(also shown on page 94)

- round flat clear-glass ornament
- pencil
- scissors
- computer-printed letter in reverse to fit ornament center as shown in photograph
- tape
- glass paint, such as Liquitex Glossies, in red, green and white
- small round-tip paintbrush
- ½" flat paintbrush
- 1" w ribbon

1. Carefully wash and dry ornament. Draw a circle ¼" outside of letter and cut out on line. Tape letter centered on one side of ornament, printed side down.
2. Using the reversed letter as a pattern, paint the letter red; let dry. Use the small round-tip paintbrush to paint a wreath around the letter using the circle as a guide and small sweeping strokes. Let dry.
3. Add berry dots by dipping the paintbrush handle tip into red paint and dotting randomly around wreath; let dry. Use the flat paintbrush to paint white inside wreath area feathering edges.

4. Let the paint dry. Tie coordinating ribbon bow to the ornament hanger.

## Dish Towel Apron
(continued from page 95)

1. From one dish towel, cut a piece 16" w by 19" long (for apron center) and 2 pieces 7½" w by 6½" long (for pockets). From other towel, cut 2 pieces 7½" w by 19" long (for side panels). Round the corners of each side panel at lower edge of each side. From the larger calico cut of fabric, cut 2 strips 3" w. Join them in a ¼" seam and cut to a total length of 70". From this same cotton fabric, cut strips 1⅞" w, joining them to make 100" in length.
2. From the coordinating print, cut one strip 1⅞" w to make a length of 30". Feed lengths through bias tape making tool, ironing as strip is pulled through the tool, to make 1" single fold tape.
3. Stitch contrasting print binding to top and bottom edges (7½" length) of pockets. Mark 4" up from the bottom of each side panel and pin pockets to toweling fabric. Stitch through all layers, following binding edge at bottom of pocket and leaving top open for pocket. Baste pocket to side panels at side seams. With wrong sides together, stitch side panels to front of apron along long side edges, using ⅜" seam. Encase the seams with binding. Apply binding to side and lower edges, easing around curves at lower corners.
4. Baste ⅜" in along top edge of apron to gather. Pull up stitches to measure 18". On waistband piece, press ¼" to the back along one long edge. Press ¼" to the back at ends

of the waistband strip. Pin band to apron, having the right side of the band to the wrong side of the apron, matching centers. Stitch in ½" seam. Iron ½" to the back on the remaining length of the tie, up to where it joins at the apron edge. Fold waistband in half to the apron front and edge stitch total length of ties and across the apron waist.

## Initial Bracelet
(also shown on page 94)

- red and silver beads
- 3 silver charms
- elastic beading thread
- red and silver spacer beads
- round-nose pliers

1. Lay beads and charms in desired order of stringing.
2. String elastic thread with red and silver beads, charms and spacers to fit wrist. Knot ends of each length securely; dot knots with glue.

## Denim Luggage Tags
(also shown on page 95)

- tracing paper
- scraps of denim from discarded denim jeans or shorts
- 3½" x 7" lightweight cotton fabric for each tag backing
- matching sewing thread

- 20" of ⅝" w grosgrain ribbon for each tag
- 4¼" x 3½" piece clear vinyl for each tag
- ¾ yard of ⅛" w decorative trim, if desired
- one grommet set for each tag

1. Trace tag pattern (page 399) onto tracing paper and cut out. For each tag, cut one pattern from denim, centering over small pockets, side seams and other interesting parts of the garment. Cut one from cotton fabric for backing.
2. With wrong sides together, stitch tag front to back, overcasting edges. Use of a heavy jeans needle may be helpful in stitching through multiple denim layers. Place clear vinyl at bottom of tag, matching bottom edges.
3. Straight Stitch (page 319) around side and lower edges of vinyl, stitching through all layers. Stitch decorative trim around outside and lower edges.
4. Apply grommet at center top of tag, according to manufacturer's directions. Fold ribbon in half and pin to top straight edge of tag about 5" down from ribbon fold. Stitch to back of tag.
5. Insert business card or identification slip into the vinyl pocket. To attach to bag handle, pull ribbon ends through grommet hole, wrap loop around handle and insert ribbon ends through loop. Pull ribbon tightly around handle and tie ends together securely.

## Country Pot Holders
(continued from page 96)

to attach and quilt at the same time. Trim around outside edges. Make 1" binding from long strip of cotton fabric. Sew binding around outside edge of block mitering corners. Sew plastic ring or loop of rickrack to one corner for use as hanging potholder.

## Cupcake Pincushions
(continued from page 97)

**For Smaller Cupcake:**
- 8" x 8" square red print fabric
- 8" x 8" square lightweight iron-on interfacing
- 2½" x 7" piece ribbing from recycled sweater
- scrap pink felt for flower embellishment
- scrap red fabric for yo-yo flower
- 8" jumbo pink rickrack
- 22" narrow red cording
- 1" rounded top red button

**1.** Enlarge and trace patterns (page 398) onto tracing paper and cut out.

**2. For Larger Pincushion:** Sew short ends of 3" x 11" pink strip together, using ¼" seam, to form a tube. Cut one large circle for top of cupcake from both the pink fabric and interfacing. Fuse interfacing to back of large circle. Cut appliqué shape for top of large cushion from red felt and appliqué to center of pink circle. Cut yo-yo circle pattern from red print fabric. Make yo-yo and sew button to center. Sew yo-yo to center of appliqué shape. Gather outside edge of pink circle. Pull up basting stitches and pin gathered circle to tube of fabric. Lightly stuff the pink top with polyester fiberfill, adding a small amount of crushed walnuts to the center of the shape and finishing stuffing with polyester fiberfill. Baste around bottom of pink band and pull stitches tight to close shape. Stitch end to reinforce.

**3.** With right sides together, stitch short ends of ribbing together in ¼" seam to make a tube. Cut circle for bottom of pincushion from pink felt. Pin ribbing tube to circle and sew in ¼" seam. Stuff lightly with polyester fiberfill, making a well in the center to add crushed walnut shells for added weight.

**4.** Insert top into ribbed bottom and pin around top edge of ribbing through top fabric at sewing line where bottom band was added. Hand stitch in place using matching sewing thread. Tack rickrack to the top edge of the sweater fabric, using hand stitches and matching sewing thread.

**5. For Smaller Pincushion:** Make in same fashion as the larger one. Iron interfacing to the same size circle for the top. Pin cording in coil pattern, radiating from the center of the circle. Couch (page 333) using matching sewing thread. Sew rounded button to center. Baste ¾" from outside edge of circle to gather.

**6.** Pull up threads to draw in fabric to the size of the ribbing tube used as the base. After stuffing top, sew bottom closed. Insert top into sweater ribbing bottom and hand stitch in place. Hand stitch decorative rickrack at the center of the bottom ribbing.

**7.** Make yo-yo from red fabric and after securing stitching in center of the gathered circle, loop thread over outside of yo-yo and into the center to pull in sections to make petals. Cut small flower shape from pink felt. Sew yo-yo flower to center of pink flower shape, stitch button in center and hand stitch to side of ribbing bottom.

## Embroidered Baby Bib
(continued from page 98)

**4.** Place band on bib front, 3¼" from bottom edge of bib and pin in place. Attach band to bib by stitching close to pressed edges.

**5.** For girls' collar, baste lace to outside edges of two collar top pieces, placing lace edge along seam line and extending to the inside of the collar. With right sides together, stitch collar side and lower edges, but not the neckline seam. Clip curves and points, turn and press. Baste collar to right side of bib at neck edge, meeting in center.

**6.** Place bib pieces right sides together with batting on back of one bib piece. Stitch around all outside edges, leaving an opening for turning. Trim batting close to stitching, clip curves and points, turn and press. Topstitch close to folded edge all around, sewing across open edge used for turning and flipping up collar to sew around neck edge. Stitch in the ditch through all layers on either side of band.

**7.** Hand sew buttons securely at center front of bib. Stitch hook and loop tape at ends of bib so that rounded edge overlaps on top.

## Crochet Toddler Hat
(continued from page 99)

**Note:** Do not join rnds; but mark beg of each with a safety pin, moving along as you go.

**Foundation:**
Beginning at the crown with green, ch 2; 3 sc in 2nd ch from hook.

**Rnd 2:** 2 sc in each sc around – 6 sc.

**Rnd 3:** Rep Rnd 2 – 12 sc.

**Rnd 4:** (Sc in next sc, 2 sc in next sc) 6 times – 18 sc.

**Rnd 5:** (2 sc in next sc, sc in each of next 2 sc) 6 times – 24 sc.

**Rnd 6:** (Sc in each of next 3 sc, 2 sc in next sc) 6 times – 30 sc.

**Rnd 7:** (Sc in each of next 2 sc, 2 sc in next sc) 10 times – 40 sc.

**Rnd 8:** (Sc in each of next 3 sc, 2 sc in next sc) 10 times – 50 sc.

**Rnd 9:** (Sc in each of next 4 sc, 2 sc in next sc) 10 times – 60 sc.

**Rnd 10:** (Sc in each of next 5 sc, 2 sc in next sc) 10 times – 70 sc.

**Rnd 11:** (Sc in each of next 4 sc, 2 sc in next sc) 14 times – 84 sc.

**For size 1:** Rnds 12-25: Sc in each sc around. Next Rnd: (Sc2tog) around – 42 sts.

**For size 2:** Rnds 12-27: Sc in each sc around. Next Rnd: * Sc in next 2 sc, (sc2tog) 20 times; rep from * again – 44 sts.

**For size 3:** Rnds 12-28: Sc in each sc around. Next Rnd: * Sc in next 4 sc, (sc-2tog) 19 times; rep from * again – 46 sts.

**Last Rnd (all sizes):** * Sl st in each of next 2 sc, in next sc (sl st, ch 2, sl st); rep from * round and fasten off.

## Flower

With Plum Wine, ch 4.

**Rnd 1:** 11 dc in 4th ch from hook; sl st in front lp only of first dc (top of turning ch-3) – 12 dc.

**Rnd 2:** Working in front lps only of this rnd, (ch 2, 2 dc) in same st as joining, (dc, ch 2, sl st in next st); * (sl st, ch 2, 2 dc) in next st, (dc, ch 2, sl st) in next st; rep from * around; do not join – 6 petals.

**Rnd 3:** Working in rem lps of Rnd 1, sl st in first st; * ch 3, sk next st, sl st in next st; rep from * around, ending ch 3; sl st to beg sl st – 6 ch-3 lps.

**Rnd 4:** (Sl st, ch 3, 3 tr, ch 3, sl st) in each ch-3 lp around; sl st to beg sl st of Rnd 3.

**Rnd 5:** * Working in back of petals, ch 4, sl st in next sl st of Rnd 3; rep from * around, ending ch 4; sl st to beg sl st.

**Rnd 6:** (Sl st, ch 3, 5 tr, ch 3, sl st) in each ch-4 lp around; sl st to beg sl st of Rnd 5. Fasten off.

Join flower to side of hat.

## Knit Button-Trimmed Clutch

(continued from page 100)

**Gauge:** In Garter Stitch (knit every row), 22 stitches = 4"/10 cm.
**Take time to check your gauge.**

### Foundation:

Cast on 44 stitches. Knit every row until piece measures approximately 16" from beginning. Bind off. Weave in loose ends on one side.

### Finishing the Bag

**1.** From cast on edge, fold up 6". Thread a 16" length of cord into yarn needle and sew each side in place. Turn right side out.

**2.** Baste batting to back of lining. Stitch ¼" around all outside edges of lining piece. Fold lining to back along stitching lines and press in place.

**3.** Pin plastic canvas to the back of half the lining and baste seam over the outside and lower edges of the canvas by using matching thread and slip stitching in place.

**4.** Turn purse inside out. Pin the wrong side of the lining to the wrong side of the purse, having the canvas facing the front of the purse. Using matching thread, hand stitch along lining folded edge, catching in yarn on back side of purse. Turn right side out. Arrange buttons on outside of purse flap and sew in place.

**5.** Cut ribbon in half. Turn back ¼" at one end of each ribbon and finger press to form hem. Place a marker on center front of bag 2½" from fold; center hemmed end of one ribbon over marker and sew in place. Fold opposite edge of bag toward first ribbon, find center, sew remaining ribbon to top of flap near the edge. Tie ribbons into a bow.

## Needle Felted Sewing Case

(continued from page 101)

### Tools

- needle felting needle
- 3-needle felting tool, such as Clover
- needle felting mat or section of rigid foam insulation
- pinking shears

**1.** Cut a 6¼" x 9½" rectangle out of the 100% white wool felt and the 35% aqua felt. Cut two 9½" long needle strips, one 3" w out of the 35% wool felt pale green, and the other 2" w out of the 100% beige wool felt. Cut two ½" x 6" long strips of beige felt for the ties. Use the pattern (page 376) as the guide to cut four leaves out of the pale green.

**2.** Place the 100% white wool back piece over the needle felting mat. Roll a long strand of brown roving to make a branch. Arrange the branch so that it extends over the bottom edge of the felt. Needle felt the length of the branch in place. Add another small twig section to the branch and needle felt it in place. Create 4 more branches alternating their orientation so they extend off the top and bottom edges of the felt.

**3.** Highlight some of the branches with strands of pale green roving, needle felting them in place. To make the flower buds, first spiral a strand of beige roving into a circle, needle felt it against the branch.

**4.** For the petal portion, spiral aqua roving into a circle and needle felt it nestled against the beige. Add one or two more buds to each branch making them smaller as they climb the branch. Highlight the base of each bud with a small strand of light beige, and the petals with a small strand of light aqua.

(continued on next page)

**5.** Fold the 100% wool felt beige stem in half and machine stitch the two layers together with a single central stem. Repeat the process with the second strip.

**6.** Trim the edge of each pair of leaves with pinking shears. Tuck a stem end between the base of two leaves. Pin the leaves together and then center the base of the leaf under the presser foot of the machine. Machine stitch your way up the center of leaf switching directions to make diagonal seams out to the leaf edge and back. Once you reach the top of the leaf, work your way back down filling in with several more diagonal divisions to complete the vein pattern. Repeat the process with the second strip and leaf pair. Trim both edges of the green felt needle strip with pinking shears then center it down the length of the aqua piece. Lay the beige piece down the center of green strip. Pin the strips in place and machine stitch along each edge of the beige strip.

**7.** Placing right sides together stack the back piece over the inside piece. Place the stems leaf side in between the layers. The stem ends should extend out the edge. Pin the pieces together and then machine stitch around the edges leaving a 2" opening.

**8.** Turn the piece right side out and hand stitch the opening closed.

**9.** Hand stitch a single bead to each finished stem, positioning it at the base of a leaf.

## Easy Fleece Hat and Scarf Set
(also shown on page 100)

- ¾ yard fleece in desired color
- matching thread
- scissors
- 3½" x 24" piece white fleece (for snowball hat only)

**1.** Cut off selvages. **For scarf,** cut rectangle with straight or decorative-edge scissors, cutting across the grain of fabric to make a strip 6"x 60". Fold scarf in half and fringe the ends by making ½" cuts through both layers, approximately 3" deep. **For hat,** cut a piece of fleece 24" (crosswise grain, with the most stretch) x 8" (lengthwise grain).

**2.** With right sides together, fold the hat together to make a piece 12"x 8". Stitch back seam, using ¼" seam allowance, stopping approximately 3" from the edge; backstitch.

**3.** On bottom edge, fold cuff under 3" to wrong side of hat. Stitch close to cut edge through both layers of fabric. Turn hat right side out and roll up cuff 2½". Lay hat flat and fringe top edge by making ½" cuts approximately 3" down. Cut strip of fleece ½" x 12" long.

**4.** Gather top of hat together and hold in your hands while using the fleece strip to tie a tight knot around top fringes. Trim strip even with other ties and fluff fringes.

**For snowball hat,** cut blue fleece 24" (crosswise) x 5 " (lengthwise). Cut white fleece 24" x 3½ ". Connect white fleece to blue fleece by zigzag stitching across the two pieces. Make hat as directed, above, using piece of white fleece to tie top fringes of hat.

## Sweet Gift Card Holder
(continued from page 103)

**1.** Using the patterns on page 401, cut a bird and leaves from felt and a felted wool wing.

**2.** For the card holder, arrange and pin the appliqués on the top half of a 4½"x6" felted wool piece.

**3.** Using 6 strands of floss, work Stem Stitch (page 319) branches and attach the leaves, bird and wing with Running Stitches. Add a Satin Stitch beak and a French Knot eye.

**4.** Fold the holder and join the sides with Running Stitches. Sew the fastener to the inside; then, glue the ribbon around the top of the holder, knotting the ends.

**5.** To personalize, string the beads on floss; knot the ends. Sew the beaded strand to a corner of the gift card holder.

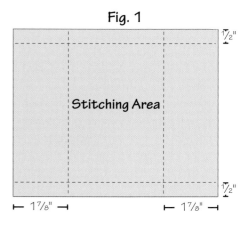

## Cell Phone Cozy
(continued from page 105)

**1.** Cut a 7"x5¾" wool felt piece. Refer to Fig. 1 to mark off the stitching area.

### Fig. 1

**2.** Enlarge the patterns on page 396 to 122%. Using the patterns, cut 2 felt leaves and one flower and flower center each from felt and fabric (we cut the centers with pinking shears). Arrange and pin the flowers and leaves in the stitching area and draw curly stems with the marker. Sew over the stem lines and hand- or machine-sew the flowers and leaves in place. Remove any marker lines with a damp cotton swab. Attach brads through the flower centers.

**3.** Follow Needle Felting (page 320) to apply berries with wool roving.

**4.** Use freeform stitching lines to sew rickrack along the top edge. Matching right sides, sew the short ends together. Finger press the seam allowances open at the center back; sew the bottom edges together. Clip the corners and turn the cozy right side out.

**5.** Thread the clasp on a 1"x2" felt strip; fold and sew the strip ends to the inside back of the cozy.

## Blooming Pincushion
(also shown on page 104)

**1.** Enlarge and trace patterns (page 398) onto tracing paper and cut out. Fuse interfacing to wrong side of both squares of fabric. On wrong side of one square of fabric, trace around the pattern for the pincushion with marking pen.

**2.** With right sides together, pin marked square with unmarked square and sew on marked lines. Trim seam allowance to a scant ¼", clip corners and curves. Cut a ¾" long slit in the center of one layer of fabric. Turn right side out. Stuff lightly with fiberfill and hand stitch opening closed.

**3.** Use 6 strands embroidery floss to insert needle into pincushion top center. Bring it out at the bottom center, up and around one of the inside points between petals, then through the top center to the bottom.

**4.** Continue stitching and wrapping embroidery floss between all petals, pulling

thread tightly to indent the pincushion. Knot securely.

**5.** Make yo-yo from smaller square of fabric and sew in center of pincushion. On back of pincushion sew one piece of the hook and loop tape to the center. Sew the other piece of hook and loop tape to the center of the shorter pocket on the front of the bag.

## Wrapping Station
(also shown on page 107)

Gather holiday wrap, ribbons, trims & tags and organize a wrapping station (we attached a vintage mailbox and a wire screen to the wall above the table for extra storage). Keep your supplies in holiday tins and galvanized containers with festive labels. With your own wrapping station, you'll always be ready to wrap!

## Wrap-in-a-Snap
(also shown on page 110)

Gather tissue or wrapping paper around an odd-shaped gift with a pretty ribbon bow. Tie a cardstock tag with a rub-on message to a basket or tote and place the package inside. Two-gifts-in-one!

## Rickrack Wrap
(also shown on page 110)

Add pizzazz to your gift-wrapped box. Adhere rickrack lengths around the box with glue or double-sided tape. Use wavy-edged scissors to cut cardstock to cover the top of the package. Cut a center slit near each edge a little wider than your ribbon. Thread the ends of one ribbon through slits on opposite ends of the cardstock topper and adhere the ribbon ends under the package. Run another ribbon under the box and thread the ends up through the remaining slits, catch the first ribbon and tie a bow at the top.

Organizing is what you do before you do something, so that when you do it, it's not all mixed UP. ~A.A. MILNE

## Fabric-Backed Cards
(also shown on page 113)

**For the Tree and Star Cards:**
- small piece of small-print fabric
- 4-5 colors of cardstock
- one patterned paper
- Christmas tree punch
- small buttons
- star punch
- twine
- paper piercer
- small punched star
- corner rounder
- small hole punch
- computer or stamp for text
- adhesive, including strong tape, glue pen

**1.** Cut card base from cardstock, then score and fold in half so that card opens at bottom. Stamp or print text strip and adhere across bottom portion of card.
**2.** Cut desired shape from cardstock, then cut into shape to fit space above text. Cut fabric and tape to the back of cardstock to show through opening. Mat in slightly larger coordinating cardstock and adhere to card. **For star card,** cut small squares of cardstock to fit in space at right. Add small buttons tied with twine on star card and on trees on tree card. Print or stamp greeting and adhere to inside of card.

## Buttons and Bows Topper
(also shown on page 112)

- cardboard box
- 4 colors coordinating cardstock
- dotted paper
- scalloped/circle die cuts for top of box
- border punch or strip
- ribbon to wrap around box
- buttons in graduated sizes
- liquid glue
- adhesive foam dots
- tape adhesive

**1.** Cover box and lid with cardstock using strong tape adhesive. Cover sides of lid in dot paper. Adhere border made from coordinating cardstock to lower edge of lid.
**2.** Wrap ribbon round sides of box and tape to top of lid. Cut scallop and circle from cardstock and adhere to lid using adhesive foam dots. Arrange buttons as desired, stacking some, and adhere using liquid glue.

## Christmas Carol Topper
(also shown on page 112)

- cardboard box
- 3 colors coordinating cardstock

- patterned paper
- old Christmas sheet music
- large scallop and circle die cut
- tag
- twine
- stapler
- hot-glue gun and glue sticks
- tape adhesive
- stamps, rub-on letters or computer/ printer (for tag text)

**1.** Cover box and lid with cardstock using strong tape adhesive. Cut mat from patterned paper and adhere to lid. Cut large circle and scalloped circle from cardstock and adhere to patterned paper on lid.
**2.** To make bow, cut 1" strips of sheet music and cardstock–two 9" long, two 8" long and two 7" long. Fold them into loops and staple at the center. Crisscross the two longest strips and use hot glue to secure. Do the same with the next two layers. Add additional layers as desired. Add loops of paper/cardstock to center. Cut "tails" from sheet music and cardstock and hot glue to box as desired. Make tag and trim with patterned paper and cardstock. Tie to package with twine.

## Dressed-Up Doggy Cards
(also shown on page 113)

**1.** To make the card base, fold the full sheet of cardstock in half lengthwise and then cut it in half widthwise (with the paper trimmer). This will divide the paper into two card blanks. The poodle card uses the natural colored card base, and the Dachshund uses the white card base.
**2.** Ink the snowflake stamp with the aqua stamp pad and randomly stamp the front of the natural card for the poodle card, and

352

he patterned paper for the Dachshund. Ink he message stamp with the black stamp ad and print it on the inside of the card.

5. Carefully rip a 1" tall strip of white paper o make the snow bank for the poodle card. Repeat the process to tear a stamped patterned paper for the Dachshund card. Trim he sides of the ripped strip to fit across the ottom of the card. Glue the strip in place.

4. Trace the dog and dog clothing patterns (page 403) and cut out. Cut the oodle shapes out of the tan paper and he Dachshund dog shapes out of brown ardstock scraps. Position the dogs on he center front of each card so that their eet stand over the paper snow. Glue each arpiece to the head so the outside edge of he ear extends beyond the head.

5. Cut the collar piece out of the patterned aper and the main coat out of the aqua elt. Cut the single Dachshund coat template out of the red felt.

6. Using red embroidery thread, make a ingle stitch in and out the center top of the blue felt coat, tie the ends into a ow and then trim the thread ends. Using off-white thread, make a series of small titches that encircle the collar of the red elt coat. Knot the ends on the wrong side of the felt; trim the ends.

7. Glue patterned collar over base of oodle's neck. Use a thin layer of craft lue to mount the blue felt coat over the oodle's body and bottom edge of collar. Use more craft glue to attach the red coat o the Dachshund. Use a thin permanent marker to add a single eye and an oval nose o each dog.

## Punched Snowflake Sack
(also shown on page 120)

- brown gift bag (ours is 8"x10½")
- 1" snowflake punch
- assorted hole punches
- scrapbook paper
- craft glue
- jute twine
- vintage buttons
- lacy trim
- emery board or fine-grit sandpaper
- rub-on holiday message and alphabet
- 2 jewelry tags
- thread

1. Leaving the bag closed, pinch the front and one front side together and punch 4 snowflakes through both layers. Repeat on the other side. Set the flakes aside. Punch tiny holes above and below the flake-shaped holes on the bag.

2. Punch 8 scrapbook paper snowflakes. Gently fold the long branches of the flakes toward the center. Working from the inside of the bag out, insert each folded flake through the center of a flake-shaped hole on the bag front and rotate the flake slightly, so the long branches cover the short branch holes in the bag. Unfold the long branches for a dimensional effect and glue or use twine to sew a button to the center of each flake.

3. Sew trim around the top of the bag using twine and Running Stitches (page 319). Punch holes in the bag to accent the trim.

4. For the tag, cut a scrapbook paper strip (ours is 1¾"x8") and sand the edges. Punch a snowflake from the bottom, and follow Step 2 to insert and rotate one of the bag snowflakes. Glue trim along the tag edges; fold the tag in half. Add a rub-on message to the front. Add buttons. Personalize the jewelry tags with rub-ons and use thread to hang them from the lower button.

## Chipboard Snowflake Sack
(also shown on page 120)

- assorted hole punches
- brown gift bag (ours is 5¼"x8⅝")
- ribbon scrap
- craft glue
- button
- 1" snowflake punch
- scrapbook papers
- alphabet stamps
- ink pad
- 2 jewelry tags
- thread
- 3" chipboard snowflakes

- brown paper lunch bag
- 1/16" dia. anywhere hole punch (optional)

1. Punch holes through the top front of the bag. Tie a ribbon through 2 holes.

2. Glue a button and a punched scrapbook paper snowflake to the bag. Stamp the tags and use thread to hang them from the button.

3. Glue scrapbook paper to the chipboard snowflakes; trim. Glue snowflakes punched from the lunch bag and scrapbook paper to the covered chipboard flakes. Add punched circles and snowflake branches where desired. (We used an anywhere punch to make holes in the center snowflake.) Glue the snowflakes to the gift bag, trimming the flakes to fit.

## Surprise Jewelry Box
(also shown on page 122)

- transfer paper
- double-sided cardstock
- stylist or bone folder
- double-sided tape
- fabric glue
- rickrack
- twill tape
- piece of jewelry (for gift)
- 2 decorative brads
- assorted ribbons
- photocopy of a 1" dia. black & white photo
- glittered wreath frame sticker (found with scrapbooking supplies)

1. Enlarge the pattern on page 376 to 200%. Transfer the pattern to cardstock and cut out. Score, then fold the box along the dashed lines. Tape the long flap to the wrong side of the opposite long edge, forming a triangular tube.

(continued on next page)

**2.** For the jewelry card, cut a 1⅝"x5⅝" cardstock strip. Center and glue an 11" rickrack length on a 10" length of twill tape. Threading the jewelry piece to the center, fold the twill tape in half. Attach the folded tape to the cardstock strip with a brad.
**3.** Insert the jewelry card in the box and tuck in the ends. Embellish the box with twill tape, ribbons and rickrack. Adhere the photocopy to the frame sticker and use a brad to attach it to the twill tape.

## Floral Bow

(continued from page 123)
**2.** Gather the ribbon between your thumb and forefinger at the streamer mark. Twist the remaining ribbon one full turn (Fig. 1).

### Fig. 1

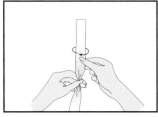

**3.** To make the first loop, place the first loop mark behind the streamer mark; gather the ribbon and twist the remaining ribbon one full turn (Fig. 2).

### Fig. 2

**4.** Place the second loop mark behind the first loop mark; gather and twist the remaining ribbon one full turn (Fig. 3).

### Fig. 3

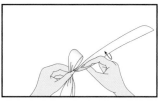

**5.** Continue to make 18 more loops. Secure the bow with wire. Trim the streamers and fluff up the loops. Add the bow to ribbon tied around the wrapped gift.

## Necktie Bow with Photo Tag

(continued from page 123)
**1.** Follow Fig. 1 to knot the ribbon around the wrapped gift, leaving a short streamer (about 9") at the top and a long streamer (about 10") at the bottom. Fold the short streamer down (Fig. 2).

### Fig. 1          Fig. 2

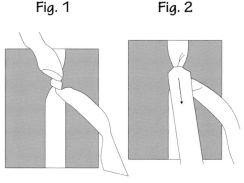

**2.** Fold the long streamer over the top and behind the knot (Figs. 3 and 4). Tuck the long streamer through the loop and pull, forming the necktie bow (Figs. 5 and 6). Trim the ends.

**3.** For the tag, stamp a deckle-edged white cardstock tag with background words using distressing ink. Use photo corners to attach the photo to a red cardstock "ribbon." Place the "ribbon" on the tag and cut a tiny slit through both cardstock layers for the button shank. Insert the shank through the slit and secure on the back with the paperclip. Clip the tag to the ribbon on the package.

### Fig. 3

### Fig. 4

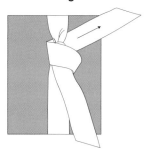

### Fig. 5

### Fig. 6

## Warm Wishes Snowman Card
(continued from page 125)

5. Adhere narrow ribbon along bottom edge of cardstock. Cut small piece of patterned paper, ink and adhere vertically to left portion of card. Ink and use adhesive dimensional dots to adhere snowman image to right portion of card. Adhere tab to upper left portion of image, tucking under snowman. Adhere button to tab using glue dot. Knot tulle and adhere to button using glue dot.

6. Adhere punched snowflake to lower portion of rectangular image using glue dot. Adhere jewels to center of snowflake. Print or stamp greeting to inside of card.

## There's No Place Like Home Card
(also shown on page 125)
- large circular sticker or stamped image; small rectangular text sticker or stamp
- 4 colors of cardstock
- 3 coordinated patterned papers
- wide ribbon
- twine

- adhesive, including glue dots and foam dots
- corner rounder
- ink for edging papers
- computer or stamps for creating inside greeting
- $1/8$" and $1/2$" circle punches
- scalloped circle die or punch
- paper piercer

1. Cut card base from cardstock. Score and fold so that card opens at right side. Round corners and ink. Cut wide strip of patterned paper, ink and adhere to bottom portion of card. Cut strip of patterned paper for left portion of card. Using a $1/2$" circle punch, notch the bottom two corners of the strip, then ink and adhere vertically to left portion of card. Cut a narrower strip of patterned paper, then ink and adhere vertically on top of wider strip.

2. Cut a small tag from contrasting cardstock to mat small rectangular sticker. Punch a hole in the end and string with twine. Ink and set aside.

3. Cut a strip of cardstock to fit width of card. Knot wide ribbon around the left portion of this strip. Before completing knot, tie twine to the ribbon, then complete the knot. Trim ribbon then adhere strip to card. Mat round image onto a scalloped circle cut from cardstock. Use a piercing tool to make small holes in each of the scallops. Ink and then position the scalloped piece at the middle right of the card, extending off edge. Trim flush with right edge. Adhere the sticker to the center of the scallop using foam pop dots. Print or stamp greeting; adhere to inside of card.

## Pink Patterned Purse Card
(continued from page 133)

1. Enlarge and trace purse pattern (page 395) onto paper and cut out. Trace scalloped topper onto cardstock and cut

out. Fold scalloped piece in half to create purse shape (fold will be at the top).

2. Fold topper in half and adhere to folded edge of purse. Use punch to make two small holes in the fold for handle. Beginning inside the purse, run cord through both holes and knot to create handle.

3. Tie short lengths of ribbon to left side of handle. Punch small circles from coordinating cardstock and glue to each scallop on the topper. Thread floss through button and adhere with glue dot. Adhere gift card or money to the inside of card.

## Holly Purse Card
(also shown on page 133)
- purse and topper patterns
- dotted cardstock plus 3 coordinating colors
- embossing template
- pearl string for handle
- border punch
- holly punch or die
- small hole punch or paper piercer
- adhesive, including fine-tipped glue
- computer or stamps for inside greeting
- adhesive hook and loop dot

1. Enlarge and trace purse and topper patterns (page 395) onto cardstock and cut out. Fold in half to create purse shape (fold will be at the bottom of purse). Fold topper and emboss the front. Adhere the INSIDE of it to the back side of the purse to create a flap/closure. Attach adhesive dot to the inside of the flap/closure and outside front of the purse. Use punch or piercer to make two small holes in the fold for handle.

2. Cut out holly and berries and adhere to flap/closure. Punch border strip and mat with cardstock; adhere across bottom of purse. Adhere gift card or money to the inside of card.

## Tinsel Purse Card
(also shown on page 133)
- rounded purse and topper patterns
- two colors cardstock
- embossing template
- wired tinsel
- small jingle bell
- floss
- narrow ribbon
- small punched or sticker snowflakes
- small hole punch

(continued on next page)

- adhesive, including liquid and fine-tipped glue
- computer or stamps for inside greeting
- hook and loop adhesive dot

**1.** Enlarge and trace purse and topper patterns (page 395) onto cardstock and cut out. Fold in half to create purse shape (fold will be at the bottom of purse). Emboss the FRONT of the purse. Fold topper and adhere the INSIDE of it to the back side of the purse to create a flap/closure.

**2.** Attach adhesive dot to the inside of the flap/closure and outside front of the purse. Use punch to make two small holes in the fold for handle. Beginning inside the purse, run ribbon through both holes and knot to create handle. Tie short lengths of ribbon to left side of handle. Cut a length of wired tinsel to fit along the flap; bend to form. Thread jingle bell with floss and tie snugly to the center of the cut piece of wire.

**3.** Use liquid glue to adhere the tinsel along the edge of the flap. Hold or weight in place to dry. Adhere small snowflakes to lower right portion of purse. Adhere gift card or money to the inside of card.

## Woodland Wrap
(continued from page 124)

**1.** Cut curved strips of "snow" from white cardstock. Adhere around base of box. Cut triangle "trees" from three shades of green cardstock. Cut small trunks from brown cardstock. Adhere the trees to the box sides as desired, using pop dots under some of them. Adhere snowflakes to box sides as desired.

**2.** Cut 2 strips of cardstock to create ribbon strips for lid. Trim the ends at an angle, then adhere to lid using strong tape adhesive.

**3.** To make bow, cut six 1" strips of white cardstock—two 9" long, two 8" long, two 7" long. Fold them into loops and staple at the center. Crisscross the two longest ribbons and use hot glue to secure. Do the same with the next 2 layers. Punch a circle from cardstock and adhere to the center of the bow (to cover staple). Hot glue a pine cone to the center of the bow.

## Stamped Paper Bag
(also shown on page 124)

- brown handle bag
- patterned paper
- decorative edge paper
- green and red cardstock
- small holiday stamp and ink
- small tag or tag die
- small circle punch
- floral wire
- pencil
- twine
- needle and floss
- glitter glue
- stamps, rub-on letters or computer/printer (for tag text)

**1.** Ink edges of bag, then stamp front of bag and color the images with markers. Add glitter to stamped images and allow to dry.

**2.** For bag topper, cut patterned paper into a square to fit the width of the bag (ours is 8"x 8") and fold in half. Cut a slit in the top for the bag handle. Cut a decorative edge along the bottom of each side. Ink the bag topper, then hand-stitch along edges.

**3.** Cut holly leaves from green cardstock; punch berries from red. Lightly fold the

leaves for dimension. Adhere to bag topper. Coil floral wire around a pencil and wrap around one side of handle.

**4.** Create tag from coordinating materials; trim with twine and tie to handle with floss.

## Torn Paper Wrap
(also shown on page 124)

- cardboard box
- white and coordinating cardstock (to match ribbon)
- brown kraft paper
- wide ribbon to wrap around box and tie
- snowflake die cuts or punches
- glitter glue
- tape adhesive
- adhesive dimensional dots
- manila shipping tag
- computer/printer or stamps for tag text
- needle and floss

**1.** Cover box and lid in white cardstock using tape adhesive. Cut and adhere a kraft paper mat to box lid. Cut a strip of kraft paper to fit around the edge of the lid.

**2.** Tear a strip of kraft paper to extend around the box. **Tip:** Tear toward your body slowly to create a rough edge. Tape to box. Tie ribbon around box and knot at top. Tie bow. Adhere glittered snowflakes to top of box using adhesive dimensional dots.

**3. For tag,** adhere white cardstock to base of manila tag. Tear kraft paper and adhere above it. Adhere ribbon to tag for color. Stamp or print text onto matching cardstock; adhere to tag at an angle. Hand stitch along the bottom of tag using white floss. Adhere glittered snowflake to tag using adhesive dots. Tie tag to lid.

## Menswear Gift Sacks
(also shown on page 126)

These versatile gift sacks vary just a bit in construction. Choose a square-corner bag with a simple drawstring, a boxed-corner bag with a double-ended drawstring or a softly gathered-corner bag with a ruffled casing for the drawstring. Use a ½" seam allowance for all sewing unless otherwise indicated.

### Boxed-Corner Bag
• 15"x28" piece of menswear fabric
• 2 yards of ⅞"w ribbon
• 5½"x6½" wool scrap for pocket
• felt scraps
• fabric glue
• embroidery floss
• black size 10 sew-on snap for eyes
• seasonal message stamp and ink pad

**1.** Matching short ends and right sides, fold the fabric piece in half. Sew the side seams. Flatten and center each side seam against the bottom of the bag; sew across each corner 1¼" from the point (Fig. 1). Turn the sack right side out and press the top edge ¼", then 1¼" to the inside. Sew along the bottom folded edge and ¼" from the top folded edge.

**Fig. 1**

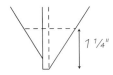

1¼"

**2.** Carefully remove the stitching from both side seams in the casing area. Cut the ribbon in half and thread 1 length through the front casing and 1 length through the

back casing; knot the ends together and trim.

**3.** Enlarge the patterns (page 413) to 200%. Using the enlarged patterns, cut the snowman appliqué pieces. Press all pocket piece edges ¼" to the wrong side. Glue the appliqués to the pocket. Use floss to work Blanket Stitches (page 319) around the snowman, French Knots (page 319) for his mouth, Straight Stitches (page 319) for the mouth corner and a French Knot and Straight Stitch snowflake in the pocket corner. Sew on the snap eyes. Stamp a corner with the holiday message. Attach the pocket to the bag with floss Blanket Stitches. For the scarf, cut ¾"x6½" and ¾"x3" felt pieces. Fringe the ends of the 6½" length. Fold and glue the scarf to the snowman.

### Square-Corner Bag
• 20"x31" piece of menswear fabric
• 1¾ yards of 1"w ribbon
• 6"x7¾" wool scrap for pocket
• felted wool scrap
• decorative brad
• embroidery floss

**1.** Matching short ends and right sides, fold the fabric piece in half. Sew the side seams. Turn the sack right side out and press the top edge ¼", then 1¼" to the inside. Sew along the bottom folded edge.

**2.** Carefully remove the stitching from one side seam in the casing area. Thread the ribbon through the casing, knot the ends together and trim.

**3.** Press all pocket piece edges ¼" to the wrong side. Use floss to work Stem Stitches (page 319) to attach a felted wool monogram (pick a favorite font from your computer) to the pocket. Add a small

felted wool circle and a decorative brad to the corner. Attach the pocket to the bag with Blanket Stitches (page 319).

### Gathered-Corner Bag
• 16"x29" piece of menswear fabric
• 1¼ yards of 1"w ribbon for drawstring
• felt scrap
• 1¾ yards of 1"w ribbon for flower
• fabric glue
• 4"x4" fabric scrap for pocket
• 1"w ribbon scraps for leaves and tag
• seasonal message stamp and ink pad
• acrylic gem brad
• embroidery floss

**1.** Matching short ends and right sides, fold the fabric piece in half. Sew the side seams. For the gathered corners, baste diagonally across each bottom corner. Pull basting threads tight and securely knot the thread ends. Turn the sack right side out and press the top edge ¼", then 2¼" to the inside. Sew along the bottom folded edge and 1¼" from the top folded edge.

**2.** Carefully remove the stitching from one side seam in the casing area. Thread the ribbon through the casing and trim the ends.

**3.** Cut a 2¾" diameter felt circle. Twist and glue one end of the flower ribbon to the felt circle center. Continue twisting and gluing in a spiral to cover the circle; trim as needed.

**4.** Press all pocket piece edges ¼" to the wrong side. Glue the flower, folded ribbon leaves and the ribbon tag to the pocket piece. Stamp the ribbon tag and add the brad. Use floss to work Running Stitches (page 319) along the pocket top edge and Blanket Stitches (page 319) to attach the pocket to the bag.

1. Enlarge the pattern on page 397 to 230%. Transfer (page 318) the pattern to cardstock and cut out. Use the stylus to score the piece along the dashed lines; fold along the scored lines. Tape the long flap to the wrong side of the opposite long edge, forming a triangular tube.
2. Place the gift in the box and tuck in the ends (tape the ends if desired). Add a seasonal message to a layered cardstock tag. Adhere the tag to the box and embellish with ribbon and a decorative brad.

## Handmade Boxes

### Open Window Cookie Box
(also shown on page 126)
• transfer paper
• patterned cardstock
• stylus or bone folder
• double-sided tape
• wrapped cookies
• ribbon
• rub-on message
• embroidery floss

1. Enlarge the pattern on page 401 to 200%. Transfer (page 318) the pattern to cardstock and cut out; discard the window cutout. Use the stylus to score the piece along the dashed lines; fold along the scored lines. Tape the box together, overlapping the grey areas where indicated on the pattern.
2. Place wrapped cookies in the box and fold down the top. Tie a ribbon around the box. Add a seasonal message to a layered cardstock tag and tie to the bow with floss.

### Triangular Gift Box
(also shown on page 126)
• transfer paper
• patterned cardstock
• stylus or bone folder
• double-sided tape
• alphabet stickers
• ribbon
• decorative brad

### Square Gift Box
(also shown on page 126)

• transfer paper
• solid and patterned cardstock
• ¼" hole punch
• stylus or bone folder
• double-sided tape
• ribbon
• rub-on letters
• photo corners
• snowflake punch
• acrylic gems
• craft glue

1. Enlarge the pattern on page 400 to 150%. Transfer (page 318) the pattern to cardstock twice and cut out. Use the stylus to score the box pieces along the dashed lines; fold along the scored lines. Tape the box pieces together, overlapping the grey areas where indicated on the pattern.
2. Place the gift in the box and tuck in the sides. Tie a ribbon through the punched holes. Use rub-on letters to personalize a layered cardstock tag. Adhere the tag and photo corners to the box. Glue punched snowflakes and gems to the box.

## Cupcake Liner Topper and Box
(continued from page 127)

**Outside of box:**
1. Cover box and lid in cardstock using tape adhesive.
2. Cut a large mat of coordinating paper for the lid. Cut strips of matching cardstock/paper and adhere to the edges of the box lid. Punch circles of various sizes from matching cardstock/patterned paper. Punch smaller holes in some of the larger circles to add interest. Adhere circles to sides of box, slightly overlapping. Place pop dots under some circles to add depth. Cut 2 lengths of ribbon and adhere to the box lid.
3. To make bow, layer several cupcake liners, alternating directions. Staple in the center, fold in half at the staple and cut slits along the edges to create "petals." Round each with scissors. Unfold and "fluff." Cut one liner a bit smaller for the center of the bow and adhere. Punch a circle for the center and adhere. Knot a short length of ribbon and adhere to the bow, then adhere the bow to the box.

## Toy Topper
(also shown on page 127)
• cardboard box
• 3 colors of coordinating cardstock

rickrack to fit around box lid
border punch or strip
wooden toys
circle punches in 2 sizes
twine
tape adhesive
hot-glue gun and glue sticks
marker
stamps, rub-on letters or computer/
printer (for tag text)

**1.** Cover box with cardstock using strong tape adhesive. Cover lid with same color and layer with 2 mats of coordinating cardstock. Adhere border made of coordinating cardstock around edges of lid. Adhere rickrack to border. Arrange wooden toys and adhere to lid with hot glue.
**2. For tag,** string twine through a large circular wooden toy, leaving length to tie. Create text for tag, punch into circle shape, mat onto larger circle, add pen-stitching with marker, then adhere to wooden toy. Tie tag to wooden toys on lid.

## Jingle Bell Topper
(also shown on page 127)

- cardboard box
- 3 colors of coordinating cardstock
- one patterned paper
- one large package of glittered jingle bells
- sheer ribbon for bow
- border punch or strip
- small tag
- twine
- tape adhesive
- hot-glue gun and glue sticks
- stamps, rub-on letters or computer/
  printer (for tag text)

**1.** Cover box with cardstock using strong tape adhesive. Cover lid with same color and layer with mats of coordinating cardstock.

**2.** Adhere patterned paper around the edge of lid. Adhere border made of coordinating cardstock to bottom edge of lid. Adhere bells to lid with hot glue. Tie ribbon into a bow and adhere with hot glue next to bells.
**3.** Create tag and tie to package with twine.

## 3-D Christmas Tree Gift Tag
(also shown on page 133)

- 3 colors of cardstock
- one patterned paper
- border punch
- punched star
- round sticker
- round stamp or computer for text
- circle punch slightly larger than round sticker and stamp
- floss
- wide ribbon
- adhesive, including strong tape and adhesive dimensional dots
- scoring blade
- corner rounder
- small hole punch

**1.** Cut a rectangle from cardstock to create tag. Round corners and punch hole at top. Cut patterned paper and adhere across center of tag. Punch a border from cardstock and adhere to lower portion of tag below patterned paper. Cut a narrow strip of contrasting cardstock and adhere just above border strip.
**2. To make tree,** cut 4 same-size narrow triangles from embossed cardstock. Score and fold each in half vertically. Adhere one side of the triangle to the facing side of another triangle until all 4 are adhered together. Adhere the flat side of this piece to the tag so that the tree "fans" out from the tag.

**3.** Cut and adhere a small cardstock trunk. Adhere punched star above tree. Create "to/from" using stamps or computer. Punch out using circle punch. Punch a cardstock circle of the same size to mat sticker. Adhere both pieces to the right portion of tag using pop dots. Tie ribbon through hole at top of tag.

## Snowflake Tag
(also shown on page 133)

- large tag cut from cardstock
- 2 additional colors of cardstock
- 2-3 coordinating patterned papers
- die cut snowflake
- wide ribbon
- twine
- large and small button
- adhesive, including glue dots
- border punch
- computer or stamp for text

**1.** Cut a strip of patterned paper and adhere across upper portion of tag. Cut two narrow strips of patterned paper and adhere below the first strip. Punch a scalloped border from cardstock then back with a lighter color. Adhere along lower edge of tag. Print text on strip of light cardstock. Adhere across lower portion of card.
**2.** Adhere snowflake to tag. Adhere large button to snowflake center using glue dots. Thread twine through small button, tie in bow, then adhere small button to large button using glue dots. Double the wide ribbon and thread through tag hole. Tie and trim ends.

## Lollipop Bottle
(also shown on page 135)

- tracing paper
- cream cardstock
- striped scrapbook paper
- craft glue
- rub-on holiday message
- glitter
- ½"w silk ribbon
- double-sided tape
- vintage milk bottle
- Candy Tree Lollipops (page 135)
- small plastic bags
- green floral tape
- wooden skewers
- ⅛" dia. hole punch
- candy-coated chocolates

This gift is sure to delight! Use the label patterns on page 394 and cut cardstock and scrapbook paper label pieces. Layer and glue the pieces together. Add the rub-on message and glitter. Thread ribbon through slits cut in the label. Add a little tape on the back and tie the label around the bottle.

For the tags, glue a scrapbook paper piece to a cardstock piece. Use the tag pattern and cut a tag for each lollipop.

Place a plastic bag over each lollipop. To lengthen the "trunks," wrap green floral tape around a wooden skewer and each lollipop stick, catching the bag ends to seal. Thread ribbon through a hole punched in the tag and tie it around the stick. Fill the bottle with candy-coated chocolates and insert the lollipops.

## Muffin Tin
(also shown on page 136)

- fabric glue
- small and medium rickrack
- vintage muffin tin (for decorative use only)
- double-sided holiday print cardstock
- hole punch
- Mom's Applesauce Muffins (page 136)
- ribbon
- rub-on letters
- jute twine

1. Layer and glue rickrack around the edges of the muffin tin.
2. Enlarge the patterns on page 398 to 143%. Using the patterns, cut cardstock muffin cup inserts and a tag. Place an insert and a muffin in each cup. Tie a ribbon bow through the hole in the tin. Add rub-ons to the tag and tie to the bow with twine.

## Party Mix Tin
(also shown on page 137)

- plastic zipping bag filled with Honey Popcorn & Cashews (page 137)

- tin with handle and attached scoop (ours is 7"wx6"dx9"h)
- vintage crocheted potholder with hanging loop
- snowflake print cardstock
- craft glue
- decorative chipboard label
- letter sticker
- sandpaper
- glitter
- decorative chipboard square (ours says "jolly")
- adhesive foam dots
- metal garter grip (available at fabric and scrapbook stores)
- hole punch
- twill tape

1. Place the party mix in the tin. Slip the scoop handle through the hanging loop of the potholder and hook on the side of the tin.
2. Cut a cardstock tag (ours is 4¾"x2½"); trim the top corners. Sew around the outer edges in a freeform style. Adhere the label to the tag; add the sticker.
3. Lightly sand and glitter the edges of the chipboard square. Attach the square to the tag with a foam dot. Add dots of glitter to the tag. Slip the garter grip pin through a hole punched in the tag. Loop and sew twill tape around the garter grip hook. Attach the tag.

## Cake Box
(also shown on page 147)

- craft knife and cutting mat
- 10"x10"x5" one-piece fold-out cake box
- double-sided tape
- acetate sheet
- patterned cardstock
- low-temp glue gun

- food tissue paper
- Blueberry Cream Coffee Cake (page 147)
- 2³⁄₄ yards of ¼"w gingham ribbon

**1.** Enlarge the window pattern (page 405) to 200% and the holly leaf pattern (page 379) to 292%. Using the window pattern, cut the shape from the center of the box lid. Tape acetate to the inside lid.
**2.** Cut 4 cardstock leaves; fold 2 in half lengthwise. Glue the crease of each folded leaf to a flat leaf.
**3.** For each berry, accordion-fold a ³⁄₄"x12" cardstock strip. Glue the ends of the strip together and add a button to the center.
**4.** Line the box with tissue paper and place the cake inside. Glue the leaves and berries to ribbon tied around the box.

## Card
(also shown on page 149)

- double-sided cardstock
- cream and dark brown cardstock
- pinking shears
- glue stick
- three ³⁄₄" dia. self-covered buttons
- red fabric scraps
- wire cutters
- adhesive foam dots
- green felt scrap
- craft knife and cutting mat
- Rustic Apple Tart (page 149)

**1.** For the gift card, match short ends and fold a 5¼"x10½" cardstock piece in half.
**2.** Print the card label on cream cardstock; cut out with pinking shears. Glue the label to the card front.
**3.** Cover the buttons; remove the shanks with wire cutters. Adhere to the card front with foam dots. Cut felt leaves and dark brown cardstock stems. Glue to the card front above the "apple" buttons.

**4.** Print the recipe or a seasonal message on cardstock and trim to a 4"x4" square. Place the square inside the card, using the craft knife to cut slits for the corners to slip into. Place the tart on a pretty plate and give with the card.

## Rice Mix Jar
(also shown on page 191)

- pinking shears
- fabric glue
- fabric scrap
- red and white felt scraps
- 1½"w ribbon
- vintage-look jar with airtight lid (ours is 8"x4" dia.)
- tissue paper
- embroidery floss
- two ³⁄₄" dia. buttons
- cream cardstock
- Savory Rice Mix (page 191)

**1.** Pinking the edges, glue a 4"wx2³⁄₄"h fabric piece to a slightly larger red felt piece for the background.
**2.** Cut ribbon long enough to go around the jar and tie in the back. Center and glue the ribbon on the background.
**3.** For the pocket front, follow the Tissue Paper Method (page 318) to transfer the words on page 379 to a 3¼"wx2"h white felt piece. Using 3 strands of floss, work Stem Stitch (page 319) letters, dotting the "i's" with French Knots (page 319). Work Blanket Stitches (page 319) along the pocket edges; then, center and glue the sides and bottom on the background. Sew buttons on each side of the pocket.
**4.** Write the recipe instructions (page 191) on a 2½"wx2⅛"h cardstock piece and tuck in the pocket. Fill the jar with rice mix and tie the pocket tightly around the middle.

## Paper Trays
(also shown on page 143)

- tracing paper
- double-sided print cardstock
- stylus or bone folder
- hole punch
- decorative brads
- snowflake punches
- flower punch
- solid cardstock
- craft glue
- mat board
- Rocky Road Bars (page 142)
- parchment paper
- 5¼"x13" cellophane bags with twist ties
- rub-on letters
- oval vellum tags
- ribbons
- embroidery floss

**1.** For each tray, use the pattern on page 404 and cut a print cardstock piece. Score, then fold along the dashed lines.
**2.** Aligning the dots, punch a hole through all layers on each corner of the tray. Insert a brad through each set of holes, piercing a punched cardstock snowflake and flower in one corner. Glue more punched snowflakes to the tray.
**3.** Place a 4"x6" mat board piece in the base of the tray. Add bar cookies on parchment paper and place the tray in a bag; close with a twist tie.
**4.** For the tag, add a rub-on label to a vellum tag. Use a brad to attach punched shapes and the tag to a cardstock rectangle. Glue on more snowflakes. Thread ribbons through a hole punched in the cardstock; gather with floss and tie to the bag.

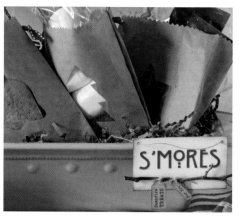

## Candy Tin
(also shown on page 173)

- plain round tin
- 2 or more coordinating scrapbook papers
- decorative-edge scissors
- drill, awl or ice pick
- hot-glue gun and glue sticks
- wire
- large decorative jingle bell
- ribbon
- pine cone and greenery picks

**1.** To create a decorative background for the tin topper, trace around bowls or other round objects that are smaller than the tin lid. Cut out 2 or more circles from scrapbook paper. Drill or poke 2 holes near the center of the lid.
**2.** Layer the paper circles, the smaller circle centered on the larger one. Center them on the lid and mark where the lid punctures are located. Poke holes through both layers of paper. Aligning holes, hot-glue the papers together and to the lid. Wire jingle bell to lid through holes. Tie on a ribbon bow and hot-glue pine cone and greenery picks extending from bell.

## S'mores Container and Decorated Tag
(also shown on page 175)

- small brown paper sacks
- small piece of cardboard to fit into sack
- crafts knife
- small cellophane sacks
- ceramic bread pan
- white and brown cardstock
- twine
- brown ink
- small hole punch
- piercing tool
- small stick
- hot-glue gun and glue sticks
- stamps, rub-on letters or computer/ printer

**1. To make the sacks,** enlarge and trace patterns (page 402). Trace around shape onto front of paper sack. Slide a heavy piece of cardboard into sack and cut out with crafts knife. Slide cellophane bag into sack to hold food.
**2. To make the tag,** print "S'mores" on white cardstock and trim to rectangular shape. Punch a small hole in the upper corners of the cardstock. Print "Campfire Treats" and "For You" in small letters on kraft cardstock, then cut into tag shapes and ink. Use piercing tool to make holes in the top of the two small tags. Cut a small stick slightly wider than the white tag. Thread twine through the holes on the small tags, then tie the tags to the stick. Adhere stick to the white tag using hot glue. Thread twine through the holes at top of tag, then tie or secure the tag to the side of the bread pan.

## Tea Jar
(also shown on page 186)

- clear glass jar with lid
- china or ceramic cup
- crafts glue
- 1"w ribbon
- small piece of felt
- embroidery floss and needle
- scrap of solid color cardstock
- scrap of white paper

**1.** Be sure the jar is clean and dry. Glue the ribbon around jar top. Glue the cup to the jar top. Set aside.
**2.** Using the pattern (page 396) cut out the felt label. Work embroidery stitches on the felt label front referring to pattern. Cut another piece of felt and lay on back of embroidered piece. Stitch around sides and bottom leaving an opening at the top. Sew or glue a piece of ribbon to the back of the felt tag. Wrap around the jar and secure in the back with a stitch or glue.
**3.** Make the instructions tag by printing the instructions on the white paper. Glue to the colored cardstock. Slide inside felt opening.

## Pie Carrier
(continued from page 144)

1. Cut a mat board circle, using the bottom of the plate for a pattern. Refer to Fig. 1 to cut four 2" slits around the circle.

**Fig. 1**

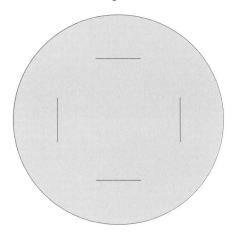

2. Paint the plate, rim and chipboard letters; allow to dry.

3. Using a thin coat of glue, apply torn paper pieces to the inside bottom of the plate. Glue the letters and add the stickers to the plate. Brush glue over the entire plate; allow to dry. Add glue to the rim and sprinkle with mica flakes.

4. For the hanger, cut two 62"-long 1½"w ribbon lengths. Cross the ribbons in the middle and thread the ends through the slits in the mat board circle. Place the circle under the plate. Pull the ribbons up around the plate. Stack the ribbons together and fold about 8" from the top. Sew the ribbons together about 4" from the fold; pull the thread tight to gather and knot the ends.

5. Tie assorted ribbons and ornaments around the gathered hanger. Insert the covered pie in the carrier.

## Cheese Ball Box
(also shown on page 150)

- transfer paper
- double-sided patterned cardstock
- double-sided tape
- acetate sheet
- craft glue
- glitter
- scrapbook paper
- photo corners
- 2 brads
- ribbon scrap
- rub-on letters
- large paper muffin cup
- plastic-wrapped Pineapple & Nut Cheese Ball (page 150)
- ¾ yard of rickrack
- vintage cheese spreader

1. Enlarge the box patterns (page 405) to 200%. Transfer the patterns to cardstock; cut out along the solid lines, discarding the window. Tape acetate to the wrong side of the window opening. Accent the cardstock design with glitter

2. Overlap and tape the top to the box along the grey area. Score, then fold the box along the dashed lines and tape together.

3. Glue a scrapbook paper house design to the lid, adding photo corners at the top. Use brads to attach a ribbon with a rub-on message. Mount a printed label on a slightly larger scrapbook paper piece and tape to the lid.

4. Place the muffin cup and cheese ball in the box. Wrap rickrack around the box, securing the spreader at the side.

## Scone Cozy
(also shown on page 151)

- cotton batting circles (one 13" and one 10" dia.)
- cozy fabric circles (two 13" and one 10" dia.)
- 6 fabric scraps for pockets
- scallop-edged fabric scissors
- clear nylon thread
- 1½" dia. button
- embellished cardstock tag (we used alphabet stamps, ink pad, chipboard label holder, decorative brads, embroidery floss and a button)
- wrapped Cranberry Scones (page 151)

*Match wrong sides of fabric unless otherwise noted.*

1. Sandwich the large batting circle between the large fabric circles. Topstitch all layers together ½" from the outer edge.

2. Enlarge the pattern (page 406) to 200%. Use the enlarged pattern to cut 6 fabric pockets with scallop-edged scissors. Center the small batting circle on the wrong side of the small fabric circle. Place the pocket pieces on the batting circle, matching the outer edges (the pocket pieces will overlap). Zigzag the overlaps in place; then, topstitch ½" from the outer edge of the circle.

3. Scallop the edges of both circles. Center the small circle on the large one. Pin at the seams so each pocket bulges enough for a scone to fit inside (the center will buckle a bit). Using clear thread, stitch over each seam from the outer edge to 1" from the center.

4. Sew the button and embellished tag to the center. Place a scone in each pocket.

## Candy Glass
(also shown on page 152)

- Chocolate Peanut Clusters (page 152)
- vintage Christmas drinking glass
- clear cellophane
- two 8" lengths of ¼"w gingham ribbon
- assorted red buttons
- patterned cardstock
- hot glue gun
- "JOY" rub-on
- black fine-point permanent pen

**1.** Line the glass with cellophane and add a stack of peanut clusters. Tie closed with a ribbon length.
**2.** Thread a button to the center of the remaining ribbon. Stack and hot glue buttons around the edge of a 2½" diameter cardstock circle. Glue the ribbon-threaded button to the top. Apply the rub-on to the center and write "peanut" and "clusters" above and below "JOY."
**3.** Tie on the tag and trim the cellophane.

## Cookie Holders
(also shown on page 155)

- double-sided cardstock
- scallop-edged scissors (optional)
- double-sided tape
- rub-on letters
- 1½" dia. circle punch
- ⅛" dia. hole punch
- assorted ribbons
- bottled coffee drinks
- White Chocolate-Cranberry Cookies (page 154)
- plastic wrap

Enlarge the patterns on page 407 to 196%. For each holder, use the patterns and cut a cardstock cookie holder and scallop-edged valance (we cut our valance following the scallop design printed on our cardstock). Discard the cookie window and bottle opening pieces. Fold on the dashed lines. Tape the flap to the holder along the top fold line. Tape the valance to the holder above the window.

Add a rub-on name to a punched tag and tie it to the holder with ribbons. Tape a punched circle to the bottle lid and slip the cookie holder over the neck. Wrap a cookie in plastic wrap and insert it in the holder.

## Pie Basket
(also shown on page 156)

- double-lidded picnic basket (our 7"wx12"lx4"h basket holds two 4½" dia. pie pans)
- liner fabric
- 1"w grosgrain ribbon (we used 2⅛ yards)
- ball fringe (we used 1⅛ yards)
- 2 Mock Cherry Pies (page 156)
- solid and patterned cardstock
- double-sided tape
- scallop-edged scissors
- letter stickers ("pie" and "cherry")
- paper flower embellishment
- adhesive foam dots
- rub-on letters
- purchased mini tag
- brown scrapbooking chalk
- black fine-point permanent pen
- hole punch
- brad
- assorted ribbons

*When sewing, always match right sides and use a ¼" seam allowance.*

**1.** For the liner bottom, measure the inside length and width of the basket; add ½" to each measurement. Cut a fabric piece the determined size.
**2.** For the liner sides, measure around the outer basket rim; measure the height of the basket and add the amount of overhang you want on the side. Add ½" to each measurement. Cut a fabric piece the determined measurements.
**3.** Matching the short ends, sew the liner side piece together, forming a ring. Matching the seam to a corner, sew the liner side to the liner bottom, pleating the excess side fabric as necessary.
**4.** To trim the liner around the handles, place the liner in the basket and arrange

the overhang as evenly as possible on all sides. Cut a rectangle from each side edge ¼" smaller than the desired finished notch (Fig. 1). Clip the corners; then, turn and sew the notched edges ¼" to the wrong side.

**Fig. 1**

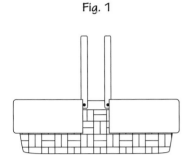

**5.** Measure around the basket rim and cut 2 pieces of 1"w ribbon this length. Cut 2 pieces of ball fringe half this length. Center and pin the ball fringe on each ribbon length, turning the short ball fringe ends ½" to the wrong side. Covering the raw edges, center and sew the trims on the right side of the liner, leaving the ribbon ends loose for ties. Place the liner and pies in the basket. Tie the ribbon ends.

**6.** For the label, cut and layer 3 cardstock circles, scalloping the largest circle. Adhere "Pie" to the label and "cherry" on top. Use foam dots to adhere the paper flower to the label. Add rub-on letters to spell "mock" on the mini tag; adhere to the label with foam dots. Chalk the label and tag edges and add pen-line dashes and dots just for fun! Attach the brad to the label and loop the mini tag over the brad. Tie the label to the basket with colorful ribbons.

## Brownie Plate
(also shown on page 164)

- vintage plate
- jadite eggcup

- clear adhesive dots
- scallop-edged scissors
- patterned food tissue paper
- acrylic paint
- paintbrush
- 3" dia. wooden disc
- craft glue
- scrapbook paper
- cardstock
- rub-on holiday message
- clear dimensional adhesive glaze
- mica flakes
- ⅝"w ribbon
- Creamy Peppermint Brownies (page 164)
- cellophane bag

Create a one-of-a-kind cake plate using a vintage plate and eggcup. Simply adhere the plate to the rim of the eggcup with adhesive dots. Then line the plate with a scallop-edged tissue circle.

For the tag, paint the disc; then, layer and glue scrapbook paper and cardstock circles to the front. Add the rub-on message. Apply glaze to the tag and allow to dry. Run a bead of glue along the edge of the tag and sprinkle with mica flakes. Glue the tag to a ribbon bow with long streamers.

Place the brownies in the bag and tie closed with ribbon. Adhere the tag and place the brownies on the plate.

## Turtle Box
(also shown on page 165)

For each box of goodies, cover a box bottom (ours is 4"x4"x2½") with holiday wrapping paper.

Fill a cellophane bag with Caramel Turtles (page 165) and close with a twist tie. Place

the candy in the box. Tie ribbon around the package, adding a bow at the top. Attach an oval cardstock tag stamped with a holiday greeting and your quick & tasty gift is ready to go.

## Cupfuls of Truffles
(also shown on page 163)

- assorted teacups (we found ours at the flea market)
- cellophane bags
- Cookies & Cream Truffles, Mocha Truffles and Peanut Butter-Cocoa Truffles (page 163)
- ½"w ribbon
- cardstock
- scallop-edged scissors
- rub-on letters
- clear adhesive dots
- tracing paper
- clear dome alphabet stickers
- raffia
- jute twine
- ⅛" dia. hole punch
- craft glue
- scrapbook paper
- miniature clothespins

For each cup, fill a cellophane bag with a truffle assortment and tie with ribbon. Cut a 5" diameter cardstock circle and scallop the edge. Add a rub-on message to the outer edge of the circle. Adhere the circle to the bottom of the cup with an adhesive dot.

Using the pattern on page 385, cut a tag from cardstock. Use a sticker to add a monogram and tie raffia and twine through the punched hole. Glue scrapbook paper to one side of the clothespin and clip the tag to the ribbon.

## Fortune Cookie Box
(also shown on page 168)

- large size paper to fit pattern
- seasonal stamps
- scoring blade or scoring board
- narrow ribbon for box handle
- piercing tool
- contrasting cardstock and matching patterned paper
- small scalloped dies or punches
- small circle punches
- stamps, rub-on letters or computer/printer

**1.** Enlarge and trace the box pattern (page 409) onto large size paper. Cut out and score as indicated. Make holes using piercing tools as specified on pattern. Fold into box shape. Unfold and stamp box using seasonal stamp. Allow to dry then refold box. Thread ribbon through holes and secure with knots on the inside of the box.
**2.** Decorate sides of box with scalloped shapes cut from contrasting shades of cardstock. Add circles to center of shapes.
**3. For tag,** cut rectangle from patterned paper. Notch the corners using a circle punch. Cut a slightly larger mat from contrasting cardstock and notch corners. Adhere the pieces together. Cut a strip of coordinating patterned paper and adhere across the center of the tag. Cut scalloped shape for the center of the tag and print/stamp with "For You". Adhere to tag base using adhesive dimensional dots. Adhere or tie tag to box as desired.

## Jar Topper
(also shown on page 169)

- 4 colors coordinating papers or cardstock
- circle cutter or template
- stamps, rub-on letters or computer/printer
- ribbon
- chipboard
- strong tape adhesive

**1.** Cut a circle of chipboard (or 2-3 pieces of cardstock) and adhere to the indented portion of the lid to create a flat surface. Cut 4 circles of coordinating papers to fit the jar lid insert. (Our jar lid measures 3".)
**2.** Fold each circle in fourths and cut apart. Add text to two of the pieces. Adhere all four pieces to the lid. Wrap ribbon around the lid ring and tie at side. (Tip: If ribbon is too wide for the ring, fold in half and iron to secure. Run a narrow strip of tape adhesive around the jar ring to hold ribbon in place.)

## See-Through Brownie Box
(also shown on page 171)

**For box:**
- large box for brownies
- wide ribbon to fit edges of box lid
- white and red cardstock
- cellophane
- crafts knife and straightedge ruler
- sanding tool
- candy canes
- hot-glue gun and hot glue sticks

**For tag:**
- embossed white cardstock
- candy cane die cut or pattern
- green dot/solid paper
- white/red dot paper
- circle punches in 2 sizes to fit text
- border punch
- black pen
- strong tape and adhesive dimensional dots
- stamps, rub-on letters or computer/printer

**1. To make box,** cover box base with white cardstock. Cut strips of red cardstock and adhere vertically to the sides of the box. For lid, determine size of opening and make pattern from scratch paper. Adhere to box lid where desired. Use crafts knife and straightedge to carefully cut opening in lid. Use sanding tool to smooth rough edges. Cut a piece of cellophane to fit over the opening, then adhere to box lid. Cut white cardstock to fit top of lid, then cut a hole in the cardstock to match the hole in the lid. Adhere to box lid. Cut narrow strips of red cardstock to fit around the opening, covering any exposed edges. Cut a similar sized piece of white cardstock to line the inside of the lid. Trim with narrow strips of white cardstock. Adhere wide ribbon around the edges of the box lid using strong tape adhesive. Adhere candy canes to lid using hot glue.

**2. For tag,** trace pattern (page 397). Trace onto embossed white cardstock and cut out; punch hole in top. Adhere green paper across the center of the tag, then add a strip of white/red dot paper below it.

**3.** Adhere border punched from red card-stock to lower portion of tag. Create cane from white and red cardstock, then add green bow. Add details using black pen and adhere using dimensional dots. Print "For You" and punch into small circle. Add dots around circle with black pen. Mat with a larger circle punched from red cardstock. Adhere to tag using adhesive dimensional dots. Attach tag to box with same ribbon used on box.

## Candy Sleigh Holder
(also shown on page 174)

- tracing paper
- pencil
- 12" square of heavy scrapbook paper
- scissors
- low-temp glue gun and glue sticks
- chenille stems
- candy canes

**1.** Enlarge and trace the sleigh pattern (page 399) and cut out, paying close attention to cutting and folding marks. Use pattern to cut a sleigh from scrapbook paper.

**2.** Fold on indicated lines and glue together. Glue chenille stem around the top edges, piecing to fit. Glue a pair of candy cane runners on the bottom of each sleigh.

## Paper Poppers
(also shown on page 174)

- short cardboard tubes
- scissors
- 2 coordinating scrapbook papers
- decorative-edge scissors
- tape
- metallic chenille stems
- cupcake liners
- hot-glue gun and glue sticks

**1.** Using one of the scrapbook papers, cut a piece to fit around the cardboard tube allowing ends to overlap slightly. Wrap the tube with the paper piece, securing with tape at the end. Using decorative-edge scissors, cut a strip from the coordinating paper, 2 inches narrower than the tube, and tape it centered around the tube.

**2.** Hot-glue pieces of chenille stem around each tube end, shaping them to fit the curve. Hot-glue a cupcake liner in one tube end. Fill the popper with wrapped candies or other small surprises. Hot-glue a second cupcake liner in the remaining tube end.

## Country Herb Spread Gift Box
(also shown on page 172)

- box for crackers
- glass container for dip
- patterned paper and coordinating cardstock
- self-adhesive jewels
- corner rounder
- ink
- stamps, rub-on letters or computer/ printer

**1.** Cut patterned paper to fit sides and tops of containers. Round corners, ink and adhere to containers.

**2.** Print "Crispy Wheat Crackers" on paper leaving space for jewels. Cut strip to fit box lid and adhere. Add self-adhesive jewels.

## Decorated Pretzel Jar
(also shown on page 173)

- clear jar with hinge top
- 2-3 coordinated patterned papers and cardstock

(continued on next page)

- circle cutter or template
- star punch or die
- self-adhesive silver jewels or gems
- adhesive, including strong tape
- ribbon or raffia
- stamps, rub-on letters or computer/ printer
- brown ink pen

**1. For jar,** cut a circle from cardstock to fit the lid and adhere. Embellish lid with stars punched or cut from coordinating cardstock. Cut patterned paper strip to fit around the jar. Mat with a slightly wider strip of cardstock and adhere firmly to the jar using tape adhesive. Print or stamp label on white cardstock and mat. Adhere stars to the bottom of the label. Add jewels to the center of each star. Adhere completed label to front of the jar using strong adhesive.

**2. For pretzel,** cut out pretzel pattern (page 379) from tan cardstock. Write "For You" with matching pen on inside of pretzel tag. Tie to the jar using raffia.

## Chip & Dip Mix Container
(also shown on page 176)

- large clear acrylic container with latched lid (ours is 9"hx5" dia.)
- Santa's Zesty Mix (page 176) in a plastic zipping bag (ours is 3"x4½") and Baked Pita Chips (page 176)
- cardstock
- scallop-edged scissors
- double-sided tape
- 1"w grosgrain ribbon

- alphabet stamps with red and black ink pads
- hole punch
- ¼"w ribbon

**1.** Tape a scalloped cardstock circle to the lid of the pita chip-filled container. Tie 1"w ribbon around the lid.
**2.** For the dip mix, cut a cardstock rectangle slightly larger than the mix bag, scalloping the ends. Fold in half. Tape a stamped cardstock label to the front. Place the folded cardstock over the bag and punch a hole through all layers (above the bag "zipper"). Tie together with ¼"w ribbon.

## Take-Out Boxes
(also shown on page 180)

For each treat box, line a colorful take-out container with patterned tissue paper. Fill a cellophane bag with Party Mix (page 180) and close with a twist tie. Knot ribbon around the bag and place it in the container.

Cover a purchased tag with scrapbook paper. Tuck a handwritten cardstock label in a purchased mini mitten (a knit, crochet or felt mitten will look great). Use double-sided tape to attach the mitten to the tag and tie it to the container with jute twine… oh-so cute!

## Soup Dinner Kit
(also shown on page 183)

- rustic wood box (ours is 14½"lx7½"wx4"h
- ivory acrylic paint
- paintbrush
- ¾"w pre-printed twill tape (ours says "special delivery")
- double-sided tape
- wrapping paper
- 28-oz. can crushed tomatoes
- cream cardstock
- oval templates (ours are 2½" and 3" long
- red pencil
- jars of Italian Soup Mix (page 183)
- scallop-edged scissors
- black fine-point permanent pen
- mini alphabet stencil
- removable tape
- fresh bread
- 2 dishtowels
- bowls
- soup spoons

**1.** Drybrush the box with ivory paint to give it a worn look; allow to dry. Tie a twill tape bow around the box.
**2.** Tape wrapping paper around the side of the tomato can. Cut a round cardstock label for the can top. Use the templates and red pencil to make oval labels for the can, soup m jars and box; cut out, scalloping the edges.
**3.** Use the pen and stencil to write names on the labels. Write the instructions to make the soup on the underside of the round label and adhere it to the top of the can with removable tape. Use double-sided tape to attach the remaining labels.
**4.** Tie a twill tape bow around bread wrapped up in a dishtowel. Tuck the remaining towel, bowls, spoons and soup mix in the box.

**Fig. 1**

**Fig. 2**

## Glittered Houses

(also shown on page 52)

one-piece fold-out brown gift boxes
 (we used three 2"hx3"wx3"d and one
 4"hx4"wx4"d)
craft glue
ruler, craft knife and cutting mat
cream and assorted colors of cardstock
thin cardboard sheets
scallop-edged scissors
tracing paper
miniature wreath
rickrack
disposable foam brush
decoupage glue
fine glitter
mica flakes
spray adhesive
white felt
cake stand (ours is 10½" dia.)
miniature bottle brush trees
vintage miniature ornaments

1. Leaving the bottom of each gift box open, fold and glue the lid flap closed. Turn the box top-side down.
2. For the roof decking, fold the straight-sided flaps together so they touch in the center. Mark the roof angles on each roof tab (Fig. 1); then, lightly score the lines with the ruler and craft knife. Cut out a V-shaped notch from the top of each roof tab to the point of the roof decking (Fig. 2).
3. Unfold the roof decking. Fold the roof tabs to the inside along the scored lines and glue the decking flaps to the tabs.
4. For the large house, glue cream cardstock to cardboard and cut a roof 1" larger then the roof decking on all sides.

Score and fold the roof in the center and glue it to the house. Repeat for the small houses, cutting each roof about ½" larger than the decking on all sides, and using scallop-edged scissors where desired.
5. Accordion-fold a 1½"x2½" cardboard piece and glue the "steps" to the large house.
6. Use the patterns on page 411 and follow the photos to cut out and glue cardstock doors and windows to the houses (we glued the miniature wreath to a solid door). Cut out cardboard chimneys and cardstock-covered chimney caps. Fold each chimney along the dashed lines with the tabs to the inside; glue on the cap. Glue chimneys to roofs as desired. Glue a 1"x3" cardstock-covered porch roof to the large house.
7. Cover the work surface. Glue rickrack along roof edges where you'd like. Brush decoupage glue on the sides and roof of each house; sprinkle with fine glitter, tap off the excess and allow to dry. Brush more glue on each roof and chimney cap; sprinkle with mica flakes and tap off the excess.
8. Apply spray adhesive in a well-ventilated area to wavy-edged felt circles (ours are about 15" diameter) and sprinkle with mica flakes. Placing one circle on the cake stand, arrange the houses, trees and vintage ornaments on the circles.

## Tractor Hat

(continued from page 53)

*Read Embroidery Stitches, pages 318-319, before beginning. Use 3 strands of floss.*

1. Fuse web to the wrong side of the appliqué fabric scraps.
2. Enlarge the patterns (page 401) to 200%. Using the enlarged tractor pattern, cut fabric scrap appliqués. Fuse, then use nylon thread to zigzag the appliqués to the felt piece. Embroider the design using Stem Stitch, Straight Stitch and French Knots. Sew the snap pieces to the tractor wheels. Trim the felt about ⅛" from the design. Whipstitch the appliqué to the hat.
3. Make a 2" pom-pom (page 320) and sew to the hat top.
4. For ear flap strings, crochet two 10" long chains, leaving long yarn tails at the beginnings. Using the enlarged ear flap pattern, cut 2 ear flaps and 2 lining pieces. Pin the finishing ends of the chains to the center of the curved edges of the ear flaps. Matching right sides, using a ¼" seam allowance and leaving the straight edge open, sew each ear flap to a lining piece, catching the chain end in the stitching. Clip the curves, turn right side out and press. Turn the raw edges ¼" to the inside and slipstitch the opening closed. Whipstitch the flaps to the inside of the hat.

369

## Mitten Puppet

(also shown on page 53)

- knit mitten
- paper-backed fusible web
- fabric and felt scraps
- 1/2" dia. pom-pom
- two 5/8" dia. buttons

**1.** Fuse web to the wrong side of the fabric scraps.

**2.** Enlarge the patterns (page 402) to 200%. Using the enlarged patterns, cut the tongue and ears from the fabric scraps and the eyes, eyelashes and ridge plates from the felt scraps. Fuse the tongue and ears to coordinating felt scraps and trim 1/8" from fabric.

**3.** Place the mitten on your hand and use pins to mark the positions of the tongue, nose, eyes, ears, and the ridge plates. Sew the tongue, pom-pom nose, ears (folding in half at the straight edge) and ridge plates to the mitten. For the eyes, layer the eyelashes, eyes, and buttons and sew onto the mitten, leaving the eyelashes free at the top.

## Gingerbread Cabin

(continued from page 54)

Follow Fig. 1 (below) to cut out the dough pieces (make poster board templates if you like). Trim the sides and chimney as shown, cutting away the shaded areas.

Bake at 350 degrees for 9 to 15 minutes or until firm to the touch.

### Assembling the Cabin

*We used a 12"x12" piece of foam core for the cabin base. Use icing as "glue" on the backs of the gingerbread and candy pieces to adhere them to other pieces, or pipe icing along edges to join pieces, holding the pieces in place or propping them up until the icing begins to harden. Allow icing to harden after each step.*

**1.** Pipe icing for the door, wreath and windows on the cabin front piece and adhere mint candies on the windows and cinnamon candies on the wreath.

**2.** Piping icing along the short edges, adhere the cabin front, sides and back pieces.

**3.** Piping icing along the bottom edges, adhere the cabin walls to the center of the base.

**4.** Adhere 1"x1/2" chocolate candy pieces to the cabin base for the porch floor.

**5.** Adhere the front and back roof pieces to the top of the cabin. Adhere the porch roof to the roof front and at the same time adhere the top and bottom of the rolled cookies to support the porch roof.

**6.** Adhere the chimney to the cabin. Adhere the 1 1/4"x5/8" chocolate candy pieces to the chimney, breaking the candy pieces as necessary to fit.

**7.** Use a knife or spatula to spread a thin layer of icing on the roof back; adhere almonds. Repeat for the roof front and porch roof.

**8.** Pipe icicles and snow on the roof and top of the chimney.

**9.** Adhere caramel-flavored candies for the "path."

**10.** Use a knife or spatula to spread icing over the cabin base; sprinkle with sugar sprinkles before the icing hardens.

**Fig. 1**

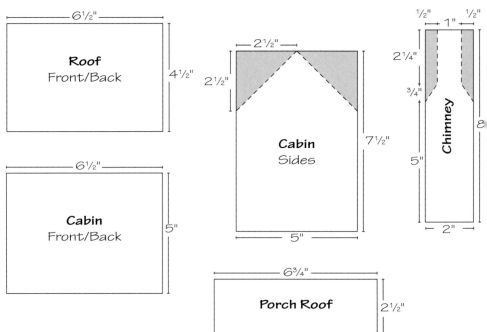

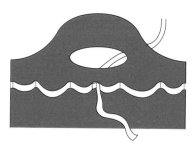

Fig. 1

## Button Wreath
(also shown on page 57)

- sturdy 14" wire ring, cut open with wire cutters
- 1½ yards total of assorted green 36" wide felt
- ¾ yard total of assorted green 44-45" wide fabrics
- craft knife
- heavy-duty masking tape
- assorted green vintage buttons
- 2 Felt Flower Ornaments (page 58)
- Gathered Rickrack Ornament (page 335)
- Flower Ornament/ Tree Topper (page 334)

**1.** Cut 104 4" felt squares. Cut 104 3" fabric squares. Fold and slit a felt square as shown in Fig. 1. Thread the folded square onto the wire ring. Repeat with the remaining squares, alternating fabric and felt.

**Fig. 1**

**2.** Securely tape the ring ends together and adjust the squares to cover the tape. Sew buttons to some of the squares and clip the ornaments to the wreath.

## Scrapbook Caddy
(continued from page 118)

**3.** Use the fabric marker to freehand stems on one front felt piece, or trace the enlarged flower stems onto tissue paper and pin to the felt piece. Use 6 strands of floss and work Running Stitch (page 319) stems. (If using the tissue paper method, stitch through the paper; then, carefully tear the paper away.) Sew a button cluster flower at the end of each stem.
**4.** Use the fabric marker to place a dot in each corner of the felt rectangles, ¼" from each edge. Sew pairs of felt rectangles together along the long edges between the dots. Sew the front and back to the sides between dots to form a rectangular tube. Pin one side of the tube to the bottom; sew the pieces together between dots. Repeat to sew the bottom to the remaining sides.
**5.** Arrange some scrapbook supplies on the divider (we chose scissors and markers). Pin ribbon across the divider, pinning between supplies to hold them in place. Remove the supplies, sew where pinned and trim the ends. Cut four 10" ribbon ties; set 2 aside. Sew one tie each to the center front and back of the divider (Fig. 1).

**6.** Draw a placement line from side to side along the inside center bottom of the caddy; hand sew the divider along the line. Sew buttons to the sides of the caddy, catching the divider side edges in the stitching.
**7.** Remove any visible marker lines with a damp towel. Center and sew the remaining ribbon ties to the inside front and back of the caddy. Tie the ribbons and add scrapbook supplies.

## Gift Tags
(also shown on page 129)

### Family Christmas Traditions
• rub-on letters
• cardstock
• pinking shears
• "traditions" word stickers
• adhesive foam dots
• ribbon
• hole punch

For each tag, write "family" and rub the word "Christmas" on a cardstock tag with clipped corners and a pinked bottom edge (ours is 2⅜"x4¾"). Add a cardstock-backed sticker to the tag with foam dots (or use small rub-on letters on a layered cardstock rectangle). Tie ribbon through the punched hole.

### Holly Jolly
• solid and patterned cardstock
• ribbons
• hole punch
• "jolly" stamp
• black ink pad
• brown scrapbook chalk
• craft glue
• adhesive foam dots

To make each tag, enlarge the patterns on page 412 to 200%. Using the patterns, cut 2 cardstock leaves, 3 berries and an oval tag. Tie ribbons through the hole in the tag. Stamp "jolly" on one leaf and chalk the edges.

Glue the leaves and 2 berries to the tag. Write "Christmas" on the remaining berry and adhere it to the tag with a foam dot.

### December 25th
• patterned and solid cardstock
• hole punch
• craft glue
• fine glitter
• ribbons
• adhesive foam dots
• rub-on letters
• glittered wreath message stickers

For each tag, clip the corners from a 2⅜"x4¾" cardstock piece. Enlarge the patterns on page 412 to 200%. Using the patterns, cut cardstock numbers and a small tag; punch a hole in both tags. Add glitter and write "to:" and "from:" on the small tag; then, tie the tags together with ribbon. Attach the numbers with foam dots and tie a ribbon around the tag. Rub-on the letters, "Dec." and apply the sticker.

## Garland
(also shown on page 129)

• solid and patterned double-sided cardstock
• hot glue gun
• tiny hole punch
• Christmas cards
• needle-nose jewelry pliers
• large oval chain links
• ribbon for garland
• assorted ribbons for ties

*Favorite Christmas cards from years past accent this sweet & simple garland.*

1. For each interlocking circle pair, enlarge the patterns on page 412 to 155%. Using the patterns, cut 2 same-size cardstock

circles (one solid and one patterned). Cut slits where shown. Slide the circles together at the slits and dot loose ends with hot glue to hold in place; punch a hole near the top.
2. Cut a small circle from each Christmas card (do not cut the slit); punch a hole in the top and bottom.
3. Using pliers, join Christmas card circles to small interlocking circles with chain links. Attach to the ribbon garland.
4. Join large interlocking circles to the garland with chain links and tie ribbons around each link.

## Christmas Bib
(also shown on page 53)

• fabric strips of varying widths (we used 8 different fabrics)
• 11"x14" fabric piece for backing
• twill tape or ribbon with holiday message
• liquid fray preventative
• ½" dia. hole punch
• felt scrap
• hook and loop fastener

*Always match right sides and use a ¼" seam allowance when sewing.*

1. Match the long edges and sew the fabric strips together for the bib front.
2. Enlarge the pattern (page 376) to 200%. Using the enlarged pattern, cut the bib front and backing.
3. Apply fray preventative to the twill tape ends. Layer and attach 2 punched felt circles and the twill tape to the bib front.
4. Leaving an opening for turning, sew the bib front and back together. Clip the curves, turn right side out and press. Sew the opening closed. Sew the fastener to the bib center back.

## Star Ornament/Tree Topper
(also shown on page 43)

- tracing paper
- assorted colors felt
- wood spools and sticks (we used vintage Tinkertoys ®)
- wood glue
- assorted size and colors wood beads

**1.** Using the patterns on page 385, cut a small star from felt. For the larger ornament or tree topper, also cut a large star from felt.
**2.** Insert sticks into the spool holes to form star shapes. Glue additional sticks to the spool edges. Glue a bead to the end of each stick.
**3.** Glue the small felt star to the back of the ornament. Glue a large felt star over the small star for the large ornament. Glue a large bead to the ornament front.

## Bead Garland
(also shown on page 43)

Your little ones will have fun while learning shapes and colors when they help craft this easy garland. Using the patttern on page 385, cut stars from felt. Use decorative-edged scissors to cut 1¾" diameter felt circles. Punch an ⅛" diameter hole in the center of each felt shape. Knot 1 end of a multi-colored hemp twine length and thread on a small wood bead, a jumbo wood bead and then a felt shape. Continue alternating jumbo beads and felt shapes until garland is the desired length, ending with a small bead and a knot.

## Hanging Birdfeeder
(also shown on page 45)

- 4" dia. clay pot with drainage hole
- 6" dia. clay saucer
- acrylic paint and paintbrush
- sandpaper
- rub-on designs
- 14" length of leather cord
- two 1" dia. painted wood beads
- Gorilla Glue®
- heavy object
- small flat chisel

*Make this clever gift for your bird lover friend... just grab a grown-up for help with the glue and chisel.*

**1.** Paint the pot and saucer. Lightly sand the edges for a worn look.
**2.** Add rub-ons to the pot and bottom of the saucer.
**3.** Fold the cord in half and knot the ends together. Thread the folded end through one bead and through the pot from the inside out. Loosely knot the folded end to keep it from slipping back into the pot (Fig. 1).

Fig. 1

**4.** Follow the manufacturer's instructions and run a thin bead of glue along the inner rim of the pot. Center and glue the pot on the saucer. Place a heavy object on the pot for 24 hours.
**5.** Scrape away any excess glue with the chisel. Untie the loose knot and thread the cord through the remaining bead. Knot the cord just above the bead.

## Bag o' Birdseed
(also shown on page 45)

- birdseed in a plastic zipping bag
- paper lunch bag
- tracing paper
- ¼" dia. hole punch
- print and solid cardstock
- rub-on designs
- alphabet stamps
- black ink pad
- ribbon and rickrack trims
- craft knife and cutting mat
- adhesive foam dot
- felt scrap
- brad

(continued on next page)

Place the birdseed in the paper bag and fold the top of the bag to the back. Using the patterns on page 385, cut and punch a cardstock tag, bird and wing. Add rub-ons and stamp "Seed" on the tag; then, knot trims through the hole. Ask an adult to make the slit in the bird and insert the wing; adhere to the tag with a foam dot. For the topper, fold a felt square over the top of the bag. Punch a hole through all layers and use the brad to attach the tag to the topper.

## Muffin Picks and Box

(also shown on page 162)

- ⅛" and 1" dia. circle punches
- red and white cardstock
- craft glue
- red and white embroidery floss
- sharp needle
- toothpicks
- Raspberry-Filled Muffins (page 162)
- assorted ribbons for ties
- wrapping paper
- one-piece fold-out pastry box (ours is 9"x9"x4")
- spray adhesive
- craft knife and cutting mat
- tracing paper
- two 1"w grosgrain ribbons
- rub-on letters
- ⅛"w ribbon
- small safety pin

*Use 3 strands of floss for all stitching.*

**1.** For each muffin pick, punch two 1" cardstock circles. Gluing the floss ends to the back, work a Straight Stitch (page 319) snowflake on one circle. Sandwiching a toothpick in between, glue the circles together. Insert the pick in a muffin and tie a ribbon around the muffin cup.
**2.** In a well-ventilated area, adhere wrapping paper to the flat box with spray adhesive. Trim the excess paper and fold into a box shape. Add the muffins.
**3.** Use the patterns on page 385 and cut a cardstock tag and "buckle." Punch a ⅛" hole in the tag. Cut slits and use the needle to pierce holes in the buckle where shown. Work Running Stitches (page 319) around the buckle. Cutting each 1"w ribbon to fit,

## Breakfast Ring Wrap

(also shown on page 161)

- tracing paper
- green and cream cardstock
- craft knife and cutting mat
- ⅛" and ¼" dia. hole punches
- spray adhesive
- ribbons and mini rickrack
- Cranberry Breakfast Rings (page 161)
- Gooseberry Patch's Merry Christmas Enamelware Plates
- cellophane
- twist ties

For each breakfast ring, use the pattern on page 411 and cut a green tag and use the craft knife and punches to cut a cream wreath design. In a well-ventilated area, adhere the wreath to the tag with spray adhesive. Tie ribbons and rickrack through a hole punched in the tag. To gift wrap, place the breakfast ring on a plate, wrap with cellophane and close with a twist tie. Tie the tag around the twist tie.

wrap the ribbons around the box. Weave the ribbons though the buckle and glue the ends to the back of the buckle.
**4.** Add rub-ons and work a Straight Stitch snowflake on the tag. Tie a ⅛"w ribbon bow to the pin and pin the tag to the 1"w ribbon.

## Fudge Box

(also shown on page 159)

- transfer paper
- 12"x12" double-sided print cardstock
- stylus or bone folder
- craft glue
- cream cardstock
- parchment paper
- craft knife
- Graham Cracker Fudge (page 159)
- ⅜"w ribbon
- alphabet stamps and ink pad
- cardstock tag
- decorative brad
- embroidery floss
- adhesive foam dots

**1.** Enlarge the pattern on page 408 to 133%. Transfer the pattern to the wrong side of the print cardstock; cut out. Using the stylus, score along the dashed fold lines.
**2.** Fold along the diagonal lines to crease; unfold. Fold the cardstock along the remaining lines and glue the flap to the opposite long edge.
**3.** Fold a 5¾"-long cream cardstock tray with a parchment paper liner that fits inside the box to hold the fudge.
**4.** When the glue on the box is completely dry, carefully push on the diagonal creases until the ends twist and meet in the center to close each end.

# Fabric Christmas Cookie Ornaments
(page 24)

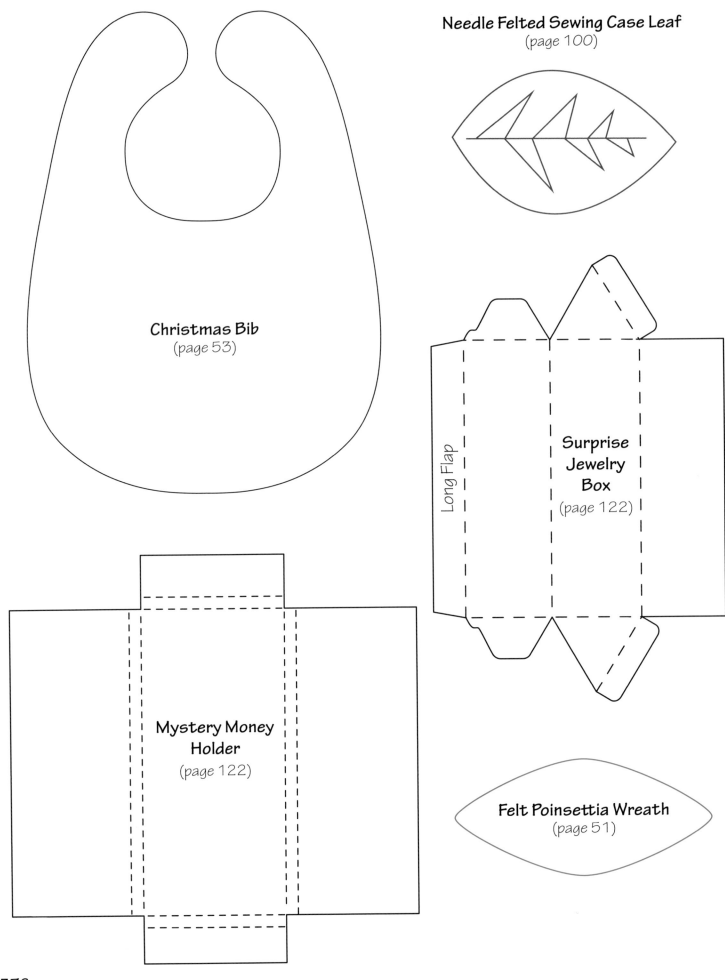

**Needle Felted Sewing Case Leaf**
(page 100)

**Christmas Bib**
(page 53)

Long Flap

**Surprise Jewelry Box**
(page 122)

**Mystery Money Holder**
(page 122)

**Felt Poinsettia Wreath**
(page 51)

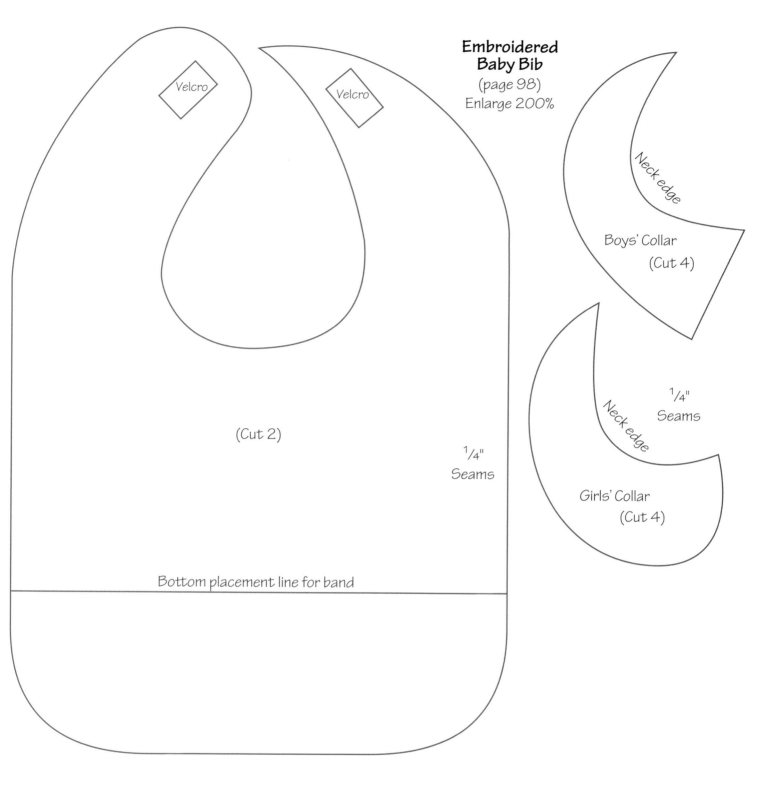

Velcro

Velcro

**Embroidered
Baby Bib**
(page 98)
Enlarge 200%

Neck edge

Boys' Collar
(Cut 4)

Neck edge

¹/₄"
Seams

Girls' Collar
(Cut 4)

(Cut 2)

¹/₄"
Seams

Bottom placement line for band

Full Size Embroidery
Pattern for Baby Bibs

# Sweet Baby
# Little Boy Blue

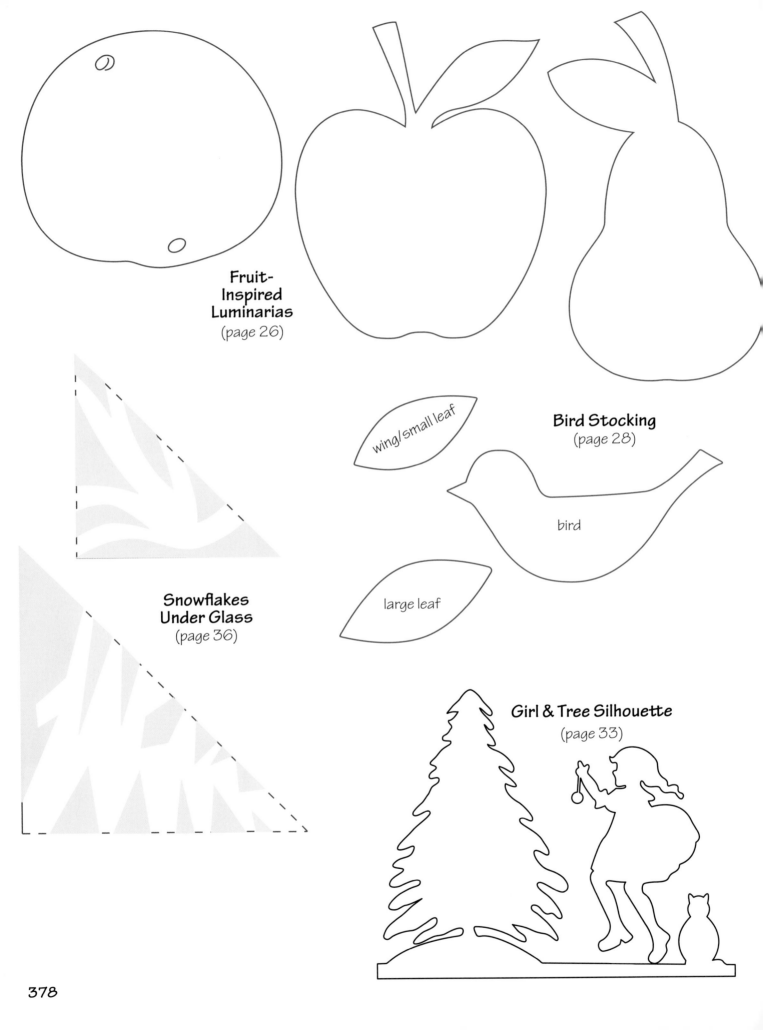

**Fruit-Inspired Luminarias**
(page 26)

**Bird Stocking**
(page 28)

wing/small leaf

bird

large leaf

**Snowflakes Under Glass**
(page 36)

**Girl & Tree Silhouette**
(page 33)

**Felted Holly Trims**
(page 27)
Enlarge
200%

holly
leaf

**Pretzels with Pizzazz Tag**
(page 173)

**Burlap Holly**
(page 14)

**Cake Box**
(page 147)

**Blooming Apron**
(page 59)

Rice Mix

**Rice Mix Jar**
(page 191)

**Santa Stocking**
(page 28)

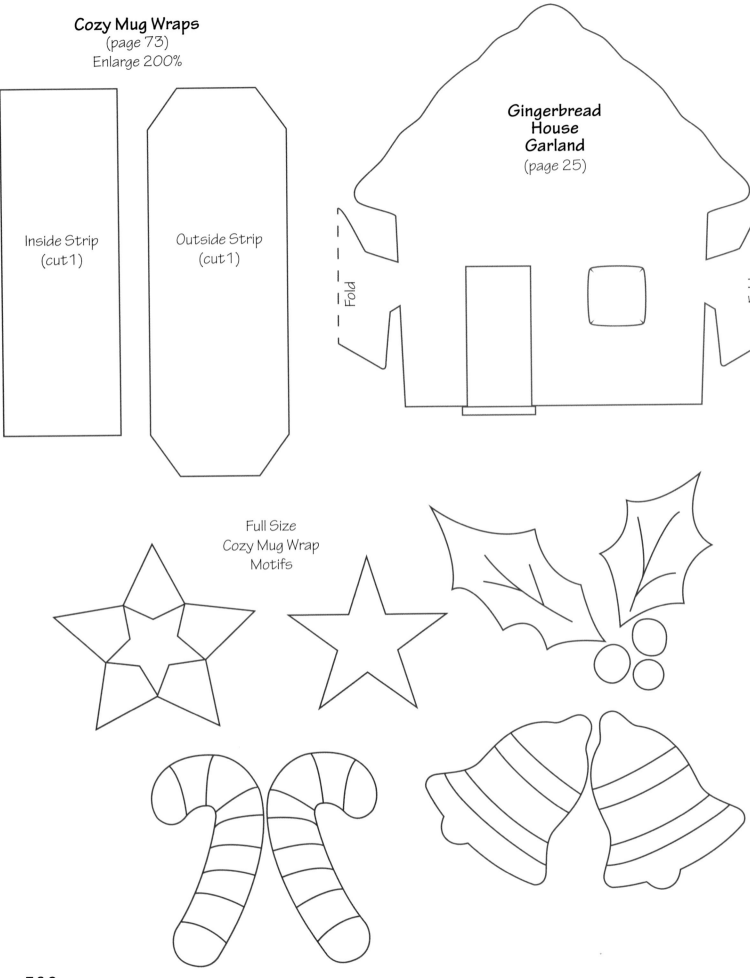

**Cozy Mug Wraps**
(page 73)
Enlarge 200%

Inside Strip
(cut 1)

Outside Strip
(cut 1)

Gingerbread
House
Garland
(page 25)

Fold

Fold

Full Size
Cozy Mug Wrap
Motifs

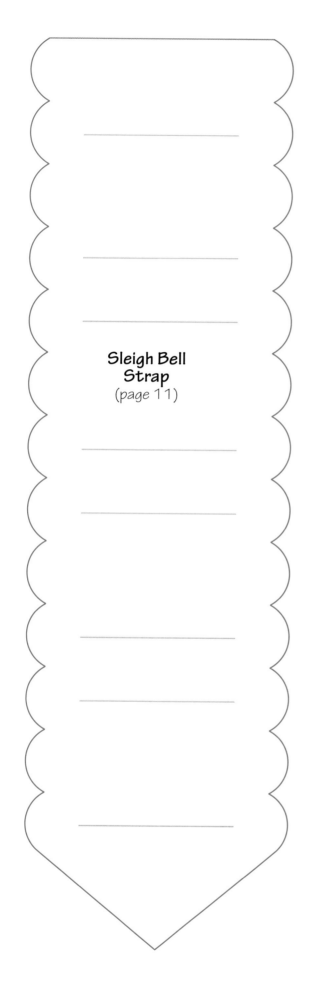

## Sleigh Bell
## Strap
(page 11)

## Lamp Post Banner
(page 11)

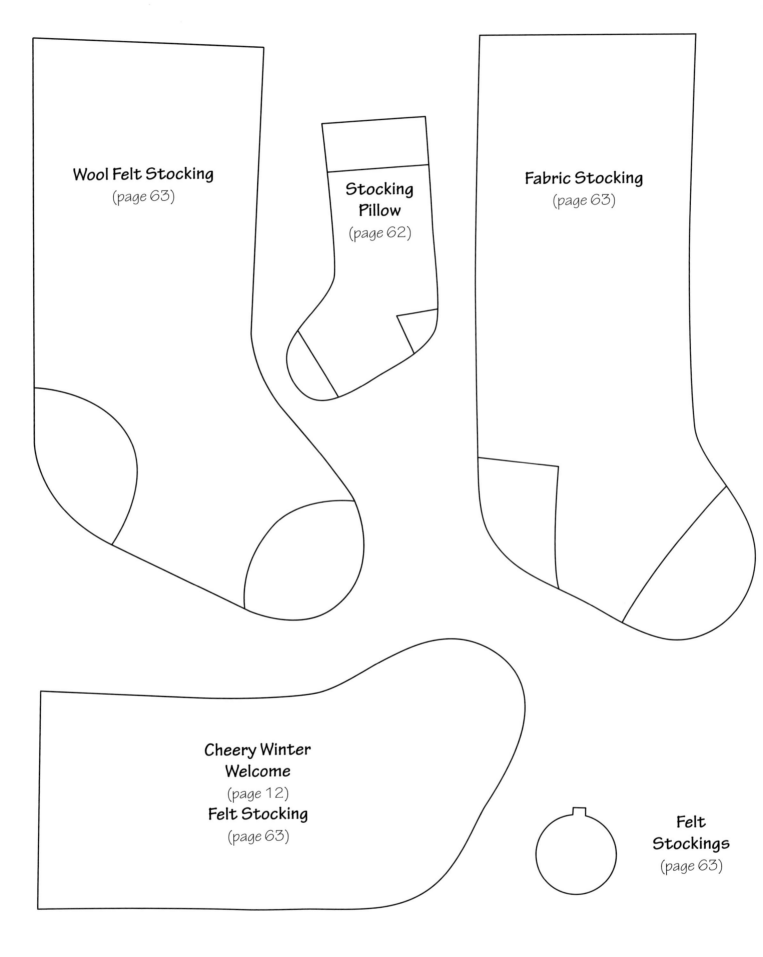

Wool Felt Stocking
(page 63)

Stocking
Pillow
(page 62)

Fabric Stocking
(page 63)

Cheery Winter
Welcome
(page 12)
Felt Stocking
(page 63)

Felt
Stockings
(page 63)

The family is one of nature's masterpieces.

Santayana

# 12 Days Ornaments
(page 18)

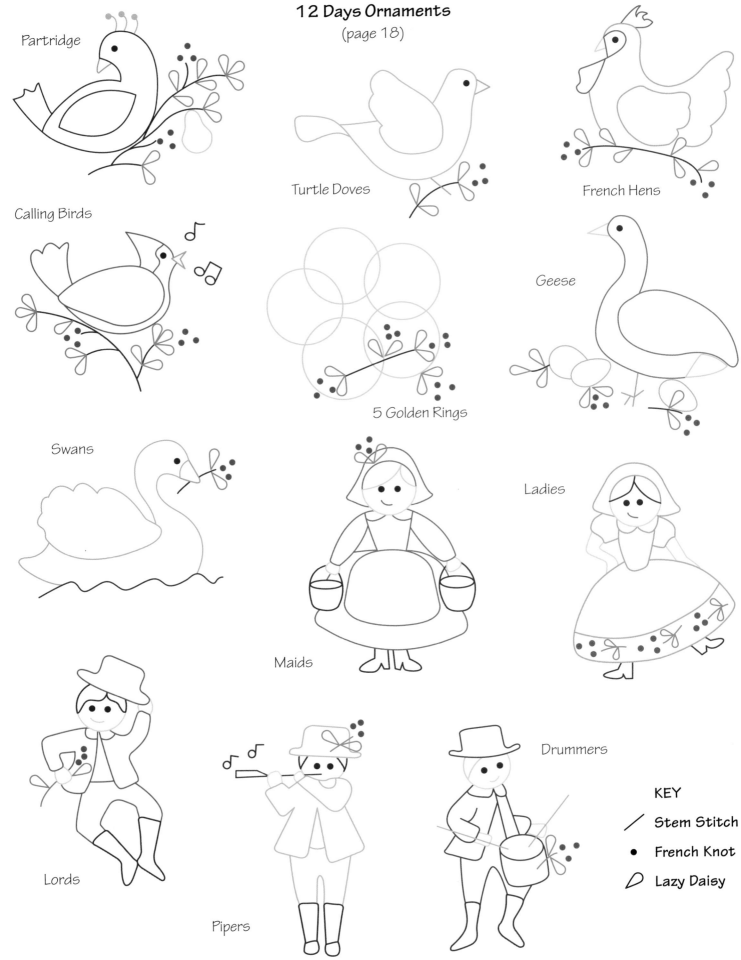

Partridge

Turtle Doves

French Hens

Calling Birds

5 Golden Rings

Geese

Swans

Maids

Ladies

Lords

Pipers

Drummers

KEY

/ Stem Stitch

• French Knot

⊃ Lazy Daisy

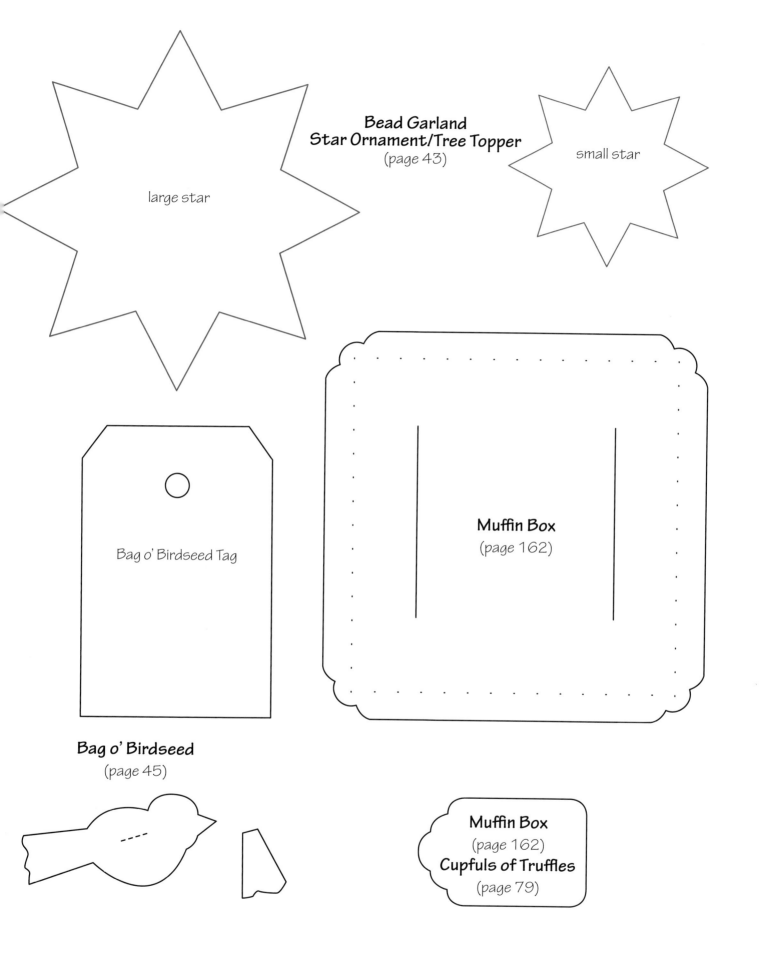

Bead Garland
**Star Ornament/Tree Topper**
(page 43)

large star

small star

Bag o' Birdseed Tag

**Muffin Box**
(page 162)

**Bag o' Birdseed**

(page 45)

**Muffin Box**
(page 162)
**Cupfuls of Truffles**
(page 79)

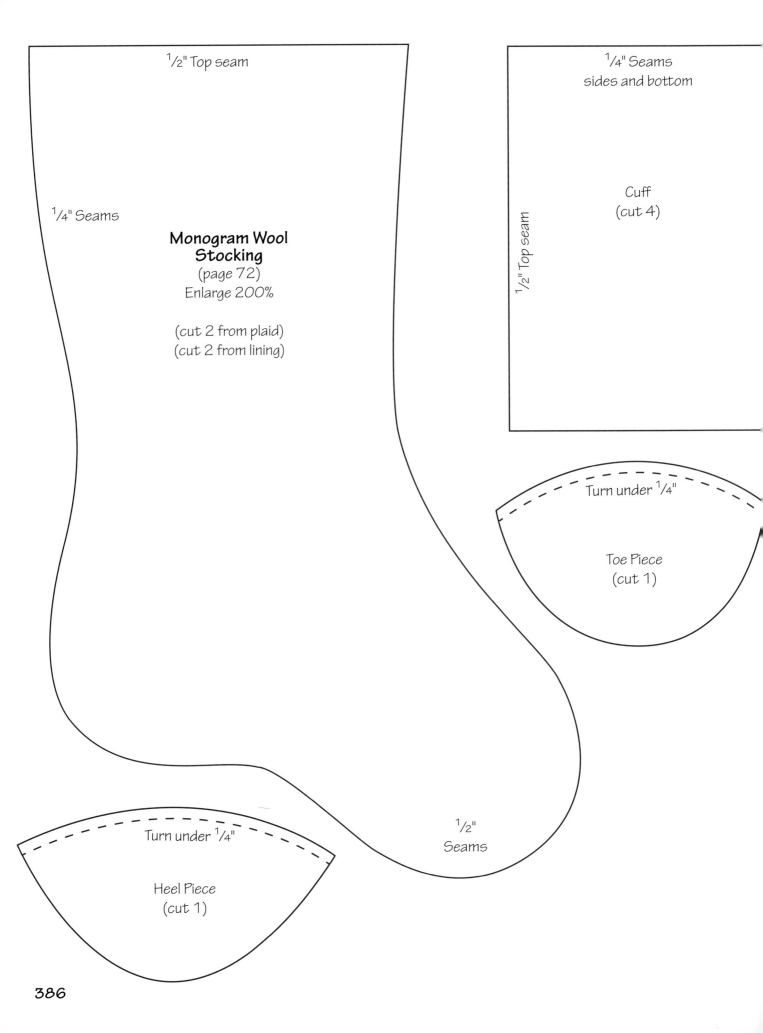

½" Top seam

¼" Seams
sides and bottom

¼" Seams

Cuff
(cut 4)

**Monogram Wool Stocking**
(page 72)
Enlarge 200%

(cut 2 from plaid)
(cut 2 from lining)

½" Top seam

Turn under ¼"

Toe Piece
(cut 1)

Turn under ¼"

½"
Seams

Heel Piece
(cut 1)

½" Top seam

386

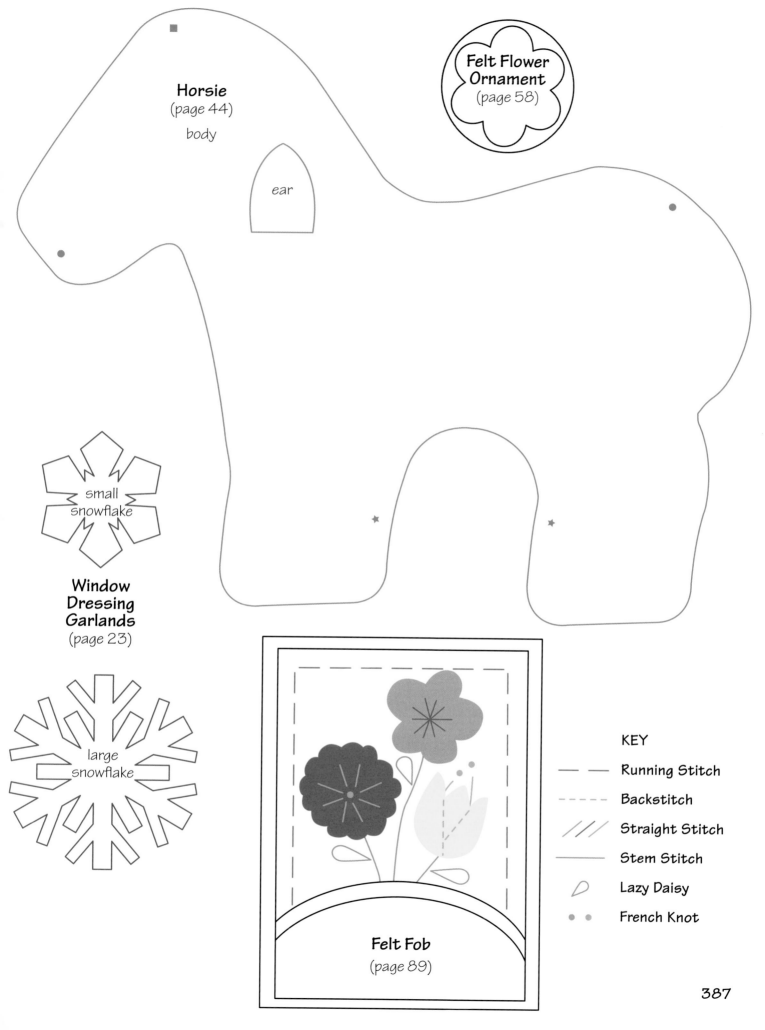

**Horsie**
(page 44)

body

ear

**Felt Flower Ornament**
(page 58)

small snowflake

**Window Dressing Garlands**
(page 23)

large snowflake

**Felt Fob**
(page 89)

KEY

— —  Running Stitch

- - -  Backstitch

/ / /  Straight Stitch

———  Stem Stitch

⬭  Lazy Daisy

• •  French Knot

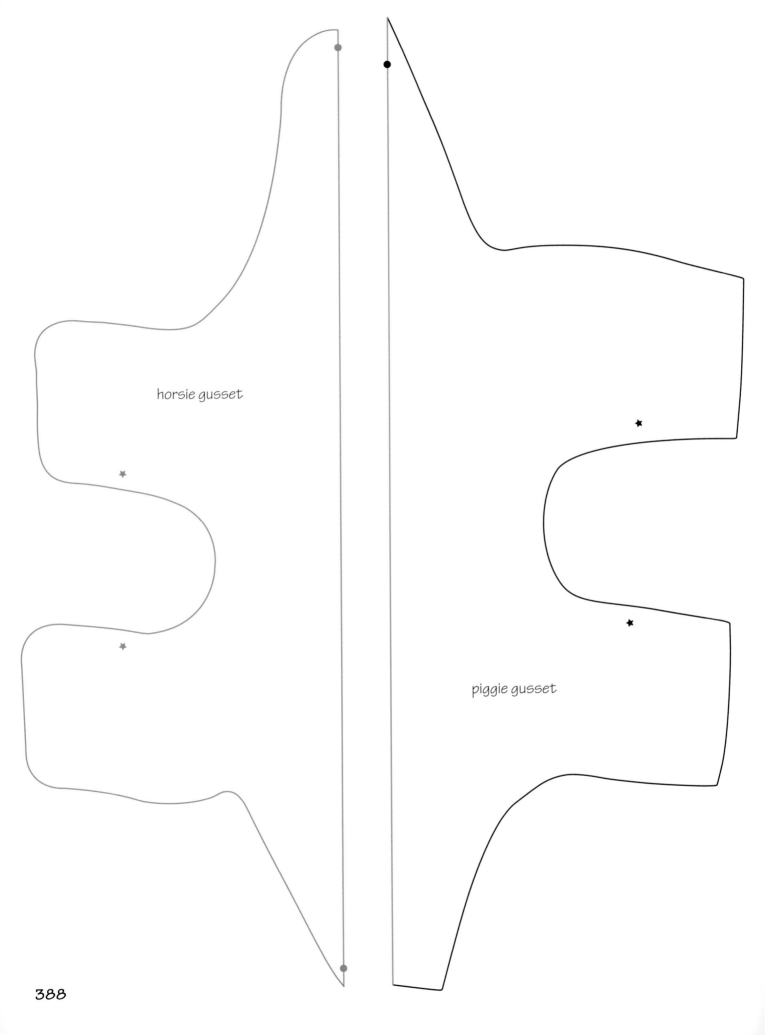

horsie gusset

piggie gusset

**Piggie**
(page 44)

body

ear

**Frosted
Jars**
(page 19)

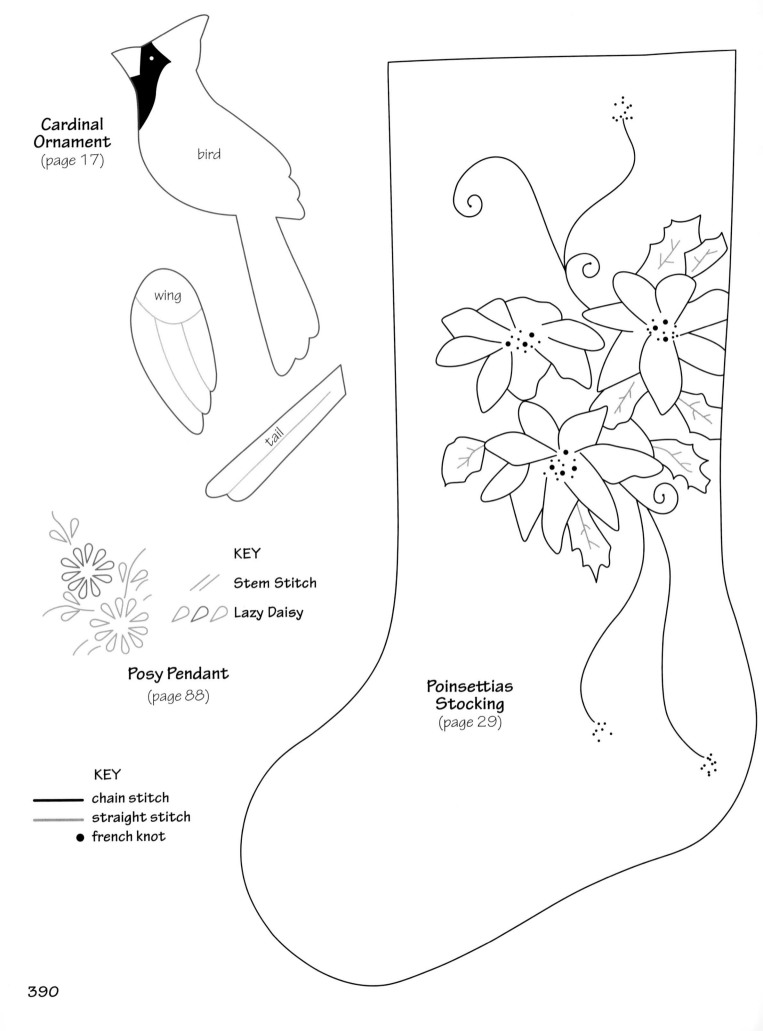

**Cardinal Ornament**
*(page 17)*

bird

wing

tail

KEY

Stem Stitch

Lazy Daisy

**Posy Pendant**
*(page 88)*

KEY

chain stitch

straight stitch

● french knot

**Poinsettias Stocking**
*(page 29)*

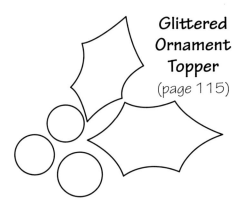

**Glittered Ornament Topper**

(page 115)

**Snowflake Topper**

(page 115)

**Reverse Appliqué Table Runner**

(page 61)

**Turtle Tic-Tac-Toe Toss**

(page 42)

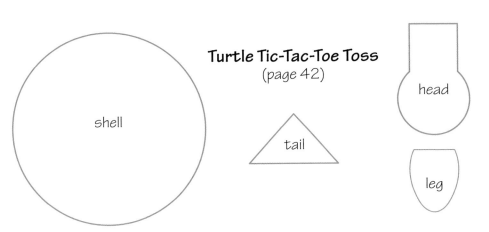

shell

tail

head

leg

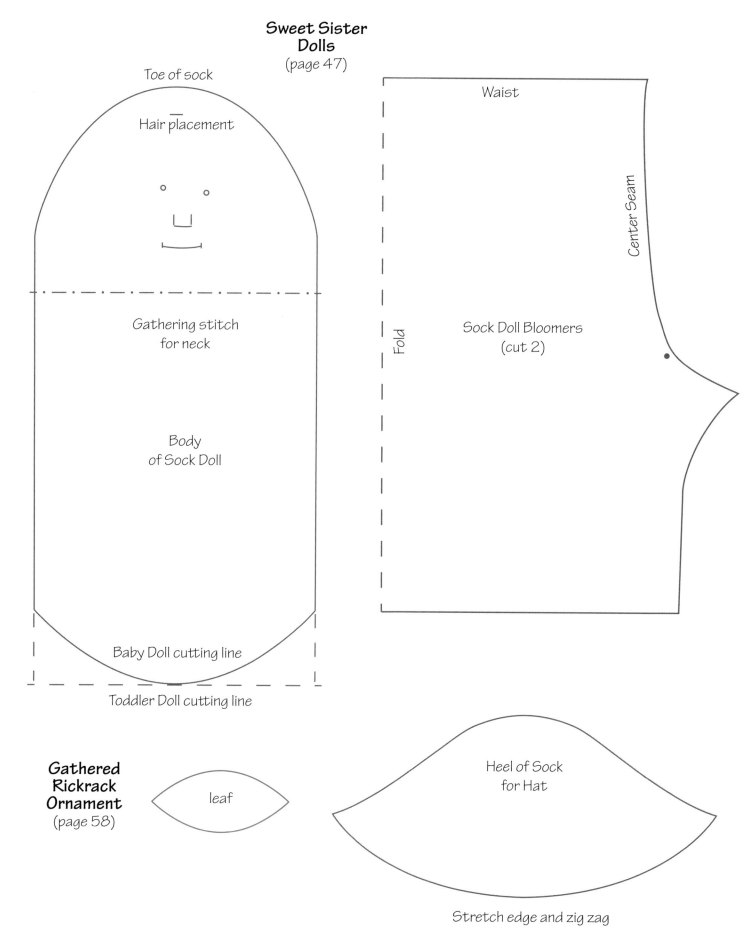

Sweet Sister
Dolls
(page 47)

Toe of sock

Hair placement

Waist

Center Seam

Fold

Gathering stitch
for neck

Sock Doll Bloomers
(cut 2)

Body
of Sock Doll

Baby Doll cutting line

Toddler Doll cutting line

Gathered
Rickrack
Ornament
(page 58)

leaf

Heel of Sock
for Hat

Stretch edge and zig zag

392

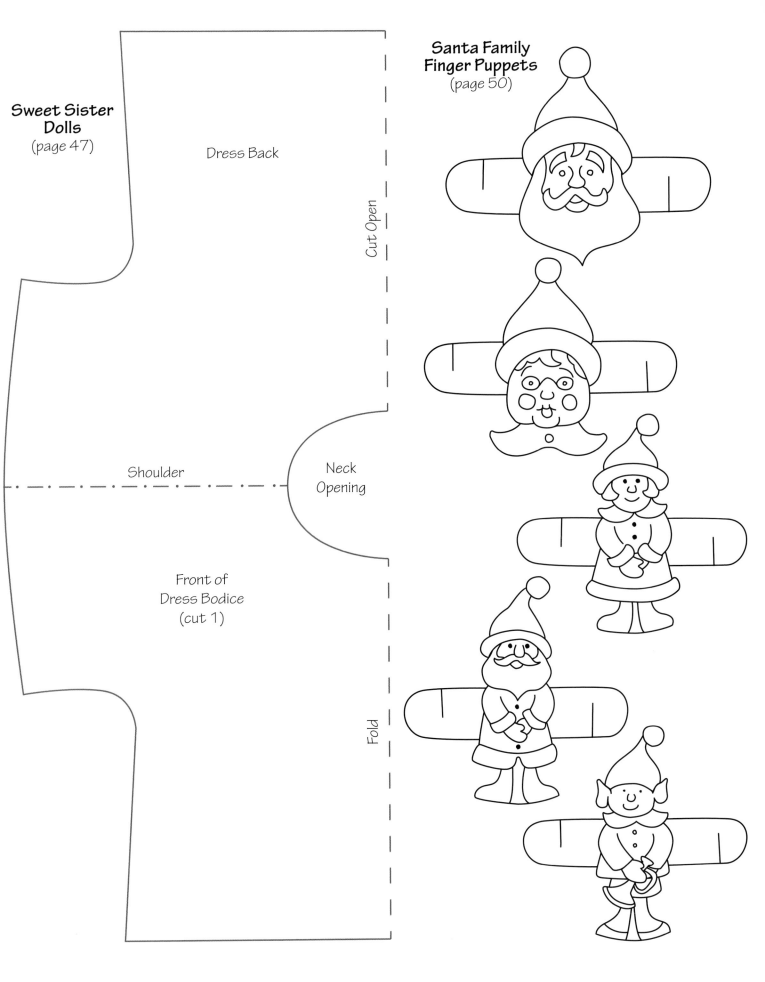

**Sweet Sister Dolls**
(page 47)

Dress Back

Cut Open

Shoulder

Neck Opening

Front of
Dress Bodice
(cut 1)

Fold

**Santa Family Finger Puppets**
(page 50)

**Snowbound Tray**
(page 90)

**Lollipop Bottle**
(page 135)

Label

Tag

**Jam Jar**
(page 138)

Carrot
Cake
Jam

**JOY Banner**
(page 85)

JOY

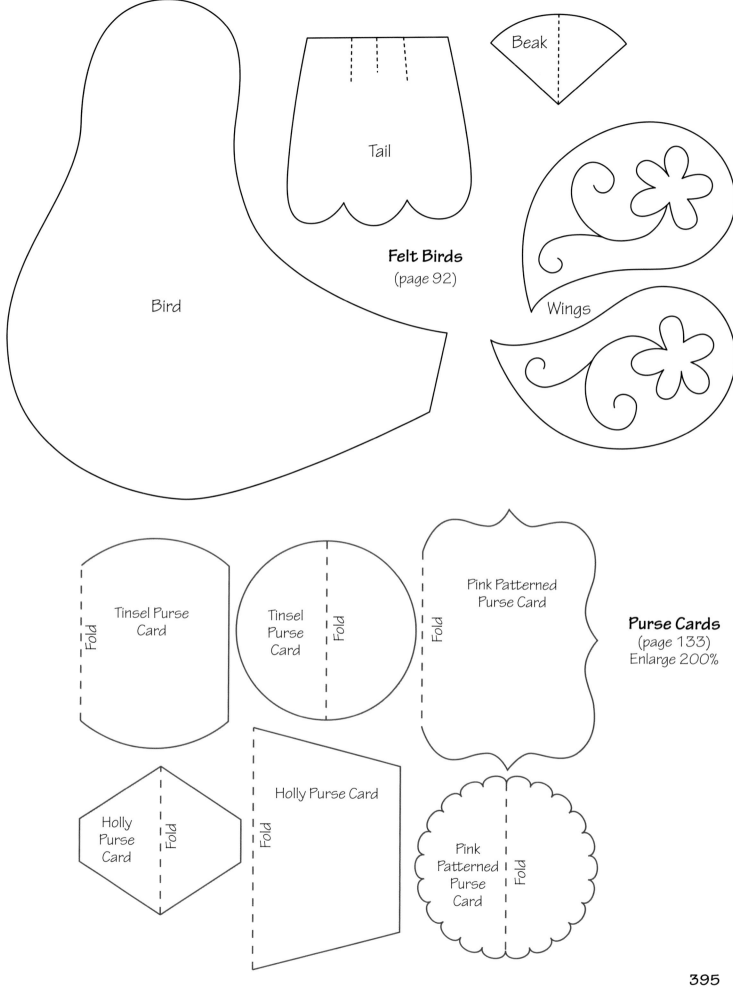

Bird

Tail

Beak

Wings

**Felt Birds**
(page 92)

Fold

Tinsel Purse Card

Tinsel Purse Card

Fold

Pink Patterned Purse Card

Fold

**Purse Cards**
(page 133)
Enlarge 200%

Holly Purse Card

Fold

Holly Purse Card

Fold

Pink Patterned Purse Card

Fold

**Paper Doll Dress Trims**
(page 48)
Enlarge 200%

**No-Sew Fabric Trims**
(page 37)
Enlarge 200%

**Spicy Fruit Tea Mix Tag**
(page 186)

Spicy Fruit Tea Mix

**Cell Phone Cozy**
(page 105)

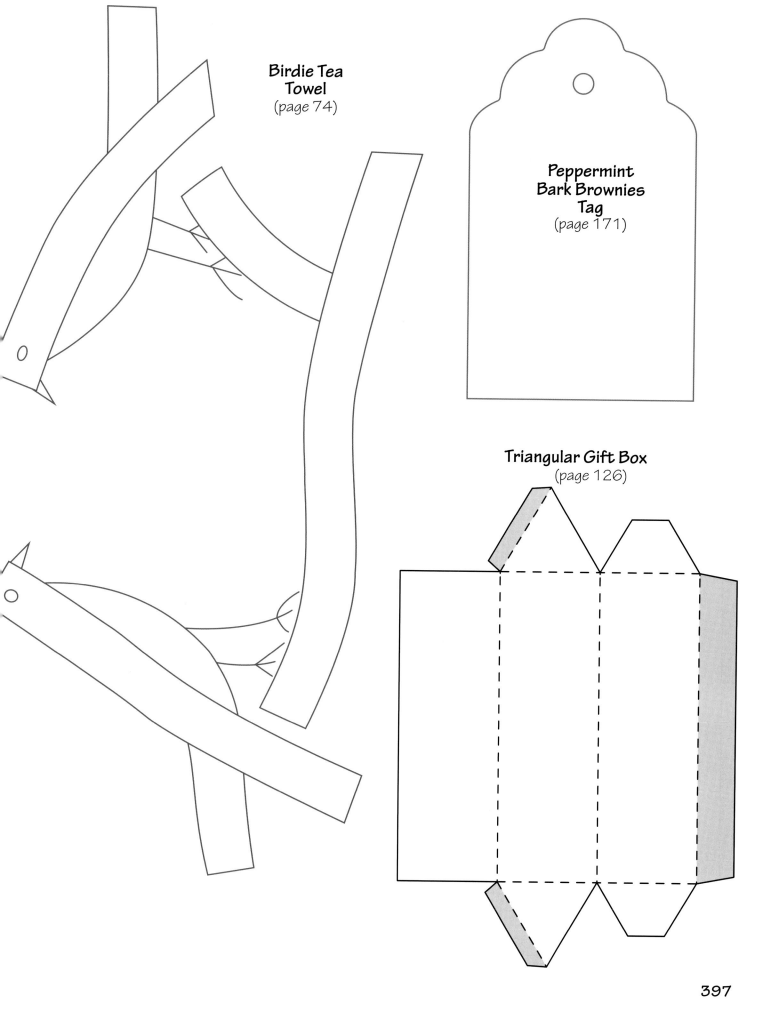

**Birdie Tea Towel**
(page 74)

**Peppermint Bark Brownies Tag**
(page 171)

**Triangular Gift Box**
(page 126)

**Cupcake Pincushion**
(page 97)
Enlarge to 200%

Yo-Yo
Center for
Cupcake
Pincushion

Bottom Felt
for Large
Cupcake
Pincushion

Cupcake Pincushion

Top
(cut 1 for large pincushion)
(cut 1 for small pincushion)

Appliqué for Top
Large Cupcake
Pincushion

Felt Flower for
Small Cupcake
Pincushion

**Handy Sewing Tote
Blooming
Pincushion**
Enlarge 200%
(page 104)

Muffin Tin Tag

**Yo-Yo for
Blooming
Pincushion**
Enlarge 200%
(page 104)

**Muffin Tin**
(page 136)

# Denim
## Luggage Tags
(page 95)
Enlarge 200%

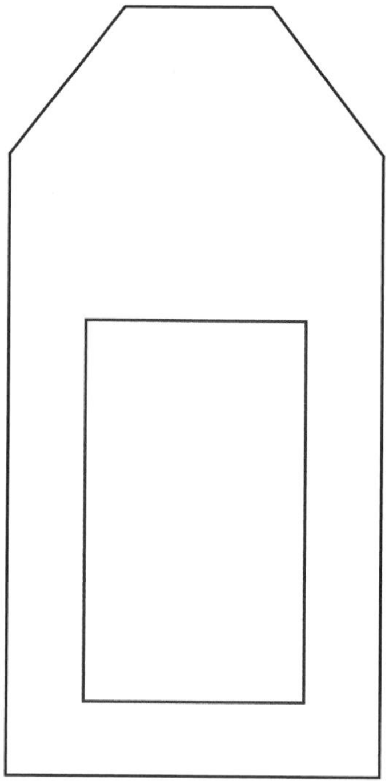

# Snowy Trail Mix
## Candy Sleigh Holder
(page 174)
Enlarge 200%

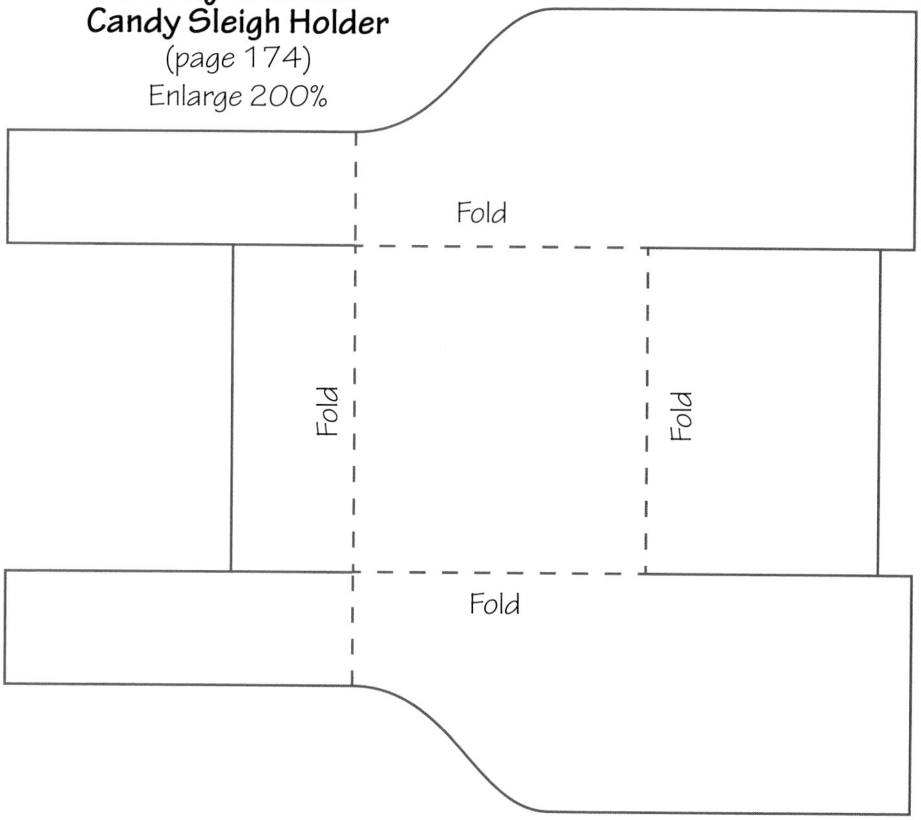

Fold

Fold

Fold

Fold

# Fanciful Journal Cover
(page 103)

KEY

● French Knot

⬭ Lazy Daisy

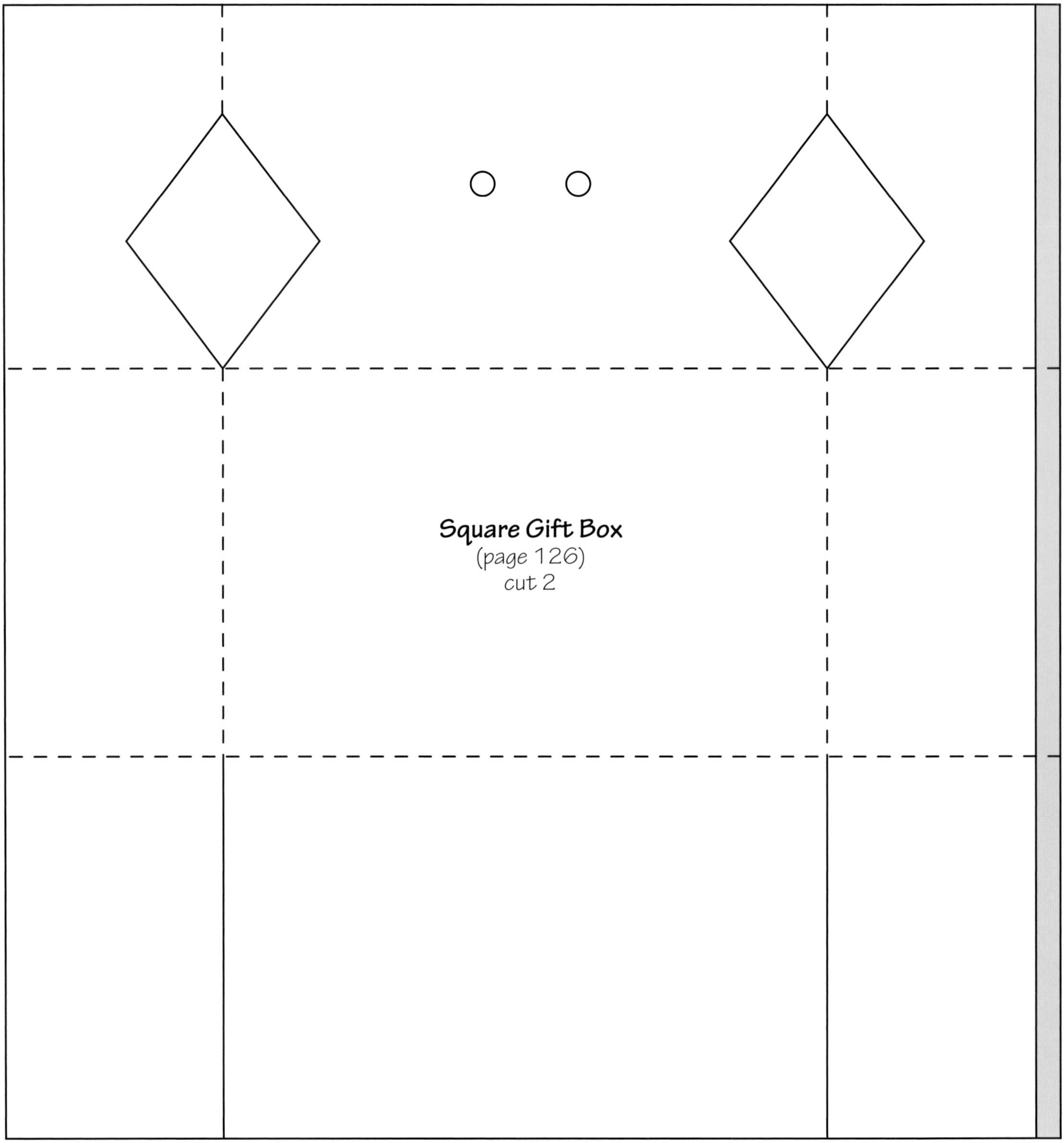

**Square Gift Box**
(page 126)
cut 2

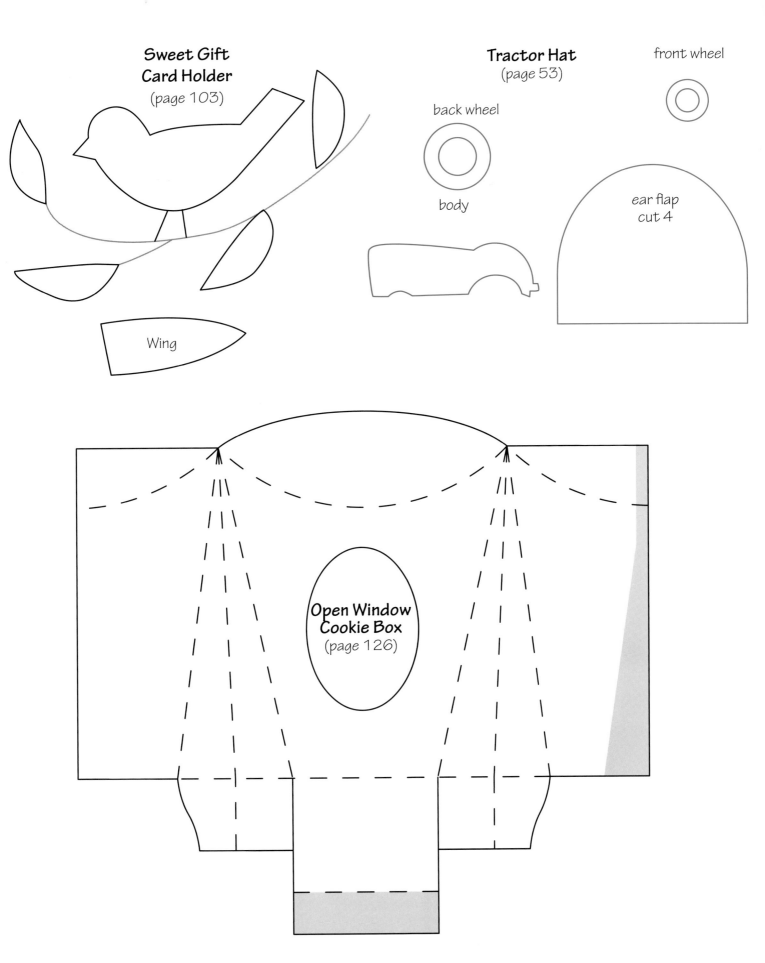

Sweet Gift
Card Holder
(page 103)

Wing

Tractor Hat
(page 53)

front wheel

back wheel

body

ear flap
cut 4

Open Window
Cookie Box
(page 126)

401

## Mitten Puppet
(page 53)

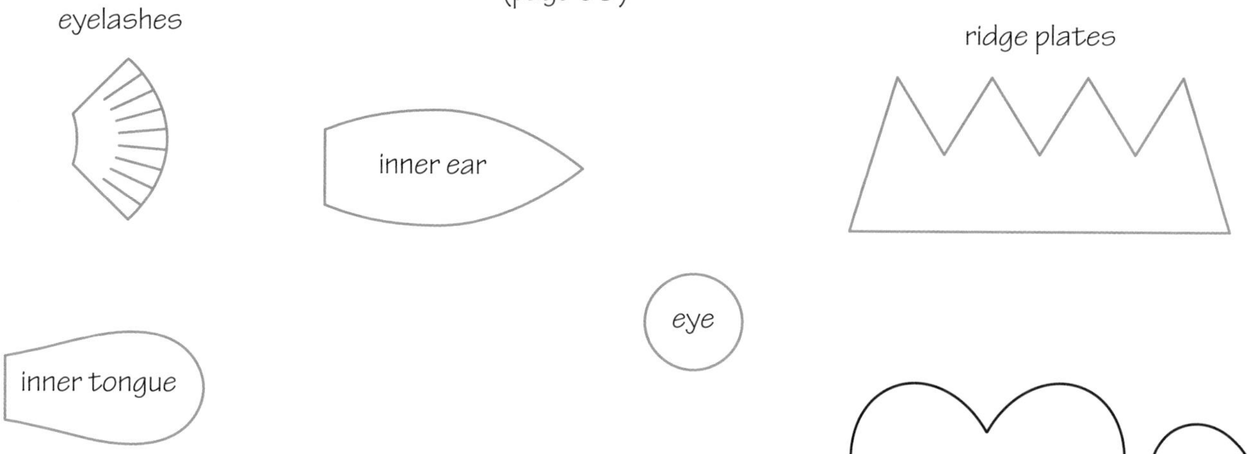

eyelashes

inner ear

ridge plates

eye

inner tongue

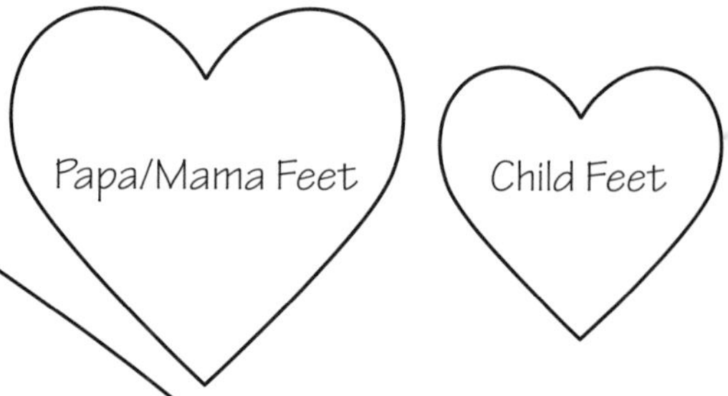

Papa/Mama Feet

Child Feet

## Spool Family
(page 45)

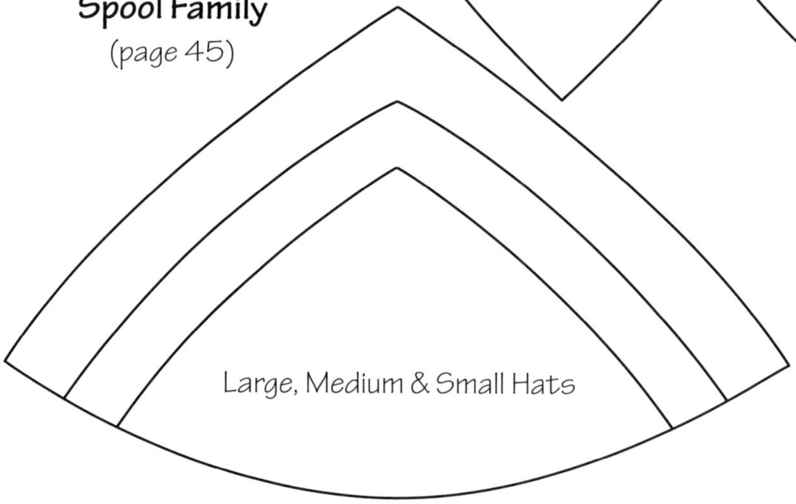

## Chubby Chirpers
(page 46)

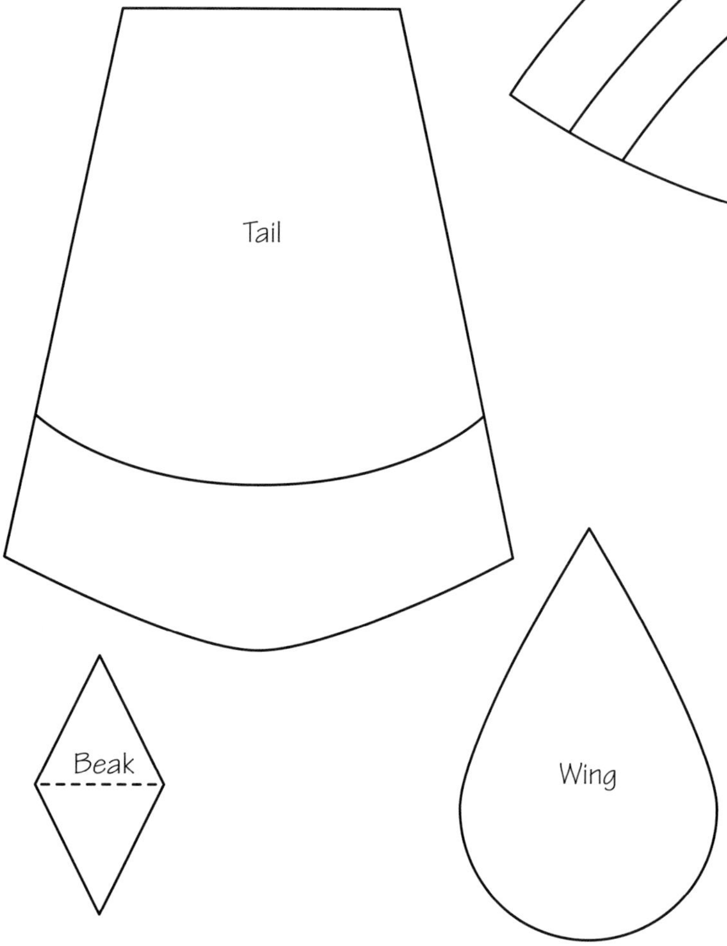

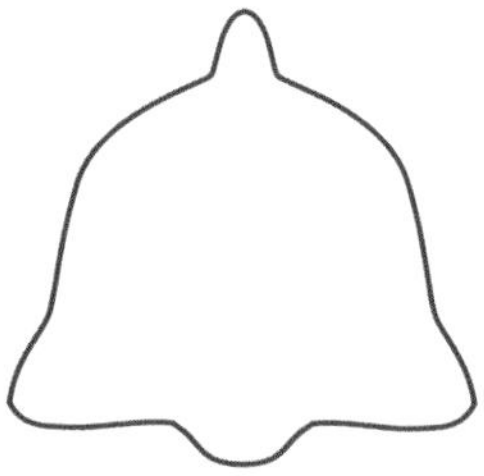

Large, Medium & Small Hats

Tail

## Homemade
## Graham Crackers
## Bag Cut-outs
(page 175)
Enlarge to 200%

Beak

Wing

**Paper Poinsettia Topper**
(page 112)

Leaf

Flower
(cut 2)

**Dressed-Up Doggy Cards**
(page 113)

Ear

Poodle Body

Poodle collar
(cut 1)

Poodle Coat
(cut 1)

Ear

Dachshund body

Dachshund Coat
(cut 1)

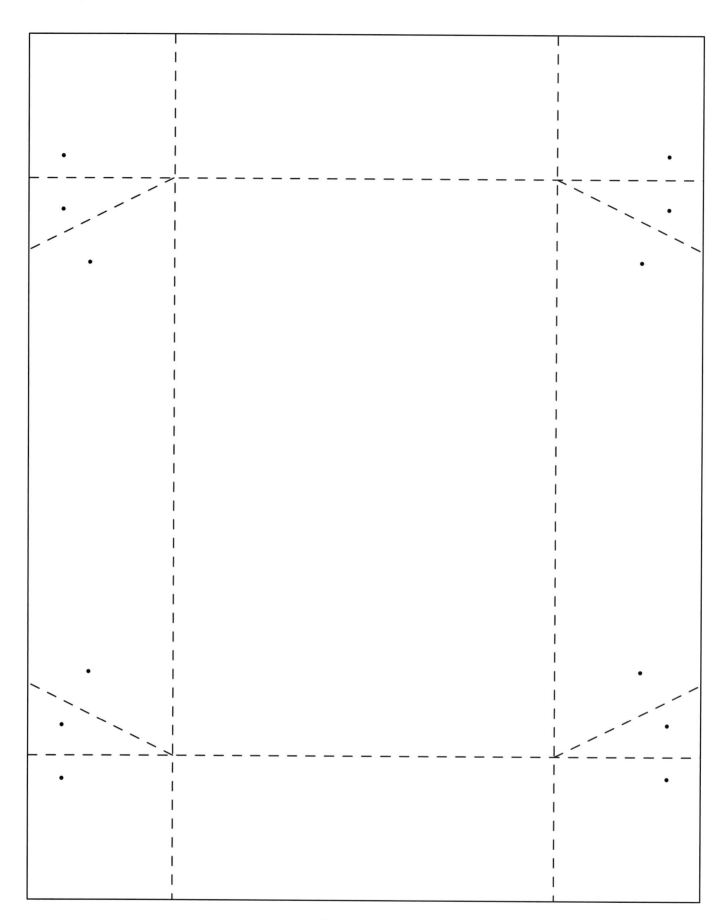

**Paper Trays**

(page 143)

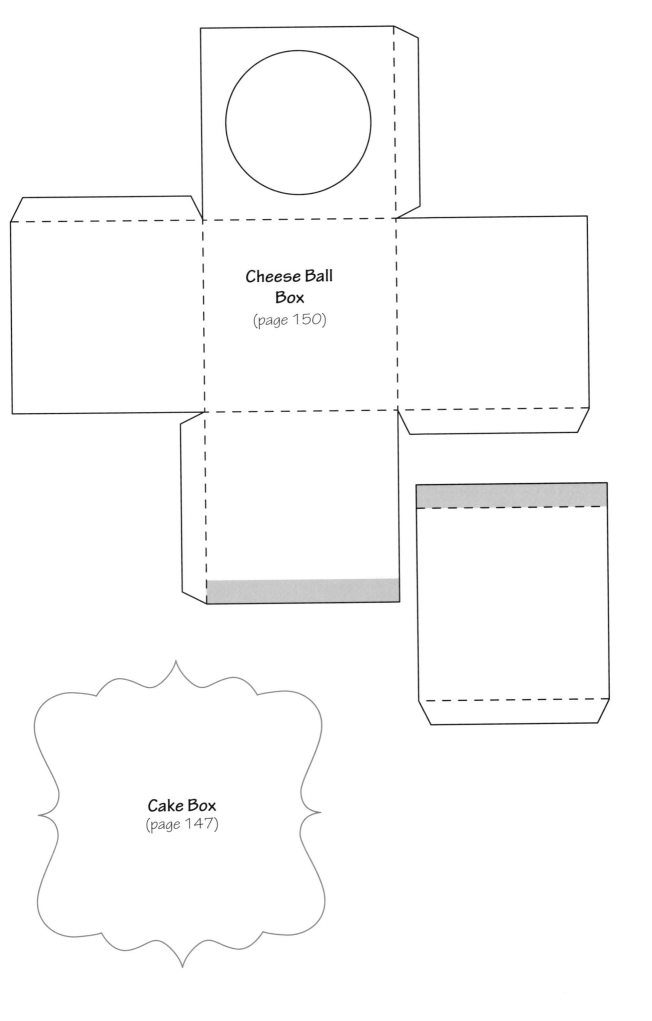

**Cheese Ball Box**
(page 150)

**Cake Box**
(page 147)

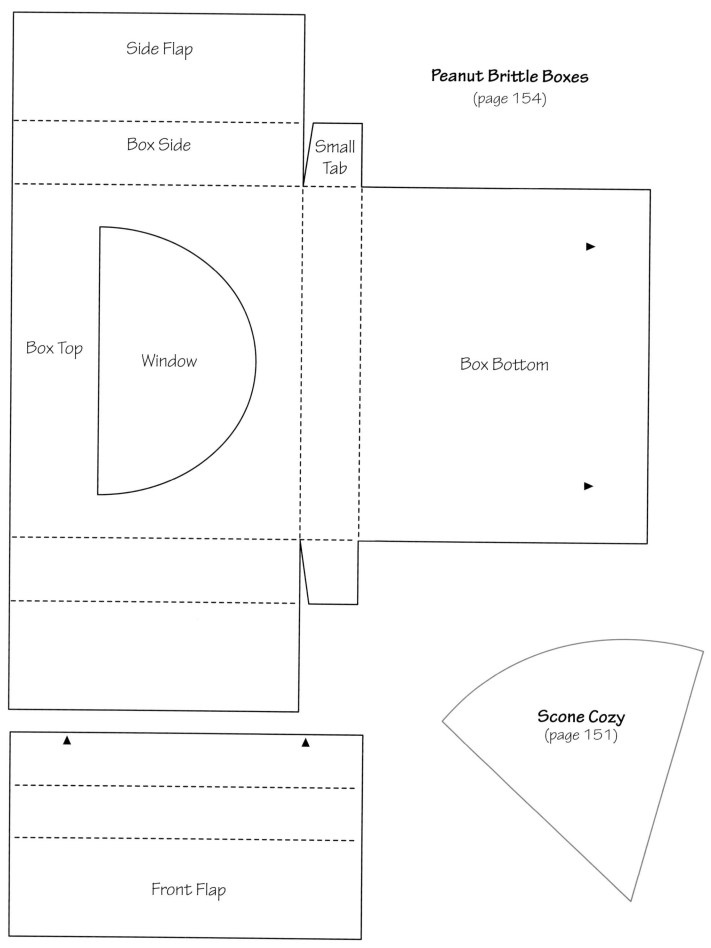

Side Flap

Box Side

Small
Tab

Box Top

Window

Box Bottom

Front Flap

**Peanut Brittle Boxes**
(page 154)

**Scone Cozy**
(page 151)

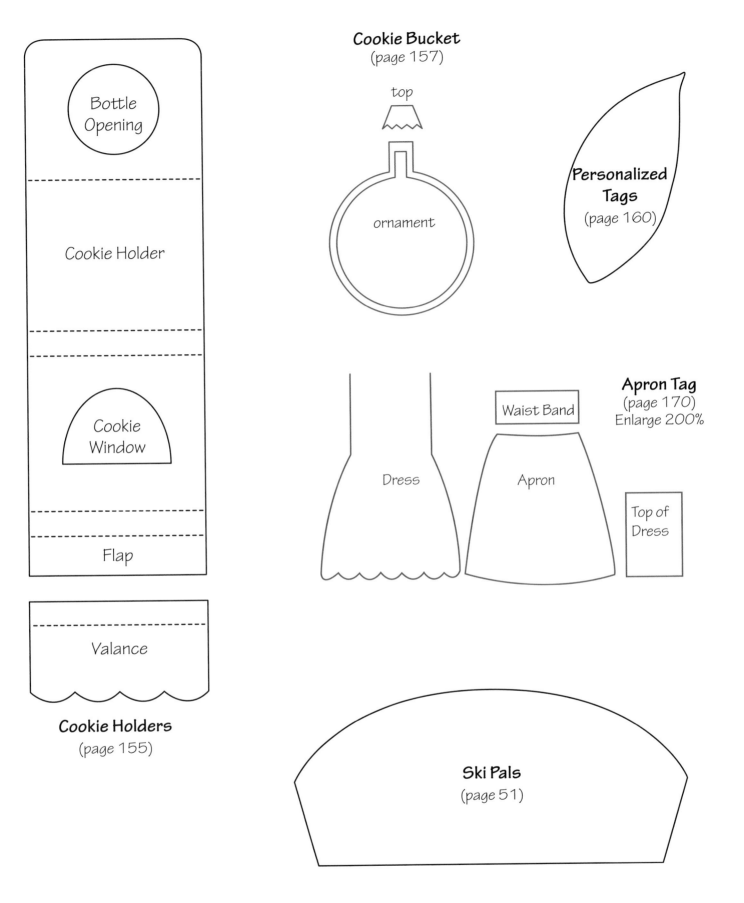

**Cookie Bucket**
(page 157)

top

ornament

**Personalized Tags**
(page 160)

**Apron Tag**
(page 170)
Enlarge 200%

Waist Band

Dress

Apron

Top of Dress

Bottle Opening

Cookie Holder

Cookie Window

Flap

Valance

**Cookie Holders**
(page 155)

**Ski Pals**
(page 51)

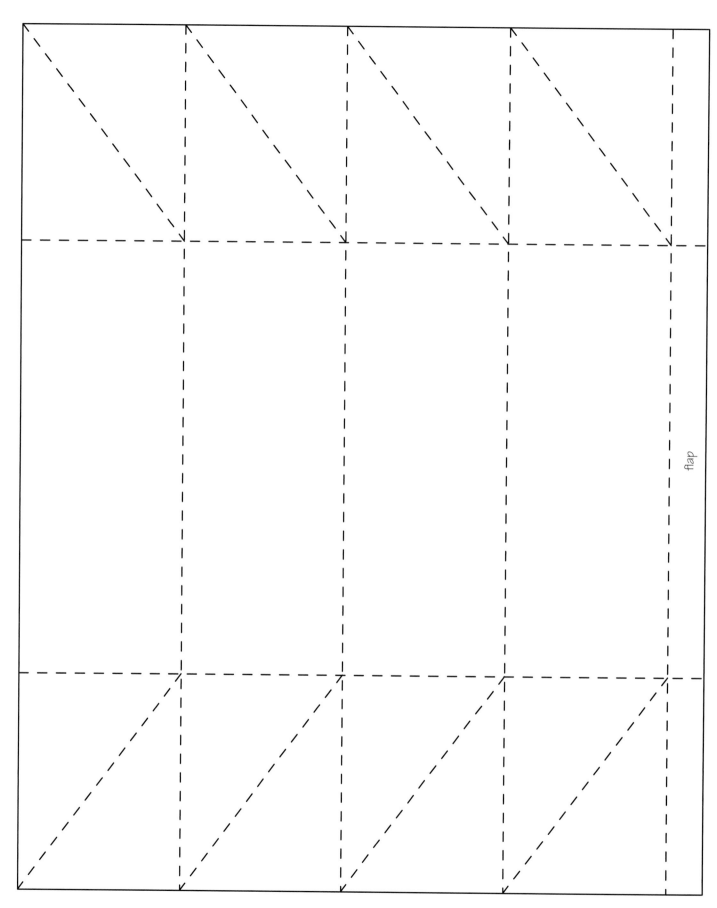

flap

**Fudge Box**

(page 159)

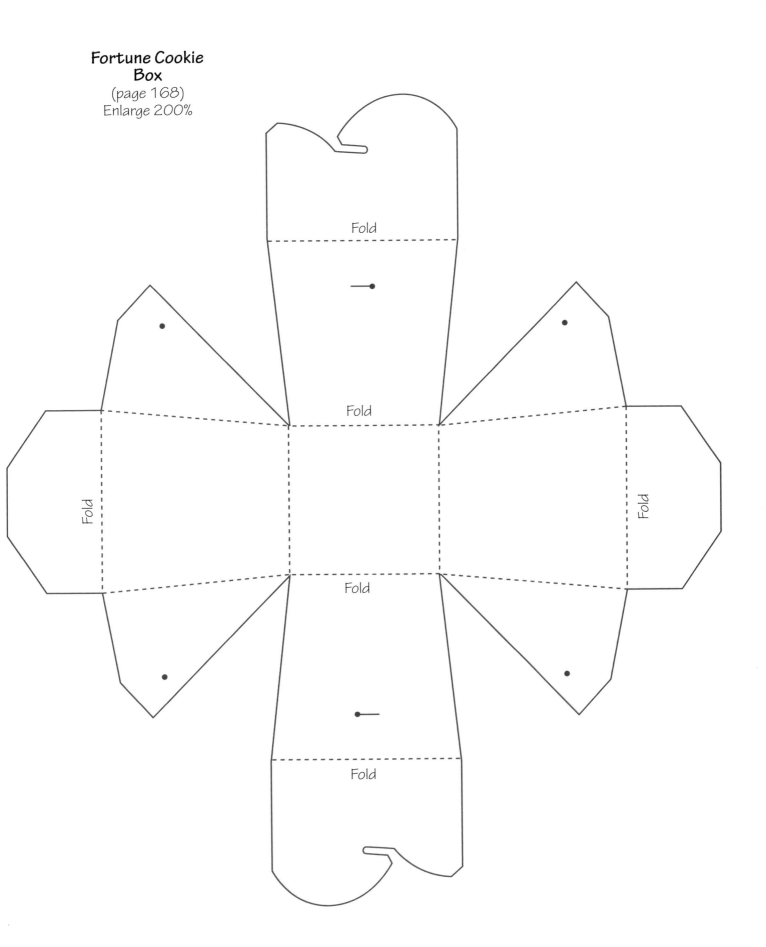

**Fortune Cookie Box**
(page 168)
Enlarge 200%

Fold

Fold

Fold

Fold

Fold

Fold

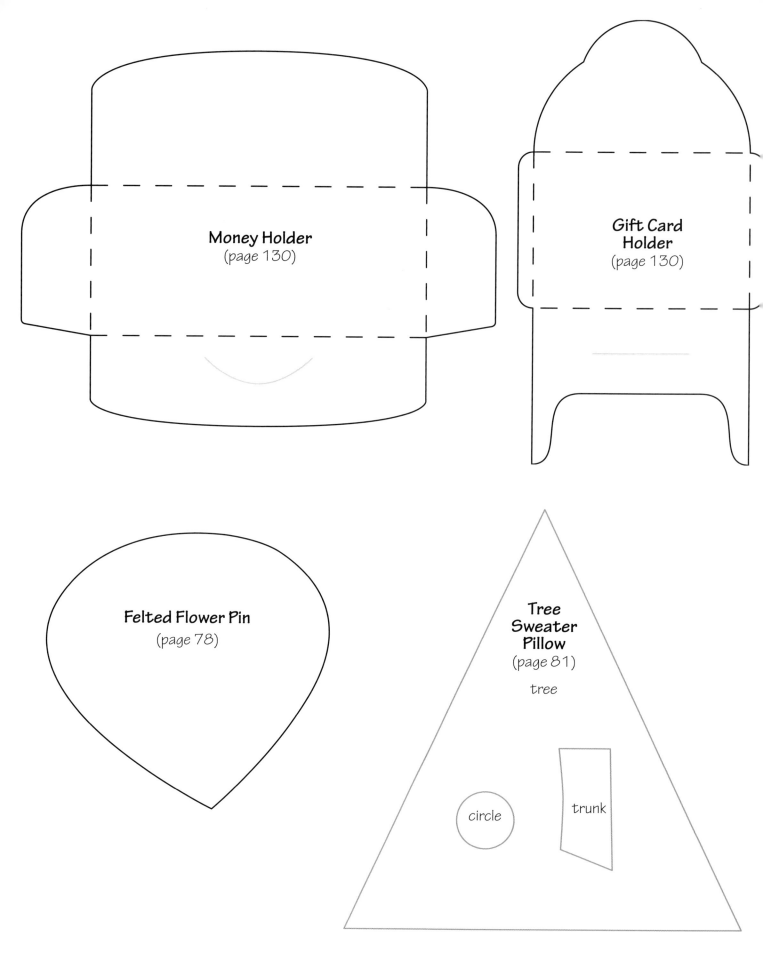

**Money Holder**
(page 130)

**Gift Card Holder**
(page 130)

**Felted Flower Pin**
(page 78)

**Tree Sweater Pillow**
(page 81)

tree

circle

trunk

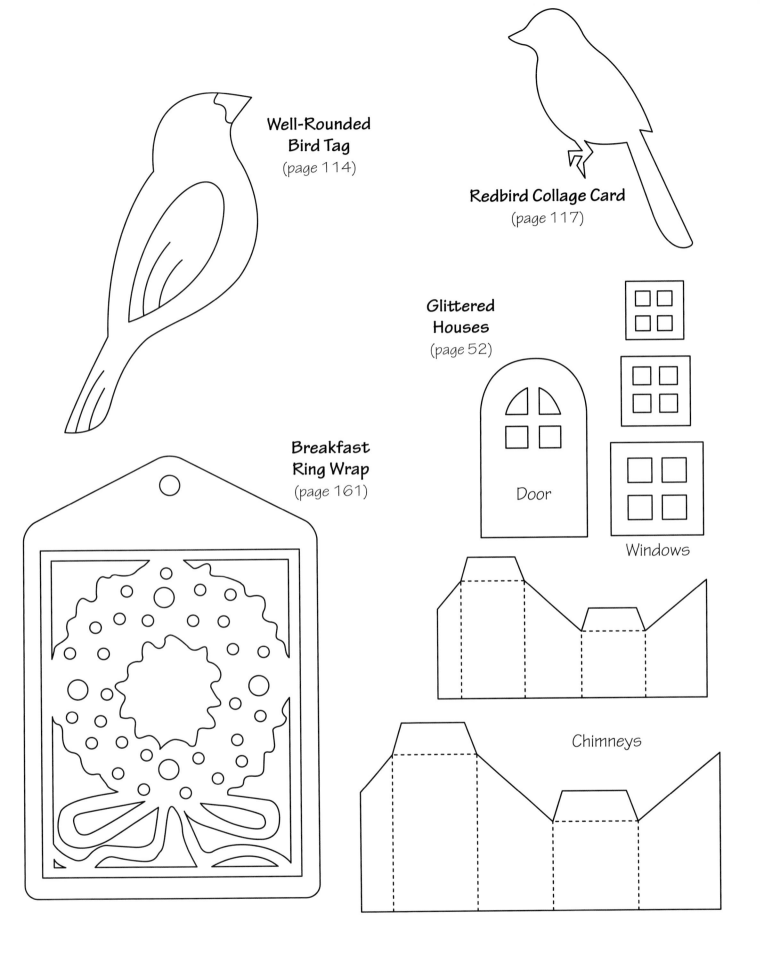

**Well-Rounded Bird Tag**

(page 114)

**Redbird Collage Card**
(page 117)

**Glittered Houses**

(page 52)

Door

Windows

Chimneys

**Breakfast Ring Wrap**

(page 161)

411

**Scrapbook Caddy**
(page 118)

Divider

Flower Stems

Large Circle

**Garland**
(page 129)

Small Circle

**December 25th Gift Tag**
(page 129)

**Holly Jolly Gift Tag**
(page 129)

Oval Tag

Leaf

Berry

**Fondue Kit**
(page 179)

Gather

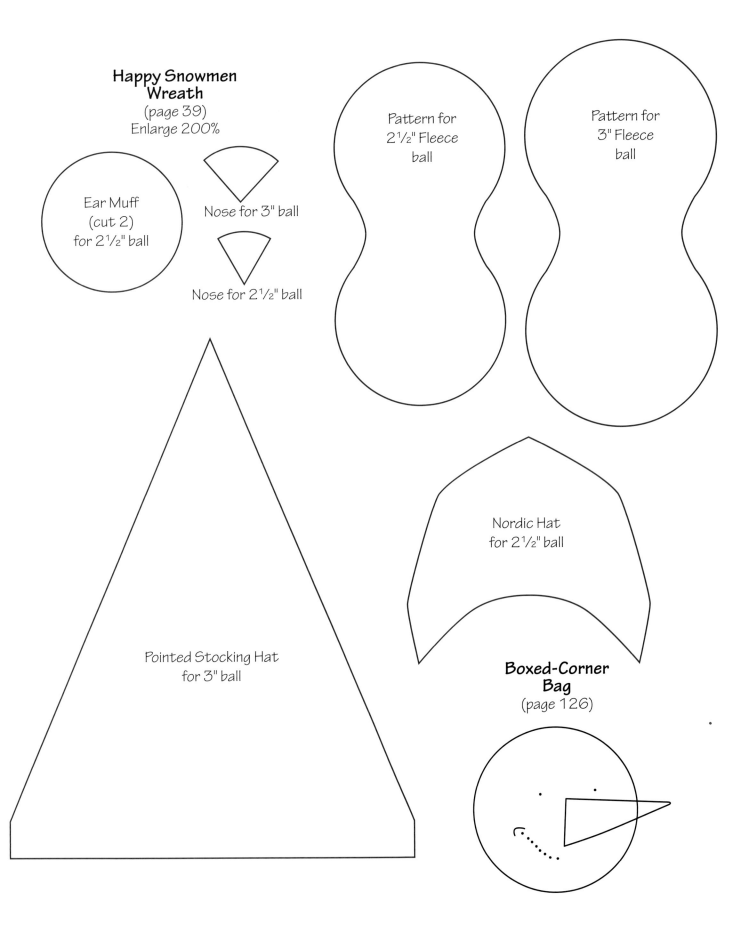

**Happy Snowmen Wreath**
(page 39)
Enlarge 200%

Ear Muff
(cut 2)
for 2½" ball

Nose for 3" ball

Nose for 2½" ball

Pattern for
2½" Fleece
ball

Pattern for
3" Fleece
ball

Nordic Hat
for 2½" ball

Pointed Stocking Hat
for 3" ball

**Boxed-Corner
Bag**
(page 126)

413

# Project Index

# Recipe Index

416